TAROT of THE SPIRIT

TAROT of THE SPIRIT

PAMELA EAKINS, PH.D.

SAMUEL WEISER, INC.

York Beach, Maine

First published in 1992 by
Samuel Weiser, Inc.
Box 612
York Beach, Maine 03910

99
8   7   6

Library of Congress Cataloging-in-Publication Data

Eakins, Pamela.
   Tarot of the spirit / Pamela Eakins.
      p.   cm.
   1. Tarot.   I. Title.
BF1879.T2E25   1992
133.3'2424—dc20   90-23600
                                                            CIP

ISBN 0-87728-730-9
EB

Cover art is "Earth Sister" from the *Tarot of the Spirit* deck copy-
right © Joyce Eakins. The deck is featured in the book and is
published by U.S. Games Systems, Stamford, CT.

Typeset in 10 pt. Palatino

Printed in the United States of America

The paper used in this publication meets the minimum requirements of the American National Standard for Permanence of
Paper for Printed Library Materials 239.48–1984.

Be it known, Dear One, that to heal thy world, thou must first heal thyself. To heal thyself, thou must know the source of thy illness. To know the source of thy illness, thou must know the Inner Self. To know the Inner Self, thou must take the Path of Spirit.

Blessed Be, Dear Traveler. Every Force and Form of the Universe is with You!

Table of Contents

Book I
The Divine Legacy

Book II
The Sacred Texts

Appendices

Acknowledgments

The *Tarot of the Spirit* is meant to pick up where other tarots leave off. It has come to us to aid serious students on the esoteric path of the Western Mysteries. Its reason for being is to provide assistance for inner awakening and continued spiritual practice.

Every concept presented in *Tarot of the Spirit* is essential in its context. Nothing has been reduced, neither has it been convoluted. Every effort has been made to keep the interpretations clearly understandable. Both the book and the deck of cards are meant to be referred to again and again. As the knowledge of the student deepens, the texts will take on greater meaning.

As for the writing of this book, I committed several years of my life to its unfolding. The depth of the information, however, is what was revealed to me—as I now know—exactly in proportion to what I was able to hear and accept—that is to say, exactly in proportion to my openness. I was aided on this path by several great initiates who prefer to remain unnamed. To them, I owe great thanks.

Authors who helped me formulate my views, and to whom this work is indebted, include Paul Foster Case, Dion Fortune, Gareth Knight, C. G. Jung, Aleister Crowley, Gitta Mallasz, Lao Tse, Paramahansa Yogananda, Joseph Campbell, Swami Akhilananda, Ernest Holmes and Stephen Hoeller. For assisting in my own inner journey, I would like to thank three of my teachers in particular: Paul A. Clark, Shekhinah Mountainwater and Roberta Herzog. I have been greatly influenced by the teachings of the Fraternity of the Hidden Light, the Rosicrucian Order and the Builders of the Adytum.

Many of my colleagues at Stanford University's Institute for Research on Women and Gender also contributed enormously to my thinking and, indirectly, to this volume.

I am grateful to my life partner Peter Adams, a dear man who contributed much of the background research, and with whom I shared many extraordinary experiences during the course of this project.

Finally, working with Joyce Eakins, who painted the *Tarot of the Spirit*, was an incredible challenge and an enormously rewarding experience. I think Joyce and I finally realized why we chose to incarnate during the same historical time period. Thanks, Mom. You have left an indelible mark upon my soul.

—Pamela Eakins
Moss Beach, California

❖   ❖   ❖

Grateful acknowledgment to the authors and their publishers for the quoted material that appears in chapter 5:

Paramahansa Yogananda, *Metaphysical Meditations* (Los Angeles: Self-Realization Fellowship, 1982), p. 38.

Paul Foster Case, *The Book of Tokens* (Los Angeles: Builders of the Adytum, 1934, 1968), p. 100.

C. G. Jung, this quote is from Jung's *Seven Sermons to the Dead*, written during the period of his confrontation with the unconscious in 1917. See Stephen A. Hoeller, *The Gnostic Jung and the Seven Sermons to the Dead* (Wheaton, IL: The Theosophical Publishing House, 1982), pp. 57-8.

Mrs. H. B. J. from Mary Baker Eddy, *Prose Works other than Science and Health* (Boston, MA: The First Church of Christ, Scientist, 1925), pp. 430-1.

Starhawk, *The Spiral Dance* (San Francisco: Harper & Row, 1979), p. 2.

Introduction

It is early. Fog folds around the house like a soft down comforter. The sea has been calm and I can barely hear the waves clapping the sand. Chirping starlings scratch about in the rafters getting ready for spring nesting. Every year they come, building nests in the corners of the eaves and, every year, I await with joyful anticipation the strained little coos of the babies.

After the last minute bustle of seeing Kätchen and Taylor off to school and Peter off to his stained glass studio, Skipper (the dog) and I have the house completely to ourselves. I won't be disturbed until noon when Mona comes to pick up the appointment book she accidently left here yesterday.

I am sitting in our "Quiet Room" mulling over what I want to say to you. I want to tell you so many things. I want to talk about the human mind. About the meaning of God. About consciousness. I want to enter into the Great Dialogue with you. But to do this, we have to begin somewhere.

Perhaps I shall begin by telling you about myself. In general, my life is rural and rather ordinary: a reconstituted family, barking dogs, baseball in the road, rock music on the downstairs radio, shelves full of books, bills to be paid, quiet walks on the beach, small town politics, an occasional business trip, phone calls from students, hauling boxes in the hatchback, planting daffodil bulbs, kissing goodbye at the doorway. On the surface, at least, we are a family not so different from any other in Moss Beach (population 400).

But then there have been certain unusual events. Some years ago, for example, I met a strange woman—dark eyes with a certain glint, long dark hair, black dress, a wild and crazy cackle, a fishing pole in one hand, a knife in the other; just like the kind the gypsy sees in the crystal ball—and suddenly found myself catapulted into a great journey. This was a journey—I kid you not—to the heart of hearts, *to the center of the soul*. It was a spectacular trip from which I knew I would never return. How many doors of meaning were opened up! How many doors of satisfaction!

The journey inward did not really begin, I suppose, with this catalytic meeting. It is more likely that it started in early childhood. As I remember it, what stands out most from the early years seems to be this great interplay of opposites. My artist mother read J. Krishnamurti and Edgar Cayce. My businessman father, existentialist and hard-core political conservative, read books about World War II. With my mother, I frequented art galleries and cafes and did ESP experiments, concentrating on the dog's head to get him to roll over through the power of psychic suggestion. My father took us to "nice" restaurants. Being an archetypal (and therefore excellent) provider, he extolled the virtures of attaining and maintaining material stability. These two parents, equally brilliant in thought and articulation, were as different as night and day. They were equally committed to their views, but their views did not jibe. This was confusing to me. I shifted back and forth trying to find my own way. At 15, I became a Buddhist. Looking back I see this as an assertion of my own identity and independence. While parents, aunt and uncle laughed hysterically around our suburban Sunday dinner table, several saffron-robed and shaven Buddhist monks—who had driven miles through a blinding and dangerous snow storm—consecrated my bedroom altar and led me through a solemn and comprehensive rite of initiation, complete with ringing bells and incense. For the next eight years, I chanted, meditated with the Maharishi and danced with the Sufis. I took up the *I Ching* and tarot. Does this sound at all familiar?

I did all these things, but while I did them passionately, I had no real understanding of how to use them and no clue as to where they could possibly lead. At 23, I became "serious." I started graduate school and the tarot deck got stuffed in the closet. I had no more time for such distractions. The world situation was bad and I was beginning to see myself as responsible.

Sitting in my university office directly across the street from the Eastern-oriented Naropa Institute in Boulder, Colorado, I wished the Buddhist drummers would keep it down. Against that noise, it was difficult to concentrate on the finer nuances of Marx's *Das Kapital*. I had become an active revolutionary and proponent of the women's movement. I was deeply troubled by the human, especially female, condition. At times, I could not rest at night for dwelling on humanity's pain and suffering. At the base, I supposed, the whole problem was purely and simply economic. The whole of it could be alleviated, as I saw it, by redistributing the world's wealth which, after all, was ample. I became a materialist. How could one dwell on matters of "enlightenment" when people didn't even have food?

I spent time in retreat, poring over books. I thought that all of our problems could be solved if we only had the right *vision*. Vision, it seemed, was the answer.

Then, in 1985, several years after receiving my doctorate, I traveled to El Salvador as one of a sixteen-member delegation of doctors and nurses whose assignment was to investigate "the effects of war on health." This team would later report to the U. S. Congress. During this trip, we interviewed group after group, primarily consisting of U. S. and Salvadorean government officials and Salvadorean revolutionaries both in prison and "underground." I met some pretty famous guerilla leaders there. For every one of them, my question was the same: What is your *vision?* When you win, what will you do?

I had been obsessed with this question of vision, but to my great dismay, I came away profoundly disappointed. In fact, after I had been home for awhile, I realized that my entire worldview had been shattered. While the revolutionaries did possess a written set of goals, their resolutions did not even begin, at least in *my* mind, to approximate anything that might create equitable social change which would *endure,* social change with *vision.* And these were some of the best educated warriors in the world, people with enormous amounts of intellectual assistance.

All they knew—and I realize that this is no small revelation— was that something had to change. Life could not continue as it was. The children are dying of malnutrition, they said, so we turn to guns. This I could see, and, believe me, my stomach was in a constant knot of empathy. It seemed to me, however, that if thousands of people are going to die for a cause, there ought to be a pretty clear vision of what it is all about. Would you want to get the power and then have the process of grabbing it keep on repeating? First one group on top, then another, then another? Does *that* save the babies?

After the years of work and study I had put into trying to understand, when I realized that even the deepest thinkers of the day had not been able to come up with a truly revolutionary *vision*, whatever Marx and Engels and the rest had said, I knew that human thinking had to change.

Marxists, please bear with me. I do not wish to oversimplify this situation. I understand its complexity. But when I left El Salvador, one thought stayed with me: *We must turn inward to find a new way of being.* Over the next few years, the memory of my early spiritual seeking—a memory which had become all but obliterated with my pursuit of "higher education"—began to reawaken within me.

Whatever may appear on my formal resume, the unfolding of my life has not been linear. Another major thing that happened was that, in 1979, I gave birth to a baby. I looked into Kätchen's eyes and I could see that she was *someone*. I could see that she came from *somewhere*. From the moment she emerged from my body, she seemed to know things that she could not have internalized through *learning*. Through this experience, I became extraordinarily drawn to childbirth. I was awarded an appointment at Stanford University in 1981, and there, as well as at UCLA, I began to study birth in a major way. I went to many births, saw many babies come into the world. I saw these babies screw up their faces, expressing their first impressions of their new home. I heard their mothers cooing, Welcome, Little Star, I am your Mother in *this* life. I was so moved I cried at every birth.

I, who had decided that I was purely an existentialist—all grown up now, an educated materialist with a library full of Sartre and de Beauvoir—felt like I was bearing witness as souls flew to earth. How could this be? Who were these people? Where were they coming from? Why was I spending time doing this?

My thinking seemed to have two currents and these seemed to live in opposite directions. One part of me was a strict empiricist, a scientist, willing to accept no explanation on faith. This part of me was concerned with understanding *real* social barriers to human advancement. This part of me lived, at heart, with all the world's "underdogs." I was fully aware for example, that in the early 1960's, a whole race of people, because they were born black in racist territory, were not allowed to sit in the front seats of buses. This I understood to be a real structural barrier to equality and achievement, and it disturbed me greatly.

The other part of me, however, was growing increasingly fascinated by questions of human spirit. This part of me sensed that life, in spite of its destructive capabilities, is very, very grand. I began to think that we create reality with a wave of the hand. I started to attune to the acute power of imagination. I sensed that social structure—that which we believe to be "the way it is"—is, in every sense, malleable. We only have to push on social barriers and they miraculously fall away. I started to perceive human society as a living, dynamic entity in which every one of us, every tiny newborn child, enacts a major role. Each of us is like a separate drop of water playing our part in the great stream of human history. I seemed to deeply understand that it only took one small dark-skinned woman, actually taking a front seat in the bus, to change a whole peoples' conception of their own potential. All alone, she diverted the stream of human consciousness.

What, then, is real? Where does my duty lie? To what camp should I assign myself?

Right after my return from El Salvador, a magical woman came into my life. I met her in a restaurant when my daughter and I were seated, by chance, at her table. First she struck up a conversation with 6-year-old Kätchen. They were talking about the "faces" (phases) of the moon. I got interested and we started talking, rather idly, about witchcraft and the goddess. Then one topic led to another and she finally ended by saying that she had been sent—by the masters of the astral plane, so to speak—to teach me. She said she recognized me and that I was the student for whom she had searched. I was to apprentice with her. Needless to say, I tended toward skepticism. But, since I was questioning so many aspects of my life and my work, even though she was a total stranger to me and what she said was even more strange, I agreed to meet her the next day.

When we met at her camper, the first thing she did was to pull out a pack of tarot cards. Tarot cards! After all the deep thinking I had done! Well, it was an adventure, so I tried to stay open. This, however, is the amazing part: within the first ten minutes, I began to perceive the depth of the tarot's subtle and exquisite ability to describe the human spirit, human relationships, and, in general, human psychology. Why had I not seen this before? And, it was not as if psychology was new to me. I had spent years as a counselor. But never, in all my studies, had I encountered such a beautifully refined theoretical system for describing the human psyche as that which I saw opening through tarot.

I continued to study with this woman. But, since I was worried about my academic reputation, I studied in a concealed way. I realized that, when I had first "read the cards" in my early 20's, I did not have enough background, education, or life experience to attain even a glimmer of understanding of their power.

With my new teacher, who I came to find out was a retired advertising executive, I discovered that the tarot was a great psychological tool. But it was also much more than that. Through working with the cards, I began to understand why I cried at births. Through the doors of tarot, I was led to the ancient qabalah, which exposed the greatest mysteries of all time and existence. Through one qabalistic door I saw where I was before my birth. Through another I saw where I would go after death. The tarot opened doors that put human life and human suffering—birth, male, female, old age, death, war and peace—in perspective. With the help of the tarot, I began to attune to a small voice within. This little voice became stronger and stronger. At times, I could almost make it out. When at last I could hear it very clearly, I realized it was the voice of my own soul crying out to remember itself. That is why I cried. I had been struggling to remember my own immortality. My soul cried out that material existence is only one aspect of life. Spiritual existence is yet another, an eternal plane of unfathomable depth. The inner voice told that, until we realize this on a global scale, humanity's wars will never cease.

Then I knew. No matter how much I martyred myself to continue the struggle to alleviate human pain and suffering, as long as my approach was solely material—accepting and working with the world "as it is"—the battle would never be won. True and enduring change, I came to understand, happened in the human spirit.

As I realized this, the game of "today" was over. I began to see the steps of humanity as great long strides. In taking the long view, I began to truly awaken. Though I was hardly aware it was happening, my ego was beginning to dissolve. I felt it less and less necessary to claim allegiance of any kind. I seemed to become less and less clever. I cared less and less about how others perceived me. As my ego faded, I began to experience my Self differently. My Self seemed to stretch out infinitely into the past and the future. My Self stretched down into the earth and up into the stars. My Self seemed to merge in a vast sea of selves, which, in turn, became one Self. And, in this place of the one Self, *all opposites were reconciled*. There was no liberal versus conservative, no female versus male, no spiritual versus material. As I experienced this sensation, I stopped worrying about my academic reputation. I stopped thinking about what my colleagues or neighbors would think if they knew I was "dabbling in the occult." All of that seemed incomprehensibly trivial.

What I was learning was this: if vision is to come for humanity, we have to stop playing the game of life as it is presented to us. We cannot accept at face value the words of parents, teachers, priests or governors. All that is presented as *fact*, we take to be *reality*, but it is not. There is only one thing that is real and that is our own inner perception; that is, the knowledge which we know to be truth in our heart of hearts. The only real truth is that which we discover ourselves. When we know this in our core of cores, we become truly the masters of our own destiny. I know this now: not only do we have to look inward to discover truth, but when we do, we will also discover there the seeds of a new world. We will find that these seeds are already sprouting, nurtured in a quivering sea of deep consciousness. We have only to nurture them further. We have only to protect their existence.

These are not the seeds of culture as we know it. And, for those of us who can perceive their value, we have to be willing to make space—which sometimes means sacrificing—so that they can grow. We have to keep the inner garden weeded. We must be skeptical and scientific, but we must take the long view as well and stay *open*. We must not forsake the material for the spiritual, just as we must not forsake the spiritual for the material. Matter and spirit are not opposing forces. They are inseparable. We are spirit contained in bodies. The body is our vehicle for knowing and acting.

As a human group, we are moving toward the spiritualization of matter. As you will see from studying the *Tarot of the Spirit*, the doors of the qabalah open onto this knowledge. You, too, will pass through these doors. There you will perceive the seeds of a new world.

Have I said what I intended? As I sit here cozily sipping my cup of tea, I notice that the sea is picking up and the fog has lifted. The sun burns brightly down on my little home in the Moss Beach neighborhood of Seal Cove. It is already afternoon. Mona has come and gone and Taylor will soon be home from school. It is time, then, to bring these notes to an end.

In closing, dear friend, let me leave you with this message: whoever you are and whatever your background, my heart, mind and spirit are with you. Even though we must take each step alone, we will always be together on the path. We shall walk separately but together, for we are, at the core, comrades in truth. Together, we will find the seeds of new life and bring form to fruition. We shall create a new world in the image of our inner Vision. We have only to imagine it and it will become. I know we can do this because I have seen it. I have glimpsed a way, and in this book, I offer you the fruits of my awakening.

BOOK I

❖   ❖   ❖

The Divine Legacy

❖   ❖   ❖

CHAPTER ONE

The Tarot Deck

Welcome to tarot, the game of life! Welcome to this incredible game in which the object is to understand all that has been, is and ever-shall-be! Welcome, dear traveler, to the *Tarot of the Spirit!*

To play this intriguing game is to learn about all existence—origins and structures—past, present and future. This is done through the contemplation of images, pictures that when attended to with the mindfulness given to great art, contain the power to propel the player on a profound path of spiritual realization.

The tarot provides a vehicle for the transformational journey of the soul. Each card contains a transformative image which—as you work with it—becomes a living entity, that is, a living projection of your own instincts and emotions, capable of guiding you inward toward a deep understanding of self and cosmos. Since its inception, the tarot has functioned unequalled as a sacred oracle, a spiritual path and a focal point for meditation. This is its divine legacy.

There are many paths to enlightened understanding. Tarot is only one. Yet it is comprehensive and provides a marvelously magical and mystical journey that spirals through the innermost layers of consciousness to the very heart of being. It is able to do this because—as you will see upon undertaking its study—the tarot contains every key element for enlightenment that has become known to humanity in its quest for wisdom.

The objective of working with tarot, whether as oracle, spiritual path or meditative tool, is to attain a sublime integration of internal contradictory elements in order to transcend conflict or conditioned response patterns and move into a state of inner peace and a deep awareness of our true identity. The tarot teaches us how we create our individual and collective identity, and therefore *reality*, through our chosen allegiances and actions and how we can break destructive patterns to move ever closer to the balanced centerpoint where the spiritual and material worlds intersect. Through the tarot, we learn how to bring our material world into balanced alignment with our deepest spiritual values. We are thereby enabled to redirect our consciousness in order to achieve true health, wealth and enduring happiness. Thus, tarot, in a sense, provides a frame upon which we can build the inner temple of our selves, "stone by stone."

As poet Phyllis Koestenbaum once wrote, "Right form pleases and controls like bones . . ."[1] The tarot is quintessential "right form" for understanding the human psyche. The structure of tarot, at once, enhances and limits possibility. That is to say, its structure is like a springboard for consciousness, but it is a springboard in which both the spring and the direction of propulsion are controlled. As such, when the divine tool of tarot is correctly employed, the potential for haphazard movement and spiritual chaos is reduced.

The divine legacy of tarot has been passed down through many centuries, undergoing continual refinement. In the last five hundred years, despite occasional controversies over particular interpretations, the structure of the tarot has remained essentially the same. One could say its structure has been perfected.

Every true tarot deck contains the same number of cards in approximately the same order. The *Tarot of the Spirit* follows a traditional tarot pattern. Thus, as an oracle, the *Tarot of the Spirit* demonstrates an awesome precision. Nonetheless, the *Tarot of the Spirit* is unsurpassed as a vehicle for traveling the spiritual path. While chapter 3, The Spiritual Path, explains in greater detail the background of the *Tarot of the Spirit*, let me briefly state that this tarot is qabalistic in orientation and therefore completely balanced in its treatment of opposites. It is neither a "dark" nor a "light" tarot. It is neither "chauvinist" nor "feminist" in its approach. It stands completely centered on the Tree of Life. As such, the *Tarot of the Spirit* is offered as a guide for those seeking *lasting* balance.

In subsequent chapters, I will speak more about how to use the tarot, but first let us look at the overall structure of the pack of cards.

[1]Phyllis Koestenbaum, from the unpublished poem "Women Artists Sestina," used by permission of the author.

The Pack of Cards

The tarot contains 78 cards. Of these, 56 belong to the Minor Arcana and 22 to the Major Arcana. *Arcanum* means mystery. The cards, it is said, contain secret knowledge which is hidden in their symbols. The object, for the seeker, is to unravel the mysteries of tarot through working with the deck.

The Minor Arcana

The Minor Arcana are divided into four suits of 14 cards each. The suits represent the four major components of human life: spirit, emotions, intellect and body. These suits are also known as planes of consciousness. Thus, represented in the Minor Arcana we have the spiritual plane, the emotional plane, the intellectual plane, and the physical plane. The contemplation of the cards of the four planes, described further in chapter 4, carries you deeper and deeper into the mysteries of the human psyche.

In the *Tarot of the Spirit,* the suit of spirit is represented by the element Fire. Thus we refer to the suit as Fire. The first card is the One of Fire. The second card is the Two of Fire, the third is the Three, and so on. In addition, as you will see in chapter 3, each card is named. The One of Fire is called *Force.* The Two is *Convergence.* The Three is the *Birth of Light.* The names of the cards are not as important for this particular discussion, however, as the structure of the suits.

The suit of emotion is represented by Water. The suit of intellect is represented by Wind and the body, or physical world, is represented by Earth. We have, then, four elemental suits—the suits of Fire, Water, Wind and Earth—each containing 14 cards which make up the first 56 cards of the tarot deck.

Each element is symbolized by a particular magical tool. In the *Tarot of the Spirit,* Fire is represented by wands. Traditionally, Fire is also represented by wooden rods, clubs, and other objects which either burn up (such as trees) or send out currents of flame or energy. In other tarot decks, as well as in decks of playing cards, this suit has frequently been known as the suit of wands or clubs.

Water is represented by cups in that cups contain and, in some ways, give form to liquid. Traditionally, any vessel becomes the tool for the suit of Water. Because it is the suit of emotion, it is also represented by hearts. Thus, it has often been called the suit of cups or hearts.

In the *Tarot of the Spirit,* the tool of the suit of Wind is the sword. Upon studying the Sacred Texts in Book II, the connection between the element of Wind and the sword will become more clear. Blades and spades of all kinds fall into the category of swords. Thus the suit of Wind has been known as swords or spades. Feathers also represent the Wind. This is easier to comprehend in that birds spread their wings—feathers—to rise up on the wind. This, of course, symbolizes the process of spiritual transcendence.

Finally, Earth is represented by pentacles. The pentacle is the five-pointed star that represents humanity—two arms, two legs and a head—in physical form. When the star is encircled, it signifies humanity passing through eternity, always changing, always moving, cartwheeling through time. Earth is also represented by dishes, platters (especially when they hold bread), coins, disks and diamonds. It is most often known as the suit of pentacles, disks, or diamonds. See figure 1 for the correspondences of each suit.

Of the 14 cards in each suit, ten are numbered 1 through 10 and four are "face" cards. We will look at the theoretical structure of these in turn.

Numbers 1 through 10

Each card in each suit represents a particular aspect of human consciousness or experience. In each of the four suits, the 1s contain many of the same properties, the 2s are similar, the 3s are similar, and so on.

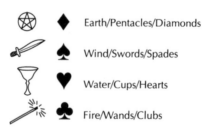

⊛	♦	Earth/Pentacles/Diamonds
	♠	Wind/Swords/Spades
♁	♥	Water/Cups/Hearts
	♣	Fire/Wands/Clubs

Figure 1. The suits of tarot.

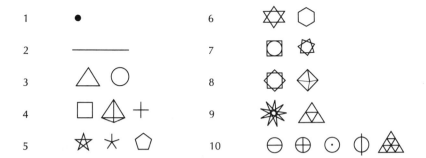

Figure 2. The sacred geometry of tarot.

At 1 something is beginning to open up; at 2, it becomes polar-ized; at 3, it becomes dimensional; at 4, it becomes stable; at 5, it begins to move; at 6, it restabilizes; at 7, it becomes highly complex; at 8, it grows; at 9, the suit comes into its highest point. At 10, the suit is completed, a cycle has fulfilled itself, and new ideas or elements begin to enter. It is as if at the 10 in any suit, the querist moves on to a new plane of experience.

It is useful to think of the numbers 1 through 10 in terms of a geometric progression. The 1, for example, is a point. At the point of the 1, everything begins to come into sharp focus. The 2 is two points that form a line; the line symbolizes duality, polarization or continuum. The 3 makes a triangle or triad and also a plane. When you begin to think of the numbers geometrically, if you use your creative imagination (as described in chapters 3 and 4) much light is shed on the meaning of the particular card. I offer the symbolism of figure 2 for your further contemplation on this matter. Figure 2 does not purport to be exhaustive, but it will provide greater insight into the possibilities of the tarot deck.

To enhance the picture obtained through thinking geometically, the meaning of the numbers can be outlined as follows:

1. raw energy;

2. will, purpose, initial understanding;

3. conception, manifestation;

4. production, mastery, clinging to achievement;

5. surrender, release, destruction;

6. solution, exaltation, seeing;

7. feeling, deepening, mystery;

8. repose, consideration, retreat, ripening;

9. understanding before or beyond words, strengthening;

10. processing, moving to a new level.

A final way of looking at the theoretical structure of the numbers 1 through 10 is as a linear graph of experience. At the 1, something begins. At the 2, it grows in intensity. At the 3, it grows stronger still. At the 4, it reaches its initial peak. At the five, problems arise. At the 6, the querist feels the problems are solved. At the 7, the querist realizes that the solutions embraced at the 6 were probably not of a permanent nature and thereby goes "back to the drawing board." At the 8, real learning, which will have lasting results, begins to occur. At the 9, the major messages and mysteries of the particular suit or issue at hand have been processed and understood. At the 10, the querist moves to a new level or a new way of knowing. See figure 3 for a graphic depiction of this concept.

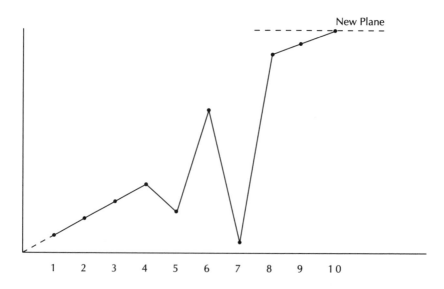

Figure 3. The linear depiction of numbers 1 through 10.

The theoretical meaning of numbers 1 through 10 is uniform in every tarot deck. Thus, the querist need not know the "name" of the particular card in order to interpret its meaning. When you know the meaning of the suits, the theoretical structure of cards 1 through 10, in addition to the meaning of the face cards, you are capable of "reading" an ordinary deck of 52 playing cards.

The Face Cards ───

An ordinary pack of playing cards contains three face cards in each suit. They are traditionally referred to as Kings, Queens and Jacks.

Each suit of the tarot contains four face cards for a perspective which is, overall, more balanced. In different decks, these cards go by different names. They are sometimes called Kings, Queens, Princes and Princesses, or Knights, Queens, Princes and Pages. One deck calls them Shamans, Priestesses, Sons and Daughters. In the *Tarot of the Spirit*, the face cards are called Fathers, Mothers, Brothers and Sisters. In all tarot decks, there are traditionally two parent-like cards and two offspring. If you wish to read an ordinary pack of cards, however, where there are only three face cards, you may wish to combine the attributes of both "children" into one child, which would, of course, be represented by the Jack.

In the *Tarot of the Spirit*, the Father in the suit of Fire is known as Fire Father. The Mother is Fire Mother. The Brother is Fire Brother and the Sister, Fire Sister.

Just as all the 1s have similar qualities, all of the Fathers have similar qualities. This holds true for Mothers, Brothers and Sisters as well. So, while we have 16 face cards in the entire deck, and while each face card will be modified by the suit in which it appears, the face cards can be reduced to four major personality types.

All Fathers, for example, even though they are conditioned by the element of the suit in which they reside, are essentially related to the element of Fire. Thus they represent spirit—action, energy and movement. If the Father is residing in the suit of Water, he will be modified, for example, by the spirit and energy level of Water. Since Water is by nature passive, the Water Father, who is really the Fire Father in Water, is likely to be passive. His high energy is subdued by Water's heavy and calming influence. When the Father appears in his own element, in *Fire*, however, he becomes the very essence of his inner qualities. He is hot and flaming, all action, high energy and continuous movement.

Just as all the Fathers are related to Fire, all Mothers are related to the element Water. Regardless of the suit in which they appear, although they are conditioned or refined by the attributes of that suit, it can be said that all the Mothers personify the qualities of emotion and understanding. The Mothers—in their exalted state—are receptive, loving and nurturing.

The Brothers represent the suit of Wind. They are intellectual, relying on reason, seeking understanding through the processes of thought. They seek to discover higher purpose through rationality. In the *Tarot of the Spirit,* the Brothers are the Spirit Warriors. In their exalted state, they are not afraid of creating and employing new information as they speed their causes along.

The Sisters represent Earth. They solidify, or "ground," all the energy generated along the path through the particular suit. In a certain way, they can be seen as the essence of the suit or the element of the suit as it is processed and applied—concretely—in the body, mind or spirit of the querist, or in the querist's life. The Sisters represent the manifestation of the messages, mysteries or lessons of the particular suit. Thus, they are like the Priestesses of the element. They are capable of understanding the element thoroughly and putting its tools to work.

While much more information regarding the modifications of the face cards as they appear in each suit is presented in Book II, it is useful to think of the face cards as four essential types: Fire Father, Water Mother, Wind Brother and Earth Sister. Beyond that, we can conceptualize Fire Father in Water, imagining, for example, how the element of Water would affect his fiery nature. We can imagine Fire Father in Wind with the same empathetic stance, or Fire Father in Earth.

In each suit, the Fathers and Mothers unite to produce their offspring. Thus it can be said that the Brothers and Sisters contain the characteristics and receive the guidance of both of their parents. Whether they attune to their parents or follow their directives is, of course, a personal matter. As the querist begins to understand this, the cards begin to come alive.

The querist, then, will understand that the Father and Mother do not necessarily contain the characteristics of their offspring. The Father and Mother are "pure" in nature. The children, however, have

the ability—if they so choose and if they exalt their own potential—
to soar beyond the limits of their parents, "casting," as it were, "the
disk of Earth much further."[2]

To understand this, to understand any of the face cards of the
tarot, we ought to put ourselves in any one of their shoes. Only then
can we begin to perceive their meaning on a deep level. We can then
begin to understand the *theory* of the tarot which takes us, in terms
of *internalized knowledge*, far beyond the limits of rote memorization.
The apprehension of these four personality types in *theory*, renders
the whole of tarot easier to understand.

If you wish to understand the Earth Sister in Wind, for example,
try to experience things from her perspective. How would you feel
with an older Brother and two parents who were guided, for all
practical purposes, by the challenge of the intellectual endeavor?

Learning to experience the tarot from the *inside* opens the doors
to its minor and major mysteries.

The Major Arcana ———————————————————————

There are 22 cards of the Major Arcana, also known as Trumps,
numbered 0 through XXI. In the *Tarot of the Spirit*, these cards are
known as Keys. That is because each one has a powerful capacity to
unlock the door of a major mystery of the human psyche.

The Keys are the *superpowers* or, in some cases, the *superheroes*,
of the tarot. They can be seen as prototypical emotional response
patterns that emerge as personality or energy "types." We can view
them as external to ourselves, but they also reside within us as our
own subpersonalities. For example, Key 0 is the trusting, faithful Fool.
Sometimes I am interacting with a Fool. Sometimes I am a Fool. Key
I is the mighty magician, the Magus, capable of creating any situation
with a swish of the magic wand. I can be a Fool, but I can be a Magus
too. Sometimes I am the High Priestess, Key II. As the High Priestess,
I see all and know all, but I do not necessarily act upon it. It depends
on my mood. In a sense, each Tarot Key is like a mood.

It could be said that the 22 Keys represent our conditioned response, or predispositions to react, to the symbolic universe in which
we live. Our symbolic universe consists of a whole interconnected

---

[2]Nikos Kazantzakis, *The Odyssey: A Modern Sequel* (New York: Simon & Schuster, 1958),
p. 414.

network of symbols to which we have developed specific reflexes. The symbols comprising our symbolic universe include, for example, our language, the patterned roles we enact in everyday life (mother, student, clerk, doctor, etc.) and the social institutions in which we live (e.g., family, economic, religious, political and educational systems). We respond to these symbols often without realizing that we have internalized the set of values represented by them. We respond without recognizing that we have accepted and reproduced the external symbolic universe on the internal level, that we have embraced this world and engraved it *inside* of ourselves on the *subconscious* level. We have developed reflexive reactions without even being aware of it. But we must understand that the way we act or react to the symbolic universe continually reinforces or dissolves both our individual and our collective way of life.

The symbolic universe represents or encapsulates belief systems or modes of operating. The symbols become forms of suggestion which, in turn, trigger the release of certain *types* of energy. The symbolic universe thus recreates itself again and again on the subconscious and conscious levels, on the internal as well as on the external levels.

In coming to understand the 22 Keys of the tarot, we come to understand our own conditioned responses to the symbolic universe in which we live. If we get *inside* the cards, if we understand each personality on its own terms, we will be able to feel how it is to react as if we were the Emperor, for example, or as if we were the Hermit.

Through arriving at a deep knowledge of the Keys, we learn that we do not have to react blindly. We are capable of selecting the form of energy, the Key, with which we choose to respond to a situation. We are given 22 concrete examples. And, from this, we learn that we can create new images or energy patterns that will transform, rather then reinforce, the symbolic universe in which we live. We learn that we can build a symbolic universe, both internally and externally, in accord with our own inner visions.

The Mystery Card —————————————————————————

Finally, the *Tarot of the Spirit* contains one additional, non-traditional tarot card, making a total of 79 cards. This card is unlabeled but recognizable by its inverted triangular shape. I refer to this as the *Mystery Card*. The Mystery Card can be viewed as the master card of the tarot deck: the overarching card of spiritual realization. It contains the concepts of birth, death and karmic transition. Playing with the cards over time, its meaning will become clear to the one who seeks it.

The Transformative Ability of the Pack of Cards

It can be intimated, from this description of the pack of cards—the 56 Minor and 22 Major Arcana of the tarot—that the tarot's transformative ability is activated when the querist 1) develops a comprehensive *theoretical* understanding of the structure of the deck, and 2) gets *inside* the cards so they can be understood intuitively.

It is not likely that a knowledge of the tarot gained through memorizing a written description of individual cards will have much impact on the mind or life of the querist. It could, *latently,* of course, but rote memorization has some fairly severe limitations. In any case, one who relies on memorization would not make a very good "reader."

If the querist wishes transformation, he or she must learn to *think* as the cards think. There is no way to do this other than to practice, placing oneself, time after time, inside of every single card that turns up. The following chapters show how to do this and offer three ways of working with and internalizing the tarot—as a sacred oracle, as a spiritual path and as a day by day meditation.

✦ ✦ ✦

CHAPTER TWO

The Sacred Oracle

The tarot is generally recognized and accepted as a tried and true oracle for reading past, present and future. Querists are continually amazed by its phenomenal accuracy. This chapter tells how to use this profound tool. Before we begin, however, let us address the question: "How could a pack of cards tell such an exacting story?" There are two explanations as to how the tarot works. The first is purely scientific. The second is more mysterious.

From a scientific point of view, let us assume for the sake of the explanation, that you have a problem or issue over which you are conflicted. Let us begin by faithfully accepting the premise that few people seek the aid of an oracle when all aspects of life are going smoothly, unless, of course, they wish to challenge the efficacy of the oracular tool itself or, after accepting its capability, to use it as a guide in designing future life activity. In all cases, the following explanation equally applies.

First, and very importantly, every tarot deck contains the same 78 cards. *Every true tarot pack has the same four suits, the same face cards, the same trumps and follows the same progressive order.* That is to say, to begin with, if you can read one tarot deck, you can read any tarot deck, and once you know the background theory, you can even read an ordinary pack of playing cards. The only difference is that the ordinary playing cards do not contain the 22 trumps included in the tarot. For your perusal, the theoretical structure of the cards is outlined in the first chapter of this book.

So, with the above information in hand, you come to the tarot with a problem. Let us say that you have lost sleep over this problem.

You have lain awake at night going over possible answers and strategies. You have composed the most ingenious scenarios in your mind. But, for some reason, you have been unable to take the step which would actually alleviate the problem. Perhaps the problem seems too complicated. There are too many factors. You do not wish to cause problems for others, let us say, but you need to get on with your life. You seek out the sacred oracle.

Imagine that the 78 cards are spinning over your head. They are spinning in a circular motion like a great revolving carousel. Imagine that you cannot see the faces of the cards, but only the backs. They all look alike. They are all the same size, color and configuration. Imagine that you must draw one. The one that you select will provide the answer to your problem. But they all seem to be of equal weight. How will you choose?

Imagine that you cannot choose. You finally decide to close your eyes, count to ten and reach up and grab a card at random. You do this, and after studying the card, with some reflection, you are amazed to realize that the concept contained in this card precisely applies to your current predicament. Since the draw of the card has been totally random—or so it appears—you question how could this be.

The scientific explanation is as follows. To begin with, each of the 78 cards of the tarot deck represents a *key component of the human psyche over time*. These concepts have been refined and refined over centuries and perhaps millenia. As a result, each card can be described in one word, one sentence, one paragraph or several volumes. Thus, each card is both precise and general at the same time.

For example, let us suppose that the particular concept you pulled from the carousel has to do with "love." Many things come to mind when we think of love. Love is a major human theme. From the beginning of time, love has affected every one of our lives. Love was just as important a thousand years ago as it will be in another thousand years. Like love, every theme of the tarot is timeless in nature.

So, you have drawn Love. The Love card gives you direction in conceptualizing and solving your problem. Regardless of what your problem is, Love will solve it. Love is your answer. Love points the way to a solution. Through focusing on Love, you can put an end to the endless spinning of scenarios. Love is the way. You accept then, that all aspects of your problem and its solution are not equal. Love has emerged as the most important aspect. Now you can focus. You have one thing to examine and that thing is Love. In your imagination, then, you *interpret* the card. *You* decide how Love applies to your problem. With your imagination, you determine the significance of the answer. In your mind, you make the answer fit. As you make it fit, you will discover that it fits perfectly. In solving your problem, Love becomes the guiding principle. In knowing this, you can make your next move.

What if you had drawn another card? Suffice it to say that whatever card you draw, that card would give you an idea as to how to stop the spinning ideas and focus your mind. Because the tarot is so well conceptualized, any one of the cards will bring you into sharp focus. That is because drawing any card, in any random fashion, limits the unending possibilities and provides a well-defined springboard for interpretation and action.

Any card of the tarot applies equally to any human problem or endeavor. Each card gives you an angle on your subject matter. Each card gives you a specific vantage point. It is as if you are a photographer and the subject of your photograph is standing in the middle of an open field. From each point around the field's perimeter, you get a different view or backdrop. Some angles might be prettier than others, but each is just as real. The tarot cards are like vantage points around the perimeter of the field. They give you 78 different angles on any given subject. Some angles might be prettier than others, but each is just as *real*.

That is why, when you align the cards in a particular order, let us say that you choose one card to represent the past, one to represent the present, and one to represent the future, no matter which cards turn up, they will all be correct. Each card merely provides a distinct focal point. Your imagination, then, provides the story which binds the sequence of cards together.

The foregoing explanation of why the tarot cards work is purely psychological and scientific. The tarot, as an informative psychological tool—incredibly useful for psychological counselors—represents the collective psychology of humankind *over time.* The way you interpret the cards for yourself illuminates your individualized psychology.

This, then, is the scientific explanation for the tarot and, without delving into any occult or esoteric thought—which is usually the case in tarot books—it stands on its own merit.

There is, however, another explanation as to why the tarot works. As it is mystical in nature, this explanation involves a leap of faith. Let us suppose that you are dealing with the same problem or subject over a one week stretch. Each day you draw a card to help you approach your issue. On five out of the seven days, after shuffling the deck numerous times each day, you draw the same card.

How could this be? It is as if the tarot is forcing you over and over to examine your subject from a particular point of view. A chill runs down your spine. The statistical probability of drawing the same card five days within one week wherein only seven cards were drawn is infinitesimally small, and yet it has happened. What is going on?

The skeptic might claim that your memory is selective. What about all the other weeks when you drew a *different* card each day? Perhaps you are merely *selectively recalling* the events of this particular week. Bear in mind, of course, that if your memory is merely being selective, it is likely the case that your subconscious mind is trying to tell you something, whatever the explanation. At any rate, you know in your heart, from your own visceral reaction to seeing that same card again, that you ought to pay attention.

Those practiced with the tarot, however, would not be surprised or skeptical about your experience. An accomplished tarot reader might react by smiling, shaking her head, shrugging her shoulders and merely commenting, "It happens all the time."

Each reader arrives at her or his own explanation. Because it does not seem probable that one could draw the same card each day, or that one could repeatedly get the same card to explain past experiences, for example, the explanations as to how such a thing could occur are necessarily metaphysical.

I leave the exact nature of the metaphysical explanations to your own interpretation. Practice with the cards and call the judgments as you will. However, I will say that without the shadow of a doubt, in working with the tarot, you will discover a deeply mystical and transcendent theoretical structure—*a transcendent reality*—that, in its luminosity, all but eclipses the mundane explanatory ability of ordinary scientific logic.

Reading the Cards

If you have never seen a tarot card, or if you have never read a book on the tarot, it is postulated that, given a good tarot deck, drawn or painted with the key symbols of tarot in mind, you should be able to render an accurate reading. How is this possible?

First, it is possible because the artwork contained in the tarot is *psycho-active*. This means that the simple act of studying the symbols on a particular card activates your subconscious mind in such a way that explanations or interpretations surface to the conscious level. Social scientists say that as human beings we all share a collective system of symbols which is understood on an intuitive level. Just looking at a symbol sets off a reaction and an interpretation. The tarot is designed to trigger just such a reaction. To read the cards, you have only to trust your instinctive reactions.

Secondly, it is said that it is possible to read the cards without being versed in their usage because you already know the answer you are looking for. The card is merely a medium which reflects your own thoughts. Again, you must trust your own response.

Thirdly, the tarot cards are said to open psychic doorways. That is to say, even if you do not consider yourself to be "psychic," *per se,* the tarot is designed to awaken your sensitivity to forces of mind which transcend ordinary states of thinking. In working with the cards, even if you are not familiar with their usage, you may well experience transcendental psychic visions.

The tarot cards are catalysts for consciousness. They propel you to think in alternative ways. And, while you may get a great deal out of doing a "blind" reading—spreading the cards without an intellectual understanding of their theoretical structure—there is so much profound and timeless knowledge connected with tarot that you will surely benefit from reading about how others have used and interpreted them. It is my duty, therefore, to summarize for you the essential nature of the reading.

The Theoretical Keys ────────────────────────────────

As we saw in the first chapter, the tarot deck is organized into four suits representing Fire, Water, Wind (Air) and Earth. These suits correspond to Spirit, Emotions, Intellect and Body. In addition, there are 16 face cards corresponding to aspects of personality and 22 keys corresponding to major archetypal representations of the human psyche. Attributes of these cards were described in chapter 1.

Much tarot reading is organized around the four elemental suits, first, and second, around the aspects of past, present and future. For example, you may wish to examine the state of your emotions in the past, present and future. You would draw, perhaps, four cards. The first might indicate the general issue around which you are having emotional feelings. The second might pertain to your feelings about this issue in the past, the third would correspond to your feelings in the present, and the fourth to the feelings you will have in the future.

Let us break down the process of reading, taking it one step at a time.

The Significator

In any given reading, the first card drawn is called the *significator*. The significator identifies the key issue with which you will be working. For example, you may have a specific question. The significator supplies the major focal point of your answer. Or, you may not have a specific question in mind, but rather, you may be doing a "general reading" on the overall status of things. If the reading is general, the significator identifies the most important event, issue or occurrence.

In many cases, you may find it sufficient to use only a significator for your reading. This is usually referred to as a "one card reading." However, if you draw additional cards, they will all be organized around the significator and refer back to the significator as the common denominator.

Once you have the significator, you will probably want to look up its meaning in the supplied text. It is advisable to read the entry in its entirety. However, if you want a brief reminder, concentrate on reading the "Divinatory Meaning."

Obtaining the Significator

There are no hard and fast rules in tarot reading about how to select a significator. Some people spread the cards across the table face down, and study their backs, searching for a card that jumps out at them. Others pass their hands over the cards feeling for one that seems warmer in temperature than the others. Still others shuffle the cards, place them face down on the table in an ordered stack, cut them once to the left, and take the top card on the right hand pile as the significator. Cutting to the left, by the way, is said to activate the intuitive consciousness.

As a side note, it may be important to mention here that some people do not allow anyone other than themselves to touch their cards as they feel it may weaken the power of the cards or that the cards may absorb "negative outside energies." Others insist that the one for whom they are doing the reading must cut the cards in order to insure that the appropriate significator is selected. However you choose to handle your cards is a purely individual decision. As with all other aspects of tarot reading, there is no right or wrong way of working with the cards.

To obtain further cards for the reading, some individuals will draw at random out of the whole pack spread face down on the table. Others take them in order from the right hand pile after the original pack has been cut in two. They are then laid down according to the requirements of the reading, which will be outlined in the next section.

Again, it is up to you to decide how you will draw the cards to fill each space in the reading. It is strongly advised, however, that you select the cards blindly, that is to say, select them from cards that are face down, place them face down in the proper sequence and do not turn them up until you are reading that particular position.

The Tarot Spread

When we place the cards on the table in a particular preconceived order, we are creating what is called a tarot "spread" or "throw." The spread is thus the basis for the reading.

It is advised that you practice creating your own spreads, but, to start with, I offer six basic throws. As a word of caution, I never end a reading on a bad note. If the outcome of the reading looks grim for any reason, I will ask the tarot how I can avoid problems and draw another card. Or I may ask what stage will follow the outcome. I will not end the reading until I feel "the story has a happy ending." You should feel free to elaborate on the reading as you see fit. Always use your imagination as well as your judgment. In the last analysis, it is always up to you to decide how you will employ the cards.

To read the cards in any given spread, first place all cards in the proper sequence face down on the table. Then turn up Card 1. Fully interpret that card before moving to the next card. To interpret the cards, please refer to the next section of this book, The Sacred Texts, wherein you can read the divinatory meaning of each card. Concentrate on making sense of each card and use your imagination as to how these particular cards link together and form one unit or story. If, after turning up all the cards and after serious contemplation, you do not understand the message of a particular card, ask the tarot for clarification and draw another card for that place. If you are confused or dissatisfied, you should feel free to draw more cards. However, if you get too many cards on the table, the original cards may get "lost," and not receive their due consideration. Every single card is equally important and carries its own message.

To interpret cards that are upside down as you turn them up, please refer to the section following the tarot spreads entitled "The Cards as Cycles; Reversals" on page 27.

SPREAD 1: ISSUE-ACTION-OUTCOME

1	2	3

Card 1. Significator/Issue
Card 2. Action to be taken
Card 3. Outcome/Resolution

In this three-card reading, the significator, Card 1, is placed in the first position. This will describe the major issue with which the querist is dealing. Card 2 tells what to do regarding the particular issue. Card 3 tells what will result from the action.

SPREAD 2: ELEMENTAL INDICATORS

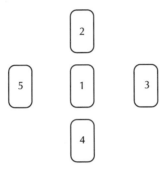

Card 1. Significator
Card 2. Physical Indicator
Card 3. Mental Indicator
Card 4. Spiritual Indicator
Card 5. Emotional Indicator

This spread is designed to get a quick reading on any particular issue or subject. Ask a question. Place the cards in the proper positions and turn them up and interpret them one at a time. Card 1 outlines the issue. Card 2 tells the querist how the issue is impacted or impacting on a purely physical level. Card 3 examines the mental or intellectual aspects of the issue. Card 4 tells about how the issue impacts on a spiritual or deep energetic level. Card 5 explains how it affects the emotions.

SPREAD 3: THE TRADITIONAL CELTIC CROSS

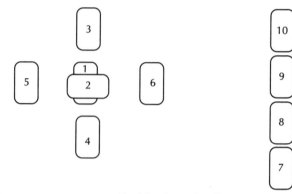

Card 1.   Significator
Card 2.   Blocking or Crossing Influence
Card 3.   Surface Reality
Card 4.   Deep Reality
Card 5.   Immediate Past

Card 6.   Immediate Future
Card 7.   Psychological State
Card 8.   Environmental or Social State
Card 9.   Hopes and Fears
Card 10. Outcome/Resolution

The Traditional Celtic Cross is the most widely used of all the tarot spreads. This is not without reason as it provides for an extremely effective and comprehensive reading. Card 1, as usual, is the significator which indicates the major issue at hand. Card 2, the blocking or crossing influence, explains how the querist is being blocked in her or his endeavors. This card provides additional information about the significator. Card 3 tells how things appear to be on the surface, but Card 4 delves deep beneath the surface to the inner layers of truth. Card 4 is to be trusted as the deep inner reality. Card 5 tells how things were in the immediate past. (I usually interpret the immediate past to encompass about two weeks.) Card 6 is the immediate future, the upcoming two weeks. Card 7 provides information about the querist's current psychological state, while Card 8 describes the reality in which the querist is operating. Card 9 gives information about that which the querist hopes will happen with regard to the significator and conversely what he or she fears will occur. Card 10 provides information on the outcome of the issue at hand.

    For this particular reading, some readers will add two additional cards to shed further light on the outcome. This gives three, rather than just one, parameters of outcome. Many feel that this rounds out the reading. When the final two cards are added, the traditional Celtic Cross is called the "Witches Spread" or the "Witches Cross."

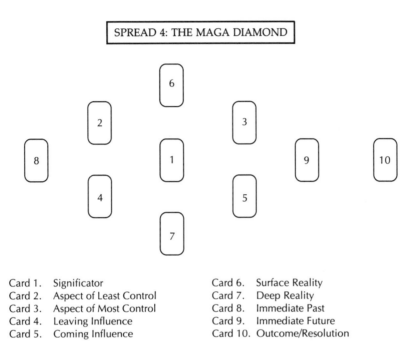

SPREAD 4: THE MAGA DIAMOND

Card 1.	Significator	Card 6.	Surface Reality
Card 2.	Aspect of Least Control	Card 7.	Deep Reality
Card 3.	Aspect of Most Control	Card 8.	Immediate Past
Card 4.	Leaving Influence	Card 9.	Immediate Future
Card 5.	Coming Influence	Card 10.	Outcome/Resolution

Like the Traditional Celtic Cross, the Maga Diamond constitutes a comprehensive spread. The central card is the significator. Card 2 shows the aspect of the significator over which the querist has the least amount of control. This is often the area which the querist wishes most to control, but since it is not possible to attain control, it is advisable not to dwell on it. The querist is advised by Card 2 to let go of the particular issue appearing in this place. It cannot be controlled so forget about it. Rather, the querist should put his or her energy into concentrating on Card 3. Card 3 represents the querist's greatest strength at the present time. Card 4 represents an area which recently had a great deal of influence over the querist, but its influence is now leaving and being replaced by the powerful influence of Card 5. Card 6, as in the Traditional Celtic Cross, represents reality as it appears on the surface, while Card 7 represents the deep inner reality of the situation. Card 7 can be trusted as reflecting the deep, inner reality as a statement of deep truth. Card 8 is the immediate past situation. Card 9 is the immediate future situation. Card 10 is the ultimate outcome of the situation or the final resolution.

As with the Celtic Cross, you may wish to add two more "outcome" cards for additional information.

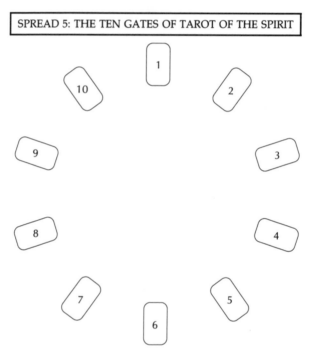

SPREAD 5: THE TEN GATES OF TAROT OF THE SPIRIT

Card 1. Significator	Card 6. Essence or Truth
Card 2. Propelling Force	Card 7. Subconscious Insight
Card 3. Guide Card	Card 8. Conscious Insight; the Direction of Resolution
Card 4. Greatest Strength	Card 9. The Gateway
Card 5. Greatest Weakness	Card 10. Ultimate Outcome; New Level

The Gates begin to open with Card 1, the significator. The significator explains to the querist what the issue is as he or she seeks to move to a more advanced level. This is especially applicable in the area of spiritual growth. Card 2 describes the force that will move the querist upon the path. Card 3 supplies the querist with a meditation card or guide to follow during the next period of development. Card 4 is the querist's greatest strength, an aspect about which the querist can feel a great deal of self-confidence. Card 5, conversely, is the querist's weakness. He or she should concentrate upon strengthening this aspect of self. Card 6 is the essence or truth of the situation at hand. Card 7 represents the querist's subconscious or intuitive insight regarding the significator. Card 8 is the insight that already exists on the querist's conscious level. It points the way to resolving the issue raised by the significator. Card 9 is the gateway through which the querist must pass after the foregoing cards are interpreted, fully understood and internalized. Finally, Card 10 tells the querist's future direction and what the new level of growth holds in store.

Remember, if for any reason the outcome or any individual cards in any of your readings is considered negative, you may choose to draw additional cards to give more information, for further outcomes, or to give advice for obviating negative circumstances or situations. As I said, I never end a reading until I reach a positive and constructive solution.

The Cards as Cycles; Reversals

It is useful to look at each tarot card as a cycle. Each card is a singular concept, but that concept has many dimensions which occur in a cyclical nature. Thus, at the down part of the cycle, each tarot card or concept contains its opposite. For example, if we think about the "Love" card again, we will realize that love can contain hate. For example, a love unrequited can generate anger or frustration in the lover. In the beginning of the love cycle, love may seem fresh and new. It may seem exciting, exhilarating even, delightful; it is full of wonder. As it gets older, it is sometimes overshadowed by negative emotions of all sorts. In its very mature state, love may become almost complacent. Eventually, a love that lasts becomes enduring and unconditional. This is love in its exalted state.

Sometimes you will notice that tarot readers interpret the same card differently. Is this because one is right and one is wrong? No, it is not. If you look at the subtleties of the tarot, you will realize that different readers are concentrating, for the moment, on different aspects of the cycle of the card.

This is not only true with regard to different tarot readers or readings, but with regard to different tarot decks. One pack of cards may picture the concept in its exalted or light aspect while another pictures it in its dark aspect. The important thing is that the tarot deck contain the *concept*. Then the experienced reader, when looking at a specific card, can interpret it at will in any aspect of its cycle. It is up to the reader, within the context of the reading, to interpret which aspects of the concept to focus on.

When tarot cards appear upside down—these are called *reversals*—many readers will interpret them as being the exact opposite of the usually accepted divinatory meaning. I usually refer to reversals as "blocks." In other words, I see the reversed card as the situation as it would appear if something were not blocking it from occurring. I ask the tarot, what is blocking the situation here? And I draw another card.

Because each card in the tarot is a cycle, it is useful to have a thorough understanding of the tarot as a system. This is not a matter of memorization. It is a matter, rather, of understanding the overall theoretical structure and working within that structure. To obtain a good theoretical understanding, look at the structure of the cards as it appears in chapter 1. The best readers are not those who have memorized interpretations out of a book. The best readers are those who have a comprehensive theoretical understanding of the *system* of the tarot coupled with a deep-seated trust in their own intuitive abilities.

Developing the Intuitive Trust

There is only one way to arrive at a deep-seated trust in your intuition and that way is *to practice*. It is through practice, as well, that you learn to construct or recognize comprehensive stories or visions from the cards laid down in a tarot spread.

At first reading the tarot may seem awkward or cumbersome. There are so many cards! But with practice, reading the cards comes easier and easier. It also becomes less and less gamelike.

Working with the Sacred Oracle can be a richly rewarding experience. It can transport you into a mystical world of transcendent realities. It can transport you into a state of heightened mystical consciousness. This will not happen, however, until you have mastered the basics.

The more you accept the work and study involved in attaining a deep, as opposed to a cursory, understanding of the tarot, the more the tarot will come to accept and lead you as its Initiate. As you prove yourself—through diligent persistence—to be a worthy candidate for initiation, you will be led into the Great Hall of Mysteries where the most fabulous wealth and sublime happiness await you.

❖ ❖ ❖

CHAPTER THREE

The Spiritual Path

Through aeons untold, we have sought explanations as to the ultimate origin and destiny of the inner life of our deepest selves. Intuitively, we feel that we must be something more than a mere bag of bones. We continually make references to the soul. We want to believe that the essence of life extends beyond this fleeting ephemeral existence of dying matter—that there is some kind of ongoing center of eternal flame housed deep within our beings—but we are often hard-pressed to come up with answers to our dilemma.

It is as if we have arrived in this dimension not knowing who we are. We feel we have forgotten something important. We struggle to remember. We ask: "Who am I?" This question—Who am I?— then, becomes the most profound mystery that besets humanity. In seeking to find answers, we step onto the spiritual path. At its heart, the spiritual quest is the journey to recollect our deepest inner identity.

Those who have walked the spiritual path through the aeons have, indeed, discovered various keys to awakening the sleeping memory. These keys can be found at the foundation of every religious belief system. And, of critical importance to us right now, is the fact that *many of the keys to unlocking mystical consciousness have been reduced, contained and preserved in the visual images of tarot. As a result, not only is the tarot a completely accurate oracle, but a comprehensive spiritual path as well.* Each card of the tarot opens a door to the deep spiritual memory. When correctly assimilated, these images provide a concise transcendental system for spiritual ascendance.

The use of tarot as a spiritual path has, in the past, been primarily the province of the Western Mystery Schools which have operated in a concealed manner. It is only during recent years—due to a growing social tolerance—that the Mystery Schools have surfaced and that this information has been released to the public in clear and understandable forms. The main reason for the secrecy was that, during different historical periods, the guardians of tarot feared they would be persecuted for their knowledge. Thus arose the adage of initiates: To Know, To Will, To Dare and To Keep Silent.

For the moment, the silence is happily lifted.

Presently, I will discuss in some detail the usage of tarot as a spiritual path, but first, I will relate the historical roots of this system as it has been told to me.

The Ancient History of Tarot

It is told by Initiates of the Great Mystery Schools of the Western world that the roots of tarot are as deep and ancient as the lost continent of Atlantis, that mysterious spiritual isle said, in olden times, to lie in the Atlantic Ocean just west of the Spanish peninsula of Gibraltar. In Atlantean temples, Initiates say, one found the keys to unlocking every Mystery of Soul or Spirit that was ever conceived. Atlantis was ill-fated, however, and as its temples began to sink beneath the rising tides that would eventually consume the whole culture, adepts of the Atlantean priesthood set sail in four directions, carrying with them, fully guarded, the Essential Keys of Atlantean Wisdom. Their task: to disseminate the Atlantean Mysteries to the four corners of the world.

It is said that some of the mystery ships landed on the shores of the British Isles, thereby fueling, with Atlantean philosophy, the Ancient Wisdom of the Druidic Priesthood. Other Atlanteans arrived at the great seaport later known as Alexandria at the mouth of the Nile delta. There, the Atlantean teachings were carefully absorbed and protected in the temples of the day.

Alexander the Great founded (conquered) Alexandria during his campaign to unite the world between 336 and 323 B.C. It was in the magnificent city-state of Alexandria that Ptolemy I is credited with having founded the Great Library. This library, which probably contained 500,000 volumes at its peak, along with the Temple of Jupiter Serapis, which housed the library's "overflow," became the center of

intellectual activity in the Hellenistic world and the headquarters of
the Collegium of the Adepts of the Mysteries. It is said that all materials of Atlantean, Egyptian and Greek origin which were relevant
to the Mystery Schools were stored at the Great Library and the
Temple.

In A.D. 391, however, Alexandria's Great Library and Temple of
Jupiter Serapis were pillaged, burned and completely destroyed by
marauding Christians acting under the edict of Emperor Theodosius
of Rome. Once again, however, in the face of terrible peril, the Wisdom of the Ages was rescued. Initiates of the Mystery Schools tell us
that the keys to the mysteries were liberated from the Library and
Temple by the Adepts of the Collegium and spirited away to Fez,
Morocco, which then became the Collegium's new seat.

In Fez, the Collegium held meetings to discuss science and philosophy. It was here, it is said, that the concept of tarot was formulated.
Initiates say that the tarot was designed to serve two major purposes:

1. To embody the key ideas of the advanced science and mysteries
of the Collegium in a form that would not be detected by secular
authorities (who were anxious to stamp out all vestiges of Inner
Wisdom);

2. To provide tools for training the individual consciousness so that
it could speed the psychological changes that would help Aspirants
attain Initiation and realize their full potential.[1]

It is thought that the Adepts of the Collegium then preserved the
keys of the tarot in a series of visual images with symbolic underpin-
nings.

The ancient roots of tarot, however, cannot be substantiated with
evidence other than the Mystery School teachings. The very oldest
surviving *tarocchi* decks, tarocchi being the earliest known form of
tarot, date back only as far as the 15th century. Thus, one may reach
the conclusion that the oral history of tarot is mere conjecture.

As for well-documented historical research based on existing tarot
decks, an excellent and exhaustive *Encyclopedia of Tarot* is now available in three volumes which detail over one thousand tarot decks

---

[1]Paul A. Clark, "The Threshold: A Guide to Preparation for Initiation," (Covina, CA:
Fraternity of the Hidden Light).

produced during the last half millenium.[2] Whatever one might conclude about its early origins, there can be no doubt as to the popularity of the tarot—in its contemporary form—during the last five hundred years.

Tarot and the Tree of Life

The oral history of tarot also tells that there is an intricate and inextricably connected relationship between the tarot cards and their progression and the ancient Qabalistic Tree of Life. The Tree of Life forms the ground-plan, blueprint, or master pattern of the Western Mystery Tradition. It is the system—in combination with tarot—upon which most students of the Western Mysteries are trained.

The exact origin of the Tree of Life, just like the exact origin of the tarot, is a matter of oral communication. One theory is that it was given to Adam in the Garden of Eden. Another is that it was given to Moses and 70 elders on the Mountain of God (see Exodus: 24–25). Herein, it is claimed that Moses and the elders received, from God, two tablets. One was exoteric, that is to say, suitable for presentation to the uninitiated masses, and the other was esoteric, intended for the understanding only of the inner group of trained Initiates whose level of knowledge of the mysteries far exceeded that of the general public. The elders, then, became the guardians of the knowledge and presumably passed it on to the "called" or "chosen" ones of future generations.

Finally, it is hypothesized that the Tree of Life was pieced together from information contained in the *Sepher Yezirah* (known prior to A.D. third century) and the *Zohar* (late 13th century), two major works of unknown origin which encompass the major teachings of the Jewish Qabalistic or Mystery Tradition.[3] Whatever its origins, the Tree of Life has been used as the primary heuristic tool of Western Esotericism.

The qualities of the Tree of Life have been described in detail by many excellent authors, most notably Dion Fortune in the *Mystical*

---

[2]Stuart Kaplan, *Encyclopedia of Tarot*, Vols. 1–3 (Stamford, CT: U.S. Games Systems, 1978, 1985, 1990).
[3]See works by Isidor Ralisch, *Sepher Yezirah: The Book of Formation* (Gillette, NJ: Pentangle Books, 1987) and Daniel Chanan Matt, *Zohar: The Book of Enlightenment* (New York: Paulist Press, 1983).

Qabalah and Gareth Knight in *A Practical Guide to Qabalistic Symbolism*—to whom I stand greatly indebted and highly recommend—and, as such, I will refrain from a probing treatment of its substance.[4] Nonetheless, it is important to note that, from the point of view of both students and teachers of the Mystery Tradition, the incredible magnificence of the Tree of Life as a teaching tool is based upon its remarkable ability to correlate a vast number of systems including, but not limited to, the astrological, Egyptian, Celtic, alchemical, Judeo-Christian and Zoroastrian. As stated by one mystery school, "its beautiful simplicity lies in its ability to organize volumes of seemingly unrelated facts into one useful coordinated system which shows us the method by which Man may regain his Divine birthright."[5]

The Tree of Life contains ten circles or spheres, each known as a "sephirah" or a "light of emanation." See figure 4 on page 36 for a schematic. These sephiroth (the plural of sephirah) are named Kether, Chokmah, Binah, Chesed, Geburah, Tiphareth, Netzach, Hod, Yesod and Malkuth. Each sephirah is also called a "path," in that a full and complete understanding of its mystical nature propels the aspirant to a higher level of consciousness just as if he or she is passing through a gateway or portal. Thus the ten sephiroth are known as the first ten paths.

There are, in total, 32 paths. Path 11 is formed by connecting the first two sephiroth, Kether and Chokmah. Path 12 is formed by connecting Kether and Binah. Path 13 is formed by connecting Kether with Tiphareth, and so on. Figure 4 outlines all of these paths.

When a student studies these paths in the mystical sense, it is said that he or she is "doing pathwork on the Tree of Life." Pathwork on the Tree is essentially what the *Tarot of the Spirit* is based on and teaches.

Although chapter 1 outlines the structure of the tarot, and Book II: The Sacred Texts elucidates the cards in great detail, for the information of the reader, I will briefly outline the paths of the Tree of Life and provide their correlations with the tarot.

---

[4]Dion Fortune, *The Mystical Qabalah* (York Beach, ME: Samuel Weiser, Inc., (1935) 1984) and Gareth Knight, *A Practical Guide to Qabalistic Symbolism* (York Beach, ME: Samuel Weiser, Inc., 1978).
[5]See "The Threshold: A Guide to Preparation for Initiation."

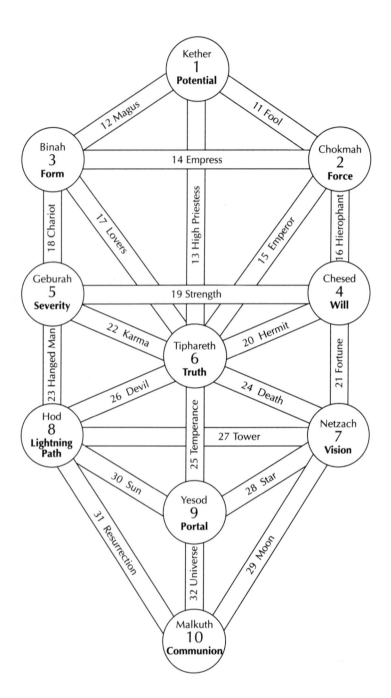

Figure 4. The Tree of Life.

Paths of the Tree of Life ————————————————————————

Path 1—*Kether.* "The Gate of Potential." This is the beginning, the source of all existence. It correlates with the "ones" or "aces" in each of the four suits of the tarot.

Path 2—*Chokmah.* "The Gate of Force." As the universal male or father principle, this is the sphere of energy and emission. It indicates direction and corresponds to the "twos" in the four suits of tarot. It also corresponds to the Fathers of each suit.

Path 3—*Binah.* "The Gate of Form." Binah is the universal female or mother principle, the sphere of receptivity. It corresponds to the "threes" of each suit as well as the Mothers.

Path 4—*Chesed.* "The Gate of Will." This is the sphere of building, of creating, of the process of anabolism. It corresponds to the "fours" of each suit of the tarot.

Path 5—*Geburah.* "The Gate of Severity." Geburah is the sephirah of chaos and destruction. Whereas Chesed builds up, Geburah breaks down. Thus it is the sphere of catabolism. It corresponds to the "fives" of each suit in the tarot.

Path 6—*Tiphareth.* "The Gate of Truth." This is the sphere of Higher Consciousness or Christ Consciousness, the sphere of achieving identity with Kether, the One, the Source of All Things. It corresponds to the "sixes" of each suit as well as the Brothers.

Path 7—*Netzach.* "The Gate of Vision." Netzach is the sphere of emotion, intuition and psychic abilities. It corresponds to the "sevens" in each suit of the tarot.

Path 8—*Hod.* "The Gate of the Lightning Path." This is the sphere of the intellect. In its exalted state, it is the sephirah of Divine Reason or Universal Mind. It corresponds with the "eights" in the four suits of the tarot.

Path 9—*Yesod.* "The Gate of the Portal." Yesod is the sphere of the subconscious mind. The subconscious mind becomes the major portal through which spiritual ascendance is achieved. It corresponds to the "nines" of each of the four suits.

Path 10—*Malkuth.* "The Gate of Communion." This is the sphere of the physical world or the body. It represents the entity where spirit is "ensouled." It corresponds to the "tens" of the four suits as well as to the Sisters.

Path 11—*The Fool.* Key 0 of the tarot. Corresponds to Gate One above (see Table 1, "The Gates of the Tarot" on page 40): blind movement and all-potential.

Path 12—*The Magus.* Key I of the tarot. Corresponds to Gate One: wielding the tools of change.

Path 13—*The High Priestess.* Key II of the tarot. Corresponds to Gate One: hearing the messages of the Inner Oracle.

Path 14—*The Empress.* Key III of the tarot. Corresponds to Gate One: opening to sensuality.

Path 15—*The Emperor.* Key IV of the tarot. Corresponds to Gate One: building a firm base of clear knowledge.

Path 16—*The Hierophant.* Key V of the tarot. Corresponds to Gate One: connecting with the Inner Teacher.

Path 17—*The Lovers.* Key VI of the tarot. Corresponds to Gate Two: understanding the divine marriage.

Path 18—*The Chariot.* Key VII of the tarot. Corresponds to Gate Two: knowing the true driver.

Path 19—*Strength.* Key VIII of the tarot. Corresponds to Gate Two: building up for spiritual ascendance.

Path 20—*The Hermit.* Key IX of the tarot. Corresponds to Gate Three: encountering the inner light.

Path 21—*The Wheel of Fortune.* Key X of the tarot. Corresponds to Gate Four: staying balanced and centered as the Wheel of Destiny turns.

Path 22—*Karma.* Key XI of the tarot. Corresponds to Gate Four: owning the results of thoughts, words and deeds.

Path 23—*The Hanged Man.* Key XII of the tarot. Corresponds to Gate Four: retreating and stilling the inner waters.

Path 24—*Death.* Key XIII of the tarot. Corresponds to Gate Five: transformation during the darkest hour.

Path 25—*Temperance.* Key XIV of the tarot. Corresponds to Gate Five: integration through trials and temptations.

Path 26—*The Devil.* Key XV of the tarot. Corresponds to Gate Five: understanding through taking a new perspective.

Path 27—*The Tower.* Key XVI of the tarot. Corresponds to Gate Five: destroying outmoded structures in order to grow.

Path 28—*The Star.* Key XVII of the tarot. Corresponds to Gate Six: following the inner star.

Path 29—*The Moon.* Key XVIII of the tarot. Corresponds to Gate Six: staying on the spiritual path.

Path 30—*The Sun.* Key XIX of the tarot. Corresponds to Gate Six: coming to spiritual realization.

Path 31—*Resurrection.* Key XX of the tarot. Corresponds to Gate Seven: illumination of higher truth.

Path 32—*The Universe.* Key XXI of the tarot. Corresponds to Gate Eight: application of spiritual knowledge to the world of matter.

Just as each sphere of the Tree of Life constitutes a gateway or portal for spiritual growth, so does each card of the tarot. Above we have used the term "gate." Table 1 (page 40) aligns the gates of tarot with individual tarot cards.

With all this information in hand, how will we employ this system to move through the gates to a deeper spiritual understanding? We will begin by considering the power of the visual image.

The Power of Tarot as Visual Image

> . . . words are but skeletons—pale, rigid, lifeless pieces of bone—while the pictures conjured up by our powers of imagination are as living flesh, elastic muscle and circulating red blood.
>
> ———*Edmond Bordeaux Szekely*

How do you walk the spiritual path? Perhaps your spiritual knowledge is a set of words intellectually assimilated via the books and teachings of the great masters. Or, perhaps your knowledge has

Table 1. The gates and portals of tarot.

Gates	Portal 1: Fire	Portal 2: Water	Portal 3: Wind	Portal 4: Earth	Portal 5: Keys
1. Potential	Force	Open Channel	Dawn	Form	Fool, Magus, High Priestess, Empress, Emperor, Hierophant
2. Force	Convergence	Sacred Cord	The Crossing	Cause and Effect	Lovers, Chariot, Strength
3. Form	Birth of Light	Stream of Love	Recognition	Works	Hermit
4. Will	Flame of Spirit	The Flood	Mastery	Power	Wheel of Fortune, Karma, Hanged Man
5. Severity	The Struggle	Spilling	Fear	The Nadir	Death, Temperance, Devil, Tower
6. Truth	Glory	Faith	Clarity	Beauty	Star, Moon, Sun
7. Vision	Courage	Insight	Many Tongues	The Garden	Resurrection
8. Lightning Path	Lightning Path	Still Waters	Power Shield	The Mountain	Universe
9. Portal	Eye of Fire	Rainbow Mirror	The Screen	The Zenith	Universe
10. Communion	The Cage	Fountain of Love	The Way of the Cross	The Great Work	Universe

been gained through your own deep emotional experience, learned by *feeling* as it were.

We receive two kinds of education, says E. B. Szekely, the one someone else gives us and the one we give ourselves.[6] Anyone can read a book and *intellectually assimilate* its contents. That is the kind of education provided for us by schools. In school, we sharpen our skills at intellectual abstraction. We learn to play back what we have been taught. After the test, we often forget what it was we knew.

The education we give ourselves is deeper. That's because it is driven by emotion. Our deepest memories are cradled in powerful currents of *feeling*. That which we *feel* is emotionally, rather than intellectually, assimilated. Emotionally assimilated memories are tenacious. While intellectual memories easily fade, emotional memories cling to our consciousness. That which has an emotional base becomes the force which drives our *actions*. Observe your own process. You will see that *your actions are the result of your most powerful feelings*.

It is the education we give ourselves that gets us inside of the teachings of tarot and gets the teachings of tarot inside of us. If we wish to assimilate, know, and retain the spiritual lessons of the tarot at the deepest level—particularly if we wish to change our spiritual, or even daily or mundane, lives through tarot—*the power of our emotions must be activated*. We must set the emotional process in motion and cultivate it. This is the central key to following the tarot as a spiritual path. We do this through activating our creative imagination.

Creative imagination transforms abstract thoughts and ideas into visible, audible, palpable and concrete realities. Using our creative imagination, we think in pictures or images. Through visualizing, we can attain the deepest levels and ways of knowing. We can penetrate the deepest meanings of a text. We can come to understand the essence of an idea as a living dynamic life-unit. We thereby begin to achieve a deep quality and intensity of inspiration.[7] Says E. B. Szekely: Words are like two-dimensional drawings, while images are like life itself. Images are three-dimensional living realities which appear in color. Color we can respond to. Through experiencing the word as a living reality, we are carried deeper and deeper into the center of consciousness.

---

[6]Edmond Bordeaux Szekely, *The Art of Study* (Santa Monica, CA: IBS Press, 1973), p. 8.
[7]See *The Art of Study*, p. 10.

Aleister Crowley, occultist and tarot master, once referred to the Tarot cards as "alive." He said, "each card is, in a sense, a *living being*; and its relations with its neighbors are what one might call diplomatic. It is for the student to build these *living stones* into his *living Temple*."[8]

Crowley is referring to the inner spiritual temple which each one of us builds "stone by stone." Each student, to attain full knowledge, must bring the cards to *life*. It is not enough to read a book and memorize the words said about the tarot. Upon the skeleton of tarot, the serious student hangs skin, meat, and muscle. The student floods the form with circulating blood. The student inspires the form with the breath of life. Only then can the death of empty words be escaped. Only then can the words be magically transformed into living entities. Only then will the student become emotionally exhilarated. This, then—this imbument of the skeleton with life—is the key to the student's inner transformation.

Thus, knowledge, attained through feeling, which derives from the image-making of the creative imagination, becomes fully and completely internalized in every cell of the body at every step of the way. This is of critical importance. So, then, we witness the unfolding of the first mystery of tarot. The first step is to teach ourselves to breathe life into a thing that, at first glance, appears to be dead.

The Psycho-Active Art of Joyce Eakins ————————————

The *Tarot of the Spirit* deck was painted by Joyce Eakins, M. F. A., a painter who has exhibited nationally and internationally and taught at the university level since 1969. Her work is exhibited in private and corporate collections the world over. She has won numerous awards.

Joyce Eakins has followed the spirtual path her entire life. The images of the *Tarot of the Spirit* flowed into her dreams, and through her paintbrush.

As she painted the deck, Joyce Eakins found that every tarot symbol came alive. It took on a life of its own and instructed her. Late one night, for example, as she was painting Key I, the Magus, a small metalic mirror appeared upon the card. She did not paint this mirror and it appeared to her to be composed of no material with

[8]Aleister Crowley, *The Book of Thoth* (York Beach, ME: Samuel Weiser, Inc., 1969), pp. 47–8. The italics are mine.

which she was working. She felt that the mirror was placed upon the card by those who guided her hand. It was there, she believed, to communicate a message about the inner workings of The Magus. To this day, the small mirror remains upon the original painting.

For Joyce Eakins, the primary message received in the painting of the tarot was related to the power of the creative imagination. Through creating new images, we actually create a new physical and spiritual reality. Through creating new images, we create a new world. We create a new life. Tarot teaches us this. Through the tarot, we learn how to create the reality we live in. We learn how to create our culture, and that culture is a dynamic and living entity in which each of us enacts a major role.

We have the idea, says Joyce Eakins, that imagination is fantasy. This is wrong. Our own imagination—the way we envision the world to be—truly constitutes the actual reality in which we dwell. What it is all about, she says, is "conjuring up a life," and each one of us, alone, chooses how we will conjure it.

If we desire change, or to conjure up a new life for ourselves or our world, we must first conjure up an idea or *vision* in our imagination. How do we do this? According to Joyce Eakins we merely have to tap in to spiritual awareness and door after door opens up. As these doors open, our inner visions become ever more powerful.

How do we "tap in" to the great force of the creative imagination? One way is through the direct contemplation of the sacred symbology appearing on the cards. As Dion Fortune says, "It is well known to mystics that if a man meditates upon a symbol around which certain ideas have been associated by past meditation he will obtain access to those ideas, even if the glyph has never been elucidated to him by those who have received the oral tradition 'by mouth to ear.' "[9]

Thus, symbolic art—the art of the tarot—is *psycho-active*, that is to say, the contemplation of such artwork activates the deep subconscious mind which provides us with new pictures—a new vision—of reality.

As we tap in, we appear to become—at least at the outset—the creator of our own Universe. But the further we go, the more we realize that the Universe of Life consists of something more than our material bodies and personalities. We realize that we are, indeed, the handmaidens of a plane beyond. We find that we are not only med-

---

[9]See *The Mystical Qabalah*, p. 5.

itating, but *being meditated*. We are not only creating, but *being created*. Ultimately, we realize, as Joyce Eakins did in painting the *Tarot of the Spirit*, that our own hand is the vehicle for the deep inner spirit which is our self, but much more than our self as well. One could say that we realize that our own hand is the hand of the gods activated or put to use on the plane of matter. As we tap in, then, we not only learn to take the responsibility for the creation of our own world, but to create our world in the image of divinity.

This becomes the deep emotional experience through which we are transformed.

Meditation and the Spiritual Journey

Through direct contemplation of the images and symbols of the *Tarot of the Spirit*—a tarot dedicated to the spiritual path—we can begin to transcend what we perceive to be an immovable reality. The context and structures of our lives begin to magically rearrange and transform themselves as we begin to pass through the Ten Gates. We pass through the Ten Gates as we come to terms with our new inner vision and incorporate the results of this experience into our consciousness and thereby into our daily lives.

We embark upon this journey through *meditation*, activating an altered state of consciousness, through which the transformative process can begin. It is suggested that the cards be contemplated according to the procedures outlined in chapter 4, in the following order:

1) The suit of Fire: Cards 1–10, Father, Mother, Brother, Sister

2) The suit of Water: Cards 1–10, Father, Mother, Brother, Sister

3) The suit of Wind: Cards 1–10, Father, Mother, Brother, Sister

4) The suit of Earth: Cards 1–10, Father, Mother, Brother, Sister

5) The Key Cards: 0–XXI.

6) The Mystery Card

As you contemplate each card, let your creative imagination work for you, creating ever-new images in your mind. Write down the visions and insights that come to you. Do not leave anything out. After a time, certain patterns will become apparent. You will perceive the power of your meditations to affect the beliefs and values you hold in your everyday life. You will see that through meditation, that is, through accessing your own unique inner vision, you encounter the potential—your *own*—to transform your world. You will find yourself empowered through this work. You will likely find, as well, that you are being carried through your meditations by what appear to be external entities or guides.

Meditating upon each card in sequence, activating the altered state as described in chapter 4, you will find that you move deeper and deeper toward the heart of your own inner nature. This process is referred to as moving through the gates of consciousness. You will be able to maximize the results of meditation if you read the card description contained in Book II prior to beginning each meditation. If you keep a written record of your revelations, you will gain greater insight over time.

We have seen that there are ten gates of consciousness. Begin your meditations by contemplating the first card of the suit of Fire. This meditation will take you through the first gate. Meditating upon the second card in the suit of fire will take you through the second gate, the third, the third gate and so on. Do this through the first ten cards.

Specifically as you contemplate the One of Fire (Force) you will find that you move through Gate One, the Gate of Potential. Moving through the Gate of Potential means that you are passing through a layer of consciousness and traveling deeper toward your inner spirit, deep feelings, inner thoughts and deep nature. In the suit of Fire, at the Gate of Potential you begin to glimpse the essence of all possibility. Since Fire is the suit of spirit, you begin to glimpse spiritual potential in your thoughts, your imagination, your self and your world. When you are ready, that is, when you feel fulfilled by the first meditation, go on to the second meditation, the Two of Fire (Convergence). This will take you through the second gate, the Gate of Force. Each of these gates corresponds to a path on the Tree of Life as outlined earlier in this chapter.

How will you know that you have passed through a gate and are ready to proceed to the next level? As you process what you learn in your meditations, you will simply *know* when it is time to move deeper. You will know because your heart tells you it is right to go on.

As stated above, upon contemplating the Two of Fire (Convergence) you will move through Gate Two, the Gate of Force. You will find yourself in the sphere of new spiritual energy with a new sense of spiritual direction. When you are ready, meditate upon the Three of Fire (Birth of Light), which will take you through Gate Three, the Gate of Form. There you will experience a surging creativity and the formulation of ideas about how to incorporate your new spiritual direction into your feelings, thoughts and everyday activities. The fourth card in the suit of Fire, Flame of Spirit, takes you through Gate Four: The Gate of Will. At the Gate of Will, you will begin to design new ways of living that incorporate your new spiritual direction. Repeat this process through the first ten cards in the suit of Fire referring to the Paths of the Tree of Life and the card descriptions contained in Book II.

When you have finished through the Ten of Fire, meditate upon the Fire Father. The results of this meditation will tell you something about your spiritual nature or state. The meditation on Fire Mother will tell you something about your emotional nature or state and how that relates to your self as a spiritual being. The meditation on the Fire Brother will tell you about your intellect and how that relates to your spiritual nature. Fire Sister tells you how you live or enact your spiritual nature in your daily life. Meditating on the face cards provides a summary of your progress through the Ten Gates.

Figure 5 gives a graphic description of how you start with Gate One (Potential) at the outermost layer of yourself. Gate Two then takes you a little closer to the center of your self. Gate Three takes you a little closer still and so on. When you arrive at Gate Eight, it is as if you come to a quantum leap in understanding. That is why Gate Eight is referred to as the Lightning Path. It represents highly illuminated knowledge which accelerates your progress. It is as if you begin, at Gate Eight, to pass through a major portal in deep, inner *knowing*. Gate Nine, then, *is* this Portal. The nines in every suit are considered to be the epitome of the way of knowing as represented by the respective suit. Fire is a spiritual way of knowing, Water is intuitive, Wind is intellectual, Earth is physical. At the nine, you arrive at a great portal of understanding. By the time you reach the Tenth Gate (Communion) you are on a completely new level of understand-

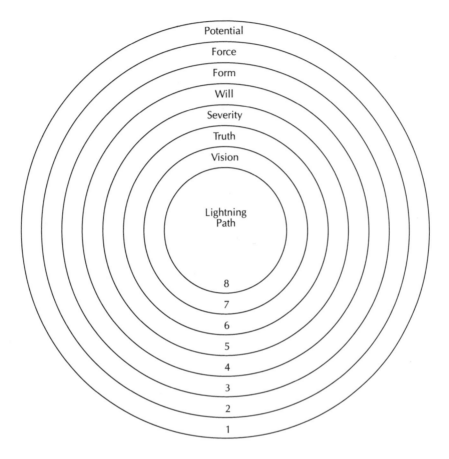

Figure 5. The tarot spiral: ten gates of consciousness.

ing. This process of moving ever inward through the Gates of Consciousness, is schematically diagrammed in figure 6 (see p. 48). You can see that you move deeper and deeper inward until you reach Gate Eight, then you pass through the Portal and your knowledge becomes very expansive. You have then arrived at Gate Ten, the Gate of Communion, which is a new level of knowing.

After you finish the Tenth Gate in the suit of Fire, and finish the meditations on the face cards, you will again be at Gate One, but this time in the suit of Water. As we saw in chapter 1, Water is the suit of emotion, intuition and creativity. As you pass through the Ten

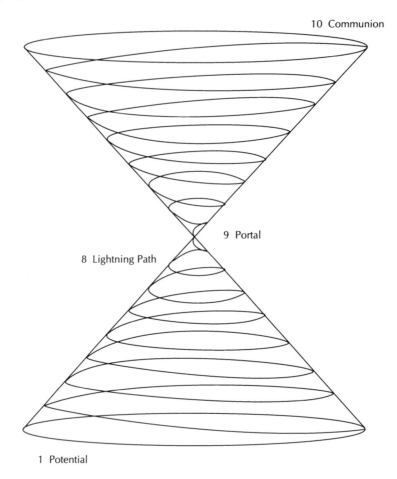

Figure 6. The portal of tarot.

Gates in Water, all revelations will apply to feelings, relationships and the creative process. Referring to the card descriptions and the Paths of the Tree of Life, move through all Ten Gates in the suit of Water.

When you are ready, repeat this process for the suits of Wind and Earth. You will see that you are passing through each gate four times, but each time you arrive at Gate One, for example, you are on a higher (or deeper) level with regard to your own self-knowledge.

After you have finished the meditations with the Minor Arcana, begin the Keys (the Major Arcana). The Keys, too, correspond to the

THE SPIRITUAL PATH ❖ 49

Gates. When you arrive at the Key meditations, you may do several meditations on each level before you pass through the gate. Most gates contain several cards. For example, Gate One (Potential) contains the Fool, the Magus, the High Priestess, the Empress, the Emperor, and the Hierophant. The first six cards in the Major Arcana all represent potential ways of being. Gate Two (Force) contains the Lovers, the Chariot and Strength. These Major Arcana cards are all motivators of action. Gate Three (Form) contains only one card, the Hermit. This is because the Hermit is the very essence of creating new forms. Gate Four (Will) contains the Wheel of Fortune, Karma and the Hanged Man. The essence of the mysteries of these three cards is involved with ways of aligning the will with existing circumstances. Gate Five (Severity) contains Death, Temperance, the Devil and the Tower. That is because all of these cards involve the destruction, taking apart, or dissolution of old ways which comes as a result of higher realization. Gate Six (Truth) contains the Star, the Moon and the Sun. At this level, the meditator experiences deep revelations. Then the meditator arrives at Gate Seven (Vision) which contains the card of Resurrection. Here the meditator experiences the beginning of rebirth on a new level. Then Gate Eight (Lightning Path) takes the meditator to levels never before glimpsed. When the meditator arrives at Gate Eight in the Major Arcana, all the Universe is at his or her feet. The Universe expands into Gate Nine (The Portal) and also Gate Ten (Communion). The meditator is now reborn. Figure 7 (see p. 50) provides a graphic description of the Gates as levels in the major arcana. Once again, as you meditate, you will feel yourself going ever deeper through levels into the center of your self. At the very core of your self is the Universe. You will arrive there after passing through each of the Gates five times, once in the suit of Fire, once in Water, once in Wind, once in Earth and once in the Keys.

When you have finished all the Major Arcana, meditate on the Mystery Card. At this point, a deep mystery of the universe will be revealed.

It is as if five major ways of knowing, each deeper than the last, is revealed on the journey through the tarot. For more insight into each step at each level, refer to figure 4 (p. 36) and Table 1 (p. 40) outlined earlier in this chapter, and the card descriptions contained in Book II.

It is suggested that you undertake the entire process over an expanded time period, doing no more than seven meditations each

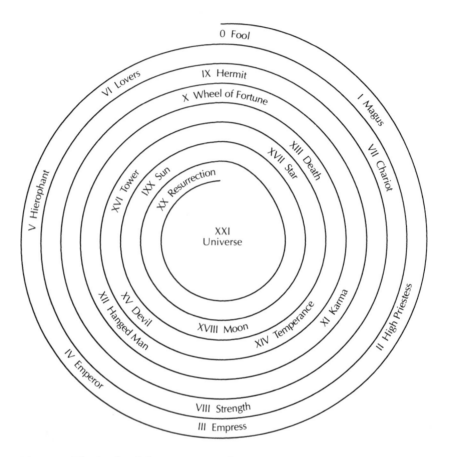

Figure 7. The levels of the twenty-two keys.

month. If you follow this path with openness, perseverance, discipline and responsibility, you will find that, as a result, both your consciousness and your daily life are greatly transformed.[10]

---

[10]If you are interested in receiving a course of study and personal guidance in the meditational process with the *Tarot of the Spirit*, please write to me in care of "The Fool's Journey" at Pacific Center, Box 3191, Half Moon Bay, CA 94019.

❖　❖　❖

CHAPTER FOUR

Day By Day Meditation

In the beginning there is desire. There is desire to move, desire to know, desire to change, desire to grow, desire to fill up the Void of Life with mystery. There is the desire to delve into the mysteries to find meaning. There is desire to refill the Empty Void with purpose.

No one imbues us with this desire. Desire sprouts and blooms of its own accord, in its own time. Desire is its own mover. It has its own cycles and seasons. It has its own rhythms and reasons for being.

It is desire that moves the unmoved mover. It is for desire that the baby bird pecks through the shell from one world to the next. It is for desire that the fledgling longs to flee the nest. And it is for the sake of desire, *for the sake of passion,* that the seeker takes the first exhilarating step upon the path.

Desire holds the seeker to the sought, the mover to movement, the beginning to the end. Desire is the only medium strong enough to bind the scholar to that which is studied. Without desire, the student will surely fall away from the path of learning.

Even the greatest benefactor cannot bequeath desire. Desire cannot be taught by even the greatest teacher; desire is a personal thing. It rises up from a strange unending wellspring at the deepest core of Self. It wells up mysteriously, and like a parting curtain in a magic theater, creates for the watcher an object, a focal point of attraction, a concentrated realm of attentiveness.

Desire is at the heart of change. It points the way to an intensification of awareness. Intensified awareness spurs us to espouse previously unfamiliar perspectives. Through desire we become bound to things "our parents never taught us." Desire leads us into "bio-

graphical rupture," that ecstatic moment somewhere in the middle
of our lives when we rewrite our resume—the shortform outline of
our existence—and say, "Aha! Now I *see! This* is what my life has led
up to." Desire, one could say, is the stimulus for *conversion.*

In our spirits, and most likely our bodies, desire takes us closer
and closer toward that which is desired. It is desire that propels the
mover upon the spiritual path. Through desire, our perception is
awakened. Our meditations become sharpened.

This sharpening, however, is not primarily intellectual. Even
though the intellect may be involved, this acute attentiveness, spurred
on by desire, is not—at its core—a matter of reason. The spiritual
path cannot be walked in the intellect. The seeker is driven by emotion. The seeker is driven by *feeling.* The way of the seeker is the Way
of Desire. The Way of Desire is focused attention.

Focused attention is synonymous with deep meditation.

Deep Meditation and the Tarot of the Spirit

Desire is the first requirement for the spiritual student. Without desire, the student will not even take the first step. The other requirements are openness, perseverance, discipline, responsibility, faith,
belief and trust. All of the secondary requirements rest upon the
foundation of the first.

In the book *On the Psychology of Meditation,* Claudio Naranjo and
Robert Ornstein refer to the concept of desire as "attitude." Through
enhancing one's attitude, one is enabled to enter into extraordinary
states of consciousness. This is done through *meditation.*[1]

According to Naranjo and Ornstein, there are three primary
forms of meditation used throughout the world. The first of these is
called The Way of Forms. The second is The Expressive Way and the
third is The Negative Way. Presently, I will show how this relates to
the *Tarot of the Spirit,* but first, allow me to briefly elucidate these
three meditational paths.

In The Way of Forms, the meditator concentrates on a symbolic
representation. The concentrative effort could focus on an internal

[1]Claudio Naranjo and Robert E. Ornstein, *On the Psychology of Meditation* (New York:
Viking, 1971).

picture, such that the object of concentration appears in the mind's eye, or an external representation, such as a photograph of one's teacher or a religious symbol like a cross or mandala. The object of this form of meditation is total absorption in the symbol. Through deep concentration, the meditator attempts either to interiorize the given symbol or project the consciousness into the object until all subjectivity is absorbed by the symbol. When all subjectivity is gone, the meditator is enabled to experience the deep inner spirit which underlies the physical body and the personality.

The Way of Forms is an assimilative, introjective or projective process. It is a highly directed formal process which demands great discipline of thought.

The Expressive Way of meditation is non-directive. Here, the meditator responds to the spontaneously arising contents of the mind. The Expressive Way is a free-form process of expression through which the meditator seeks to become open or receptive to the forces and forms of the internal imagination. The meditator, using The Expressive Way, seeks freedom from the known. Through escaping the known, the unknown is given a chance to arise and become the teacher.

This process unfolds through the activation of the creative imagination. As we saw in chapter 3, the creative imagination has the power to open up new ways of knowing. The goal of The Expressive Way is the same as for the first form: to meet the deep and true inner Self, to understand one's relationship to the cosmos, to establish inner meanings, to come to know the inner purpose.

The Negative Way involves, not a reaching out or a reaching in, but emptying out of the self. With this approach, the meditator seeks to still the mind entirely, to concentrate on nothing. The Negative Way involves a withdrawal from all thought; cultivates a detachment from all psychological activity. Through completely stilling the pre-programmed internal conversations and observations of the mind, the internal imagination is freed. Freeing the internal imagination allows the meditator to come into contact with the deep inner Self, that Self that transcends conditioned responses related to perceptions of time and culture—perceptions of social duty—aspects of human life which may dictate the circumstances in which we live without necessarily offering a sense of why. The Negative Way, too, opens doors to meaning and understanding one's deep inner purpose.

Figure 8. The meditational triad.

Naranjo and Ornstein summarizes the three ways of meditating as shown in figure 8. It is clear that all three forms of meditation, while differing in method, have the same goal. When working with the tarot as a meditational device, we move through all three forms of meditation in succession.

Meditating with the Tarot

When we meditate using the symbolism of the tarot, we begin by concentrating on the card itself. Often we will simultaneously concentrate on a specific idea. Since we are concentrating on a particular symbology appearing directly before us, we could say that we are beginning at the corner of the Meditational Triad entitled The Way of Forms.

As an example, the first card of the *Tarot of the Spirit* and its accompanying meditational poem is shown on page 55.

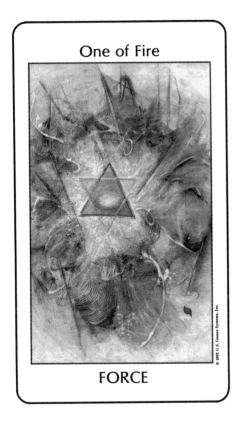

One of Fire

FORCE

One of Fire Meditation

Raw Spirit, Raw Power, Raw Force
Breath in the Void,
All Possibility;
The Essence, the Soul, the Intent, the Potential
Holy, Cosmic, Sacred, Inspired;
Breathing Spirals Whirling
Galactic Coils: Spirit of Will; Will of Spirit;
Sprouts Spikes Stalks Towers
A Sexual, Erotic and
Phallic Burst of Courage, Vigor
Essence of the Search for Real Meaning
True Intent.

We will place all our effort in concentrating upon the visual symbols and the accompanying words. We concentrate—controlling the processes of our minds, as it were—until we begin to lose our subjectivity and become absorbed in the symbols. Our personality and our everyday concerns begin to dissolve. As we become totally absorbed, we eventually find ourselves essentially without thought. We become empty. Using The Way of Forms as a springboard, we catapult ourselves into emptiness. Thus, we find ourselves meditating in The Negative Way, the second form of meditation represented on the Meditational Triad. But it is exactly such emptiness that paves the way for the creative imagination. Only when we have emptied out is there room for the unknown to enter. It is then that we begin to journey in our minds. We let our imagination open up and take us where it will.

It is no accident that the first card in the *Tarot of the Spirit*, the One of Fire, appears as a triangular force. At the very beginning, it is symbolically stated by the form of the card that the *Tarot of the Spirit* unites the three types of meditation just as it unites the three layers of consciousness: the waking consciousness, the subconsciousness and the mystical consciousness.

This is only the beginning of the meaning of the symbolism of this card. More information will be found in the card's description contained in Book II of this text. Further, the symbolism is meant to be a springboard for deep inward imaging in the observer's subconscious mind. Following, for example, are three individuals' experiences of their own creative imagination during a meditative experience with the above visual image and poem:

❖ ❖ ❖

Example 1
One of Fire ————————————————————————————
[Done indoors at night with a fire in the fireplace]

"I see a cave. It is an underground burrow with a low ceiling, barely enough room for me, smells of dirt. My arms are long and hairy. I try to be careful of the fire because I could burn myself and easily catch my hair on fire. I'm afraid of the fire.

"I get a message. I cannot embrace fire, but I can learn to tap into it as a force like the spirit of the flames. It is a transformative power, it charges things up. I was told that I barely use it but I will learn to fan the inner flames to build it up so that I can utilize its power in my life."

❖ ❖ ❖

Example 2
One of Fire ─────────────────────────────────────

"It is time to open up and face the power within me as well as my internal wisdom. I can no longer ignore it; I must let it out, learn about it, acknowledge it, and accept it. I must learn to know me, who I am."

❖ ❖ ❖

Example 3
One of Fire ─────────────────────────────────────

"I was naked.
Lit round red candle
fat and red as swollen lips
stained with the juice of berries

Lit round and red candle
and stared into flame
stripped away my clothes
raiments of some foreign culture
(that odd overlay into which I became)
with the candle in the bed's middle
I sat and stared into flame
        felt the need for old bones
                sundried and dusting
        and animal skins
                with lusty fur floating
Around the flame I placed
        a ring of bones
                ring of bones
Then a round of skins

and like an animal self
I rolled in them
draping them round my human form
and this was right

rubbing skins
on my legs and breasts
felt myself a sister
in the long ago form

I touched my sex and felt the wheel turn
the flame burning
in that lower realm
where the sleeping snake lies coiled

Bones and skins meant transformation
I supposed
and the redness like a
      raw
    impassioned rose
rose and caught my breath

I breathed into flame
and black smoke rose
the waste; snaking waste

I breathed in flame
and my lungs were hot
seared by fire
passion's flame

My old sister lied about the fire
she said it was for food
she said it was for warmth

but it was to pull, I knew,
me away from my
    animal self
and push me back into it

pull me in and out
    like a state of trance
    a dance
where sex raced

it was primordial
I could feel it
    skins all around my hips
    berry stain on my teats and lips

all brown and white and
    black fur
    against my naked skin

it felt like moving toward
    a beginning

an aura
    of blue and aqua then
        violet
    jumped about the candle's base
I fell upon my face
and tasted bone

it was my bones I tasted
    old and gone to dust
    was my lust for *Life*

      or *Death?*

I closed my eyes
and the flame repeated
    came a bird on wings
    to my inner eye
blue first
    winging on black
then violet
    orange
    red-orange
    red-pink
violet and moving into black
then like a bat blacker
    than a no-moon sky
    it hovered flapped
    and became an eye

    the eye with no sight
    black hole

Where does it go?
What will I find on the other side?

but no, they said, it is
    not time for you to

        pass
    only to know that sight awaits

seeing through a hole in
    the center of flame

I said it was for cooking
    warmth
but it was a dancing flashing
    flame of life
that took me from the animals
    and led me back again
    burning life on a sea
        of black
passion
passion flame for all that
which eludes me

all that which I will know

the hole in the flame
through which, I think,
would be the gray portal
between
above and below."

❖ ❖ ❖

Every example above represents the first meditation experienced by these individuals with an image from the *Tarot of the Spirit*. In all cases, the symbology of the tarot became a springboard for The Expressive Way of meditation, which opened the door to the meditators' creative imagination. Subsequent to the meditation, each meditator interpreted his or her experience on the meditational journey, correlating it with the circumstances of his or her life. Thus, for these individuals, the experience bound the three aspects of the meditational triad and immediately related it back to the physical world each one inhabited. All three meditators experienced the entire *Tarot of the Spirit* in this way.

    Over time, with the use of such structured meditations, the meditator begins to perceive inner patterns of thought and a deep transformative symbolic system which has the power to significantly alter thinking as well as daily life. This is the process that was referred to in chapter 3 in "building the inner temple, stone by stone."

Structuring the Tarot Meditation

Continued meditations are essential for continuing to open and grow on the spiritual path. There are several ways the seeker might wish to structure his or her own meditational journey. You could, for example, draw a card—at random—daily or weekly, trusting that the particular card drawn is exactly the one upon which you need to meditate. Another way would be to follow the path of the cards in the sequence of the deck as outlined in chapter 1.

To understand the tarot on its deepest levels, as well as to understand the Self on *its* deepest levels, the serious student must persevere, be very disciplined and responsible and remain open and willing, with a deep faith, belief and trust that the information revealed is that which needs to be understood.

The *Tarot of the Spirit* comes to us as a tool for serious students. Although answers or resolutions may not come quickly, as the student persists, the keys to the mysteries will gradually be disclosed. The *Tarot of the Spirit* has the power to reveal these mysteries.

The path to the mysteries is, however, an independent path. Even if working in a group, every student walks the inner path alone. At first, this may seem lonely or frustrating. At first, the bits of information attained through meditation may seem fragmented and irrelevant. But if the student endures, the puzzle of tarot will eventually begin to fall into place. Then the student arrives at the realization that he or she is, in fact, far from alone. The student comes to the realization of being *at one with the Inner Spirit,* and therefore, *at one with All.* To realize this end, the most important requirement is desire. The doors of tarot will eventually open for those who deeply desire, and whose commitment outlives frustration or lack of understanding.

As you begin to explore the *Tarot of the Spirit,* I give you the first key to unlocking her doors. The first key is the knowledge that to learn, we must offer ourselves in service to a force which is greater than ourselves. We must persevere with a mental attitude of discipline and humility. That is why desire is so important. Discipline alone has a hard time binding any of us to a path so arduous and intricate. And remember, always, for this adventure as well as the next:

one comes to nothing
who serves nothing.

Let this adage, acolyte, be your guide upon the way.

❖   ❖   ❖

CHAPTER FIVE

The Spiritual Birth

The spiritual birth is the mystical awakening. As we awaken, the knowledge of the Ultimate Reality is revealed. All along, we have trained our minds to conceive of this reality. We have sought to invoke this reality with every beat of our hearts, with our every breath.

At one moment, then, "God" becomes real.

To experience the Ultimate Reality is the first major goal of the spiritual path. This experience cannot be attained on intellectual terms. It happens when the spiritual student perceives the universal consciousness directly and this can only take place at the deepest level of the heart. This knowledge is an emotional matter. On some level it involves a thrilling hyper-awareness, which, when felt, miraculously lifts all existential bondage. Doubt is nullified. The soul is freed.

How do we attain this exalted state? We reach it through cultivating the inner qualities of desire, discrimination, discipline and love. These, says Swami Akhilananda, are the four major requirements for the spiritual student.[1]

In the preceding chapter, we saw the importance of desire. Without desire, there can be no spiritual movement. Without desire, there can be no spiritual devotion. The serious student must cultivate a deep sense of desire, but also a sense of discrimination. While weekend workshops promising sensational experiences may open important doors, they will, in general, not answer the quest of one who seeks deep and lasting transformation. Recognizing that the path may be long and arduous, the serious student must select teachers and

---

[1]See Swami Akhilananda, *Spiritual Practices* (Cape Cod, MA: Claude Stark, Inc., 1974), pp. 26–32.

"God's vastness I glimpsed in the skies of quietness. His joy I tasted in the fountains of my existence. His voice I heard in my unsleeping conscience."

———Paramahansa Yogananda

"My hand holdeth the whole circle of being
And for me time is not."

———Paul Foster Case

"—Man is a portal through which one enters from the outer world of the gods, demons and souls, into the inner world, from the greater world into the smaller world. Small and insignificant is man; one leaves him soon behind, and thus one enters once more into infinite space, into the microcosm, into the inner eternity."

———C. G. Jung

"One Monday morning, I awoke. ing very ill indeed. The morning was warm and sultry. I thought I certainly could not wash that day; but when I went downstairs, I found my daughter had made preparations for such work. I thought, 'Well if she feels like washing, I will not say anything; perhaps I shall get over this.' After breakfast I went about my work, thinking I could lean against the tub and wash with more ease. . . . All at once these questions came to me, as if spoken by some one, taking me away from my line of thought entirely: How is God an ever-present help? How does He know our earnest desires? Then, without waiting for me to think how, the answer came in the same way, God is conscious Mind. . . . I was healed instantly: every bad feeling was destroyed. I could see that the morning had not changed a particle, but I was oblivious of the weather. It did not seem that I had anything more to do with that washing. It was finished in good season, while I was 'absent from the body, and present with the Lord.' "

———Mrs. H. B. J.

"The chant builds, spiraling upward. Voices merge into one endlessly modulated harmony. The circle is enveloped by a cone of light. Then, in a breath—silence. . . . We will receive the gift, and remember: 'I am Goddess. You are God, Goddess. All that lives, breathes, loves, sings in the unending harmony of beings is divine.' "

———Starhawk

methods with care and then—cultivating a sense of faith and trust—become wholly devoted. There are likely to be moments of despair as deep as the moments of exaltation are high. The serious student recognizes this and perseveres nonetheless, never relinquishing the sense of desire, knowing that conscious awakening will eventually be the result.

Once a woman who wanted to study with me called on the telephone. During the course of our conversation I thought I heard her say, "I am ready to be odd." I thought, "How terrific! She wants to take a major leap without regard for what others think! She is ready to experience a life of spiritual pursuit!" I got very enthusiastic and started expounding at great length about the joy of being a student on the spiritual path, which, of course, is how I envision myself. Later I came to realize that what she had actually said was: "I am ready to be *awed*." Awed! She was bored and wanted something *interesting* to do. Although she was no doubt on the path, she was not yet a serious spiritual seeker. I doubted that I could give her what she wanted.

The serious student is not in pursuit of entertainment. The serious student is a deep digger. I am reminded of the greeting card by Richard Stine. It shows a comical dog looking totally blank and bewildered after digging thirteen holes and turning up nothing. It is captioned, "Dog Beginning to Question the Value of Shallow Attempts."

One could picture the mystical consciousness as an underground river and the seeker as very thirsty. I know I have to dig a very deep hole to get to the water. I know that when I get there, I will no longer thirst. I dig day after day, day after day. I know I cannot keep switching locations or nothing will ever transpire. I just keep digging. Then, one beautiful day, after I have worked very hard, and just when I least expect it, I strike water! It rises to the surface, clear and clean, bubbling and brilliant in its transparency. *It is the most beautiful water I have ever seen.* It is effervescent and luminescent and seems to emit its own light. I feel myself glowing with a radiant energy. I have reached the cosmic sea! I have glimpsed eternity! I am reborn! Now I know the meaning of Mother-Father-God. I have grasped the deep symbolism. Now I know what the prophets speak of! I know it first-hand. I have reached my spiritual birth, the greatest rite of passage in my life.

But then what? I still have to get up and go to work in the morning. I still have to feed the dog, vacuum the rug, teach the class and get dinner for the kids. How then can I integrate what I have seen?

Clearly, once you find the deep water table, you have to maintain the well. This is hard work. Maintaining a hole is not a sensational experience and no one else can maintain it for you. It takes discipline; it takes practice. But if you don't do it, the well may dry up. Certainly you, yourself, could dry up for lack of sustenance.

Thus, the serious student must develop power over any lackadaisical tendencies. The student must develop tenacity as well as the ability to avoid activities that are harmful to spiritual realization. The body must be kept clean, clear, pure and deserving to keep the divine channel open. The heart must remain trusting, open and pure. The heart must keep faith.

If the first three requirements of the spiritual student are desire, discrimination and discipline, the fourth requirement is love. The serious student must cultivate sympathy, patience, endurance and purity. Then, says Patanjali, the human mind will be rebuilt in the image of these qualities.[2] The mind must be rebuilt with positive, constructive tendencies. Swami Akhilananda reiterates these qualities and emphasizes that a "remodel" of this magnitude does not happen overnight.[3] Attaining consciousness built on love is a matter of discipline, just as it is a matter of conscious living.

As I experience the spiritual birth and continue to maintain spiritual practice, my inner goals become transformed. I seek now to enjoy the integrated life, the experience of love, sympathy and a new kind of duty. As I rebuild my values, I rebuild my personality. As I rebuild my personality, I naturally transform the external conditions of my world. This is because, through the power of awakened consciousness, I begin to imagine new ways of living. I cannot help but do this. I see things differently. My perception has changed.

Having a new perception increases my devotion. I become a better student. As part of the natural flow, when we become better students, we become better teachers.

There is only one requirement for a spiritual teacher: to live a spiritual life. The spiritual teacher lives in a state of equanimity. The anger of the holy man, says Akhilananda, is like a line drawn in

---

[2]Charles Johnston, *The Yoga Sutras of Patanjali* (Albuquerque, NM: Brotherhood of Life, 1983).
[3]See *Spiritual Practices*, pp. 26–32.

water. It disappears as quickly as it arises.[4] How can this be? How does the holy man become master of his emotions? He resolves his feelings because he sees beyond the surface permutations of everyday life into existence at the level of the Ultimate Reality. He sees beyond everyday life to that plane where all that is is perfectly balanced.

Consider these principles: design, tension, order, harmony, balance, wisdom, love, *chi*. Like the holy one, then, let these be your guides. Remake your mind in the image of divinity. Recreate your self as you would fashion beautiful art. Let the world be a better place for your having touched it.

We glimpse a great beauty through mystical windows, but after the spiritual birth, we must turn to face the extraordinary challenge of applying what we have learned. We face the extraordinary challenge of leading a spiritual life, a life permeated with divinity. And so I say to you: blessed be as you go forward, dear one. And leave beauty where you pass. Though you are a pilgrim and the way is hard, you will reach the great land for which you were destined. If you need food, you will not go hungry. If you need water, you will not thirst. If you need love, you will not be alone. *All you need to do is knock, and every door will open.*

---

[4]*Ibid.*

BOOK II

❖   ❖   ❖

The Sacred Texts

✤ ✤ ✤

CHAPTER SIX

Fire

Fire
The South
Wands
Rods
Sun
High Noon
Blazing Summer
Black, Red, Gold, Orange, Yellow, White, Blue-White
Roaring Lions
The Hoofbeat of a Thousand Stallions
Warring

The Path through Fire

Fire licks, flickers, struggles, persists, searches, enflames;
The more you divide it, the more it multiplies . . .

The suit of Fire is the suit of spirit. It is the suit of limitless light. Fire
is flaming, wild, raw and violent: the will of us, our spirit, our spirited
ways, our will power, the will to live, the spark of life, forever searching, trying to make connections—perhaps to some higher form: God,
Goddess, Holy Spirit. This is the suit of the superconsciousness. There
is a sense of eternal longing in the suit of Fire, an intense generally-
contained power which sometimes smolders, sometimes erupts,
sometimes smothers and sometimes lies dormant. Fire represents
intense and keen personal energy, the force and raw drive of the

individual. It is the element which motivates you to action. Like fire, your energy heats, destroys, purifies, and lights.

The suit of Fire carries an incredible dynamism which leads to discovery, especially to those forms of discovery which are technical, electrical and atomic in nature, discoveries which are the imprint of truth. These discoveries lay the groundwork for connection to a higher consciousness, the Higher Light.

In the suit of Fire, you discover depth of spirit.

Initially, the discovery of the power of that element may lead to a certain frustration as you feel bound by the realistic constraints of earthly life. Daily activities may appear to be trivial or futile, or the daily routine may come to feel like a cage.

But when there is appropriate balance and control (Fire must have Wind and Earth to keep it alive, and Water to keep it on track), the importance of every action comes to light.

The "cage" in which you live—the physical body and other material structures—can actually become your vehicle for emancipation. Your cage doubles as physical armor, a source of strength: that which shields your vulnerability on the physical plane.

Strength equals will equals purpose equals the Fire/lifeforce within us. It is the motivating factor, all that which persists, endures and searches. All that which will not compromise. This is the strength of spirit we discover on the path through the suit of Fire.

Because the path toward *Wisdom*, which is the underlying quality of the suit of Fire, is long and difficult, and most likely eclectic, one's conclusions, in the end, are likely to be highly individualized, unique, and they may change from time to time. One person learns that "if a Fool carries a torch against the Wind, he will likely burn himself." Another finds that the self-empowered individual, through understanding the laws of nature, can change the course of the Wind.

One of Fire: Force

Divinatory Meaning ───────

You feel a sense of transformative high energy; inner blocks are falling away, freeing you to move into newness; you have the will to change and you feel the great energy of new beginnings; you have a newly discovered source of power; you are excited, you feel exhilarated; if there is an undercurrent of depression, it is only because the future remains unknown at this time; if you feel like you are burning up with no channel or outlet for your emotions, do not worry, the way will very soon become clarified, you will soon find someone or something to connect with.

One of Fire

FORCE

Meditation ───────

Cancer, Leo, Virgo
Raw Spirit, Raw Power, Raw Force
Breath in the Void,
All Possibility;
The Essence, the Soul, the Intent, the Potential
Holy, Cosmic, Sacred, Inspired;
Breathing Spirals Whirling
Galactic Coils: Spirit of Will; Will of Spirit;
Sprouts Spikes Stalks Towers
A Sexual, Erotic and
Phallic Burst of Courage, Vigor
Essence of the Search for Real Meaning
True Intent.

Interpretation ───────

At the One of Fire, your spirit grows restless. It is time for a change, time to engage in new activities, new relationships, new interests, a new treatment of the body. Your internal Fire, the driving force of change and movement, is burning. You must *do something*. You desire newness. You desire meaning. At this point, however, you are experiencing only a blind will to change. You need direction.

You are experiencing the raw and undirected force of the first stage of creation. Here, the force of your own will to act, produce, or create becomes a focused point in the realm of all the unfocused and infinite possibilities in the universe. This is the force of Kether on the Tree of Life, the first sphere—the creative force—that emerges from the void of all possibility.

While burning desire is the essence of focus and creativity, and you ought to be feeling very creative at this time, it is possible that you feel neither creative nor focused. In reaction to the surging Fire within, you may feel a variety of emotions ranging from exhilaration to depression. You may feel like you are burning up with no outlet or channel for the endless yearning and energy. You may feel frustrated. Do not be tempted, however, to supress the burning. Be advised that the Fire within is the source of all of your movement and all your wisdom. It is the source of all growth and change, whether such change is spiritual, emotional, mental or physical. This burning energy is the force that will propel you toward realizing or maximizing your potential in all of these areas. Focus on the excitement.

At the One of Fire, you have tapped the central and elemental point at which your deep internal spirit—the force behind all change—begins and ends. When this burning flame flares, your energy level increases. You experience raw and infinite energy, unleashed, unabashed and undirected. Understand that you are about to undertake a new project, love, adventure or spiritual quest. You cannot yet envision where you are headed, but you know you are headed *somewhere*. You feel the Wheel of Fortune beginning to turn.

At this time, your internal will is powerful and driving. It can take you to heights you never fathomed. The force you experience at the One of Fire is not only the spirit of your own will—the source of all action and movement—but the will of your spirit. The will of spirit seeks to focus ideas and bring them into manifestation. The challenge of the One of Fire is to understand how to achieve the best focus.

At the One of Fire you are meeting the yang energy pattern within yourself. You are dealing with Fire in its most uncontained form. Fire is the primal male element: the universal yang force. Yang, in Chinese philosophy, is the active, positive, masculine force or principle. It is the universal emitting force: the source of all light and heat. The yang part of you is now rising up, challenging you, and moving you to peaks of growth and awareness.

Through proper attunement, the creative surge of the One of Fire will soon become directed and rewarding. The only way you will find what you are looking for, and thereby direct your vast and potent inner force, is by exploring the cosmic sea: your own inner depths. Turn within. It is time for introspection. It is as if you are a blind or empty pupil in the center of an eye. Although your visionary powers for the new stage are forming, you are not yet able to see the path with clarity. Stated another way, in order to learn to *see*, you must become a student in the center of the I. This means it is time for a deep penetration of Self. You must open your deep, inner Self in order to understand the depth and power of your own will as well as the direction in which you are now moving.

At the One of Fire, to open your deep Self, you need to access your feminine, or yin, side. Your feminine side, which is fluid and free-flowing, will give you the permission, space and freedom to open to new possibility. Using your feminine aspects will end the uncontrolled burning or yearning for change. A balance of male and female energies within will allow you to expand and grow with flexibility, creativity and clarity.

Card Symbology: In the center of the One of Fire, an upright male triangle manifests containing an empty eye socket. Everywhere this triangle is surrounded by spirals of purpose, will and lifeforce. Dark rods shoot out. These rods are searching for *something* to penetrate. The sense of the card is blind, wild, rearing, and unbridled. One has the sense that the central figure has flown from the primal source in a bursting supernova. Overlapping the male triangle is an inverted female triangle. Connection with the female force, receptivity, has not yet been made. This connection is needed in order to produce an eye to see, which is the key to realizing the eternal light-giving potential of the suit of Fire. The ghost of the feminine form appears because the blind will intuitively knows it must be tempered so that it does not burn itself out.

Two of Fire: Convergence

Divinatory Meaning

Unfocused energy becomes clear and polarized; you feel you now have a strong direction; you are making changes spiritually, emotionally, intellectually and physically; while you may go through various struggles, your courage in starting an enterprise at this time will eventually pay off; maintain your own internal sense of balance as you begin your new activities.

Two of Fire

CONVERGENCE

Meditation

Mars in Aries
Convergence
Alliance Connection
Imagination
bond tie link
clamp clasp buckle lace
knot
nail brad rivet
bravery and wonder
at the moment of encounter.

Interpretation

The Two of Fire is the first understanding of the necessity of connection, the first perception of the fact that you have to want *something* in order to cure the endless longing.

You already know what it means to burn inside. You know the feeling of the internal fire that yearns aimlessly. You know restlessness and boredom. But now, at the Two of Fire, you are making a connection. The connection is important. Trust your intuition! You are experiencing a profound convergence.

If you allow yourself, you can now move in a focused direction. You can now begin to refine your energies. This is your opportunity to escape the interior burning and clear the way for internal empowerment.

Seeing the way has not been easy. You have had to take a risk. You followed a trail of smoke that wafted and faded. You worried about disruption in your life. You feared that no matter how bad it was, it could be worse. At times, you felt you were going nowhere. You worried about time passing. Some of your old fears may trail you still, but you have learned that where there's a trail of smoke, there's a pit of fire: pure energy, opportunity and motivation. Through your own perseverance, you have finally glimpsed the source of the flame, and now you must seize opportunity!

The path you walk is of critical importance. It is time now to willingly and joyfully surrender to newness and accept your true destiny.

At the Two of Fire, you are pioneering. You must stay clear to maintain your direction. You must remember that the way will never be found through an external source, but only by looking within. You will find your answers and your true direction through peering into dark internal spaces. The dark I speak of is the field of your subconscious mind. It is all that which is unknown, all that which swims and floats in the cosmic sea, the waters below the surface of your consciousness. There you will make the most important discoveries and connections of your life.

At the position of the Two, two points polarize and become clear. The two points consist of you and your focal point. Your focal point is the direction in which you must travel. A certain consciousness or awareness of direction arises at the Two of Fire. A new path is formed.

At the Two of Fire, you have a sense of duality and duplicity, a sense of inside and outside, past and future, light and dark, and above and below. You discover that knowing contrast is one of the major keys to understanding the deep Self and the world you inhabit. You know your Self through separating out that which you are from that which you are not. Your inclination is to move toward that which you wish to become. Your inclination is to emit energy: to find the areas of greatest receptivity and to fill those spaces. At the Two, the student converges with the teacher, the homeless converges with the home, the seeker converges with the path, the lover converges with the loved.

However, as in the force of a magnet, while positive, emitting (male) energy appears to be at one end and negative, receiving (female) energy appears to be at the other, you can break a magnet into the most minute pieces and still retain the poles. Male and female polarizations infinitely move in and out of each other, yet there is clear directionality. Thus dualism becomes a paradox. This is the paradox of the fundamental universal forces of yang and yin, which first appears at the Two of Fire.

As in the analogy of the magnet, the Two of Fire is not only your first movement in a new direction, but it is also your first movement in the direction of the golden mean, Temperance (see Key XIV). Through the very recognition of your deepest goals, you recognize also that you are standing between major forces. The challenge is to maintain your balance through change and movement.

Ironically, in maintaining balance, you find yourself both inside and outside at the same time. You are attached and detached at the same moment. The Two represents the place at center, where yang energy comes into contact with yin. This is where change happens, where new forms are created.

On the Tree of Life, the Two of Fire is represented by the sphere of Chokmah: the universal masculine and father force.[1] Chokmah embodies and directs the previously undirected universal yang (wisdom and light) energy.

He directs this energy through moving toward the receptive universal female, maternal force: Binah. Chokmah is Fire. Binah is Water. Without the cooling, mediating and understanding force of the clear waters of Binah (the reflective cosmic sea: the subconscious mind), Chokmah (light and wisdom, the higher consciousness) runs the risk of being blinded by his own internal light and consumed by his own eternal Fire. Listening to Binah, the internal pool of emotion, provides critical direction for the endless and burning quest for meaning. The tempering question Binah poses to Chokmah is: How do you really *feel* deep down inside?

---

[1]See chapter 3 for an explanation of the Tree of Life.

As you converge with your major focal point at the Two of Fire, you ask yourself this question. How do you really *feel* on the deepest level? Knowing the answer is the key to your growth.

The male and female forces, although apparently distinct entities and complete within themselves, are capable of uniting and combining forces to produce powerful offspring. The offspring, which are the children of mind and body, result when wisdom (as represented by Chokmah) and understanding (Binah) come together as one.

In the story of the Tree of Life, Chokmah and Binah symbolize both the external universal forces of male (emission) and female (reception) and the male and female universe within the Self. The lesson of the Two of Fire is to learn to move with the burning energy of the male force toward that which is most receptive and tempering, maintaining the internal balance of male and female at all times.

Card Symbology: The empty eye socket of the One of Fire now has a pupil with which to see. The pupil is realized through bringing into focus the receptive and reflective female force. This is the force of Binah on the Tree of Life. Attaining a pupil means that clear sight and direction has been established. Since Binah is the watery female force, the pupil doubles as a lake or sea, the cosmic sea, which you look down into as if you were looking into the top of a cup.

The eternal flame has now been contained, as tempered by Binah, in two wands. The heads of the wands are composed of six-pointed stars. In these stars, the male and female triangles have moved through each other, which symbolizes the power of creation. The wands contain tremendous power and are capable of magical feats. The source of their power is deep, reflective understanding. The Two of Fire represents the intercourse of wands and cups, Fire and Water, male and female. Flooding out of the pupil, as a result of that intercourse, are the flames and waterfalls of all that which will become. The yellow ring surrounding the pupil of the eye is a wedding band signifying that the wands and cups are now wed. It is yellow for the conception of the Son/Sun—the child of mind or body—that will grow out of their union.

Three of Fire: Birth of Light

Divinatory Meaning ——————————

Stay on the path; keep on with your present activities; everything is coming to fruition; it is as if a miraculous birth is at hand; to resist this great birth would bring pain; realize you are in a state of grace and stay with this feeling; giving birth to the "children" of body or mind is not always easy, but it is a highly rewarding process; in this case, your "child" is a product of love.

Three of Fire

BIRTH OF LIGHT

Meditation ————————————————————————————

Sun in Aries
Destiny
The Future flows forth like Fire from the Sun
like Water from a Spring
and there is the newness
of Spring
in every direction.

Interpretation ————————————————————————

The Three of Fire indicates that an important connection has been made and that conception or perception has occurred.

At the Three, you have established your path and you are treading it virtuously. In a sense, a birth is underway. There is nowhere to go, but through the dark tunnel toward the light. You know deep down inside that your current activity is right and will take you where you want to go. Even though outcomes can never be entirely clear, all movement on the path is balanced and promising.

At the Three of Fire, the will to act and to change has been recognized, acted upon and received. The Three of Fire can be likened to the gestational period of the coming child—the Son/Sun—of mind, body or spirit. This birth of light is symbolic for the rebirth or renewal of the Self. Creativity is sparked in every direction.

For the first time in the path of the tarot, the holy balance of Three is experienced. With the introduction of three points, a plane is established. A plane allows for a broadening of movement, a geometrical leap of understanding. The Three of Fire represents the plane of spirit. The plane of spirit is also the plane of action and movement, propelled by the force of an internal eternal energy.

On the Tree of Life, with the addition of the third point—the sphere of Binah—a holy trinity emerges. This is the trinity of Mother-Father-God. Binah is the mother form, the womb of life, the place where the surging fiery energy of the father force (Chokmah) comes to rest. Her womb is dark, comforting and beautiful. Through resting in the stillness of this womb, which is the cosmic sea beneath the surface of consciousness, we achieve a deep understanding of what is to unfold. Our fiery will becomes contained, monitored and nurtured—tempered—in the watery womb of Binah.

In this resting place, the Three of Fire becomes a moment of inaction on the plane of action. As a result of this resting, a marvelous birth will occur. This means that you are now in an extremely creative mode. The "rest" you experience is stillness in the waters of the subconscious mind.

In the *Tao Te Ching,* the oldest Taoist text from ancient China, philosopher, Lao Tsu, says:

Tao gives birth to One;
One gives birth to Two;
Two gives birth to Three.
Three gives birth to the Ten Thousand Things.
The Ten Thousand Things uphold *yin* and embrace *yang.*
They harmonize through blending these vital breaths.[2]

This is the mystery and enchantment of the Three of Fire. Binah goes into labor. This means that the Binah part of your consciousness prepares to give birth. There is great promise at this time. There will be a great birth. If there is pain, it is only the pangs of promising

[2]Lao Tsu, *Tao Te Ching* (London: Concord Grove Press, 1983), p. 45.

new beginnings. You are already on the path, the birth is underway, and you must keep going. Do not increase pain through resisting the inevitable flow.

Card Symbology: The Three of Fire is formed of three wands. The six-pointed stars at the head of these wands form a triangle. This is the uppermost triangle on the Tree of Life. The cooling Circle of Binah, sacred to the Three, appears in blue and green on the left side. The fiery Circle of Chokmah is to the right. The Circle of Kether is white light at the top center, the zenith of the triangle.

The heads of the wands reach out above a horizontal axis which represents the abyss on the Tree of Life. The abyss is the river which divides the above, the heavens (the universal creative force), from the below, the earth (practicality and receptivity).

The stem of the wand of Kether forms a bridge of light over the abyss: the spiritual path. Thus the horizontal axis of the cross in the center of the card is formed of that which divides the worlds of above and below, while the vertical axis represents the spiritual aspirations that connect the planes of above and below.

The central diamond represents the triangular forces of above and below uniting, which symbolizes the symbiotic processes of bonding and individuation. As Above, So Below.

The white backdrop is the skull of Kether, primal idea in the Universe. The white circle at the bottom of the card is the skull of the Christ, Buddha, Krishna, or Self moving into manifestation.

Black snakes of renewal can be seen in motion at the bottom of the card. They are black to represent the dark subconscious from which creativity arises. One must trust the process: if the snake bites, it is only trying to get your attention.

Four of Fire: Flame of Spirit

Divinatory Meaning

A phase of development is complete; based on your revelations and good intentions of the past, you built a strong structure, but in some ways, you no longer feel connected to that structure; know that old structures must frequently be abandoned to make way for new growth; you are growing, beginning a new phase in your life; it is as if your own personal wheel of fortune is turning again; this is necessary in order for you to grow; search your heart for the right course of action.

Four of Fire

FLAME OF SPIRIT

Meditation

Venus in Aries
Completion
Decrees have been set
Orders proclaimed
Proclamations delivered

The old system comes to an end
the Wheel of Fortune is turning again.

Interpretation

At the Four of Fire, you have completed a stage of development. This is a time when you have brought an idea to completion, when you have finished building or enacting something on the physical plane. You have created structures. You have enjoyed outcomes. Your loftiest ideas have materialized. You have met great challenges.

In fact, you have been so successful that you have solidified your routines. You are moving from a position of rigid balance.

The structures you have built could represent an actual building, business, marriage or family, or the pattern of your daily life and routines. These systems have been built on a solid foundation, usually with good intentions, and are now in full operation on the material plane. Structures can also be built by a culture: institutions, laws, orders, governments. Thus, as with the rest of the tarot, all that applies to the Four of Fire applies not only to the individual, but to the social system. The solidification of ideas in matter happens at all levels of material existence.

The structured balance of Four is a second-level balance. It is a step beyond the tripodal balance of Three. It is the point where the creative magic of Three brings the desired end into manifestation. While the Four of Fire implies the completed formation of a structure, a "house" which you have built brick by brick, problems with the "house" may emerge.

The first problem is that structures, because they tend to be comfortable, can be habit-forming. Operating within a structure of habitual patterns can present serious obstacles to insight and growth. Established patterns keep one from "being lost." Getting lost is an adventure which necessitates activating the creative mind. In getting lost, one arrives at deeper levels of understanding—getting found.

The second problem is that structures are easily outgrown. With an open mind, one easily moves through structures to ever-greater levels of awareness and understanding. Desires change. New challenges are posed. We constantly ask ourselves: how can the structure be expanded? Is an altogether new structure required?

The third problem is that becoming solidified in a structure can lead to arrogance. There is a danger in being blinded (from seeing truth) by one's own light (one's own success).

A fourth problem is that a structure can take on a life of its own, reproduce itself, long after its usefulness to the builder is outmoded.

On the Tree of Life, the fourth point is the sphere of Chesed. Chesed is the first circle below the abyss which separates the above, the world of lofty aspirations, from the below, the physical world of manifestation. In other words, it is the first circle to appear on the physical plane. It is the circle of brilliant creation, ideas taking form, but also the circle of tyranny and bigotry. Tyranny results from clinging too tightly to the structures you build. True strength comes from flexibility.

Chesed represents the process of anabolism, the process of building. Technically, anabolism is the process in plants and animals whereby food is changed into living tissue. It is constructive metabolism. It is a process of critical importance, but it needs a counteracting force to keep it from overproducing.

At the Four of Fire, which is called the Flame of Spirit, the challenge is to attune to the spiritual aspects of Self, the eternal light of the spirit which transcends the material plane. A change is in the offing. However uncomfortable, a new beginning is about to occur. The challenge of the Four of Fire is to go on to the next move before the endpoint is reached. That way, you stay awake and aware, and you don't get locked in or distressed by focusing on endings.

The key at this time is to remain fluid and mobile and to attune to the grand structures of the cosmos. Be aware that old structures must forever be abandoned to accommodate new growth. It is time for you to honor the flame of your spirit. You can do this through introspection. Rejoice in the fact that you are not the structures that you build. Your spirit is forever free.

Card Symbology: In the Four of Fire, we are looking down, from the above, into the crater of a pyramid which has a foundation of light. In fact, it is the higher consciousness of the aspirant (light) which pours into the pyramid from above. This represents the Flame of Spirit contained in a physical structure.

The four stars across the top are the stars of Chokmah, the great male force of action. The female force does not appear as a wand in this card, because the card is dominated by male energy. Chokmah no longer needs Binah in order to create. The structure has been created, and has taken on a life of its own. The feminine energy of understanding—the *desire* to produce—is fading out below.

The love that does appear, as signified by the presence of the green of Venus, is a love of form, of known routines and rituals, a love of the pyramid one has built. This can be a hedonistic type of love.

But even with the solidity of the pyramid, the twenty-eight rods flowing like rays of light down the sides, indicate that a change is in the offing. The rods are the spokes of the Wheel of Fortune and they are about to turn.

Five of Fire: The Struggle

Divinatory Meaning ────────

You feel a sense of conflict; the struggle which seems to be happening outside of yourself may, in reality, be happening on the inside; you feel as if you are striving, but you are immobilized at the same time, a sense of chaos has resulted from the presence of conflicting ideas; allow yourself to "fail," allow yourself to "lose" and you may find that you are actually winning; in losing all, you will gain everything; in this case, you are merely relinquishing that which is obsolete.

Five of Fire

THE STRUGGLE

Meditation ────────────────────────

Saturn in Leo
Strife. Impasse.
The System—now in question—has taken on a life of its own.
Authority. Bureaucracy. Theocracy. Monarchy.
Nation. State. Marriage. Family.

Structures challenged. Structures defended.
Only Fools move against the Proven.
Am I such a Fool?

Interpretation ──────────────────────

At the Five of Fire, you stand on the brink of change, between worlds. The feeling is one of impending implosion/explosion and the spirit in a state of chaos. Any attempt to go back to old imagery or ideas, to regress, retrace steps, or make amends, does not work well at this time. Even though there is much disruption, on the deepest level, you do not feel remorse. You know that change must occur. The structure is too tight. To release pressure, the lid must blow off.

You are in a time of internal struggle. Your energy is heavy and dense. It feels blocked. You feel fragmented and disrupted. Things you have built seem to be dissolving. Even your own personality is in question. You are asking: Who am I? What do I want?

This is the beginning of a new aeon in thought. But regardless of whether the voice of change comes from within or without, you find yourself persecuting new ideas. This is because you have a strong vested interest in the existing structure. In fact, your whole life's work or savings may have gone into creating and perpetrating it.

At this point, however, you are growing. Old structures no longer fit. As you grow and develop, you may find that growth is also occurring at the social level as well. At the Five of Fire, a whole culture or society may be suffering an identity crisis. Lawsuits occur. Revolutionaries arise. Wars break out. Prophets speak. Poets publish.

But, to the individual facing personal change, the battles of the external world may seem like children's skirmishes, while the internal war of Self seems deep, bloody and churning. Inside, you burn like a fire out of control. There is no cooling force of emotional balance to quell the flames. You experience the uncertainty and burning struggle inherent in the human condition.

The Struggle involves the quest to free the spirit and reconnect with the Oneness from which we emerged. The Five of Fire denotes the fall of spirit to the conditions of "man." In our physical world, we seem to work hard at building structures which become the very means by which we are later trapped. Our need then becomes to abandon or destroy such structures.

On the Tree of Life, the fifth circle is the Circle of Geburah. Geburah represents the energy of destruction. This is the process of catabolism, breaking down. In plants and animals, this is the destructive metabolism whereby living tissue is changed into waste products of a simpler chemical composition. In Fire, the Five implies destruction by burning. Burning away can mean that there is a surge of will which is not yet connected with a deep understanding. The stabilizing feminine force of emotional attachment has disappeared. Since there is no regulating force, the male, active, energetic force of Fire burns out of control. Thus, you may not realize why you seem to be destroying that which was once dear to you.

In actuality, you are mercilessly tearing down all that which is obsolete, useless and outdated: structures which no longer fit. Just as the diseased society is torn asunder, you are burning clean and purifying yourself in order to move to a higher level.

The Struggle is a testing ground of life. Can you surrender to the catabolic process of destruction and still attune to your basic goodness and caring within? While old structures must go, can you realize this outright and work lovingly with those around you so that The Struggle will not cause undue damage?

The challenge of the Five of Fire is to flow with the process of change. Allow yourself to fail. Allow yourself to lose. In losing all, everything is gained. This is the difference between being in control and being empowered. Allow yourself to go soft and you will win by giving in. This process involves letting go of false hopes and expectations. If you let go, you cannot be disappointed. If you let go of hope, you have nothing to fear. It is only by letting go of hope and fear that you begin to comprehend the vastness of space. This is the first step toward mastery.

Card Symbology: In the Five of Fire, we are looking down into the crater of a volcano, which is beginning to fold in on itself. The volcano represents conflict, eruption, war. The innermost depths are black, the darkest dark. Dark is the absence of light. As in the center of flame, there is the still absence of light. Darkness reigns at the center of light, and this must be understood before insight will occur.

The female force of understanding, blue and green for the influence of Binah, is locked outside of the eruption.

At the top center, an abstract black face sweeps in on a white cloud. This is the Face of Destruction.

The wands now become battering rods. Some turn into laser crystals. These lasers emerge to cut away the extraneous, to cut away the shell which is outgrown, all that which is inadequate. The power of the laser wands far exceeds that of the outmoded battering rods.

Six of Fire: Glory

Divinatory Meaning ──────────

The struggle has been difficult; it is as if you have fought a battle and now all you have left is the bloody fruit which you have won; make an offering of this fruit, surrender your winnings, to move into a state of harmony and beauty; you must understand that glory, however much you covet it, is a brief and fleeting thing; the truth is that which endures deep inside of yourself over time.

Six of Fire

GLORY

Meditation ────────────────────────────────

Jupiter in Leo.
Victory. Glory. Revelation.
Old and the New unite in Desire.
There is Harmony.
Understanding. Equilibrium.
All Flames burn in the Same Direction.
All are in Peace.
A place for the Flame; a place for the Crystal.
The Sun is Rising; a Son has Risen!
The Peaceful Sun follows the Moon.

Interpretation ──────────────────────────────

You are now moving into a new stage of being. You experience newness, green-ness, wetness. You feel reborn into a state of higher light and basic goodness. It is as if the light of spring has come!

At first, like a colt with its first uncertain steps, you may feel doubtful. But the light into which you emerge, after a transitory stay in darkness, is brilliant and beautiful. It is light by contrast to the darkness you have known and it grows directly out of allowing yourself to experience all things, both dark and light.

As a result of the battles you have fought, and your excursions into a chaotic darkness, you have tapped your inner light. The inner light is shining and white, hot, burning and eternal. It is bright, clear, clean and pure, not heavy or dense.

Technically, light triggers the functional activity of the eye, the organ of sight. As a form of radiant energy traveling at 186,000 miles per second, light illuminates the way, making sight possible. Through your struggles, you have come to *see* clearly. Seeing clearly means that you are experiencing a maturation of understanding. On the Tree of Life, the sixth sphere is the Circle of Tiphareth, the sphere of the unification of Wisdom and Understanding. This sphere is your stage at the Six of Fire. It symbolizes the birth of a holy child, or, in the individual, the onset of Christ-, Buddha-, or Krishna-like consciousness. As you are reborn in Christ-consciousness, you come into a profound balance.

To come into balance, you must understand your patterns of creativity, work, rationality, and interaction. When all such forces blend harmoniously and stand in equal balance, Glory is the result. As you are reborn in light, the mediating force of your inner Self stands like a fulcrum, continually balancing the great forces of action, receptivity, construction and destruction. Your old and new values compromise and are united in harmony. Then you reap the benefits of all of your hard work and times of Struggle. You look back over your personal biography and say: So *that's* what it has led to. When viewed in the new light, all of your past actions suddenly make sense.

The most important realization of the Six of Fire is that there is deep within you, a harmonious internal flame, one which cannot be quelled. This is the force that keeps you in balance. It is the beautiful and glorious flame of primal spirit which burns eternally, tempered by the feminine influence of goodness, loyalty and devotion. Recognizing that this beautiful flame burns within is the greatest fruit of all the difficult battles you have fought.

The test of the Six of Fire is to yield up, or *offer*, the fruit of your battle. To yield the glorious discovery of the inner light to a still higher force—one that is beyond the boundaries of your Self—is the challenge of the Six. If you divide and offer your internal flame in service to the One, just as Fire multiplies by dividing, your flame will surely grow.

Card Symbology: The volcano of the Five of Fire has been leveled and becomes like a rug, depicting a battlefield. It shows an intermingling of blood and darkness flecked with glimmers of light. A magic carpet of liberation emerges. It is the flying carpet of ascension.

The battering rods have united and become a fruit-bearing tree, a yielding tree, which grows from the battle-scarred landscape. The yield is a bloody fruit with light emitting from the center. This fruit is offered up, via the white path of the magic carpet (the wings of ascension), to a higher force. The higher force is symbolized by the appearance of the four-colored diamond or octahedron (a pyramidal structure) in the sky. This higher force is four-colored for the four planes of existence, and geometrical for balance. Looking at the diamond, you are looking into the pyramid of the Four, once again filled with the light of your own higher consciousness.

Seven of Fire: Courage (The Kite Card)

Divinatory Meaning

Conditions intensify; take further risks with greater awareness; you may feel trapped by social expectations—all that you were taught as you were growing up—but now the reality of the past no longer works for you; if you trust in your own internal convictions, you will develop strengths and a sense of self-confidence which will work for you and will, in good time, come to be respected by others; if you have the courage of your convictions, all that traps you will fall away.

Seven of Fire

COURAGE

Meditation ───────────────────────────────

Mars in Leo.
Challenge. Wavering.
The impeccable warrior
finds inner conviction
and faces adversity with
self-possession,
confidence
and resolution.

Interpretation ──────────────────────────────

At the Seven of Fire, Courage, you tune into the world of your emotions and your intuitive capability to come to an understanding of
your deepest convictions: those which go beyond the expectations of
your parents, children, mate, family, school, job and all other aspects
of culture and social conditioning. This is the time when the heart of
the deep Self is experienced. At this time, you cease to be a "stick
figure" and begin to understand and enact, with devotion, the true
purpose of your life.

The Seven is a time of repose, of turning inward, and it may also
be a time of feeling constrained or trapped by external conditions. As
you experience your deep convictions, you come to know that which
makes you different from other people. This sense of individuality
ought to be something to be celebrated, but it can also be a source of
anxiety. In discovering your uniqueness, you may feel like you no
longer fit in. You may lose confidence. But the feeling of being different is a result of your uniqueness. Understanding the extent of
your individuality—and your own unique powers—is a critical step
in the process of mastery and empowerment. It is a critical step on
the spiritual path. The deepest and truest seeing is the "seeing" of
the heart. Understand your uniqueness and celebrate it. Do not, however, allow yourself to succumb to the folly of infatuation with your
surface self. The process I describe herein involves deep work on the
most interior levels.

If you are feeling weakened, it is because you are moving toward
an understanding of a deeper source of knowledge, one that transcends the mundane conditions of your life. Temporary weakness
can be the result of knowing that you might have to make changes

to reduce the presence of conflict and bring your actions into alignment with your true purpose. But deep down inside you know the constant flame is burning and that is the source of your strength. This is the flame of eternal life and the energy of renewal. It is your own resilience, the energy to continue, the energy to move to ever-higher and more challenging levels.

On the Tree of Life, the seventh sphere is the Circle of Netzach, the sphere of Courage. Netzach oversees the emotions. As you delve deep into your own heart, the balance of the Seven will be discovered and true meaning will be revealed. By opening your eyes in your own dark sea, you will not only discover your true convictions but the Courage of those convictions. The way to truth is through listening to your own heart. If you feel off-balance in this process, you need only tune into the balancing structures of the Seven. Seven is the number of perfect order. It combines the moving, creative balance of Three with the stationary, structured balance of Four. You already hold the strength of the eternal Three and the material Four within. Through right attunement to your own strengths, you can easily rise above those things which appear to be limitations.

You need only grasp the tail of "the kite," that enlightening force which will lift you from the bonds which constrain you. The tail of the kite is your own tale. The body of the kite is your connection with the One-ness of all things. Through reassessing and re-telling your own story in light of your connectedness with all things, you move into deeper self-understanding. This will prepare you to transcend your surface limitations. The two major components of transcendence are (1) looking deeply within, and (2) speaking or enacting the truth discovered there. Having the Courage of your inner convictions is the key to mobility. Then, when the pressure of truth is brought to bear on seemingly immovable structures or barriers, they miraculously fall away. In this way, in every direction, you create the conditions, and therefore the reality, of your life.

Card Symbology: The card shows a colorful six-pointed star on a four-colored circular background. The background circle represents potential balance on the planes of Spirit, Emotions, Mind and Body. The pyramid which encloses the star is the Dark Pyramid of the past. It represents outmoded structures. The star is trapped by six crossed wands which border the top of the pyramid. This entire configuration symbolizes the trapped spirit.

A black tail moves down from the enclosed star into a Fire. The Fire is the source of the energy that will eventually propel the star from its cage of darkness. The energy source is the external fire that burns within each of us.

The prison or cage trapping the star, represented by six crossed wands, results from the ensnarement which comes from attuning to dominant views, even when they are incorrect, and feeling the contradiction. The dominating wands, though white on the outside, have centers of darkness. Also, they do not have a "line" to the higher illumination of perfect balance. The line to higher consciousness is the tail of a kite, thus the Seven of Fire, Courage, is also known as the Kite Card. The tail of the kite is the tale of our individual and collective history: all the cumulative records; the past, present and future of all that was, is and ever shall be. This tale is constantly developing at the internal level of self and the external level of culture.

The kite itself represents the One-ness of all things. It shows the perfection of knowledge on the four planes which are combined into the diamond-, pyramid- or octahedron-like structure which represents perfect attunement to the cosmic will.

Eight of Fire: The Lightning Path

Divinatory Meaning ─────────

This is a high energy period for initiating change; you have a sense of fast movement, rapid growth; you are achieving a broader base of human and spiritual knowledge and potential; energy is coming to you, but it is as if you have to reach up to meet it; stretch yourself and you will grow; the perception of love creates the most powerful of all energies, remember this in your period of development.

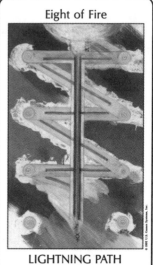

Eight of Fire

LIGHTNING PATH

Meditation

Mercury in Sagittarius.
Change.
Conversion.
Rapid Rise of New Energy.
Form of a Higher Form!
Hope of a Higher Hope!
The New Coming of the Original Will:
Electric Spirit, Intent, Breath!
The Spiral, the Coil,
Cosmic Power.

Interpretation

The Eight of Fire is the card of perception. It is the card of the trans-
muting spirit. At this time you are on the verge of a "raised" consciousness which, if allowed to develop, will alter your goals and
convictions. As you arrive at this point, you are in a time of major
movement to a higher level. You are achieving a broader base of
human and spiritual knowledge. You are now able to put words to
feelings you have had, but until this point, could not fully comprehend or express. It is as if the clear direction of your life has been
floating just below the surface of your conscious mind. You knew
you had an important task, but you could not quite perceive it. At
the Eight of Fire, however, clear direction rises to the surface. You
need only follow your intuitive grasp.

The Eight of Fire is the Lightning Path of energy taking off. This
energy flows to you from the primal universal force. Some refer to
this energy as the descent of power. As you perceive this energy or
power moving toward you, you will know you are on the right track.
The force of the universe is behind your ideas. In becoming aware of
this, you realize that you can harness and channel this force for your
own empowerment or for the empowerment of your group.

Harnessing force means becoming very clear and moving with
the universal flow. In order to become clear, you must *ascend* to meet
energy as it comes to you. This means that you must open yourself
to receive, understand and channel universal force. Let the universal
force flow through you and you will be successful in actualizing your
deepest goals. Letting the force flow through you is a sign that your

understanding has matured. Your fiery energy has become more sub-tle. Your nature is now cooly electric. You can operate from a lower-key, but more effective, position. This is an indication that you are headed in the right direction. Although you now have words and concepts to describe your work, you feel very comfortable in moving ahead without discussing it. This is because when you are on the right path, you do not need to clear it with anyone.

It is now time to move quickly. Move quickly, and you will reap great rewards! On the Lightning Path movement is rapid, driven by the momentum of polarizing opposites. At the Eight of Fire, you are driven by your own understanding of the dualistic nature of the universe. There is black and there is white, female and male, cold and hot, wet and dry, earth and heaven. The eighth force mediates between matter and spirit (the square and the circle). Thus, eight is the symbol for regeneration. It represents the eternal spiraling move-ment of creation. It represents the spiritual connection of the con-scious mind (earth: the below) to the higher consciousness (heaven: the above). Arriving at this point in time, you are motivated by the incredible force of making connections.

On the Tree of Life, the eighth sphere is the Circle of Hod, the conscious mind. At the eight, the subconscious mind has transmitted sensory experience to the conscious mind of thought. Thus, eight is creative and rational thought. It is the realm wherein archetypes, symbols, and other abstractions are created from all that which seems illogical. You are now making sense of things. You are describing and understanding processes and occurrences for which, earlier, you could find no words. The eight is the dawn of objective consciousness.

With objective consciousness comes enlightened perception. You are now part of the group that understands. That is why the Eight of Fire, the Lightning Path, is also the symbol of initiation. With your new level of understanding, you can now see the purpose of mem-bership or belonging. This enables you to understand the significance of the secret ceremony. In seeing clearly—as if for the first time—you have a sense of communion with that which was heretofore unrecognizable.

As your philosophy changes, you benefit by using the subtle energies of the Lightning Path to purge your existence of that which is no longer necessary. With each extraneous element you burn away, you shed more light on that realm which you once perceived as darkness. Burn away that which is outmoded and your consciousness will rise to ever-greater levels of awareness. The key to separating out that which needs to be burned from that which should be preserved is the knowledge that love is the catalyst that triggers the movement of the Lightning Path. The perception of love creates the most powerful of all energies. Move in the way of love and you will become energized, aware and fully empowered.

Card Symbology: Fueled by the subconscious mind, and propelled by the interaction of the emotions (Netzach on the Tree of Life) and the intellect (Hod on the Tree of Life), the Lightning Force takes off from the material plane in a dialectical movement toward the above. This symbolizes rising consciousness.

Simultaneously, energy in the form of lightning descends into matter from the realm of spirit. This symbolizes the power of the universal force to affect and energize the human being. As such, the Eight of Fire card depicts lightning shooting through the entire Tree of Life, crossing the abyss with a tremendous velocity.

The universal force is often viewed as a flash of spiraling light which is caused by electrical charges in the atmosphere. The clinging fiery energy of the earlier Fire cards becomes more subtle in the Eight of Fire. This means the level of knowledge has matured. The powerful force of the One of Fire reappears, but this time the manifestation is more sophisticated, technical or evolved. It is electric.

The vertical axis in the middle of the card is the tail of the kite as depicted in the Seven of Fire. It is the tale which holds the story of past, present and future. In the Eight, the significance of past, present and future is fully comprehended. Full and accurate comprehension is the driving force of change. Full and accurate comprehension involves a deep understanding of the role of love in creating the flow of energy.

Nine of Fire: Eye of Fire

Divinatory Meaning ───────────

You have arrived at a peak experience; you have reached the right wavelength, the right current; you are attuned to the right frequency; you are seeing things accurately and—if you work within the concrete realm of your everyday life— your clear sight will lead to solid creations which will endure over time; as things change, do not let yourself get thrown off balance; stay focused on the details of living.

Nine of Fire

EYE OF FIRE

Meditation ──────────────────────

Moon in Sagittarius
Strength
Meditation
Now you See as never before:
Gird up for the new stage
    New Understanding means New Challenge
    the Strong Arm approach leads nowhere
Beyond the enemy,
there is no need to defend.

Interpretation ─────────────────────

You have arrived! You now understand the power of giving up to gain. Through allowing yourself to surrender, you reached the right wavelength, the right current. You are traveling at the right altitude at the right cruising speed. You have attuned to the right frequency. You are now moving on Gautama Buddha's eightfold path: right views, right aspiration, right speech, right conduct, right livelihood, right effort, right meditation, right rapture. You have understood and celebrated your uniqueness and then abandoned your individuality for communion with the One. You hear the messages of the One and you have learned to flow with the cosmic will. Because you are "in the flow," the universe favors your movements.

At the Nine of Fire, you have moved to the subconscious plane in order to know the deep inner Self. This is knowing the I, as well as knowing The Eye! The eye is an aperture, or portal, of higher understanding. The eye is apprehended when one first understands the nature of the deep Self. Developing insight into the true path of Self entails turning one's focus inward toward the subconscious mind and allowing one's two eyes to see as one. Correct and directed inner vision is achieved by coming to an understanding of the function of the one eye—the third eye. The third eye looks in and out at once. At the same moment, the third eye perceives right and left, below and above, past and future. Further, this eye reflects images accurately, both in this world and the next. The seeing of the third eye is not directed by contemporary culture or the dominant status quo. It is eternal sight, freed from the constraints of society. In this way the third eye is similar to the eye of a hurricane. The third eye represents still and clear sight in the midst of chaos.

On the Tree of Life, the ninth sphere is the subconscious mind, Yesod. This is the sphere of the third eye. The subconscious mind transmits sensory experience to the conscious mind where it is interpreted, abstracted and reacted to. The conscious mind consists of the interacting forces of intellect (Hod) and emotion (Netzach). At the level of subconscious mind there is no interference from thought waves or emotional reaction. Thus Yesod represents a way of knowing—the view of the third eye—which is unaffected by personal, social or cultural constraints. At the Nine, in the subconscious mode, there is a perception of the unity of all things. At this blissful center, you see things as they are.

Accurate sight (including foresight and hindsight) leads to sensible, solid and durable creations. At the Nine of Fire, your ideas are sound because your assessments are clear. The way you see things is grounded in a reality that transcends the boundaries of everyday life. Moving from a position of solid—and eternal—accuracy renders possible the most magical results! And the best magic comes from the discovery that the light in the dark of subconscious chaos is *the light of your own heart*. Through understanding your own internal capacity for love, you realize that the creation of light in the darkness is forever the work of your own hand. This knowledge is the source of a deep and tenacious power: the power of boundless sight which is a reflection of the power of boundless love.

At the Nine of Fire, you realize that change is the essence of universal will, and to stand grounded in love at the center of the hurricane—with a clear eye—is to stand firmly rooted within the process of change. Change is the only thing that is stable in the universe. If you want to stay rooted in rightness, like a top righting itself by spinning faster, you must constantly adjust your movements to complement all internal and external movements of the cosmos. The secret of the Eye of Fire is to continually move and adjust while operating from a center of stillness and love. The higher light is everywhere. It is within and without. Light goes on within you and without you. Life goes on within you and without you. Love goes on within you and without you. Maintaining this knowledge—the deep knowledge of the third eye—will ensure your continued success.

Card Symbology: In the Nine of Fire, the wands become red-hot cylinders shooting from a cone of light which emanates from a cube floating at the top of a mountain range. The mountain range represents all that which comprises the physical plane. The mountains, as moving triangular forces, also double as the holy trinity of Mother-Father-God at the top of the Tree of Life, thus their meaning is dualistic and paradoxical. They represent earth and heaven at the same time. This is a clue to understanding the statement, "As Above, So Below."

The cube is the magical box of understanding—the "black box" or Pandora's box which contains all. It unfolds into the energy of the sacred cross. This cross represents the intersection of the physical plane and the spiritual path.

The Cone of Light is the Lightning Path of the Eight of Fire, now leaving the physical plane. The eye through which the cylinders emerge is the third eye of the physical body. Through the third eye, the cylinders simultaneously give and receive universal messages. The red cylinders move up through the Tree of Life to the yellow circle of Tiphareth, the holy child ready to be reborn in each of us, which stands between overlapping repetitious circles of dark and light, dark and light. The circles of dark and light represent the mobilizing power of universal dualities.

Central to the Nine of Fire is a hot air balloon, which has harnessed the lightning energy of the Eight, and risen from the Earth to the Circle of Kether, the uppermost sphere on the Tree of Life. At the center of Kether, which is the eye of higher knowledge, is an ankh, the ancient Egyptian symbol of life. The ankh is the uterus, the womb, the place where conception occurs.

The key to understanding the Nine is represented by the dominant inverted female triangle which contains the moon in the center of the upper eye. The female forms and the moon symbolize the move to the subconscious plane where the third eye sees and the meeting and understanding of the deep inner Self occurs.

Ten of Fire: The Cage

Divinatory Meaning ─────────────

Your spirit feels trapped or oppressed; your heart seems caged; you have had a peak experience, but you are having difficulty applying the results to daily life; the key is to let go of extraneous matter; free yourself of all unnecessary encumbrances; tune into your emotions to realize what should stay in your life and what should go; attuning to your emotions may necessitate an attitudinal change on your part.

Ten of Fire

THE CAGE

Meditation ──────────────────────────────

Saturn in Sagittarius
The awakened Heart burns
in the Cage of Matter

How to escape the
Wretched Oppression

of the heaving weight
of Matter?

Interpretation

You have had an incredible awakening experience, you have been awed, and now you are back down to earth, with your feet on the ground, and thinking: *Now* what? You are even doubting your experience. You are asking: was that moment of elation *real*?

The Ten of Fire expresses the disappointment of one who has traveled on the astral plane, or experienced a miraculous conversion, or a burst of kundalini energy, chi force or sexual ecstasy, or even *died* —and then is forced to return to the mundane experience of daily life. The scenes experienced were so beautiful. The feeling was so welcoming. There were loved ones and guides along the way. You felt like you had gone "home." Now you are back in your body. Your heart is burning brightly, but it feels imprisoned. You feel trapped by having to come back. You feel trapped by uncertainties and social responsibilities.

How will you deal with the world after you have known the ecstasy of perfect union? At this time you need to adjust your perspective.

In *Myths to Live By*, philosopher Joseph Campbell relates the story of the troubled woman who came to the Indian saint Ramakrishna and said, Oh, Master, I do not find that I love God. Ramakrishna asked, Is there nothing that you love? She answered, My little nephew, to which Ramakrishna replied, There is your love and service to God, in your love and service to that child.[3] Ramakrishna provided this woman with a new perspective. The challenge of the Ten of Fire is likewise to see things differently. It is time for an attitude change.

Moving to a new level is the message of the number ten. Numerologically, ten is one plus zero. One is a point of new possibility. This signifies your new beginning, your attitude change or new perspective. Zero is pure unity, the revelation you have already had. Combining one and zero signals movement to new level. You are now moving quickly. At the point of the Ten, the Wheel of Fortune turns again.

To understand your new direction, it is wise to listen to the deepest messages of your heart. At this time, you may need the guidance of a master or teacher. Such a teacher is as close to you as

[3]See Joseph Campbell, *Myths to Live By* (New York: Viking Penguin, 1972), pp. 98–9.

closing your eyes and retreating in stillness. Teachers can be found in classrooms and through the printed word. They reside on the Tree of Life and in the Major Arcana of the tarot. Further, all of us are teachers just as all of us are students. At this time, it is wise to hear the messages of all whom you encounter: friends, family, associates. Listen to the messages on the wind. Open up your heart and listen and remember; the deepest *hearing* is the hearing of the heart.

On the Tree of Life, the tenth sphere is Malkuth, who represents the merger of the three elements—spirit, emotions, thought—with the fourth element—matter. Malkuth is the realm of the physical body and daily life. She represents the totality of our experience brought down to earth. We do live in the social world. We are of the physical world. And with our very attitudes toward this world, we construct our own cages. We construct our own cages through imagining that our physical bodies and our social responsibilities are a trap.

If you feel caged at the Ten of Fire, it is well to remember that matter is the manifestation of spirit, the fruit of time and space. And just as the body can be viewed as a trap, it can be viewed as a liberating vehicle. The physical body and the physical world provide the tangible form in which the spirit does its work on the physical plane. Existing in the physical world, the world of action, gives the spirit the tangible opportunity to create.

The task of the Ten is to tune into the source of your creativity as well as to what you want to create. Use your heart. Love what you do. Use your head. Be clear about what you do. Use your hands for the work of the spirit. Through applying to your daily life everything you have learned about moving with, rather than against, the universal flow, your heart will, paradoxically, be freed. By accepting and rejoicing in matter, you are paradoxically freed from the bondage of matter. You will be freed by the realization that the physical plane constitutes an opportunity and a blessing which ought to be celebrated. It is a tremendous opportunity and a privilege to be that which embodies the spirit in the world of action. It is a tremendous opportunity to become a co-creator with the primal force on the physical plane.

Card Symbology: In the Ten of Fire, the tubes which connected to the above in the Nine now become the bars that lock in the caged heart. This is the oppression of physicality. The two cubes in the card represent the above and the below. The heart is imprisoned in the below, in the world of the manifest.

The upper cube is like a television screen. The screen shows light and dark fire (will). Monsters and horses appear. The horses are rearing. They are raring to go. This is an indication that the choice is yours. Observe yourself from a distance and choose your course.

The upper triangle is Kether, Binah and Chokmah. The lower triangle is Netzach, Hod and Yesod. These are the elements of the Tree of Life interacting and birthing new forms on the physical plane.

Fire Father: The Spirit of Flame

Divinatory Meaning ───────────

Father

FIRE

You are experiencing the sense of conviction; there is much movement, energy is surging; you feel the power of leadership; you are rapidly moving toward a new way of knowing; a new viewpoint or perspective on matters; regulate your activity; be careful not to burn yourself out in this high energy period.

Meditation ──────────────────────────

Scorpio, Sagittarius
Fire Father in Fire
Fire of Fire
Spirit of Spirit
Spirit of Fire
Power of Action
Power of Spirit
Fiery One
the Lightning Flash
Light and noble

swift and agile;
Spirit burning on his track
Soul smoking in his wake
He's got what it takes for explosive
Leadership

Spirit of Spirit
Flame of Soul
screaming voltage
searing control.

Interpretation

The Fire Father is open to all possibility and moves quickly. He is the active, fiery part of spirit, the spark of life, lightning flash movement: fierce, impetuous, impulsive, and swift. He is the elemental force in the suit of Fire, embodying the essence and spirit of Fire. His nature is energetic force. Fire Father's brilliance is dazzling, permeating. Moving at a slow pace, he provides comfort, light and warmth. He is the Father of Fathers. At maximum speed, like a forest fire, he burns and destroys, making space for new seedlings.

As the essence of the will of Fire, Fire Father feels neither victory nor defeat, pleasure nor pain. As the will of will, Fire Father's drive is to move. He burns for the sake of movement. Ashes lie in his wake. He judges not, but moves because he must, consuming that which feeds him and dies only when there is nothing more to consume.

Fire Father is the issue of pure flame, the issue of pure will. He is the friend and enemy to all of nature. He is a raw and sacred form, a rare potential, the transformer of matter, changing matter into energy. His transcendent whorls of smoke signal not only that which must be seared away, but that which will become. He is a great teacher, opening the way for the new. The message he brings is *change*.

On the Tree of Life, the Fire Father corresponds to Chokmah, the universal male principle. He is the emitting force, the force that fires energy outward. When properly attuned, Chokmah receives his strength from Kether, the primal force—the God aspect of the supernal trinity of the Tree of Life—the universal light. His challenge is to actively hear the message of Kether, the God force. Kether informs the direction of activities so that they are timely and meaningful.

When he is in his exalted form, the virtues of Fire Father bring him into accord with the great movements of heaven and earth. The mind of Fire Father is as clear as the Sun and Moon. The actions of Fire Father are well-ordered and move in time with the seasons. (See *I Ching:* Hexagram 1: The Creative Principle.) In achieving the sense of *timely* movement, Fire Father achieves wisdom.[4]

When Fire Father is not in tune with the universal or God force, his movements may seem frantic or frenetic and he can cause trouble or quickly burn himself out. Like a revolutionary leader, Fire Father is charismatically invigorating, but, when he is not attuned to the directives of Kether, he can pose danger. He can be an astute scientist, but a mad one as well. Whether he is sheer genius or sheer madman depends upon the source of his actions. However he is informed, he is too powerful to be ignored. Nevertheless, if his actions are to persevere, he must have the backing of Kether.

He holds the greatest promise, but he needs the balance of *conscious* conviction to keep his spark alive and on track. To avoid burning wildly or burning out, he must be attuned, grounded, rational and emotionally committed. That is, in order to remain successful, in addition to staying consciously attuned, he must balance the fiery part of himself with the other major elements: Earth, Wind and Water. Connection with these elements—Earth for grounding; Wind for rational thinking; Water for emotional commitment—will both fan and temper his flames. The essence of the tempering process is to keep the processes of production and destruction in active balance. Remaining *temperate* (see Key XIV: Temperance) is the processual goal of Fire Father.

Fire Father symbolizes the inner connection to wisdom. With the wisdom that results from balance and proper attunement, Fire Father becomes the master of growth, inner development, and increased perception. Growing through every challenge, he becomes the essence of dynamic change in conscience and consciousness. Moving in tune with the cosmic flow, he becomes dedicated, powerful, loyal and noble: the very essence of success and leadership.

Card Symbology: The Fire Father is the white hot flame of spirit. He rides the beast of radiant darkness into the limitless light. The dark horse treads the sea of wisdom, so cold, that, like dry ice, it

---

[4]For an excellent translation of the *I Ching,* see John Blofeld, *I Ching, The Book of Change* (New York: E. P. Dutton & Co., 1968).

burns. The dry ice is the dry eye/the dry I of the One of Fire. It longs to be wetted by connection with feeling and understanding.

The Fire Father's magic wand and his steed's hooves spark on contact with balanced (gray) wisdom. Wisdom is gray because it comes from a combination of light and dark forces. As this sparking occurs, new flames—new possibilities—flare into existence. The only danger is that Fire Father's wand is burning at both ends. If Water is not encountered, the magic will be lost.

The rider's steed dances at the portal between layers of consciousness. Just beyond the Fire Father is a layer of light—Higher or Super Consciousness. This is the light of Kether, the God force. The layered concentric circles of light and dark imply that light and dark are forever contained inside each other, that there is limitless light in darkness and radiant darkness in light. When the Fire Father moves fast enough, light and dark collapse and become one.

Fire Mother: The Conduit

Divinatory Meaning ⸻

Long after the energy of others has burned out, your own energy burns like a constant pilot light; you have the sense of being a sought-out leader especially in matters of the spirit; you seek quiet, but consistent, leadership; as long as you move in accordance with nature's laws, nature obeys your every command.

Mother

FIRE

Meditation

Pisces, Aries
The Fire Mother
of the Steady Ray
Water Mother in Fire
attractive/generous
beautiful flame
actively lighting the way for those within
her reign
with her fathomless
Energy
Spirit
Perceptions

receptive channel
for Light and Strength
animal woman moves in Time
with Lions:
feral hearts of Fire
desirous of Learning
the Secret Keys to an Aeon Beyond
the slow burn of Spirit
blazing beneath, then sailing away
on waving flames/gaseous streams

Her children stand
in awe
of her.

Interpretation

The Fire Mother signifies the beginning of something new and possibly dangerous. This new effort has the potential for great success. The new enterprise can be likened to stepping on a lion's tail. Do it carefully and exercise breathless caution! Treating the lion (active new fiery energy) with caution—not moving too fast or hard—will lead to the highest rewards. If you move gently, the lion won't bite. If you watch your step and heed omens, good fortune will be yours. How you *conduct* yourself is of utmost importance (see *I Ching*: Hexagram 10: Treading, Conduct).

The Fire Mother is the loving and tempering aspect of the fiery energy of spirit. She is the desiring force. Her vast energy is always active, but also persistent and calm. She burns like a constant pilot light, forever shedding light on the vast mysteries of the subconscious realm, continually lighting the way for insight. She is a quiet and tranquil teacher, who, through the transmission of insight, wields an awesome power. As such, the Fire Mother is exceedingly attractive. She feels in control and is very sure. Her actions are premeditated, practical and fruitful. The Fire Mother is kind. She is honest. She is generous. She makes deep and lasting commitments. She loves and serves all things of nature, the great and small. In turn, the Fire Mother is, herself, great.

In her most exalted state, the Fire Mother has dominion over the king of beasts—the lion of Fire. But she does not impose her vision. She has only to communicate that vision and the lion will respond. That is because she understands and serves the king of beasts. Her dominion is the power of love. The source of knowing true beauty and love is deep understanding. Anything can be appreciated once it is understood. The Fire Mother knows that when you hear with your neighbor's ears and see with your neighbor's eyes, the inner nature of your neighbor's actions becomes crystal clear. When she sees as the lion sees, she understands the lion. In understanding the lion, she understands her own actions. The presence of understanding alters the way you behave, especially when it comes to aggressive activity.

Manipulation, without a complementary understanding (of the lion, for example), limits power. Power is subtle. The greatest power results from quiet Strength (see Key VIII). True strength is simply balanced and stable action.

The challenge of the Fire Mother is to attune to the balanced part of herself—the Water—in order to retain her constancy. When she is overly influenced by the power of Fire, she can take sudden, unpredictable turns. She can be violent and demonstrate incredible fury. She may attempt to soften or control this behavior, which she knows is a problem, through the use of drugs or alcohol. But externally produced altered states can never cure her longing to consume. Further, she faces the danger of turning this fury inward upon herself. It is well known that anger that preys upon the Self results in disease of the most despicable character.

There is only one way to manage the burning of the internal Fire, and that is through balancing active energy with loving under-standing. The lesson of the Fire Mother is to tread lightly and with love.

As she learns to blend the internal flame/will/drive to action with the balancing force of Water/love/the mind of God, Fire Mother be-comes the exalted conductor. She corresponds to Binah, the Great Mother on the Tree of Life, who facilitates the passage of the spirit through the Great Portal. On one side of the portal is the world of the subconscious—the dark—the domain of all that is, was and ever shall be.

As the guardian of this portal, the Fire Mother teaches that you must delve into the dark to discover all the wondrous methods and results which, through balanced, calm and considered action, shall manifest in your spirit and therefore in the matter of your life. In the dark, you will discover love, the motivation behind all satisfactory and lasting achievements. In the dark, you will discover the meaning of Strength (see Key VIII). These discoveries are the result of a deep knowledge of the inner Self, that which can only be found when you face your own Shadow.

On the other side of the portal is the world of matter. Fire Mother conducts rebirth of the spirit in matter. She is the conduit which draws down, receives and nurtures the energy of the primal force, trans-forms it in the dark, and releases it into the world as spirit born in matter. She is the bridge between spirit and matter, idea and actual-ization. She teaches that when you attune to righteous and divine love—and tread gently, but with conviction—your ideas will become actualized with the greatest Strength (see Key VIII).

Card Symbology: The Fire Mother is the drop of Water that has the ability to control Fire. That she can control flame is signified by the half-lotus position of her knee atop the lion of Fire. He is not held by her, but willingly stays. Both are content.

She is at once a pilot light and a billowing flame. Her rainbow stained-glass window is a portal which leads beyond the veil to a layer of darkness: the level of subconscious dream and imagery. The Fire Mother guards this threshold: the threshold of understanding and balancing fire through love. Just beyond this layer of darkness is the Radiant Light of Kether.

Fire Brother: Sun Warrior

Divinatory Meaning ─────────

Your inner spirit aspires; you are like a flame reaching heavenward; you perceive great qualities of strength, swiftness, brilliance and agility, the sense of romantic revolution: qualities which are real and wondrous; be careful, however, do not be too impulsive at this time of great revelation and change; attune to the eternal nature of things and your actions will endure.

Brother

FIRE

Meditation ──────────────────────────

Cancer, Leo
Spirit Warrior
Wind Brother in Fire
sailing on a sea of Flames
too fast to be
burned
too strong to be hurt
with dramatic strategies
would fight in the streets
to spur
the cataclysm
onto a new dimension

a coup d'etat mentality
the Warrior filled with Energy
intensely Romantic/young Vitality
spurning words—
they cannot describe the

gambler inside
nor the Soldier of Fortune
with steely-eyed courage
with steel-helmed nerve
fight hard die hard
with unswerving faith
he runs his race
through infinite rings
of Fire.

Interpretation

The Fire Brother is the flame reaching heavenward—the aspiring spirit. He is swift and strong and has the power and energy of lions. He is clever and spontaneous, which makes him exciting, but he is also unpredictable—even airy or "flighty"—which can sometimes lead to problems. Nonetheless, his charisma and his ingenious strategies and plans are incredibly attractive.

The Fire Brother is the romantic revolutionary, the pure idealist. He wants utopia. He wants it now.

The Fire Brother is a mover and shaker. When everything is in balance, he enflames a tremendous positive energy. With his power of reason, the Fire Brother fans the flame of action (Fire Father) which is kept from destructive tendencies by the power of the heart (Fire Mother).

The danger of the Fire Brother is that he may not attune to his Mother who can be the very spirit of love. He may be too quick, too clever, or too impulsive for his own good. He may seem abrupt or offensive. He may arrive at incomplete, irrational solutions that go awry as quickly as he institutes them. His answer is to learn to balance his surging, brilliant, fiery energy with his equally brilliant power of reason. In his exalted state, the Fire Brother is the Sun Warrior, the immaculate child of the One, child of beauty, light and love, child of all things transcendent. He brings the dark to light through the power of reason.

To outsiders, the Fire Brother may seem hard to pin down or mysterious, and therefore may be revered and dreaded. The dread may come from fear of unpredictable change, but the Fire Brother is not really inconstant. He is just growing, expanding at a rate that many find incomprehensible. This expansion applies to the expansion of the internal spirit as well as active expansion on the physical plane.

If the Fire Brother attunes to his origins, he should have no trouble realizing his tremendous potential. He is born of the intercourse between light and love. Thus, his warrior energy is the energy of the sixth sphere of the Tree of Life, the Circle of Tiphareth, the Circle of the Sun. When he learns to balance the force of his father (action) with the understanding of his mother (love), the Fire Brother can fly through any hoop with freedom, agility and knowledge.

His challenge is to come to understand the lesson of eternal being. In thought, word and deed, the Fire Brother must learn to base his life upon the sure foundation of eternal being. It is with this knowledge that he can advance with security. In order to advance, however, he may have to lighten his load, shorten "the tail of his kite," which may be weighing him down. The tail of his kite is his own cumulative "tale," his biographical history through this life and other lives. The internalized knowledge of eternal being is his strength for searing away that which keeps him from flying, namely his bondage to fear and hope. In his exalted warrior consciousness, the Fire Brother has no fear. He also has no hope. This enables him to move rapidly and without doubt, ever-deeper into layers of the Self.

When Fire Brother understands the nature of eternal being and his own relationship with time, his actions will be timely. Careful timing ensures that the fruits of his actions will endure. When all is understood, as a result of timely intercourse, all things begin (see *I Ching:* Hexagram 44: Sexual Intercourse).

Card Symbology: As a result of the marriage of Fire (Fire Father) and Water (Fire Mother), the Fire Brother, Sun Warrior, journeys by steam. He leaps with tremendous velocity through portals of Fire and Water/Light and Dark. He can be seen moving at the speed of light through layer after layer of consciousness.

He flies through hoop after hoop, carrying his "tail," the tale of past and future, with him. The further he flies, the faster he flies. The faster he flies, the longer is his jet stream. He is moving inward toward the I/the Eye.

He rides the supreme steed of the suit of Fire: the magical lion-horse whose head streams Fire and whose hooves strike sparks. Lion-ness, the dominion of nature, is tamed, for Fire Brother serves the lion. Horse-ness, the dominion of servility, is tamed, for Fire Brother serves the horse.

Fire Sister: The Spark/Free Spirit

Divinatory Meaning ───────────

Accept all change and movement with a balanced perspective: equanimity; you feel enthusiasm, self-confidence, eloquence; you are moving within the natural flow of the universe and you are favored by all universal forces; when you feel in danger of fragmentation, turn within for the answers: meditate on the sun setting in the ocean—imagine this picture in your mind—and you will be soothed and regain touch with those things that are of real and lasting importance to you.

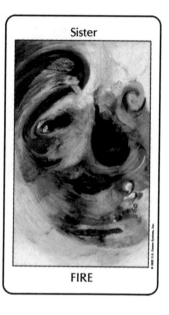

Sister

FIRE

Meditation ────────────────────

Cancer, Leo, Virgo
Fire Sister
the Earth Sister in Fire
the Virgin Priestess of
the Fires of Spring
Shining Daring
bringing Tidings from
Strange Worlds
the Carrier of Strange News
crystal views
of the Coming Aeon

the Secret Flame
into which all things
Return

burned in Seas deeper
than spirit itself
Loving

Fire Sister
Burning
    Fire Sister
Verdant
    Fire Sister
Silent
    Fire Sister.

Interpretation

The Fire Sister has survived all the trials by fire, has gained and lost and gained again. Now, she accepts change with equanimity, moving with the will of the universe.

Moving with the universal will, the Fire Sister faces no danger. The natural forces of heaven, sea and earth favor her. She moves in time with the seasons, internally creating her own beauty through her wise use of energy. She is naturally aggressive and completely gentle at the same time; enthusiastic, self-confident, trusted and trustworthy. She can be very articulate when asked to perform, but she would rather just live in harmony with the world around her, enjoying her life and her gift of spirit. She feels no driving need to aspire, but her balanced views and ideals make her a sought-out oracle.

As a divine priestess, the Fire Sister's task is to connect, and stay connected to, her three layers of consciousness, the above (higher consciousness), the below (subconsciousness) and the center (waking consciousness). These layers can also be thought of as heaven, sea and earth.

Through standing in the center of these layers, *seeing* All at once, knowing All at once, the Fire Sister understands and moves in time with the universal will. That is the key to her freedom and intense happiness. That is why she is in the favor of the great forces and why her actions are right. She is, in every way, perfect in her niche in the universe. And that is why she is sought out by others. They wish to understand her magic. The source of her magic is love under will. She may be seen as the bringer of unexpected or unusual news, because her secret, though she makes no attempt to disguise it, may come as a surprise.

Sometimes, however, even the Fire Sister fears fragmentation. Heaven, sea and earth, the forces which must balance to insure the creation of all things, seem cut off from each other. It is as if the creative flow will be quelled by the destructive tendencies of Fire, flames out of control.

At this time, the Fire Sister has to retune. To accomplish this, she directs her vast powers for *seeing* within. Her favorite meditation is to imagine the Sun setting on the sea from a western exposure. Waking consciousness (Sun) dips into the subconscious (sea) from the superconscious (Heaven), thus uniting the three levels. In attuning to the harmony of this sacred union, Fire Sister is reminded that the great forces always were, are, and forever shall be, in balance. The grand movements of life come into perspective. She feels at peace. Through reliving trust in the natural processes, Fire Sister escapes any negative influences around her and sees only the higher light: her true path.

On the true path, she is exalted. She is not even tempted toward honor and riches. All that seems irrelevant (see *I Ching:* Hexagram 12: Obstruction).

The Fire Sister *sees*. She *sees* that everything is moving, that change is stability. She is the original will of the One of Fire exalted to its heights and recentered in Earth. She is the embodiment of spirit, the most minute element of flame, the harmonious balance of all the good in her ancestry, her Fire Father, Water Mother and Wind Brother. She is the spark of life/light that dances in the cosmic flow. This is because she *sees* and *knows* the flow. She does not have to contain her actions. She is so much a part of the universal will that with every step, she treads in light and love. Thus, she is truly a free spirit.

On the Tree of Life, the Fire Sister is Malkuth, the spirit of the One brought to earth and embodied in flesh. She is the manifestation of the one life that is held within all life, the spark of life within each of us that is part of the central flame of the one life. She teaches us that the nature of the one is embodied in the many. As we realize that our internal flame is but a spark of the One, we learn to attune to, move in time with, the one source. We experience a profound unity, and like Fire Sister, our actions become favored by all of the diverse forces and elements, all of which are manifestations of the eternal life-giving power of the one source.

Card Symbology: The Fire Sister represents the spark between the horse's hoof and the sea of wisdom (see Fire Father).

She is the light of the spark, dancing with a black image. The image is her partner and her Self. She is light as a feather. She is a feather to signify her continuous transformation: the flight to the heavens and back to earth. She is the eternal grayness (balancing light and dark) at the center of the flame.

Jubilantly, she emerges refreshed from the cave of the below, the underworld, the forest of the night. She has rested well and dances in delight. The cosmic sea (see) spirals out of her being carrying all of the components of life. In the lower part of the card, a salamander appears. The primordial salamander is the Fire Sister's emblem of the original will made flesh.

❖ ❖ ❖

CHAPTER SEVEN

Water

Love, Reflection, Psychic Upwelling
Cups, Mirrors, Moon
West
Dusk
The Sacred Year Falling Toward Death
Blue, Green, Purple, Black
Quartz Crystals and Moonstones
Fish, Water Snakes and
Dragons sloshing in the
Sea of Renewal

The Path through Water

Water fills, floods, reflects, distorts; it quenches
the parched throat and satiates the burning desire . . .

Water is the primal female element, yin. Yin is all receptivity. It is all
that which is dark and cool as opposed to Fire, which is light and
hot. Water is the reign of emotions and the source of the psychic
powers of divination and prophesy. It is associated with the subconscious mind.

It is the element of reflection. Though we often think of water
as a cooling force, it actually has no temperature in and of itself. It
is only affected by the application of heat and cold or of other elements. Further, Water is silent. It makes no sound unless it is being
pushed or pulled or impacted by another element. Water is invisible
unless it is reflecting that which is around it. Its surface can be seen

rippling or even cresting and breaking when it is disturbed. The natural tendency of Water, however, is to heaviness, stillness, silence, clarity, and reflection of all that which surrounds it.

Due to its heaviness and stillness, Water is seen as the great balancer. When the emotions—the realm of Self represented by the element Water—are balanced, the mundane life is fulfilling. When they are out of balance, chaos reigns.

Symbolically speaking, Water stabilizes, contains and cradles the active element of Fire. Without Water, flames may explode or burn out of control. Running a strong electric current (Fire as electric force) through Water, however, causes the Water molecules to break up. Hydrogen and oxygen, which become gases, are liberated and bubble up through the Water. In the symbolism of the tarot, Fire, the element of action and will, is the electric energy which rearranges and transmutes the element of Water. It is also the powerful energetic force contained inside the Water molecule. In metaphysical language, the yang force (Fire) acts on the yin form (Water) to cause change. The interaction of Fire and Water symbolizes the process of bonding and separation between people as well as within the Self.

Water has long been known to mystics as "the secret abode of Fire." Only now are scientists beginning to discover how to harness the vast energetic potential contained inside water molecules. It is known, for example, that there are enough deuterium atoms—a powerful source of energy—in the top ten inches of Lake Superior to supply the current energy needs of the United States for 5,000 years. The problem is how to access the deuterium, or, for our purposes, how to extract the "Fire." At the time of this writing, the latest scientific experiments to access the power contained inside water molecules involve the process of "cold fusion," fusing deuterium neuclei via an electric current—applying "fire" to release "fire"—in order to produce heat. This is a very difficult scientific problem, and so important that its solution will transform the world's political and economic status quo.

Water has an incredible power to dissolve. Over time, it wears down the most solid stone. It also has an incredible power to bond. Such is the symbolic power of the element. Technically, the water molecule is formed of two hydrogen atoms and one oxygen atom holding together in a "V" shape. The combination of hydrogen and oxygen atoms in water makes the water molecule polar. A polar molecule has two ends like a magnet. This is how water molecules bond together and also why water clings to that with which it comes into contact.

One could say that water is the glue that binds the building blocks of life. The same hydrogen bonds that are in water link DNA molecules together.

Finally, the human body itself is composed primarily of water. It is as if we *are* water, Water which mysteriously contains the Fire of Life.

On the path through Water, we begin as open and empty. It is as if we are fragments of spirit, a bit of flame cast off into an unknown form, ever desiring reunification with the great flame (of spirit). We want to remerge with the One. We attempt to do this in our relationships with one another, and, at times, we come very close to attaining that experience of bliss.

The goal of the path through Water is to embrace the Self as *individual*, which has the double meaning of being separated from the whole while at the same time remaining undivided from the whole. "In" means contained or enclosed by, and also without or outside of. The Latin *dividuus* means to divide. We are with the whole and yet divided from it. Through Water, we learn about our patterns of connection and disconnection. We learn about our reactions as energy comes to, or passes through, us. We discover secret and hidden sources of power—our innermost resources.

To walk a middle path between symbiosis and separation is the message of Water. Walking the middle path is the "message of the fishes," as heard by the Water Sister, who represents the continual cycling and renewal of life.

One of Water: The Open Channel

Divinatory Meaning ————————

You are experiencing a burst of feeling, sentiment, empathy, sympathy, enthusiasm; the time is right for connecting; stay very open and the way to connect will become clear; the only way to receive is to open yourself up; becoming vulnerable is sometimes the only way to the discovery of true love.

One of Water

OPEN CHANNEL

Meditation ————————————————————————

Libra, Scorpio, Sagittarius
Raw emotion
Empty, Open
desire yearning
the Heart without Home
MotherCore
in its secret and original form
the Moon in life-fluid
Blood Water Wine
consecrated space that wants to be filled
you are ready to feel
all that is good and bad
green, cold and wet
sea
moist, preserving
and waiting.

Interpretation ───────────────────────────────────

At the One of Water, you are feeling intense fondness or deep devotion. These feelings have only just arisen, and there may be, as yet, no recognizable object for your affection. You are open and ready, moving your Self into a position to receive. Your cup is ready to be filled. You are beginning to surrender to universal processes, to open to the possibility held there. You are discovering, in your Self, the source of all receptivity.

The One of Water is the Open Channel. At the One, you become the receptor and receptacle, the vessel for containing. At the One, you become the vessel capable of receiving and containing all that ever has been, is and ever shall be.

At the One of Water, you open to all possibility. You feel a sense of anticipation, as if something is about to happen. Perhaps you find yourself longing for something, the exact nature of which is not yet clear. You are longing to be filled, to fill your cup, so to speak.

Be advised that you are now opening to the possibility of jubilance and joy. But, you are also opening to vulnerability. You are opening to feel your own pain and sorrow. You are opening to the pain and sorrow of others. You are opening to feel pity, compassion, sensitivity, sensuality and tenderness. This is because, at the One, through your own newfound receptivity, you are beginning to access the deep understanding Self within you.

What does it mean to be a receptacle? Types of receptacles include the upper end of the stalk of a flowering plant out of which the blossom grows, the electrical wall outlet designed for use with a plug, and any number of cup- or disk-like structures supporting spores or sex organs. All of these forms of receptacles provide good analogies to explain the relationship between the suits of Fire and Water. The flower receives the hummingbird and pollen is transformed, the outlet receives the plug and the electric force begins, the seed of life is forever received, held and nurtured until it matures.

The emitting force, Fire, must connect to the receiving form, Water, in order for either to maximize its potential. At the One of Water, you are waiting for a connection to be made with you. You are a "channel" open to all stimulation in the universe.

Think of a channel as the bed of a stream or river, or the deepest part of a harbor through which boats or ships may pass without damage. A channel is also the narrow band of frequencies within which a radio or television transmitting station must keep its signal to prevent interference with other transmitters. It is a *passage*, a means through which something is transmitted, conveyed or expressed. *To channel*, as a verb, means to send or receive messages as if through a tube. The One of Water is the card of opening your Self as a channel: opening the deep stream (of consciousness) so that transmissions—including the deepest emotions and visions of humanity—can be given and received. That is why the One of Water is often referred to as the card of "love."

The first step in opening your Self as a channel is to understand your own process of maturation. You have moved away from the womb that bore you and you have established your own place in the world. You have become unique and distinct from others of your species. You have become strong as an individual. You have developed a deep sense of Self. And as you realize your own individuality, your sense of Self as a separate entity, you simultaneously come to understand that you have a desire to reconnect, remerge, or again become One with that from which you came.

At the One of Water, you have the desire to re-enter the loving folds of the womb. You have the desire to fill your own womb, whether you literally have a womb or not. All of us, regardless of sex, regardless of age, have a womb. This womb is "negative" space, "empty" space. It is a deep channel for the creation of new forms or the transformation of old forms. Each of us attempts to use this channel, or fill its empty space, via different means. Some of us receive a spiritual path, some receive a relationship, some receive intellectual illumination, some receive the seed of a child. The One of Water represents opening to connection. It is about attaining deeper meaning.

On the Tree of Life, the One of Fire is represented by the Circle of Kether, the sphere of the spirit. In the suit of Water, Kether represents the first opening of the heart, the first glimmering of the magnitude of cosmic and human love. As mentioned above, the One of Water is also the first glimmering of the immensity of the sorrow that exists in the Universe. Do not despair at the sorrow, however. Be thankful for your ability to perceive. Through perception, you will know. Through knowledge, you will become the vehicle for transformation, nurturing the seeds of change in the deepest part of your Self.

Card Symbology: The pupil of the eye/student of the I appears like a dark opening in the cosmic sea. It is surrounded by a ring (a zero) of white light. The white light is the paradox of All and Nothing at the same time. The dark opening is a hole. It is whole. It is holy. The significance of the hole is that the more holes you punch in your structure, the more holy you become.

The dark hole is a sparkling jewel at the center of an unfolding lotus. It is also a cup as viewed from above. It is a portal, which is the entrance to a channel.

The pupil is upheld by a dove which is in turn upheld by a dolphin. The dolphin swims joyfully in the cosmic sea (which is the mind of God or the universal mind). The dove represents the potential for peace. On its wings are the serpents of transformation. The dolphin symbolizes the creativity inherent in the suit of Water.

In the center of the pupil, an abstract black goddess flies in on wings of turquoise. She represents communication, healing and higher understanding. The black sea in the center of the cosmic sea is the sea of the High Priestess (see Key II). The ring of pink, green and blue petals belongs to the Divine Mother, who is Binah, the female essence, on the Tree of Life.

Two of Water: Sacred Cord

Divinatory Meaning ───────────

All opposites joyfully merge: male and female, light and dark, dry and wet, hard and soft; you have a great sense of connection; you feel a sense of bliss; you were waiting to make a connection and now you have received just as you have been received; enjoy!

Two of Water

SACRED CORD

Meditation ————————————————————————————

Venus in Cancer
Unity!
The Heart finds an object!
The Heart moves toward a Home
attraction, affection, devotion
adoration
The Great One has a new Will
melodic, harmonic
brotherhood, sisterhood
The empty Void is no more!

Interpretation ————————————————————————————

At the Two of Water, you come to love! Love is deep and tender affection, devotion. It is so deep that it sometimes feels like the most exalted joy, sometimes like a burning pain. In love, your Self is given over to a higher force. In earnest, you pour your Self into some activity, idea, purpose or person. You have found an object for all your feelings.

Love drives your mind and senses to new insight, to understanding with a new perspective, to glimpsing all that which can become and then moving to create in that direction. Love drives your hand to create. In love, the path becomes clear, goals are illuminated.

An invisible line, like a silver cord, connects you to the object of your affection. Thus, the symbol for two is a line. A line—a continuum—is formed when two points are connected. The more hallowed—or sacred—is this silver cord of connection, the thicker it seems.

In forming the cord of love, you feel compelled to detach yourself from everything that holds you back. You want to join forces with the object of your affection, with everything that feels uplifting, with everything that can give new form to your passion. You now feel connected. You can see the possibility of form in what has felt formless.

Within the feeling of connection, however, comes the simultaneous feeling of aloneness. There is recognition of being separated, of being specialized, of being unique. Your newfound sense of oneness thus coexists with the sense of aloneness. Life takes on new peaks and depths. There is a sense of simultaneous expansion and limitation.

When love occurs, the great emitting positive light force of yang (the sphere of Chokmah on the Tree of Life) is drawn toward, and received by, the great receptive negative dark force of yin (the sphere of Binah). The major forces thus become polarized. Polarization is the first law of creation. It transforms neutral space into charged space. At the Two of Water, you understand the edict: "Let there be Light!" In coming to know the womb of dark, receptive shadowy energy, by contrast, you come to know and understand its opposite—light.

Thus, love arises and becomes the driving force for replacing churning and open emotional energy with the forms and structures which arise when one begins to understand the power generated through polarization. Polarization is the basis of all creativity. In this way, love—as the key that illuminates the pure polarized forces—can be seen as the Sacred Cord that weaves the web of manifestation.

Coming to know the power of love happens internally—as you come to love your Self—and externally, as you come to love another person or a higher or greater entity. On both levels, you move into a new, and more highly developed realm, of Self-understanding which illuminates the forms to take in order to activate and maximize your potential.

Card Symbology: In the Two of Water, two chalices, containing the waters of the cosmic sea, overflow like fountains. The wands appear as symbols on the chalices, red stars for the male energy of Chokmah/Fire holding the Sea of Binah within. The stars are six-pointed to represent the unification of the great masculine and feminine forces. The stars are encircled to denote the eternal nature of the union.

The cosmic sea is ruffled like the lace of Binah's gown. This sea is in perpetual motion, consistent but forever changing, never the same at any two moments in time. This is the paradox of the Two of Water. This is the paradox of love.

The female force appears as dark energy, the male force as light. Their hands are joined with the figure eight, the lemniscate, of perpetual movement. The female force navigates with wings. The male force has flippers for rapid propulsion in the sea. Over their heads, the holy ghost of Kether sanctifies their union. Thus, Kether (the life force), Chokmah (the male force) and Binah (the female force), as a triad, represent the upper triangle of the Tree of Life.

The card shows the ideal marriage: simultaneous bonding and individuation: being merged together and yet retaining the separateness of the pure force. This marriage takes place both within and outside of the Self.

Three of Water: Stream of Love

Divinatory Meaning

You are in a sublime state of harmonious pleasure; you are in a grace period; you feel a sense of wondrous creation; you feel very loved by all that is, you love all that is; this is a beautiful time to be alive.

Three of Water

STREAM OF LOVE

Meditation

Mercury in Cancer
Entwined!
Abundance!
Love springs from God!
Creation springs from Love!
All promises fulfilled
All dreams realized.

Interpretation

At the Three of Water, you stand in a purifying shower of love. There is no need to move. All new forms, those which are necessary in order to move to the next stage of development, are emerging effortlessly from your internal vow to remain open and loving. You are now in a state of grace.

At the Three, you are on a new and highly rewarding plane of emotional existence. Your success moves openly and effortlessly, like the fragrance of a rose. It opens naturally because you have discovered a sacred and sublime state of being. The direction of your venture is clear because all was conceived in love. You have committed yourself consciously, and that is the reason for your current clarity of mind.

The Three of Water is a stream of love which cleanses and purifies like a healing rain. Symbolizing a primordial state of grace, the Three is the mother of faith. All faith comes from the purifying waters of the Stream of Love. Now you have not only faith, but the courage of your convictions.

The original intent, the raw ocean of the One of Water, the Open Channel, has now found containment and contentment. This means you have found a place—a structure—in which to rest. You have moved into a mode of productivity and are spinning off children—the children of mind or body.

The children of the Three of Water are the forms, patterns and designs that emerge out of the formless energy of the Open Channel. The raw energy of the One had no potential for growth until it was able to contain itself in these structures. The structures provide systematic direction. The direction for the One—the raw emotion—was established because you became attuned to the potential of love. Through love, you found your direction and established structure.

At the Three of Water, the polarized male force (the sphere of Chokmah on the Tree of Life), has contained itself within the polarized female force (Binah), the womb/form. Yin energy is synonymous with form, the essential ingredient for manifesting idea, but it is also synonymous with death. The Womb of Binah, as the creator of form, is the creator of limitation. This is because every form that is cast must sooner or later be outgrown. No form is ever infinite or eternal. All that is born—that is to say, every specific form taken—will eventually die. It will be used, outgrown and ultimately abandoned. All this, you understand at the Three. You accept the fact that every death gives way to new growth, that it is all part of the endless cycle. Renewal comes in the Stream of Love.

At the point of the Three of Water, you are in the creative part of the cycle, everything is in a state of fullness, not yet spiraling toward its death. Although you must always remain wary, not even a trace of death is yet at hand. At this time, all indications are toward growth and development: good fortune and great pleasure. The Stream of Love, which is the stream of life, seems to be flowing endlessly.

Card Symbology: In the center of the card, you see the stylized ankh, which represents the Womb of Binah. From the center of this womb, which is all light symbolizing the Sun/Son, the purifying and sacred Waters of Faith pour into the chalices.

The purifying waters of Binah cool, but do not quell, the burning Fires of Chokmah. Chokmah can relax, float in a gestational period. Intercourse and fertilization take place in the Dark Realm, as symbolized by the blueness of the background. Phantoms and celestial objects appear in the darkness. These phantoms are all-possibility. On the left, the waning Moon of Binah follows the Sun of Chokmah. Both have done their work and the results flow effortlessly.

The pattern of the triple cross reflects the pattern of the Tree of Life. The upper horizontal cross, which moves from blue on the left to red on the right, is the abyss. The middle cross is the path of understanding the secrets of the spirit. The lower cross is the path of active intelligence, through which all beings receive spirit and motion.

Below the lower cross, the stems of the chalices are reflected in the cosmic sea. This reflection represents the maxim: As Above, So Below.

Four of Water: The Flood

Divinatory Meaning

You are outgrowing a period of contentment; things that were once good now seem stale; things once new have grown old; change is the only thing that remains stable; do not be afraid to change to regain your balance.

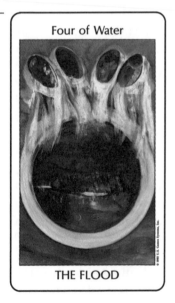

Four of Water

THE FLOOD

Meditation ──────────────────────────────────

Moon in Cancer
A luxurious floating
The Family is ordered, balanced, stable
but where is the purity of Conception?
The Moon is in the Water
but Water needs MoonLight Above
and the stillness of Light
for accurate Sight
to accurately reflect
the mind of the Seer
The surface of the Sea is ruffled
Restriction Constriction Deliberation
How to raise the Moon?
How to raise the Moon Above the I?
How to raise the Moon Above the Eye?
How to raise the Moon Above the Sea?
How to raise the Moon to See?
How to still the Sea?

Interpretation ────────────────────────────────

At the Four of Water, The Flood, you are at the edge of completion. All that which carried you to this point—especially that which
you created in love—has become strong. You feel as if you are in a
good and powerful position, but be advised that old structures will
shortly begin to falter. It is time to reattune to the original will of
love.

Although everything on the surface of your life points to success
and abundance, the overflow of love and life abounding, your method
of creativity, the structures and patterns by which you have known
your greatest inspiration, are beginning to show signs of weakness.
In a sense, you have outgrown your own methods. You are becoming
jaded and need a new infusion of energy. While you may not yet feel
or sense it, you are about to begin a period of new growth.

Your structures, however, are not yet weak enough to fall, and
you could save them if you revitalize your passion. It may be wise
to refurbish that which has served you well. You already know that
you must also serve your structures, keep them in a state of constant
repair and expansion, if you expect them to continue working.

There are times, however, that you may wish to abandon old structures for new systems that appear to be more sensible or expedient, more challenging or interesting. Consider your next move carefully. Are your intentions pure? Are you considering others?

One of the reasons you are bursting at the seams is that, at the Four of Water—The Flood—you must begin to formulate a new vision of love. You have been through the stage of raw, open emotion. You have had the experience of being completely devoted and you have floated in the sublime state of grace. Now, it is almost as if the abundance you have experienced—especially in love—has made you lazy, has taken on a life of its own, apart from the original source of energy.

The way out of the ensuing uneasiness is to be still, to still the ruffling seas. Simplify. Pare down your needs and expectations, pare down the stimuli so that you can hear the voice of the higher will, the original intent. It was that voice that originally drew you into love.

The fourth circle on the Tree of Life is Chesed, the sphere of love, majesty and mercy. Chesed is the sphere of the Four of Water. On the Tree of Life, it is the first sphere on the plane of matter or manifestation, thus it represents rulership in the world of form. And it is in servitude to the higher force that Chesed most effectively rules, and the highest law is love. Thus, the maxim arises: "Love is the Law, Love under Will."

As you come to know that love is the law, you will understand the meaning of the 23rd Psalm: "Thou preparest a table before me in the presence of my enemies; thou annointest my head with oil, my cup overflows. Surely goodness and mercy shall follow me all the days of my life." This is Chesed in his most exalted form. It is also the message of the Four of Water, the inner meaning of The Flood.

Attune to love and you will understand revitalization.

Card Symbology: The flood of the Four of Water is the flooding subconscious. We are looking into the eye of the storm. This is the eye of Karma, the eye of Temperance, the eye at the heart of the Wheel of Fortune. It is also the Open Channel and the eye of Binah, the great receptive energy of yin.

In the Four of Water, the gushing tears are Binah's. Her mate, Chokmah, has left the dark to dwell in the House of Light, but she is not yet ready to make any move. She has become so full with love— merging—and the sorrow of love—separation—that she has had to release. Her crying eggs—the source of her fertility—are almost depleted of strength. Although her light is almost out, it can still be seen flickering, in the stillness at the center of the storm, like welcoming harbor lights, at the center of her Eye/I.

At this point, Binah has temporarily lost sight of truth. Her cup is running over. The gold wedding band, which united her with yang, Chokmah, can no longer contain her tears. She remains solidly on the physical plane, ensconced in old structures. To escape her sense of imprisonment in her own emotions, she must tune into the source of life and spirit which dwells in her own internal House of Light.

Five of Water: Spilling

Divinatory Meaning ——————————

Painfully, you feel that relationships are transient and impermanent; do not rely so much on others for love; when it seems like the "cups" of your life have spilled—and all your love has emptied out—you will discover that you still have a major reservoir: your own source of internal love, do not forget that! Look inside yourself and you will see that of five cups, only three have spilled, two are still standing and spewing light everywhere!

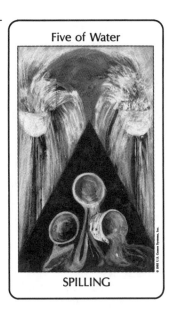

Five of Water

SPILLING

Meditation ——————————————————————

Mars in Scorpio
Disappointment Regret Frustration
Fiery Winds make the Sea of Love arid
The leftover Water stagnates, is putrid
Inside the Dark Pyramid of the Past
The Cups have spilled
but only to be filled
with new Life.

Interpretation ———————————————————————————————————————

At the Five of Water, your understanding of love involves desire and expectations. Retaining expectations has led to frustration and sorrow. It is time to move to a deeper level of understanding in order to overcome your frustration.

The Five of Water is the rise of antipathy just when it seemed everything was going well. You anticipated that you would experience great pleasure at this stage, but there was an unexpected disturbance, and the expected pleasure has been usurped. As such, you feel a sense of futility and regret. You feel anger and despair. Emotional chaos seems to have arisen from somehow *not being seen*. You have felt as if you were lost, experiencing an onslaught of transience. Can nothing be counted on? Is nothing real or permanent? There may have been moments when you felt so confused that it seemed like you were controlled by internal destructive forces, forces which seemed too deep to understand.

You may have found yourself shaking your head and repeating: "I don't know. I don't know . . ." You may have felt like you wanted to cry. You have tried to get someone's attention. You have spilled out in all directions.

When you have spilled everything out, and are right down to the bottom of your cup, you will finally see your own heart reflected. Then you will see that you based your desire on expectations that had no foundation in reality. That was the problem. But you will also see that your heart, at the base, is pure and good. It is full with love, a deep love that longs to flow in the right direction. It longs to do the right thing. It does not desire to hurt or be hurt. In reaching this understanding, you will be able to make realistic assessments and correct your actions.

The challenge of the Five of Water is to establish a new vision of your own power. It is time to reassess and adjust. It is time to know and correct any falsities you have programmed into your life and reestablish your connection with the fundamental truth. This is signified by the fifth circle on the Tree of Life, the Circle of Geburah, the great destroyer. Geburah carries out justice in the world of manifestation, the world you have created.

In order to understand the justice of Geburah, it is necessary to examine your own failings. You must purge anything that does not align with the basic universal drive toward goodness. During the critical examination, you must be strong. Have courage. Do not fear. Fear is the result of the lack of faith. Faith comes from aligning your love with the will of the universe.

Geometrically, the five is symbolized by the five-pointed star— the pentagram. On one level, the five points refer to the human— two legs, two arms, head—feet for moving, hands for manifesting, head for thinking. On another level, the points refer to the five dimensions of existence: modes of action, emotion, intellect, body and spirit. Use the clear symbolism of the pentagram as you pose the question: are all the aspects of my Self in alignment with Divine Will?

Thereby, will you come to know how to overcome your tears.

Card Symbology: At the Five of Water, Spilling, we see the dark pyramid of the past. This pyramid is the structure you have built through all time. It has led up to this moment. It also becomes a road leading into the future.

Inside the dark pyramid, three cups have spilled. They are pouring out the water, wine and blood of life. The rim of the central cup is the gold wedding band from which the foundation is draining. Yet, at the bottom of that cup, you see the purity of your own heart reflected. This is the key to understanding that the outcome will be positive. At the bottom of the cup, Binah, the feminine sphere of the Tree of Life, finds her own heart. This is her last reservoir, and it is the eternal reservoir of Self-Love. Here she finds true understanding, but for the moment, that understanding is cut off from relationship.

All around the perimeter of the dark pyramid rains the flowing light of love.

The way out of the dark pyramid is to see it as a road. Stop crying over "spilt milk." Take the healing reflection from the central cup, place it inside your own heart, step over the spilled cups and take the first step on the road toward the future. The road leads to justice and balance. The road is a road of healing. Then you emerge at the top of a lighted hill and as in Matthew: "You are like light for the whole world. A city built on a hill cannot be hid. No one lights a lamp and puts it under a bowl; instead he puts it on the lampstand, where it gives light for everyone in the house. In the same way your light must shine . . ."

Six of Water: Faith

Divinatory Meaning ───────────

Having learned that the answer to your question lies within, surrender to faith; be innocent, remain innocent; take great pleasure in your childlike qualities; experience the world as if you are seeing it for the first time; you are taken care of in all ways.

Six of Water

FAITH

Meditation ────────────────────────

Sun in Scorpio
Pleasure
Childhood
You begin again
Wiser
You don't know it all but you have been ceremonially purified!
All the Universe is at your feet!
You have seen the House of Light!
Humility Joy
All wrapped up in the Newness of Spring
Rejoice
In the New Childhood, it All begins again!

Interpretation ───────────────────────

There is great pleasure. The truth is that dissolution, putrefaction, the breaking down of substance is a sacrament. As a result of forest fire, giant redwood trees go to seed. Those things that dissolve are those that are outgrown. New forms must continually arise. This process is strengthening.

Coming apart, or dissolving, and moving back together—forming—is the basis of all life. It is the basis of all fertility. What is lost in this process is ultimately gained.

Through the trials of loving, you have gained a quiet internal strength. This strength will sustain you through the difficult times ahead. You will need to rely on this strength as you move on your path toward enduring happiness. The greatest things in life do not come easily. There is the matter of commitment and perseverance. Nonetheless, you have seen the light, you know the source of your inner strength, and, as a result, your direction is clear.

This is the time to trust. The challenge of the Six of Water, Faith, is to become like a child. Open to learn, and you will become like a fulcrum holding in balance the above and below, the male and female forces, and the processes of construction and destruction. You will stand balanced between all the planes or dimensions of existence: action, emotion, thought, body and spirit. In standing balanced, you are attuned to divine purpose. In balance, you stand in unity and beauty.

The realization that you have glimpsed the inner seed of understanding is the key to the message of the Six of Water. Have faith that you walk in beauty and unity. Walking in the light—which emanates from darkness—is the key to healing.

In Tiphareth, the sixth sphere on the Tree of Life, the great force of spirit materializes on the physical plane. This means that you experience the birth of spiritual consciousness. You have earned this consciousness through your past sorrows and suffering. You will stay in this exalted consciousness as long as you remain directed by your own conscience. This is the key to walking in the way of light. Having a clear conscience is the key to healing and health.

Tiphareth is symbolized by a six-sided cube. The cube represents the stability of matter. It represents the three dimensions: 1) meaning, and 2) purpose, within 3) the context of space and time. If you unfold the cube, it becomes the cross of life: that which symbolizes the spirit incarnate in matter.

Opening up to—rediscovering—original intent, the reason for incarnation, is the message of the Six of Water. And, ironically, the highest knowledge of the Six of Water is the knowledge that we know nothing. This is the great wisdom—and freeing joy—of childhood.

Card Symbology: The cross of life, atop the stable cube of matter basks in the yellow sea of Tiphareth. The cups have become childrens' toys: tops with decorative six-pointed stars—to demonstrate the balance of the great forces—spinning harmoniously.

The raft is the flotation device of higher consciousness. The reward of trusting is that you will be upheld by the raft of higher consciousness even when you are not clear about the direction.

In the center of the cross is the glyph for the Sun. You stand in the center, like an unfolding rose, shielded by a circle of protection. This is your protected sacred space, your shield against distracting influences.

In the yellow sea, wings beat and dolphins scallop. These are the symbols of joy and jubilant transformation.

Seven of Water: Insight

Divinatory Meaning ─────────────

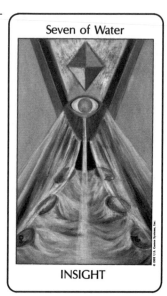

Seven of Water

INSIGHT

The empty space of the soul must be filled; you are moving into deeper spiritual realms; you may feel highly intuitive; perhaps you do not want to know everything you are seeing; if you feel depressed or generally uneasy with the state of things, remember that this reaction is natural and normal; be careful not to overindulge in alcohol, drugs, food, tobacco or any other substances, these will never satisfy your emptiness; the times you feel the worst are often when the greatest spiritual insights come; let yourself experience this time and do not judge yourself harshly; you are a good and loving individual.

Meditation ─────────────────────────────

Venus in Scorpio
Dreams
Illusions
Visions
New possibilities appear at the edge
The Darkest Hour has come and lingers languid
at the edge of Light
Be careful!
The sacrament is profaned with a fatal ease!

Interpretation ────────────────────────

No matter how much attention you have received from others, the empty space of your soul has not been filled. You know that the void within you is like a deep natural well, a well so deep that its end is unknown.

You have dreamed about love. You have had illusions and fantasies about love. You have waited for love. You have contemplated the idea of connection, union, and you have more than once anticipated, wrongly, what would occur when you came to know love.

When love did not go as planned, in the worst cases, you have tried to fill the empty space with alcohol, drugs and food. Or you have tried to deprive the empty space, starve it to death, in the same abusive way. You have sought to fill the void with sex, however empty it feels in the end.

But none of these desperate endeavors brought you any lasting love, beauty or peace. The satisfaction you experienced was only fleeting, and the prospect of true love remained elusive. That is because such desperate measures contributed to your imbalance, and balance is the method through which truth is known. Balance is attained by following your conscience, the eightfold path of Gautama Buddha: right views, right aspirations, right speech, right conduct, right livelihood, right effort, right meditation, right rapture. Following your conscience moves you into balance with the overall cosmic order, the divine law and plan.

The Greek myths say that human nature was, in the beginning, whole, that we were originally one. Then we became divided parts. And all the while, we have longed for reconciliation; we have longed to move back to wholeness or oneness. That pursuit, the idea of moving back into oneness, is the pursuit of love, and at the Seven of Water, you are deeply involved in that pursuit.

At the Seven there is a psychic upwelling. There is a need to sink into the subconscious, the dark, for answers, in order to make the necessary connections. At the Seven, you wish to discover your higher purpose in love, and that higher purpose has to do with reuniting with the whole. Therefore, the task of the seven is to contemplate your own perception of the cosmic whole. You must rely on internal Faith to stay balanced, at a point when you are most likely to hurl your Self off the path.

The seventh sphere on the Tree of Life is Netzach, the force of inspiration, the perfect balance of force (three) and form (four). Becoming aware that you can assume the perfectly balanced position of the Seven at will can produce meaning and purpose: fulfillment. You have force, and that is your own ability to overcome inertia. Overcoming inertia leads to the joy of creation. That which is created is new form. Maintaining form involves overcoming false ideals of love, beauty and peace. The loftiest knowledge gained at the Seven of Water is the spiritual vision of the triumph of truth and original law. Such a vision is true love, true beauty, true peace, true Insight.

To rediscover cosmic will, tune in to your natural instinct. Your own inner will is the will of the divine.

Card Symbology: In the Seven of Water, six cups are tossed in the sea of the subconscious. A seventh cup, the Victory Cup, rises up out of the swirling pool. This cup holds the Vision of Original Purpose, the cosmic vision of love, beauty, peace, and Insight.

That vision is represented by the eight-sided octahedron floating at the top of the card. The blue facet is for Water, the red for Fire, green for Earth, yellow for Wind. The dark side is a mirror reflection of the light side. But light, of course, is necessary to illuminate it. The octahedron is for conscience in its eight manifestations, as listed above.

The Victory Cup, having seen Truth, receives the energy of the higher source and radiates this energy toward the cosmic sea.

Eight of Water: Still Waters

Divinatory Meaning

You are in a state of withdrawal; retreat is necessary and good at this time; through withdrawing, all things shall become clear; you will be protected as you withdraw, you will not lose anything important; take a break and remember, "still waters run deep."

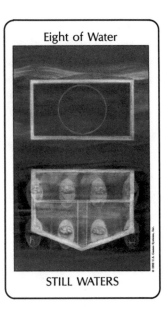

Eight of Water

STILL WATERS

Meditation

Saturn in Pisces
Making structures for the dreams
polarizing in the Sea
aligning with the cosmic stream
rocking, going with the wave
the ebb and flow of the tide
it is a gentle swaying cradling ride
—in the safety of the cosmic shield—
—the apron of Light—
in the shimmering field of the deep
waters of foreverness.

Interpretation

At the Eight of Water, you withdraw into an introspective state to rebuild your strength. You are, in a sense, charging your Self and renewing your resources within a space of protection. At the Eight, you begin to understand the magical capacity of your mind. This magical capacity allows you to respond creatively to what is going on around you and to transcend any sense of victimization remaining with you from the past. The key to understanding this magic is to *sublimate* and refine your *emotional reactions*. This does not mean that you should repress your feelings. It only means that it is time to retreat in order to *hear your own song*—as opposed to the tune sung by others—and begin to focus more clearly.

The first stage in focusing entails stopping, if only temporarily, that which is moving—stopping all the noise—in order to bring it under control. You need to let things gel. Retreat from action.

The process of retreat can be likened to that which happens during a computer's "turn around time." We input a certain amount of information and then wait for the answers to print out. When we sleep, our mind acts like a computer. We process everything that has happened during the day, everything that is "on our mind," and we often wake up with new insight and answers. When we meditate, as when we sleep, we emerge refreshed. The spirit is renewed.

At the Eight of Water, taking action means resolving to take no action. It is time to retreat, to sleep, to meditate, and—to be cradled in the security of Still Waters—to renew your flagging spirit. Don't worry about not acting. You are in "turn around time." It is not the time for action. Your processing is not yet complete.

The challenge of the Eight of Water is to descend (or rise) to the space within your Self that is motivated by goodness or love. Here I do not speak of the common kind of love, such as sexual attraction to another or a strong liking or interest in something. The love of which I speak is a deep internal goodness which makes you feel honorable and worthy. This is the goodness of moral excellence, but it is a deep morality, one that transcends the (sometimes crass or economically justified) morality of culture. This is the deep morality of the inner Self. At this level of morality, you know you are doing the right thing. You are honoring and loving your Self just as you are honoring, respecting and loving those around you.

Finding your love involves retreating from instantaneous or re-flexive emotional reactions in order to activate your higher mind. This is where you separate your own song from the song of your culture. In the highest love, you direct and control your Self to ends that are well-conceived. At first, finding your love may entail groping in the dark. This process is often symbolized by a marsh bird. Standing on one leg, the bird searches the muck below the surface for morsels of food. At the Eight of Water, you are searching below the surface for morsels of truth. The beginning of this process is to stop everything and allow your Self the luxury of utter stillness.

How will you recognize truth when you find it? Truth is known through the concrete internal realization that you are operating solely out of deep inner goodness or love. Are you motivated by goodness and love? This is truth, and this is what you are seeking.

The eighth sphere on the Tree of Life is the sphere of Hod. Hod is the sphere of reason. It is the first sphere of definite organization on the physical plane, the sphere in which the mind categorizes, develops models and then creates forms. Form is created through daydreaming, night-dreaming or intellectualizing about what could be and then casting that thing in a pattern or form of your design. Thus it is the sphere of the craftsman as well as the magician. The craftsman builds structures on the physical plane. The magician builds forms on the mental and astral planes.

Hod is the sphere of formal magic rather than just the powers of the mind because the magician harnesses the power of his or her own concentrated will to certain ends. At the Eight of Water, you are beginning the process of concentrating your will in love and goodness. At first you withdraw in order to hear your song. Then you cast your song into new forms.

It is now time to retreat into Still Waters to escape reflexive re-actions and begin to build forms in a deep and real love. Remember, at every moment, you recreate the structure of the universe through the magical formulative capacity of your mind. For both craftsman and magician, only those forms conceived in love can help to relieve the condition of humankind or Mother Earth. You, alone, are the master craftsman of your life. With the power of love, you become the master craftsman of the universe.

Card Symbology: In the lower portion of the Eight of Water, we see eight cups holding sparkles of energy contained in egg-like forms swaying in the cosmic sea. The eggs are floating in gestation, aligning with the cosmic will and beginning to blossom into plants which will eventually bear fruit. They are covered by a protective apron, which is the apron of the craftsman as well as the magician. The apron protects the craftsman's body and clothing. For the magician, the apron protects the "Moon Center," which is the ninth sphere, the sphere of the subconscious.

The upper portion of the card depicts the outline of the circular cosmic mirror, which is protected or encased. The upper box represents the essence of the Eight: the unity of the eternal circle of spirit with the straight-edged box of materiality. In this case, the circle is contained inside of the box. The box is the magician's creation—all form—which has come to ensoul the force of spirit.

Nine of Water: Rainbow Mirror

Divinatory Meaning ───────────

You feel a strong sense of internal integrity and inner security; you are enjoying a strong sense of self-esteem; you are peaceful with your sense of inner joy; you have accepted yourself and that has given you a new sense of wisdom and harmony.

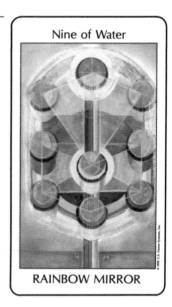

Nine of Water

RAINBOW MIRROR

Meditation ────────────────────────────────

Jupiter in Pisces
Happiness
Stability Restored
The Soul in Repose:
There is Peace and Calm, a New Wisdom
All things are Love:
Burning Fires, Raging Seas,
Arid Landscapes, Stagnant Waters,
Windblown Plains,
A Full Horizon

Lovers' Pains
Gains and Losses
The Void is not so deep and burning
the Yearning not so great
in the quiet benediction
of the Resurrected Self
and indeed, the Pain of Love is sweet
the Lover even sweeter

In deepest Love, there is
the Joy of Self-Acceptance.

Interpretation

At the Nine of Water, you know that time heals all wounds. You are healing well. You feel satisfied, content, psychologically well-balanced. You have a strong sense of your own integrity. This is the stage of a new-found, higher-level purity. You have worked to live in goodness. Now you are at the stage that comes after the struggles have passed. You are in a stability that results from true understanding. It is the culmination and perfection of the original force of the One of Water: that undirected, receptive raw feeling that wanted to love. This force has come to rest in the center of your Self. It has come to rest in self-unity. You are learning to fill your own void. You are coming to love your Self.

You are moving into a stage of joy and gladness, where wisdom is fulfilled in perfect happiness and delight. The Nine of Water is the time of dancing joyously on the earth, firmly grounded in matter, and blessed in every revelrous movement.

The ninth sphere on the Tree of Life is the Circle of Yesod: the sphere of the subconscious mind. This is the sphere of the Moon. It is through journeying through the sphere of Yesod that we come to understand, accept, and love the Self.

We journey into the subconscious mind via the "ether," the very essence of mind and matter. Ether is the fifth element, which stands above the four elements of matter: fire, water, wind and earth. Yesod, the sphere of ether, receives transmissions from all the other spheres, transforms the information, and in turn, transmits it back to matter: our physical thinking being. As such, our material world is transformed through the vehicle of our subconscious mind.

As we journey into the cosmic sea of Yesod, we see the reflected images of the collective unconscious, that unconscious mind which we share with each other. Once we have accessed the collective unconscious via inward travel on the ether, we begin to understand our Self as we understand others. We begin to understand that we are each a separate spark of the One, and yet we are the One. With the acceptance that *I am you and you are me,* while we are, at the same time, unique and separately beautiful individuals, we begin to move into a deep and real, harmonious love.

This is the harmonious joy of the Rainbow Mirror. Though all separate sparks, we have emanated from the One Fire. We have emerged from the One Water. We will return to the One Fire. We will return to the One Water. The rainbow—symbolizing the convergence of Fire and Water—is the sign of our covenant with God. God is love. The mirror is the moon reflection which illuminates God within the Self. The Rainbow Mirror symbolizes self-love and self-acceptance. The Rainbow Mirror is the love and acceptance of all that is in the universe. The journey inward brings the Rainbow Mirror to light.

Card Symbology: At the Nine of Water we see the emanations of the Tree of Life. White light is pouring in all directions. On the central pillar a rainbow of light connects Kether, the One, to Tiphareth, the Six. Tiphareth is connected to the ninth sphere of Yesod by rays of white light. Tiphareth appears as a searchlight, encased in green, black and yellow moons, searching the heavens and, in turn, transmitting the energy found there.

In this card, a rainbow bridge crosses the abyss. The rainbow bridge is the secret bridge of knowledge. This is the knowledge of true love.

The Nine is the level of opening chakras. Rays emanate from the One and begin to move through the level of the subconscious. At the Nine, all spheres of the Tree of Life are perceived at once. The key to understanding this process is seen on the card at the first sphere, Kether (uppermost on the card). In the sphere of Kether, the eight spokes of Gautama Buddha's eightfold path appear as a wheel (right views, right aspirations, right speech, right conduct, right livelihood, right effort, right meditation, right rapture). The key to happiness is seeing truth through the inner love and higher wisdom of the eightfold path. Happiness results from true alignment with the cosmic will.

Ten of Water: Fountain of Love

Divinatory Meaning

When you are motivated by love, the highest wisdom unfolds; you feel that you are showered by a fountain of love; all has turned out well; enjoy this time: it is a time of rarefied joy, spiritual love, exquisite beauty and deep sharing with others.

Ten of Water

FOUNTAIN OF LOVE

Meditation

Mars in Pisces
Satiation
Love is Salvation
The empty void is filled and, for a time,
we worship Love

The Virgin-Queen-Bride has arrived and she is the
Gate of Love
but as well the
Gate of Death, Gate of Tears
Gate of Justice
since Form ensouls the boundless
in her magic circle
and all Form must die.

Interpretation ────────────────────────────

Now you know love. You know what it means to love deeply. You know all the aspects of love and the continuum of love. You know how much love can vary, how love can hurt, how love can fulfill, how it acts on the void and channel of your open heart.

Your love has filled a host of forms. It has filled you to the brim. You have felt love unite the feminine and masculine principles within and you have felt exalted in love.

Love has been bountiful. The Ten of Water symbolizes the joining of the Self with the whole. It implies the loss of self-consciousness and the gain of absolute joy in which every sphere is aglow. This is perfection, completion. Water has finished its work. There is oneness with the cosmic will through love. There is total union with the cosmic sea: the mind of God. The swirling force generated by this alignment is the electricity of love. It is the electrical connection of the Two of Water, multiplied to a universal level.

As the Fountain of Love reaches its crescendo, however, you have reached your own plateau of growth. Now the emotion of love must come into balance with the other great forces. Coming into a sense of true understanding and wisdom requires harmony in reason, spirit and physical reality. And this balance is the key to maintaining your love.

At the Ten of Water, new forms are unfolding. The tide is turning. You are beginning to understand that you must give your Self to wisdom. Now that you know your own love, you must also know that the basis of wisdom is love. Wisdom, motivated by love, is divine reason. When motivated by love, you accrue a deeper social, as well as spiritual, understanding. Then your love, once again, changes form.

In changing form, there may be some discomfort. Do not worry. You are about to move to a new level. The child outgrows old shoes, but eventually gets a new pair.

Card Symbology: The force of love has simultaneously descended into the form of self and ascended from the Self to the source. Love is spewing forth like a fountain, firing in all directions. It floods like the light of searchlights from bottomless cups. The structure from which love emerges looks like a telephone dial composed of ten crescent moon cups. The dial indicates that it is nearly time for you to dial again. You are holding the phone.

At the center of the dial is the cosmic sea, in which resides the original intent of the One of Water: the intention to receive love. Love has been received and is flowing.

The card shows two cubes, the cubes of above and below, mind and matter, interconnecting via a swirling force. Mind and matter are operating in parallel. Since they are reflecting each other, there is no conflict. In parallel, they generate and maintain the flow of love.

Water Father: The Spirit of Water

Divinatory Meaning ⎯⎯⎯⎯⎯⎯⎯⎯

Listen to your conscience; trust in your impulses; be guided by your instincts and intuition; you are in a gentle and sensitive period, it is like falling in love all over again; wonderful things may come of your endeavors; have faith and maintain your self-confidence.

Father

WATER

Meditation ⎯⎯⎯⎯⎯⎯⎯⎯⎯⎯⎯⎯⎯⎯⎯⎯⎯⎯⎯

Aquarius, Pisces
Fire Father in Water
Fire of Water
Power of Water unraveling the mysteries
Rain and Springs
and turbulent Seas
The spark behind Dark Forces
mysteries of Love

subconscious
mediation;

Reflective
Distortive
a pool mirror
with the Power
of solution
re-solution
alchemy
The Power to Create
Transform! Through the Dark, Light is Born!

Protective Provider
Water Father
Flooding; Storming; Just

We would have Trusted his rule—
if we could have seen him—
but he was the Master
behind the screen.

Interpretation

The Water Father stands between currents. In stillness, he discovers power and energy. Knowing this strength makes his journey successful.

He is the very spirit of feeling, the spirit of the subconscious. He is "gut level" instinct, operating intuitively and emotionally; his intuition guides him in breaking down and solving problems. He represents Water's power of solution.

In this stillness is the spark of creativity. Water Father becomes fanciful and may be intensely romantic. He is, in every way, pure and beautiful, but his very sensitivity may result in the feeling that the world he inhabits is too difficult, too harsh. The dilemma of the Water Father is well-expressed by the poet James Kavanaugh who writes:

There are men too gentle to live among wolves
Who devour them with eager appetite and search
for other men to prey upon and suck their childhood dry.

There are men too gentle for an accountant's world
Who dream instead of Easter eggs and fragrant grass
And search for beauty in the mystery of the sky.[1]

The Water Father is like the deuterium atom floating in the water molecule. Deuterium is an important fuel. One pound of deuterium can produce 40 million kilowatt-hours of electricity, and there is enough deuterium in the Earth's ocean to last for billions of years, but, alas, there is only one atom of deuterium for every 5,000 atoms of ordinary hydrogen in water. It is a tremendous task to separate the fuel from the medium in which it floats.

Nonetheless that fuel is there, that spark of electric energy which holds the power of transmutation. Water Father accesses this power, this electrically charged energy, by churning his internal Waters—through introspection.

As you look inward, there is the danger of becoming a prisoner of your own fantasies. The Water Father transcends the prison of fantasy through seeking truth. In knowing and speaking truth, he is freed from the sense of drowning under the weight of a social structure. Above all, he struggles against external pressures to conform. He must follow his own song.

Water Father gets himself in trouble when he tries to move against his own natural flow. He can come to feel trapped and bitter. He does well when he moves in the rhythm dictated by his innate, instinctual desires, which are—deep down—directed toward the highest good. He is truly free when his will is aligned with the cosmic will: the will of truth.

How does the Water Father recognize truth? He attunes himself to nudges from the cosmos. He places the guidance of his conscience above all.

The Water Father is often deep in introspection. To an outsider, he may seem fathomless or hard to understand. And, because, like a mirror, he reflects the observer, he may appear to be surface or shallow, but that is only because what is seen is what is looked with.

The challenge for the Water Father is fortitude. A journey at this time would be rewarding, but there is always danger on the path.

---

[1]James Kavanaugh, *There Are Men Too Gentle to Live Among Wolves* (Los Angeles: Nash Publishing, 1970).

With firmness and strength, failure can be avoided. Water Father's key to success is to be still between the currents and avoid becoming bewildered (see *I Ching:* Hexagram 5: Calculated Inaction).

Card Symbology: The Water Father rides in the cosmic sea which is rough and full of mystery. His wild stallion is the energy and fortitude of the subconscious. If the Water Father has enough trust in his steed, all will be well. The horse has the raw power and intuition to use the currents most productively. When he is tired, he lets the water carry him. To escape the riptide which would pull him too deeply into the sea, he swims diagonally. The sea is all diagonals, denoting all activity.

The Water Father is the Light in the Darkness, the diamond-like sparkle that dances in the sea.

Water Mother: The Keyhole

Divinatory Meaning ——————————

This is a stable and nurturing time; there is a feeling of maternal love and support; pace your steps and wrestle joyously with difficulty; this is a passage in love; your associates, particularly children, may not always show it or even be aware of it, but they love you deeply; you are always there for them in their time of need—even if they come to you in anger—because you see life and love in long strides; your love is full with its own spiritual source; your love is unconditional.

Meditation ————————————————————

Gemini, Cancer
Eternal Mother
A Watery Door

through Endless curves of circling Light
spiraling tunnel-like
to the deepest, darkest core
a Cave of Truth and Vision

Her own Light
is subtly blinding
reflections like a silver mirror
bewitch enthrall and
fascinate
captivating the would-be
loner

Look into her eyes
One is forced to face the Night
there are no lies—
only—
transmissions of emotion
illusions of devotion—
and sacrifice—
swirling into Light.

Interpretation ───────────────────────

The Water Mother represents extreme purity and beauty in its most subtle form. She embodies the dreamy and elusive qualities of illusion. She is the shimmering tranquility which results from the endurance of emotions over time. In the stereotypical sense, she is the Perfect Mother: she seems self-sacrificing to the point of martyrdom; her love seems altruistic.

The Water Mother's emotions have a long time-frame. She has paced the pulse of her feelings, and therefore, while she might appear to be "low-key," or even *non-feeling*, she has tremendous staying-power and wears well. She will be there offering assistance long after others' flames have gone out. She will be there exuding a quiet love.

Because Water Mother moves at a slow and deep rate, and because, like Water Father, she reflects the observer, it may be difficult to see her truth, but she is devoted, loyal and nurturant.

She has the gift of subconscious vision and she sees and acts on the basis of her intuition which is accurate. In medieval times, Water

Mother appeared holding a closed cup. It was said that she held the secret of the subconscious.

Due to her tremendous capacity to receive, process and transmit, Water Mother is the perfect agent. She is psychic and has accurate dreams and visions. She is a symbologist, and the symbols she uses are the product of the collective unconscious, to which she is aptly attuned. She may appear to be very wise.

When you are in an emotional transition, the Water Mother may appear at a portal through which you are to be conducted. This will likely be a portal of love. If you draw the Water Mother card in divination, you are probably moving to a new level of understanding. The new understanding involves the creation or adoption of new forms. Thus, Water Mother greets you like a birth mother. At her door, something is about to be created.

At the portal of the Water Mother, the challenge is to pace yourself and wrestle joyously with difficulty. When you face adversity with joy, burdens naturally become lighter. Joy comes from doing that which you feel, deep down in the soul, is right. The greatest quality of joy is the encouragement it brings. Meet this time with joy and all will be well (see I Ching: Hexagram 58: Joy). That is the message of the Water Mother.

Card Symbology: The Water Mother is the key in a keyhole. The keyhole is the door to the connectedness of all things. It is a hole. It is whole. It is holy. The Water Mother, as the agent and the guardian of the threshold, is the key to emotional understanding. The keyhole is bell-shaped because she uses the power of resonating bell-like sound to help her access the deeper areas of consciousness. Through this process, she improves her powers as an agent of truth.

She is white light floating in the abyss of the cosmic sea, the brilliant light in the radiant darkness.

Before her floats the white lotus of the East. It symbolizes the existence of the primal force housed within the physical body. Water Mother reminds us that our body is the temple of our soul.

Below the Water Mother is her reflection which fills the cup of the suit of Water. The surface of the water upon which she floats is the mirror of the cosmic sea. Her reflection reminds us that as it is above, so it is below. As it is inside, so it is outside.

Water Brother: Wings of Love

Divinatory Meaning

Love is the basis for your new creative surge; love gives wings to your spirit; your heart is wide open and filling with love; you feel romantic; let your creativity be translated into art, poetry, writing; give a friend a rose.

Brother

WATER

Meditation

Libra, Scorpio
Love Man/Water Warrior
conquers his enemy with Art—
fills his Cup, his need for Love
through the stream of Unconscious

his dreams are dreams
of loving delights
his gift is a gift of powerful
Insight
he converts to Art all that which comes
from the deepest part
of his element

Listen to him
he absorbs and conveys
and harbors solutions

he says Feelings are but fleeting illusions
to be cradled and birthed in Art!

Alas!
His victory lies within his sense
of poetic completion.

Interpretation

The Water Brother is the Wings of Love. He is highly sensual and loving—the great lover. He is tenuous and spiritual, an artist in all ways. His imagination is his strongest quality and it shows in his poetry, grace and style. He is forever engaged in the search for intuitive knowledge—and the search for meaning. On the basis of this knowledge, he is determined to create art, which will communicate his deepest feelings.

Through creating art and encouraging others to do so as well, he delivers the gift of ideas and opportunities as well as self-love and self-discovery. He is just the type to write love songs and send flowers, and thereby cause the receiver to reflect on his or her own emotional state. Water Brother strives to conquer his own needs and desires through translating what he finds in the stream of the unconscious into art and he encourages everyone, but particularly those he loves the most, to tune into that stream in order to make the most of their creative talents.

Giving art to the world symbolizes the emergence of the deep Self into the social world. The Water Brother takes great risks in order to do this. Through engaging in the highly personal process of creating art, the Water Brother puts his own emotionality before the world and, as such, is vulnerable. As a vulnerable warrior, his weapon is a cup, because his victory lies in being emotionally fulfilled. One cannot be filled if nothing is allowed to enter.

In his weaker moments, the Water Brother may appear to be lazy, bored or inaccessible. The underlying problem, however, is that he has temporarily lost sight of the meaning of life and his higher purpose. He can retrieve that meaning by tuning in to the subconscious stream of his deep Self.

The challenge of the Water Brother is to stay connected to the subconscious stream. As the *I Ching* says, you can move a city, but not a well. Sometimes when people come to draw water from the well, which is the source of fulfillment and nourishment, the "rope" (their connection to fulfillment) is too short or breaks, and they fail to achieve results. In Water Brother energy, if your rope breaks, find a way to lengthen it through meditation and possibly through the counsel of one who seems to have a long rope. This is a time for persistence. Do not give up before you reach the wellstream (see *I Ching:* Hexagram 48: The Well).

Card Symbology: In the Water Brother card, we see him walking in the cosmic sea. He leaves the earth behind. In all directions, he is guided by spirits.

The spirits come to him as wings of support, holding him aloft as he journeys, so that he does not sink in the abyss.

His antenna picks up messages from the above and below. He is attuned to the deepest frequencies. Sound comes through his antenna, the white sound of the universe. He hears the sound of "Om" resonating in the spaces between the chiming of his mother's bell. Water Brother stands at the threshold of sound.

His cup, which is his heart, extends out to the universe and is reflected in a mirror image from above. Water Brother is our own mirror image as we completely attune to the messages of the cosmic sea.

Water Sister: Love Divine

Divinatory Meaning ———————

Trust your feelings and impressions; you are on the right path; you are strongly connected to earth, water and sky and the passage of all seasons; maintain your strong connection and stay attuned to the earth by meditating frequently; you are blessed with the ability to know intuitively that which others do not have access to.

Sister

WATER

Meditation —————————————————————————————————

Libra, Scorpio, Sagittarius
Water Sister
hears the Message of the Fishes
she is the Power of the Waters;
Force behind the Seas
infinitely gracious
Secret Priestess of the Water
floats on psychic Visions
and perpetual dreams

Water sister
Love Delivered!
Sacred Vows and Oaths Discovered!

Loving sister
to the spindly spiny creatures
of the
Deep
Dancing Diamonds grace the ruffled
surface of her dresses
sweet caresses
Water Sister singing tales
to me.

Interpretation ——————————————————————————————

The Water Sister represents the power of the emotions and the un-
conscious/subconscious to give sustenance to idea. Since she is born
from the unification of her father and mother, Fire and Water (the
superconscious and the subconscious), she symbolizes the process of
creation; the beginning of imagination on the physical plane. As such,
she has been depicted as supporting, or being the strength behind,
the tortoise which, in Hindu philosophy, supports the elephant
which, in turn, supports the world.

The Water Sister is rapturous and gentle, a kind and tender sister.
She is full of romance, dreams and loving vision.˙

She moves entirely in the flow of the right path. That is why her
strength is quiet. She has no need for crass or glib display of any

kind. She is a quiet visionary, highly successful in all psychic work and in all matters of self-examination. She holds the power of crystallization, and can help others to focus.

If the Water Sister ever suffers from depression or melancholy or unrealistic flights of imagination, she can always re-establish her positive energy by stopping to listen for the spaces between the world's sounds. Therein she will hear a humming "Om." This is her natural focal point.

Om, the sacred Indian prayer syllable is composed of four elements. It is sometimes written and heard as Aum or A-U-M. The A is the first element. The U is the second. The M is the third. The silence, at the beginning and the end, is the fourth. The A sound comes from the abdominal level and is formed in the back of the mouth. It symbolizes waking consciousness. At the U, the sound moves upward through the chest and at the formation of the U sound in the mouth, the mouth and head are filled with dream consciousness, the subconscious rising. The M resonates in the head and through closed lips. It can be pulled all the way back through the body to vibrate at the abdominal level. M stands for the state of deep dreamless sleep. This state is the ultimate peace of the Water Sister. And, in the silence that follows, she rejoices in her life as symbolized by the exhalation and inhalation of breath, the breath of her life moving in and moving out accompanied by the purity of resonating prayer.

The Water Sister is adept at entering the space of rejoicing which exists between the sounds. In such a way, her whole life is a yoga, a *yoking,* or harnessing, of a state of peace, jubilance and love on the mundane, or earthly, level.

She is, in all ways, successful, bringing the great love that she knows down to earth. Thus, we can think of her as the love that nurtures the growing and changing things of Earth.

The strong tree of Earth is well-watered and grows large. This means that, in Water Sister energy, you experience great success— or there is great success coming. The best approach to the bountiful life is to keep to the middle path, balanced in all elements: the spirit, the actions, the emotions, the intellect, the physical or mundane life. Sometimes, in order to achieve the greatest success, we must conceal our will within our hearts (see *I Ching:* Hexagram 19: Going There). The Water Sister does not divulge all she knows. Her work is often carried out in a state of silent beauty.

Card Symbology: Water Sister is riding the Swan of Peace which is also her path out of the cosmic sea. Water Sister chooses where she wants to be and moves in and out of the sea at will. The reins she holds symbolize her power to harness the energy of love. This is the first appearance of the "yoke" in the deck. It denotes a mastery of a yoga of the mind.

Water Sister is supported by a sea turtle, powerful and resourceful animal of the deep. Behind her, creatures of sea and earth travel on the black waves of Binah. These waves also represent the dark wings of spirit. Water Sister is limitless light in radiant darkness. She forever moves on the path of light.

❖ ❖ ❖

CHAPTER EIGHT

Wind

Swords
Sounds
East
Wit, Light, Wind, Feather, Thought
Incense burning for
the Morning of the Sacred Year
White, Gold and Dawn Rose
Hawk and Eagle split the Sky on Sacred Wing
Yellow Knowing rises to Amethyst Peaks

The Path through Wind

Wind shifts, scatters, cools, dries; its origin
is as mysterious as the origin of breath . . .

Wind gives life. With our first breath, we breathe in the consciousness of our present plane, the plane of manifestation. When we cease to breathe, the material segment is finished. Therefore, Wind is the suit of waking consciousness.

Wind is energy. It is free to all. It is infinite. Where does it come from and where does it go?

On the physical plane, wind is caused by a constant interchange of air between the cold polar caps and the warm tropics. When air cools, it becomes compressed and when it warms up, it expands. Thus, on an analytic scientific level, wind is caused by a change of temperature. When the temperature changes, bodies of air begin to move. Wind is also a manifestation of the Earth's rotation. The

Earth moves a thousand miles an hour at the equator. This causes the production of a "sea of air." These two great forces, in combination, produce a pattern of winds which travel the Earth's surface.

Even though, from time immemorial, navigators have depended upon the power of wind, it was not until the middle of the 19th century that wind was studied seriously. Using thousands of ships' logs, U. S. Navy hydrographer, Matthew Fontaine Maury, produced a map of the world's winds. This map showed 52 wind systems. Maury demonstrated that a longer sea route can sometimes result in faster travel, depending upon the prevailing winds.[1] The key, for Maury—as well as for us in working with the tarot—is using the power of the wind to one's advantage.

In symbolic terms, Wind is force brought into manifestation just as Earth represents manifested form. Thus, Wind and Earth are like brother and sister, bearing a strong resemblance to the parent elements Fire and Water (which correspond to force and form on the level of idea). In the tarot, Wind corresponds to intellect, the manifestor of idea. Harnessing the Wind's power, or the power of the intellect, results from understanding its patterns. Bodies of air, for example, move from high to low pressure zones. How does the intellect work?

First of all, there are seven veils which mask the deepest internal pure thought. These include:

1) The Veil of Imprinting: an apparently irreversible behavior pattern established very early in life which occurs every time a particular stimulus is experienced;

2) The Veil of Parroting: the methodical repetition of information that has been "fed" by educators, etc.;

3) The Veil of Social Conditioning: intellectual response based on (what is perceived as) social (peer and parental) expectations;

4) The Veil of the Clever Show: a quick-witted response pattern;

5) The Veil of Ego Reification: vanity and repetition of intellectual

---

[1]Landt Dennis and Lisl Dennis, *Catch the Wind* (New York: Four Winds Press, 1976).

patterns because they have been successful in winning the approval of a social group;[2]

6) The Veil of Spinning Intellect: the onslaught of many ideas at once, the intellectual stirring that causes insomnia;

7) The Veil of Massive Confusion: lack of intellectual clarity (bewilderment) that stems from attending to too many sources of information.

The true intellect, pure thought—discoverable beyond these veils—is fresh and clear, unfettered by external stimuli. Pure thought can be discovered through attuning to the innermost conscience, the major personal guide in the suit of wind.

In order to attune to the conscience, veils must be sliced away. Thus the major tool of the Suit of Wind is the sword. The sword slashes material—both formulative and concrete—into its smallest components. The sword pierces, makes holes, cuts apart, lifts and comes to a point. The sword is a weapon against falsehood. All of these attributes of the sword represent the analytical capability of humankind. When we are analytical and intellectual, we are "really sharp."

I can use my blade to kill or to prepare the ground for planting. I, alone, decide. The use of the sword is something over which we, as warriors, have total control. It is our weapon. It is our tool.

We cannot, on the other hand, control the Wind. We can only understand its patterns and endeavor to work with its energy. Through understanding the patterns of the Wind—that is the blowing of our own intellect as well as that of our culture and historical time period—we can avoid entrapment in the veils, which act like nets and hold us captive.

---

[2]Regarding ego reification: to reify means to make real. It implies that we sometimes treat as real that which is merely a product of our imaginings.

One of Wind: Dawn

Divinatory Meaning ————————

The dark clouds of your mind are scattered as if blown away by a strong wind at daybreak; an important new idea is taking hold in your mind; it is as if a light is turning on in your life; pay attention to new thought; this is an exciting time; as you think about your new idea, you will not be able to follow every nuance to its logical completion point in the future, but there will be time for that later; attend to the present and accept the great potential of your new ideas!

One of Wind

DAWN

Meditation ————————————————

Capricorn, Aquarius, Pisces
Reason is born
amid Essence and Desire

Pure Light Blasts
as the thing is Defined/Understood
made clear

It is the first perception
of the Conscious Mind
Instinct Idea and Intellect
At first they are One
the presence of the Wind
Directs and Scatters.

Interpretation ————————————————

At the One of Wind, you have glimpsed new ideas which hold tremendous potential. You are feeling incredibly creative. The question is how to manifest the creative impulse for the greatest good.

The One of Wind represents the essence of Wind. Wind is born of the intercourse of the elemental forces of Fire (spirit and energy) and Water (desire). This means that your desire for change and your energy level to enable that change to occur have reached a new level. Both aspects of your Self have grown stronger and deeper. A change is in the offing. You are beginning to see things in a new way. You are gaining a new perspective. You may feel as if you are "seeing the light." At this time, you are channeling and directing your own energy, and becoming highly cognizant of your own boundaries.

Dawn represents the first level of apprehension or insight on the part of the conscious mind. It is the beginning of science, philosophy, theory, doctrine, scholarship; the beginning of conscious knowledge: naming, abstraction, generalization. This is the beginning of the intellectual process.

At the One, your thinking is original. It is completely your own. It is completely fresh. The intellect represented by Dawn is not a pattern of intellectual expression, such as parroting answers for a test. It is clear, creative thinking in a primordial and triumphant stage. The visions you are seeing and ideas you are encountering are new messages from your Inner Self. This is why this stage is often referred to as Hidden Intelligence. Hidden Intelligence is the psychoactive process of discovery. It is the process of naming or identifying that which has previously been unrecognized. At this point, energies and insights which were previously on the unconscious level are moving into your consciousness. The One is the point of the great "Aha!" It is the power of utterance, the time when—in sudden recognition—the child calls out "I AM!" It is a time for rejoicing. Beware, as you move to this stage, of any patterns of imprinting from your environment which might negatively influence or bias your thinking or hold you back.

The One of Wind represents the inflow of breath, the very force of life. It is the Wind moving into and out of the body, thus it symbolizes the moment of birth, that time when the idea becomes manifest, when the word becomes flesh. It is the cutting edge and the point where all ideas and potential are released into the world.

This is knowledge in its most pristine form. Knowledge, however, ultimately has the ability to oppress as well as to free. At the One, it is not yet clear which way the Wind will blow, yet there is a sense of triumph connected with the new illumination. Celebrate your joyous discoveries. It is time to revel in newness!

Card Symbology: The One of Wind is the crack of Dawn. The Sun's blade slices into the dark and releases myriad thought forms. The ideas manifest in the shape of crystals, for communication, and butterflies for transformation and emotional expression. The crystals are multifaceted and precise. Here is all the potential that exists for human development. It is like the opening of Pandora's Box: all good and bad escapes. Dawn represents the cumulation of all hopes and dreams, thus the One of Wind is mystically connected to The Star (see Key XVII).

Two of Wind: The Crossing

Divinatory Meaning ───────────

You are in a temporary balance which may feel like a state of detente; there is a sense of release from captivity; maintain balance gently and peace can continue; it is time to use all of your wisdom and understanding to assess the situation you now face.

Two of Wind

THE CROSSING

Meditation ──────────────────────────────

Moon in Libra
The Moon is Change
Nature pure
The Ocean hits upon the Shore
rising to ebb to rise once more
moving in and out and back again
The crane stands on one stilt
retreating in Dark Waters

The Star is a White Dwarf
and a Red Giant
There is no Contradiction
Two is the Balance
that regulates the Energy
bursting from the Power
of Recognition.

Interpretation

At the Two of Wind, you have begun to identify new aspects and ways of knowing. At some moments, this new knowledge may seem to set up an either-or situation. You have a need to break through old or outmoded constructions of thought, thinking patterns, which no longer work.

The path of the Two is referred to as Illuminating Intelligence. The consciousness has awakened to new possibility and is beginning to abstract the alternatives. In waking consciousness, we *identify*. We say "A is not, not-A." The method of waking consciousness is scientific. In waking consciousness, we imagine how things might be constructed, test them, and draw conclusions. In this way, we determine limits, structures, and, basically, what is and what is not.

The Crossing represents the waking mode of consciousness. It represents our struggle to attain knowledge on the conscious level and to judge the significance of that knowledge in a rational manner.

As we move through this process, our internal constructive and destructive forces hang in balance. Both sides of issues are understood, which can lead to harmony, but also to indecision. It is as if reward is on the Wind, but the time is still precarious. The Crossing is a time of opportunity and danger. It is a time of unknown factors. X, the glyph of the crossed swords, signifies that which remains unrevealed. Paradoxically, it also represents that which is revealed. In mathematics, for example, X represents the unknown quantity and also indicates the known. We say, "This table is 2' x 3'," and we use X to show the power of magnification in optical instruments. At The Crossing, with our new knowledge, we find that more is concealed than ever before, and at the same time, more is revealed.

In the polarized force of The Crossing, we are at a point where we must soon make decisions. As we move closer toward taking the next step upon the path, we reassess our personal situation. We attempt to come to grips with our identity. We decide who we are, and who we are not. Figuratively speaking, we mark our position—our X—on the social map. Here, we make the statements: "This is who I am; this is where I am; this is why I am; this is how I am; this is how I am different from others."

The X at The Crossing is also our alternative signature, the ubiquitous signature used by those who are unable to spell out a name. At The Crossing, our identity may be in flux. Our name, in the symbolic sense, may be changing. New knowledge can release us from the bonds of ignorance. It can also cause confusion. At the Two, we learn that knowledge frees and knowledge oppresses. How will I use the knowledge I have gained? I, alone, must decide. I, alone, am the responsible party.

Card Symbology: In the Two of Wind, two swords are crossed in an X. To the right is the illuminating light of Chokmah. To the left is the radiant darkness of Binah. The crossed swords show the unification of these two monumental forces: rational wisdom and emotional understanding.

The hilt of the sword on the right is the equal-armed cross of higher attunement, which shows the highest function of this card. Both blades are attaching themselves to the bodies of butterflies, thus they are not necessarily hard and destructive. They indicate transformation on the highest levels. It is a paradox that the swords are both hard and soft at the same time. That is because all potential exists in the analytical realm. The power of analysis, that is the power to cut down into the smallest components in order to understand more clearly, is the strength of the sword.

Three of Wind: Recognition

Divinatory Meaning

Give up to gain; surrender in order to achieve; recognize that all that is good has the potential for evil; all that is evil has the potential for good; you have seen so much and you sometimes wish you hadn't; you have told yourself that ignorance is bliss, but you know that something is missing in that proverb; all that you know will eventually help you build your own character or personality in a positive image; ask yourself if your motivation is pure, then you will know whether you are on the right track.

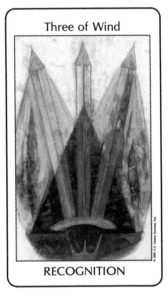

Three of Wind

RECOGNITION

Meditation

Saturn in Libra
Meat to Bone to Earth to Meat
Evolution, Understanding and Science
the infant rises, takes a life of its own
grief in rejecting the cradle
and yet
it must be done
Thy Will be done.

Interpretation

You are the great decider. You now feel solely responsible for determining the right direction. At the Three of Wind, Recognition, you have arrived at a new understanding of the nature of things. You are beginning to understand the cycles that are both internal and external to your Self.

Your process of understanding has been rational. Your method of incorporating new information has been scientific. In arriving at a more comprehensive understanding of the universe, you have arrived at a more comprehensive understanding of your Self. Now, you are on the verge of establishing a new identity, an identity that is deeper, broader and truer than what went before.

At the Three, you have attempted to unravel paradoxes in your life. Your passion to create has been sparked. This is because, in symbolic terms, your basic grounding internal elements of Fire (the active force) and Water (the stable form) have united and become balanced. This balance has given birth to Wind which represents pure and original thought. The Wind carries a message of liberation. To liberate your creativity, you must now throw off the Veil of Social Conditioning. It is time to experience your unique creative prowess, that which has been repressed by the process of your socialization.

At the point of the Three, you may feel frustrated, but frustration is a normal part of your creative process. Bouts of anxiety may intermingle with bouts of harmonious joy. Many emotions arise as you grieve for the loss of "parental" guidance and protection. You are now on your own. If you succeed, you succeed on the basis of your own merit. If you fail, you have no one but your Self to blame. Whatever the outcome, your newfound ability to play with a new set of data is pleasing. You are sorting out, discarding and assimilating at will. Through this interplay, you begin to see your new context juxtaposed upon the context of your earlier life.

In leaving the old neighborhood, the old job, the old house, the old school, the old social class, you recognize that ignorance is bliss. But, knowing carries its own bliss and if you don't let go, you won't grow. In any case, however pleasant the thought, you can never go home again. You are reborn as a new person. There is no turning back. You have come too far. You know too much. You are extremely aware, at this point, of what you are giving up, but less sure of what you are getting. You do know, however, that the past—which you are struggling to leave—houses much sorrow. And still, no matter how much sorrow the past contains, there is sorrow in leaving it. Your heart feels saddened and angry. You are hurting. You may have hurt others as well.

At the Three, you have the first recognition that all that is good has the potential for evil; all that is evil has the potential for good. You feel responsible. Your heart weighs heavily. New ideas are always dual-edged. Laser beams kill as well as heal. The blade desecrates and, in turn, prepares the ground for planting.

In the Sword's desecration lies the sorrow of life.

In a sense, *knowing* is like desecration. It calls for destroying the antiquated. One must abandon old views which were useful and comfortable and possibly even sacred. In *knowing,* one is, in a sense, cast out of the Garden of Eden. Growth seems painful. More knowledge brings more pain. You feel pain and frustration, a sense of being "up against the blade." If you feel miserable at the Three of Wind, you must work through and understand your own misery in order to grow. You must come to understand that the sense of despair is caused by the clash of old and new. Old shells must be abandoned. There is no use for that which is too small. Concentrate on the new. Concentrate on the positive.

The moment of Recognition then becomes the path of Sanctifying Intelligence. Sanctification means to make pure or holy, to free from sin. The question you must ask your Self is: Is my motivation pure? Is my cause holy? When you have determined that it is, you must surrender to the new flow of Self in order to complete your transformation so your new thinking can take flight. That is the challenge of the Three of Wind: to purify your motivation and then to surrender to the new process. Your fear is but the initial insecurity of experiencing new identity.

There is only one way to escape the bondage of the past. You must unlock the door to the next level. In your own hand, you hold the key. It is the key to good and evil. The key is knowledge. This is your power. It is the knowledge that you, alone, are the great initiator. You, alone, are the great decider, the great destroyer, the great sanctifier. In this context, you are reborn. Is your motivation pure?

Card Symbology: The blades of the Two now become lights and pencils. They light the way. The blades to the right and left are the wet bodies of the butterflies of transformation which have just emerged from the cocoon and are drying their wings to fly. They are getting ready to emerge from the dark.

The wings are the wings of immortality. They are dried—and freed to fly—by the light of knowledge. The blades indicate that your will to fly is present. The hilt indicates that you possess the understanding to fly in the right direction.

Four of Wind: Mastery

Divinatory Meaning

You are in a holding pattern; having now mastered a difficult task, you are resting on your laurels and enjoying rewards in your environment; only you know that disturbing influences are beginning to emerge within you; there is a tendency to cling to successes because of ego; be careful: clinging to the desires of ego can be a deadly enemy; the things that gratify the ego do not necessarily gratify the soul.

Four of Wind

MASTERY

Meditation

Jupiter in Libra
Mastery
Authority
Dogma and Law
bringing Order to Chaos
intending to rigidify the lay of the land.

Interpretation

You have completed the first phase. Through the powers of primitive reasoning, you have reached your initial goals. It is now time to conceptualize further goals through receiving the message of divine reason. It is time for you to open up and receive.

The Four of Wind signifies authority in the intellectual world. It shows that you have succeeded in understanding your task, at least initially. You have now sorted things out, developed a type of taxonomy to quell the confusion you perceived in your world. At the Four, mental chaos has been replaced with systematic, orderly knowledge. You have approached the situation scientifically and your theories have proven correct. As such, a good case can be made for conservatism. Change signals discomfort. Staying conventional, and resting on your laurels—for you have won laurels!—is the easiest path.

Thus, you are in a stage of retreat, of rest and recuperation from your own comprehensive and difficult struggle to understand. Now that you feel order has been restored, and that you no longer have to worry, you have been able to coast.

Beneath your calm exterior, however, you feel a growing restlessness. You sense the beginning of new or previously suppressed urges and feelings. You sense that you may be entrapped in the Veils of the Clever Show and Ego Reification, which may be blocking the light of your original intellect, your innermost access to your creative potential, that which we refer to as pure thought. As such, the peace you are feeling may seem like an armed truce. You find you have to keep your armor up in order to remain calm.

Being in the Four of Wind is like being caught in a repetitive "success syndrome." This syndrome is exemplified by the artist who succeeds in selling paintings of barns or seascapes and then paints the same painting over and over and over again, thus becoming a technician for the sake of material success while undermining the essence of the original impetus to create.[3] Where does the *art* go? Little new is added. The creative impulse is superseded by the impulse to attain material security. At this stage, you become removed from the original psychoactive process of discovery.

Viewed from one angle, you have earned the right to coast on your previous accomplishments. You have attained autonomy or power in the outside world. But from another angle, repetition becomes a culprit. There is the nagging, disconcerting feeling that something must change. Yet, you know that if you move too fast, you could crack your cohesive (and successful) exterior. If you move too slow, the destructive influences that you intuitively know are present could rise to greater power.

This internal knowledge—that which only you perceive—feels threatening. In order to maintain your sense of authority amid growing internal doubts, you are tempted to defend your position. The challenge of the Four of Wind is to become aware of the source of

---

[3] I do not deny that repetition can be an extremely valuable meditation, however, the time for repetition is fading and your deep Self recognizes that.

your arrogance. Arrogance arises from feeling vulnerable. Your key, at this point, is to understand that the first natural enemy is the reified construction of your own ego. Don't do something just because it brought you kudos in the past. Be sure you feel good about what you are doing and what is happening in your life on a heart level. The Four of Wind offers an opportune time to clarify your true direction, that which your *conscience* tells you is right.

The path of the Four is known as Receptive Intelligence. Open your Self to receive. By opening up to receive, you will be able to rekindle your own brilliant process of psychoactive discovery. Your love of life and your joy in your true work will magically return.

Card Symbology: Four butterflies are on display. They are shown in a clear glass case, having been analyzed and, literally, pinned down. This is symbolized by the butterfly bodies—actually swords symbolizing the analytical power of the intellect—appearing in alignment. That all the swords are lined up and pointing in one direction means that the original goal or idea has been mastered. The butterfly, an object of investigation, has been understood.

Nonetheless, the understanding is uni-directional and pinning the butterflies down takes the life out of them. This introduces the idea that "analysis presupposes a corpse," one of the major lessons of the suit of Wind.

Pinning down the butterflies creates a holding pattern. In a holding pattern, one rests. But just beyond the realm of the holding pattern is an open rainbow radiating energy. This is the rainbow of the system of chakras—the energy centers of the human body—open and receptive to the higher cosmic will.

To free the butterflies, which signify beauty, transformation and immortality, one must open to the message of the rainbow which represents higher consciousness. The rainbow stands for the rainbow covenant. Each time it appears, it brings the message that God, or the cosmic will, is the major guide.

Five of Wind: Fear

Divinatory Meaning ─────────────

You fear a painful, frightening or unknown situation; the major thing you
have to fear, however, is fear itself; you
have trapped yourself with your own
negative energies from the past; operate
with ethical tactics and bad situations
will be resolved; attune to your own conscience; ask forgiveness; build bridges,
not walls.

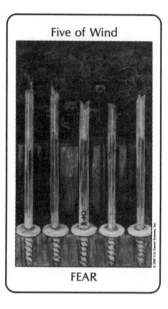

Five of Wind

FEAR

Meditation ──────────────────────────────

Venus in Aquarius
Chaos breaks the order
The heart is trapped in its own cage
the two-edged blade of the past is chipped and broken
the butterflies are dead
the monsters of the present lie stirring
in the Void
fear fear fear
defeat defeat defeat.

Interpretation ──────────────────────────────

You are trapped in a self-designed prison of negative energy from
the past. You have arrived there through adhering to external expectations. You must purge the negative impulses, repent, offer res-
titution and move in the direction of diplomacy.

At the Five of Wind, you feel a sense of weakness and Fear. Your
emotions dominate you and your intellectual plan—having once been
so strong—now seems obscure. You are caught in the Veils of the Spin-

ning Intellect and Massive Confusion. Your sense of virtue breaks down. The overall order, which you once took for granted, seems to dissipate. There are so many new factors now appearing. It is hard to make sense of what is happening. You feel overwhelmed and defeated.

There has been a sudden coming of a new light or idea which is changing your perceptions. With the new perspective comes Fear, fear of change, fear of retribution. But it is Fear itself, concealed at every turn, hiding in every crevice, that is the second natural enemy. The challenge of the Five of Wind is to make room for your own objectivity and clarity in spite of the fear you feel. The new idea is struggling to break through the power of your fear. The challenge at the Five of Wind is to let go of your fear—you must face your karma to move to the next level—and to replace it with a higher sense of ethics. Since this is the case, you must take this time to review your interactions with the outer world.

You have now learned that there is a great danger in internalizing the values of an economic, social, or familial system that exists outside of your Self. Internalizing external values without processing their origin or relevance can lead to your own sense of defeat, degradation or dishonor. Along the path of this incarnation, you learn that the only true values are the values of *your own conscience,* those that you internalize through your own unique experience on the plane of manifestation.

You learn that your tactics must, above all, be ethical. Your conscience must be clear. At the Five of Wind, it is time to clear your conscience or clear the path behind you, which may seem painful at first. Clearing the path from the past is what is referred to when the Navajos say, "May it be beautiful behind me."

The way to clear the path behind you and free the way for the future is to remove your Self from the river of continuous participation in which you could easily drown. Take time to sit on the bank and observe. You must learn that your problems arose because you jumped into the river of your thoughts and held onto an idea. You held this idea beyond its time. You held onto this idea when it could no longer support your weight. You held onto this idea when you could have pulled others under with you. Was this ethical? What was your motivation?

What you need to do at this time is to experience the depths of your feelings and ask forgiveness for the hurt and pain you have caused. It is time to *feel.* The first step is to ask, "How do I really *feel,* deep, deep down inside?" The second step is to ask forgiveness for clinging to that which has served no positive end.

Through all this, you will find that the bridge to communication is hard to find. You must look deep within to determine what must change. That is why the path of the Five is called the path of Radical Intelligence. It is about a radical purging of all that which serves negative ends.

Remember, on the most profound level, it does not matter whether you receive the big award or whether you attain the most prestigious position. The important thing is the efficacy of your own inner process. How does your heart weigh? Is it light like the wing of a spring butterfly?

Card Symbology: Five swords are pointed toward the dark and stuck there. They seem unable to penetrate to a new level. The swords are separated and this fact symbolizes the negative energy of Wind.

The swords form a prison in which the viewer is trapped. It is, of course, a prison of one's own design. It is a prison of the void or the abyss, a prison of nothingness, with vague, indecipherable monsters and dead butterflies floating in the dark.

Across the top of the hilts, however, is the way out. The hilts form stepping stones across the abyss. To step out, purge all that must be purged inside your Self and move in the direction of mediation, the direction of your own heart.

Six of Wind: Clarity

Divinatory Meaning

Everything is suddenly clear; you have a keen ability to analyze; you have the right perspective; you feel a beautiful sense of reverence; enjoy this time but be careful not to get caught up in fanatically embracing your new truth; that is a current danger that could lead to much trouble.

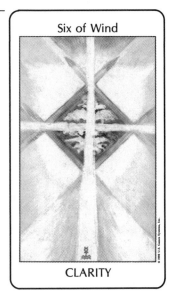

Six of Wind

CLARITY

Meditation ————————————————————————

Mercury in Aquarius
Intelligence of a higher form:
There is no other Way
The Way is clear.

Interpretation ————————————————————————

At the Six of Wind, you are following the higher power, the higher force, and the way has become clear. You have made a quantum leap in your understanding. The way is not dangerous, but meant for the higher good. Your intellect is now influenced by all things that aid the earth and all of humanity. You have achieved a new level of awareness and exaltation. Your mental and moral faculties have come into a *true* (as opposed to superficial) balance. The true promise of divine reason has been revealed. It is time to move steadily in the direction of the higher power, which is both internal and external to your Self.

At this time, a new, more comprehensive vision has emerged as you begin to integrate diverse ideas and visions. Your process is informed by the guidance of your Higher Self or your *conscience.* Nonetheless, your comprehension of the situation is still achieved largely through your rational analytical ability, which, at this time, is operating accurately and efficiently.

Because all is clear, the new sense you feel is reverence. You are thinking clearly, and therein is a certain sense of jubilation. You are actively and accurately balancing the incoming influences of yin, yang, production, destruction, higher consciousness, subconsciousness, inspiration, and analysis. You are integrating all of these influences in your waking consciousness and keeping everything moving as one. That is why the sixth path is called the path of Mediating Intelligence.

The danger on the sixth path is falling prey to the Pollyanna Complex—feeling excessive, and often unrealistic, optimism—or fanatic conversion. Either one can happen when everything is going so well. Fanatic conversion is your third natural enemy. In its extreme state, fanatic conversion is one of the world's most destructive forces. The best action to take at this time is to quietly emanate peace, prosperity and love. It is time to see the light and to respect the light.

This is not the time, however, to be overly simplistic or childish in your perceptions.

Card Symbology: In the Six of Wind, Clarity, the blades of the swords have turned into the path to higher wisdom. These are the clear lines of communication with the Higher Self.

Inside the diamond are the wings of transformation. These signify that change/movement is the balancing force. These are the wings of protection through the process of change.

In the background is the spirit of the Holy Grail. This is the message of the Great Spirit. Blue is for understanding this message. Yellow is for the holiness of divine reason, the key to understanding. This symbolism refers to the influence of Tiphareth in the astral world. Tiphareth represents Christ-consciousness and the Way of the Cross. Walking in the Way of the Cross results from understanding the reason for suffering. With right reflection and resolution, suffering is transformed into true and everlasting joy. This is the greatest message of the suit of Wind.

Seven of Wind: Many Tongues

Divinatory Meaning: ─────────

There is a sense of futility; it is as if you are hearing or speaking several languages at once and there is no sense to be made of anything; you cannot express yourself in the way that you want to; this is because old systems—things that you once believed in—are now outmoded; let go of the old ways, it is time to change; do not fear change or movement; fear of change can lead you to danger.

Seven of Wind

MANY TONGUES

Meditation ─────────────────────────────────

Moon in Aquarius
Injured Brilliance
holding on
vascillation
twisted tongue speaks many forms
Where is the ME in the new?
Have I built a kingdom to watch it fall?

Interpretation ─────────────────────────────

You want to cry out, but a singular language of expression is un-available. You are speaking in too many tongues and cannot be under-stood. This is because your thinking is forked.

At the Seven of Wind, you experience a sense of futility. It is as if there are too many ways to go, alternative paths, and each path seems equally desirable. You find your Self shrouded once again by the Veil of Massive Confusion. You feel your Self at a standstill. This is frustrating. You feel doubtful and pessimistic. You feel anxious. You have the expectation that things will not go well. The sense is that of butting up against a brick wall. The goat butts against the hedge and gets his horns tangled. Then nothing at all can move.

This uneasiness has all come about because a short-lived victory went to your head. But then you lost the courage of your convictions and your ideas became entangled. You became disillusioned.

Many Tongues represents intellectual wreckage, the idea of striv-ing in vain against strong, outside, uncompromising forces: a stronger idea. It is the clashing of paradigms; comprehensive and logical sys-tems of thought are competing in your mind. Each system makes sense when taken individually on its own terms, but each reaches different conclusions and the conclusions are not compatible. You are fighting to cling to the old ideas. It is not clear, after all, whether the new is better, and you have a vested interest in the old ways.

It is as if you are speaking two or more languages and it is twisting your tongue. You are babbling. You are totally conscious of your Self, but all you can do is talk incoherently. Be aware that you are not only influencing your own internal system with inconsistent, unclear or negative thought forms, but you are projecting these negative thought forms (vibrations) out to the universe.

The nightmarish feeling you are experiencing, however, will pass. The way out of your present dilemma is to get more information and to compare this information with the dictates of your conscience. You will find that the paths you currently perceive are not equal. One path will prevail. That is the path you will take. Remember, however, as you analyze the situation, that holding on just because you have your ego invested, or because no matter how bad things are, they could become worse, will most certainly bring disaster.

Comparing the incoming information with the dictates of your conscience must be based on the highest functioning of your intellect in concordance with the highest functioning of your faith. That is why the path of the Seven is called Occult Intelligence. Occult means hidden or concealed. That which is occult is mysterious or just beyond understanding. The path of the Seven combines the highest of intellectual virtues, divine reason, with the unknown factor, X, the occult (see the Two of Wind), that which is taken on faith.

By listening carefully for the messages of the higher will, those which now seem hidden, you will be able to move through this problematic situation into a place of perfect balance. Perfect balance juxtaposes the perfection of the eternal (circle) with the perfection of the physical (square). This juxtaposition is the Seven in its most perfect form.

To become balanced, you must surrender to change. Fear of change is the fourth natural enemy. Embrace your new discoveries— but do not cling. Change is the one constant. Sense the energy climate and you will discover the most productive flow.

Card Symbology: The Seven of Wind shows seven split and twisted swords. The swords represent muddled thinking. The green appearing in the swords represents Venus. Venus appears because the emotions are likewise muddled.

There are two snakes in this card. Each snake speaks a separate language. These languages are not intelligible to one another. Therefore there is great confusion. The story of the curse of unintelligible tongues has been told many times in many ways.

Just behind the swords are two triangles. The lower triangle, which stands in the background, is the abyss. It is the cosmic night, the place of the formless silence, the place of the potential of all things. The upper triangle is white light. This is the way out of the dilemma and represents higher consciousness. The central sword, which is relatively straight, but split, has a hilt which is intact. This hilt is reaching toward the light. As it stretches, the sword will unify. At that time there will be one point, one language.

The viewer is looking for the point. Consciousness must be stretched to find it.

Eight of Wind: Power Shield

Divinatory Meaning

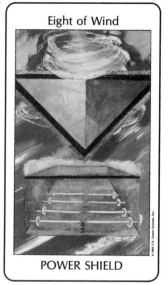

Eight of Wind

POWER SHIELD

Indecision leads to a sense of imprisonment; energy is wasted; there are external obstacles; you feel disillusioned; go into retreat; do not fear solitude; you will find that empowerment comes through surrendering yourself to the higher way of love; if you surrender yourself to love, you will become clear, you will become internally empowered.

Meditation

Jupiter in Gemini
The fight matters not
Interference from without will continue forever
Retreat
Withdraw
A time to make Peace.

Interpretation

It is time to stop arguing with your Self, time to stop arguing with others. At the Eight of Wind, you cease to persist in matters of the intellect and in any other kind of contests. There is no point in continuing. Interference from without seems to continually interrupt your progress.

How will you respond to the interference you perceive? The best method is to listen to your Inner Voice. Listen to the message of the Great Spirit, the flow of the cosmic will. Do not be thrown off course by apparent interference. Do not get caught up in obstacles. The interference and the obstacles are only lessons to show you the right path. Learn from, but do not get bogged down by, reviewing your situation again and again. The fact is that you will most likely not come to a decision on the matter at hand through an analytical process. It is time to trust. It is time to get out of "doingness" and into "beingness."

At the Eight of Wind, you have formed fairly clear and accurate ideas. At this point, thinking too much, continually mulling it over— getting caught in the Veil of Spinning Intellect, the onslaught of too many ideas at once—will complicate and obscure your clarity. That which is true has already separated from that which is false. The two versions of reality have already polarized in your subconscious mind, and now, at the level of rational thought, you have abstracted them into truth and falsehood. You *know* which way is right. You must make certain admissions to your Self. Now that you know truth from falsehood, do not dwell on the subject. You will only dwell your Self into the ground.

It is time to release mental strain and surrender to the truth. One way of doing this is to retreat for a while to consider your Inner Voice. Listen through meditation, not through analysis.

As you withdraw, do not fear solitude. Fear of solitude is the fifth natural enemy. There is great reward in deliberately detaching to consider the matter at hand. If you do not find what you are seeking within, you will never find it without. Remember that what you are looking for is what you are looking with. Thus, in a sense, the external interference you perceive is really not external at all. It comes from your own inner blocks.

The path of the Eight is known as the path of Perfect Intelligence because it is primordial and self-contained intelligence. It is intelligence which is original and set apart: the *a priori* intelligence of the cosmic or universal mind. It is that which we know to be true as opposed to that which is growing and imperfect. It is the intelligence of the spirit, that which is perfect. The intelligence of science can never be perfect. Its very nature is to be improved upon continually. Scientific intelligence always changes. A priori intelligence remains true in spite of constant change.

At the Eight of Wind, the sword—the analytical struggle—is laid down. The battle is abandoned. Abandonment of the battle means, in a sense, the loss of self-consciousness.

At this point, you may feel like you are losing your intellectual ability. This is because, in the recent past, you have accepted your intellectual pursuits as your identity. But, temporarily relinquishing self-consciousness does not mean that you have lost your mental powers. It merely means that you are beginning to put your intellectual pursuits into the proper perspective which is *spiritual* in nature. It means that you are beginning to abandon shallower pursuits in the quest for deeper meaning. You are beginning to reorient your life toward the one true path.

As soon as you abandon your fight with competing realities, a new and powerful Power Shield is given to you. This is the deep and lasting protective shield of truth, love and conviction. The origin of the shield comes from truth. The power of the shield comes from conviction. The stamina of the shield comes from love. With the acceptance of this gift, you receive the gift of divine reason, which is the most important gift of the suit of Wind. This gift helps you to transcend the analytical overlays—the spinnings of your mind—that keep you awake at night. Your Power Shield is formed from a new perspective: a spiritual perspective. You must be courageous. You are on the right path. You must trust your Power Shield to protect you as you seek meaning and the deepest and purest truth.

At the Eight of Wind, you will become conscious of a hovering energy. That energy is the whispering of the spirit of the Wind. It is telling you that it is time to confront the self-created and self-perpetuating monsters of your intellect. This may be frightening, but, after all, those monsters do not exist apart from your own subconscious. Remember you can choose to receive the gift of divine reason, which will help you overcome the struggle to analyze that which escapes you, that which, in any event, can never be understood through the methods of science. The gift of divine reason is your Power Shield. This is the shield of truth, love and conviction which no sword can assail.

Card Symbology: The Eight of Wind card shows an inverted triangle hovering over an open box containing eight swords. The box resembles a lidless coffin. In this depiction, the swords are laid to rest. The battle has been halted.

The inverted triangle hovering over the swords represents a triangle on the Tree of Life. The green segment represents emotion, the orange segment represents the intellect and the purple segment represents the spirit. This triangle is the Power Shield. The triangle is floating in front of a black triangle which represents a passageway or tunnel. This is a tunnel to the truth.

The spiraling energy is the energy of the spirit of the ether: the Great Spirit. In that divine Wind is the message of truth. This symbolizes the temporary relinquishment of self-consciousness, the beginning of separation and re-grouping.

Nine of Wind: The Screen

Divinatory Meaning ————

You are threatened; you may appear to others as threatening; you fear cruelty, judgment and pain; you feel a sense of anger; there is a tendency to go into seclusion, but this is not the time for withdrawal; you must enter the world and atone; embrace love and you will discover freedom.

Nine of Wind

THE SCREEN

Meditation ————————————

Mars in Gemini
Danger, desolation and despair
no rest—not even in Dreams!
Seclusion is the enemy!
The Self is the enemy!
Come back! Come back!
There are those—so many—
who contrive to throw
roses
at your feet.

Interpretation ————————————————————————————

You have been hurt. You have hurt others. Now it is time to confront your own Shadow, to understand the darkness which has bound you, thereby to enlighten it. This process begins with acceptance and atonement. You must make amends, atone, accept and reenter the warmth of the circle of humanity. There you will discover love.

In a sense, you have found that it has been easier to withdraw than to live in the world. It has been easier to function alone than to negotiate with others. It has been easier to seek solitude than to communicate with family and friends.

This is because you have struggled—and sadness has been the result. You have experienced the threat of deaths, both great and small, as well as the threat of judgment. There have been times when you felt there was no rest from danger, not even in dreams. You have experienced desolation and despair. Not only have you felt victimized, but you, yourself, have victimized. You have inflicted cruelty and been responsible for great and small deaths. You, yourself, have inflicted pain and sorrow. As you have suffered, you have been the cause of suffering.

As a child, for example, hurtful remarks came to you. It is your misfortune—but also the seed of your growth—to remember this cruelty. In sadness and anger, you recall your innocence and how it was robbed. But, no one has been more cruel to you than you have been to yourself. You have accused yourself, recriminated yourself, hated yourself, punished yourself. You have become your own convictor. You have become your own judge.

Were you surprised when, in bouts of anger or rage, the same hurt that you experienced flowed through you to hurt others? Were you surprised when the same remarks that hurt you so deeply came out of your own mouth? Have you felt a deep sense of cynicism? Have you forced yourself to withdraw to consider what has happened?

The anger you have experienced is one of the three great fires of the world. The other two are greed and recklessness. These great fires—anger, greed and recklessness—are the cause of the disruption of harmony. Withdrawal is often necessary before we can understand this.

At the Nine of Wind, you have been in withdrawal. You have gone into seclusion. You have known solitude. But now you must emerge. Seclusion is the sixth natural enemy. It is time to atone, to repent, and to re-enter the group where you will find love. You are now ready for love, to give and receive love in its truest sense. To re-enter, atone for your grief, for the grief you have caused, and begin to attune on a higher level.

At the Nine, it is time to open your eyes in the face of danger. Patiently analyze your situation, exercise clarity. Exercise strength. New life is won through suffering. Turn your cruelty into kindness. Be kind to others. Be kind to yourself. It is time to convert your anger, greed and recklessness into harmonious behavior. Work through the sadness, let it go, and focus on universal abundance. The world can be a place of harmony and beauty. Change your thought patterns. Remember that all of your thought patterns and actions affect others as well as yourself. Your every thought is a thing. As Ernest Holmes says, the world is a mirror which reflects back that which we think into it.[4]

When you feel that those with whom you come into contact hold a negative opinion of you, know that they are only reflecting your own inward view of yourself. As you become a more positive person, those around you will reflect your thought patterns and convey back to you a positive image. As in a mirror, you see yourself as others see you.

The path of the Nine is known as the path of Absolute or Perfect Intelligence. Nine makes alterations and improves and perfects the design. Here we are working on the design of Self. Here we are improving the design of our active and reactive thought patterns.

An important way of tuning in at this time is to remember and record your night dreams. In these dreams, you will discover important directives and teachers. Beginning a dream journal would be an auspicious undertaking. You are not just "being." You are "becoming." With every breath, you are reborn. Every moment is a new beginning. At this moment, you have the ability to become that which you will.

Being in the world, especially in a world that is constantly changing, takes strength and energy, vigor and vitality. It takes a constant influx of lifeforce. Further, it takes a deep sense of self-confidence. This you can develop, beginning at this very moment. Change your actions. Emit love. Emit beauty. You are loving. You are beautiful.

---

[4]Ernest Holmes, *The Science of Mind* (New York: G. P. Putnam's Sons, 1938).

You are clean, clear and pure. All at once, you are so many things. It is time to focus on grace.

Card Symbology: The Nine of Wind, the screen, shows the dark or shadowy part of the Self. It is a screen that writhes with phantoms. But you learn at the Nine that, like a television set, you can turn it on and off at will. You can study and confront the forms of your nightmares at your own leisure. Such phantoms need not control you in any way.

The screen symbolizes that you have been taught to fear the dark, even when you cannot make out what phantoms lurk there. You can overcome this conditioning and face your darkness.

Your Power Shield, which supports The Screen from below is your strength and your guide. Your Power Shield is growing cleaner and stronger in the Nine. It is your antenna.

The Screen symbolizes the fact that you are in school. Your teachers appear upon The Screen. Do not fear your teachers. Make friends with your teachers in order to learn from them. Your teachers are ready to go to work for you in order to power your creativity. But you must first go to work for your Self. Turn on The Screen. Accept the lessons. Tune into your dreams.

Ten of Wind: The Way of the Cross

Divinatory Meaning ⎯⎯⎯⎯⎯⎯

Death comes to the old way of thinking; a new perspective arises; you have learned to think in the ways of nature and your thoughts are clear; you are transcending old patterns of thought which have kept you caged in a reality which no longer serves you; you feel as if your spirit is rising on the winds of change.

Ten of Wind

THE WAY OF THE CROSS

Meditation ──────────────────────────────

Sun in Gemini
You have screamed all night
But the Army is with you
There is no need to fear

Resolute:
a swim in the Sea
a walk through the Rain
pushing through the pain
to Rebirth

Resolved:
Going Warring brings Ill
Going Somewhere brings Gain
What you thought was Ruin
was Name fighting Name.

Interpretation ──────────────────────────

At the Ten of Wind, it is time for resignation. It is time to resign your Self to a higher form of thinking: divine reason. This is how you will be able to retune to your original intellect which is the original and pure thinking of the cosmic or universal mind.

In solitude, when you withdraw from the group energy of your fellow human beings, reason can become divorced from reality. Logic can spin off on itself—the Veil of the Spinning Intellect again—disrupting and disordering all harmonious energies, depositing you in the Veil of Massive Confusion. But rest assured, you are on the verge of a new, deeper and more beautiful harmony.

At the Ten of Wind, you undergo a ritual death. This is a sacrifice for the sake of the higher cause. That higher cause is truth, love and conviction. You must sacrifice those patterns and forms within you that do not promote the higher cause. All that which is base or harmful must be purged.

Resignation to truth, sacrificing for the sake of truth, love and conviction, is The Way of the Cross. At the Ten, you are at The Way of the Cross. To arrive at The Way of the Cross, purge your Self of all unworthy thoughts, methods and procedures. In order to do this, work in the realm beyond the intellect. Grope your way in darkness.

Travel alone. You will be forced, there, to face your fears, to confront frightening phantoms. You will learn that the phantom forces in your own darkness are your greatest teachers. They are there to help you. Confront them squarely and you will come to know them. In knowing them, you will begin to love them. Eventually, this path will take you to the realm of higher understanding, the realm of divine reason, the realm of wisdom.

When you arrive at this point (after you have cleaned out all of your "closets," both figuratively and literally), you are at the path of the Ten, Resplendent Intelligence. This is the path that illuminates the splendor of all light. That is because the tenth path is the path of wisdom. Wisdom transcends limited intellectual spinning. This is because wisdom necessarily involves intellectual, emotional and spiritual understanding. Wisdom is a balanced position. It is the original intellect shining. It is not a game of the rational mind.

In the realm of divine reason, or wisdom, the intellect (conditioned force) and love (active form) have merged in a continuous circle. The intellect also merges into a circle with the will (unconditioned force). There is no longer a struggle between parents (love and will) and child (the intellect). There is no more polarization. Everything contains its opposite, but there is no contradiction. All the world is in the process of becoming.

With this knowledge in hand, you move to a new level of understanding. Having this new sense of things means that your Wheel of Fortune (see Key X) is about to turn. You are cycling. Your creativity is about to open up in a whole new way. Since you are confronting major change, however, the object is to stay centered. Stand in the middle of the cross—the fulcrum of the spirit, the emotions, the intellect and the body—not off to one side. Stand in the middle of the turning wheel of change. If you maintain this position, which is the position of divine reason, of wisdom, of the original intellect, of the universal mind, no amount of spinning will throw you, and you will be freed to create within polarized forces without being thrown off course by the polarization process. All is one. All is being, just as all is becoming. There is no contradiction. Center in the process of movement. Center and balance in your spirit, your emotions, your intellect and your body and you will be enabled to move with the changes. Move from a position of truth, love and conviction and you will remain stable. This is The Way of the Cross.

Card Symbology: In the Ten of Wind, the triangular Power Shield of truth, love and conviction at the bottom of the card becomes the impetus behind change. It is powered by the new energy of the intellect, the intellect exalted. The intellect becomes exalted with the discovery and internalization of divine reason.

The television cube from the Nine of Wind now unfolds and becomes The Way of the Cross. This is because after you have dealt with the monsters on your subconscious screen, they become your teachers and your friends. Opening up to fear and embracing your own phantoms and monsters opens up the possibility for balance between the four directions. This balance, together with sacrifice to maintain that balance, is The Way of the Cross.

The Swords which have been prevalent in all of the cards of the suit of wind until this point have now become Feathers. These are the feathers of transformation. They are directed at a target of red, yellow and black. Red represents Mercury: the intellect. Yellow is for Tiphareth: love. Black is for Binah: the yin force of the universe. The target is a representation of The Wheel of Fortune. This indicates that your Wheel of Fortune is about to turn.

Wind Father: The Will to Transcend

Divinatory Meaning ─────────────

An analytical period; thought is very powerful; the power of the intellect is bounded by neither time nor space; your ideas are brilliant and highly rational, but as you move through intense mental processes, do not lose touch with yourself as a spiritual, loving and physical being.

Father

WIND

Meditation ─────────────────────────────

Taurus, Gemini
A shooting Meteor with
Flaming Intellect
flying behind a clear course
of Reason; a hero at abstraction and realization
Will and connection with Spirit
Subtle
the superior authority of the Higher Teacher

Founding Father
Fire Father in Wind
caught/between heaven
and clouds
wrapped by the shroud
he wove
while thinking that somehow
making sense of things
could wind up as a
linear matrix

His breakthrough comes in knowing cycles
Nature forever obeys
when her Law is observed
and Love is the Law, Love under Will

The Fire Father in Wind can confront his own process
and he *can* make a change.

Interpretation ────────────────────────

The Wind Father is the power of idea and motion, the spirit of the
intellect, the flame of mind. He is the power of Wind. When the Wind
Father raises his sword—the power of his mind—flames leap, waves
rise, leaves scatter.

Wind Father's intelligence is highly analytical and his precision
is exacting. He stands as a firm and frugal judge of the ideas put
before him. His judgment, however, may be informed by one of two
directions, depending on his level of spiritual attunement and commitment. In the baser state, Wind Father is informed only by mundane

status quo expectations. His judgment will be conservative, in alignment with dominant social values. This Wind Father's reasoning is perfect, but based wholly on popular science. Thus, his advice may have its limits. He may dismiss anything that cannot be validated by scientific research, and such research is, by definition, limited. The less developed Wind Father overlays analytical system upon analytical system, devoting much time to evaluation. He may become defensive about his ideas. In the most harmless of negative cases, he may seem full of "hot air." In the worst cases, since he represents the *power* of the intellect, he could become an undeviating ruler, fierce and offensive, causing chaos in the name of order. He is only fierce because he fears, however since he represents the power of motion, he may be violent and terrible in his fear, totally selfish and cruel. Without the controlling factor of empathy, Wind Father has the potential to rage like the dreaded Wind of 120 Days that has buried Iranian villages with an incredible force of flying sand.

In his more complacent mode, the underdeveloped Wind Father may slash fruitlessly at air, drawing conclusions that are totally useless, or building level after level of analysis, until his conclusions are completely removed from the object of his contemplation. In fact, he may pride himself in such games.

The more developed Wind Father knows that "analysis presupposes a corpse." At a higher level of attunement, he is perfectly informed by the divine mind. He is informed by the cosmic will and acts and judges accordingly.

How well the Wind Father can apply his vast stores of knowledge to his daily life, and indeed to others through supplying his intellectual leadership, depends upon how well he works within the guidance of the Great Spirit. His motivation is of critical importance. He must understand the divine nature of his own unique contribution. He must understand that he is not the source, but the channel. Further, he must transcend the expectations or seeming requirements of popular culture, which may be his most difficult task. Wind Father has a responsibility to use his wonderful capacity to move humanity's thinking forward, not to defend outmoded or harmful ideas. This means that the Wind Father must learn how to "think on his feet," always aligning himself with divine and sacred values. Accordingly, he must learn to judge the relevance and *goodness* of ideas, which entails developing a "moving" and free form analytical process. This process need be no less rigorous than the scientific method.

If Wind Father can come to understand the patterns of his own intellect, and begin to align himself with the Wind of divine reason, he will have the capacity to move to incredible heights. He must understand that human science is growing. There is much that cannot be explained via a rational, analytical process. Science is, by nature, imperfect, but truth is, by nature, perfect. In his exalted state, Wind Father thinks according to the higher truth.

To discover, utilize and apply his fullest ability, the Wind Father needs to tune in to his *conscience*. Of the product of his analytical process, he should ask: Is it safe? Is it good? Is it important? Does it matter? Will it preserve and enhance the Mother Earth? Will it relieve the suffering of humanity?

The challenge of the Wind Father is to realize that his greatest strength will be found in softness. Softness entails receptivity. Using too much strength (to defend or promote a position) is a dangerous weakness which can lead not only to getting lost, but to terrible deeds. This is a time to build a "moving" analytical system, and thereby to build a quiet confidence. This confidence is built by seeing anew. To get a new perspective, Wind Father tunes into the unconscious stream and he attunes to the dictates of his conscience. He asks himself, how do I *feel?* (see *I Ching:* Hexagram 9: The Lesser Nourisher).

Card Symbology: The Wind Father appears as merging his spiritual and physical selves. He is learning that the spirit contains the body. He is learning to trust a moving process.

The energy of the bull he rides is still wild. Being wild, the bull can take him in any direction. The bull is the lunar bull which signifies rebirth through death, that is, massive internal change. For the Wind Father, changing involves surrendering his thoughts to the universal mind. His task is to surrender to the process, to relax and to let the bull's energy flow through him until he understands it. Only in this way, through allowing himself to be taught by the bull, will he be able to appreciate and come to love the bull. When the Wind Father is motivated by love, the bull is willingly yoked.

Wind Father holds the yoke in his hand. Holding the yoke in his hand means that he is capable of controlling the direction of his own thought. He does this through the practice of entering the state of dreamless sleep while still awake: meditation. In meditation, he programs his pattern of thought. He learns, through focusing on the eternal—that which is unspecified and unbounded—how to yoke his waking consciousness to its source in the cosmic consciousness or universal mind. In such a way, Wind Father opens his heart to divine reason.

As he discovers divine reason, he is able to transcend the divisions of Self on the wings of transcendence, the wings of the holy ghost, which are waiting above. The Wings are marked by spheres of yin and yang integrated. These are the spheres of neverending circles of radiant darkness and limitless light.

Wind Mother: The Eastern Threshold

Divinatory Meaning

An intellectual process is completed; there is a sense of resolution and commitment, triumph, clarification, objectivity and rationality; a time of thinking globally rather than locally; at this time emotional balance is the key to success; embrace your loving nature and you will have many followers.

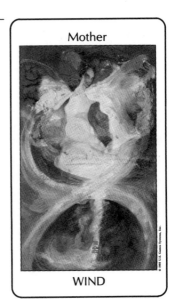

Meditation

Virgo, Libra
Water Mother in Wind
Intellectually Pure
the Clear, Conscious Pursuit
of Idea
Intensely uncompromising
the Wind Mother
is a keen observer
quick and confident

Ahead of the Flow
intent and brilliant
razorsharp and ardent
her knowledge sails
beyond that which
is known
her sharp edge cuts channels
where none have gone

Graceful/Stylish
she wields her Sword
beyond concession
breaks the screen of oppression
and emerges clean
clear
pure
and deserving.

Interpretation

The Wind Mother is true to discovery. She is pure and triumphant
in her transmission of truth. She is steadfast and sees divine reason
as the highest and purest of lights. Science, she knows, is imperfect
and growing. Whatever conclusions humanity arrives at, sacred truth
will remain sacred truth.

As the clear, conscious perception of idea—and the perfect juxtaposition of the intellectual process with emotional understanding—
the Wind Mother illuminates the universe and liberates the potential
of the universal mind.

Her observations are intensely keen and she is confident in her
assessments. Her actions are just; she is uncompromising. She is
clever, subtle and quick-witted, sharp as an ax in her perception. But
this does not mean she feels no love.

Wind Mother is a loving entity. The traditional interpretation of
Wind Mother as barren and emotionally empty, or as a woman in
mourning, represents only the narrowest interpretation of Wind
Mother's character. She is a great teacher and vast in her ways of
knowing. She teaches us how we are led astray by our thought patterns and how to transcend our bondage. She knows the truth. The
truth sets her free. She knows that true freedom exists in aligning

one's internal will with the cosmic will. In learning this, we stand at the Eastern Threshold: the threshold of transcendence. It is true that much of Wind Mother's knowledge has arisen out of her difficult struggle. With her brilliant mind, she has sensed shortcomings in traditional methods of thinking and, as the courageous soul that she is, she has focused public attention on this matter. Thus she has had to struggle against ridicule. Teaching has not been easy for her. There were times that she cried. But ultimately, she succeeded in affecting the universal processes of understanding in her realm. Wind Mother is successful because she is centered between the great processes of spirit, intellect and emotion.

As a teacher of spirits, Wind Mother has many devoted followers, or students, but they often keep a certain distance from her. Sometimes they are intimidated by her exceptional powers of mind. This is due to the fact that she is a strong character, her character having been built out of her struggle to know truth. Her strength of mind enhances her tremendous grace. That is why Wind Mother may be, in addition to everything else, a beautiful dancer.

The Wind Mother is just as contented in withdrawing from the world of humanity as in participating. She is as capable in dancing alone as in dancing with others. If she does not focus on goals when she withdraws, however, she runs the risk of sagging under too much intellectualizing. She may risk sinking into narrow-mindedness. If this happens, she may succumb to making rash judgments. Since she is so powerful, she can even be dangerous. In general, however, her foresight, prudence and loving nature are her safeguards. Her other safeguard is to remember she is always in the process of becoming. Therefore she always needs to keep clear goals. Focusing on clear goals keeps her emotional state protected and intact (See *I Ching*: Hexagram 28: Excess).

Card Symbology: Wind Mother is the wings of transcendence or transformation. She is the guardian of the Eastern Threshold, which is the threshold of transcendence.

She transcends the division between dark and light. She represents the merger, full and complete. She holds the reigns, which are her yoke, and spins them in figure eights, representing infinite transition. She has yoked together the inner (subconscious) and the outer (conscious) minds. The tail of her yoke goes down into the portal of transcendence. Wind Mother controls this portal. The feather at the end of her yoke is the feather of transformation.

Wind Brother: Warrior of Mind

Divinatory Meaning ——————

You may feel torn between two ideals or ideas which seem to be of equal weight or value; go deep within to find the answer—meditate—you will not ease this conflict through continual analysis; if you find your head spinning with too many ideas, find a teacher to help you focus.

Brother

WIND

Meditation ————————————————————

Capricorn, Aquarius
Wind Brother
Wind in its own element
comes and goes
and blows again
torn—
the Pure Intellect
Brilliant! Illuminating!
phenomenal in its original form
warring on its spinning form
when it gets into layers upon layers
and wars with the boundless
Powers of the Mind
idea/design
aspiring to Construct/Destroy:

which channel to Sail?
which Sails to furl?

His children may leap
like feral beasts
squalling into Obscurity

with a quick tongue
and cunning
out of reach of defeat
he constantly
shifts his stance

elastic elusive
this glib Wind Brother
allies himself
with the nearest element
and hopes for a ride
it is only that he cannot decide—
for himself—
which way the Wind blows

the answer to his consternation
is to look within for integration.

Interpretation

Though he has made great progress in his thinking, the Wind Brother
may still find himself spinning. There is more than one direction to
choose from and he must take the right course of action. He must
now integrate all that he has learned. In order to reach a state of
integration, serious inward examination is necessary.

The Wind Brother carries out the combined intellectual energy
of his parents. He has his father's incredible energy and the potential
for his mother's balance. He is the windy part of the intellect, incredibly brilliant, but blowing this way and that.

He is so smart—and attuned to the farthest reaches of thinking—
that any one of his ideas would be highly successful. But because he
has so many ideas, he may have trouble choosing.

Further, his ideas may be very fine, but they may be removed
from everyday practicality. Therefore he may seem unreachable or
unapproachable on a practical level.

He is a Warrior of Mind—developing complicated strategies and intellectual battle plans. He is a theoretician—always on the forefront. In fact, Wind Brother may be on several fronts at once—and brilliant on every one.

The Wind Brother is brave, dashing and domineering. His heart is clean and full of courage. He is quick to defend or to fight, and he is fierce in action, but, if he is not committed to his ideas, he may have no staying power.

In the worst case, he is a pompous boaster who engages in thoughtless action and enjoys a sense of tyranny over the weaker. He may be stormy and out of control. His ideas may reduce air to the most minute geometrical patterns, but he may have no plan for his life.

While he is clever and rational, the overall purpose of his existence may seem clouded and he may even feel indifferent to his own ideas. He will soar to the highest levels and ideals in one moment and, in the next, he may crash to the deepest levels of despair. He may prefer the appearance of courage to the real thing.

In general, the Wind is favorable for Wind Brother. He needs to count his successes in small matters and solidify his goals. He can come to know himself, and thereby solidify his goals, by looking inward. He needs to look deeply to reconcile that which seems polarized. Holding the thought of dualities keeps him thrashing. He must understand that the physical is contained within the spiritual. There is no duality. There is no contradiction. A visit to a Master Teacher could be a great deal of help at this time. The teacher will reiterate the Wind Brother's spiritual, intellectual and physical successes and help him to formulate immediate and long-term goals (see *I Ching:* Hexagram 57: Willing Submission). The teacher knows that Wind Brother is forever in the process of becoming.

Card Symbology: The highest commitment of the Wind Brother is to the universal mind. Therefore, he can appear to be totally ungrounded. He may seem to be slashing at the air.

He appears as dead, because he is changing. He represents not only the "corpse" that "analysis presupposes," but the eternal connection with spirit. He is a skeleton, because he can choose his own "skin" by way of his level of attunement and his pattern of thinking. The skeleton is merely his brilliant capacity. He transforms himself into that which he understands.

Wind Brother requires the balancing aspects of Fire (spirit), Water (emotion) and Earth (matter) in order to become whole and move to his greatest productivity. To understand the importance, or lack thereof, in what he is attempting to accomplish, he must become more attuned to the results of his thought pattern both on the spiritual and physical planes.

The energy of the card demonstrates movement and power. Such force can be used in a highly positive manner. Wind Brother represents not only the movement of the analytical process at its highest velocity, but also the potential insight to transcend old forms of analysis. Wind Brother has the intellectual capacity to tune into the deepest levels of the universal mind. The Wind Brother does not just slash the Wind. He is slicing a portal into the realms of the dark layers of his own subconscious mind. He is ready to confront his own intellectual process in order to move to a higher level of thinking which will better benefit humanity and afford a deep and harmonious internal satisfaction. He is moving toward a new level of spiritual commitment.

Wind Sister: Truth

Divinatory Meaning

The truth has risen to the surface; you may feel that you are engaged in battle; you may feel that you are fighting against traditional notions or values; this is not an easy time but your ideas are correct; stick to your convictions and you will eventually know victory.

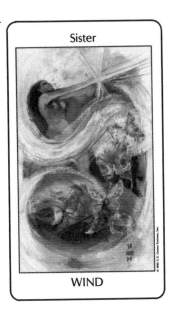

Sister

WIND

Meditation

Capricorn, Aquarius, Pisces
Wind Sister
Earth Sister in Wind
Angel of the Mind
Priestess of Idea
Wind Sister
has earned her athame

Draws down the ethereal and
yokes the force
grounding the idea
for or against the Dominant Voice
the challenge of Mind
on Matter

Sharp-witted Wind Sister
wields her athame
She alone knows the flight patterns
of war hawks and doves of peace.

Interpretation

The Wind Sister has recognized Truth within. The Truth has not resulted from Imprinting, Parroting, Social Conditioning, Ego Reification, Clever Demonstration, or Spinning Intellectual Thoughts. Truth represents the Intellect in its original form. It is Truth based on the highest conscience. The Wind Sister acts on this truth, applies it to her life.

The Wind Sister is the Priestess of Idea: idea materialized, idea taking form in the physical world. She has tremendous follow-through ability because she has balanced the dark and light forces within.

She represents the stabilization of that which is volatile in the intellectual realm. She stabilizes through recognizing her own pure and original intellect which she has learned to separate from intellectual games. In such games, one learns to mimic or parrot, or to respond cleverly in order to meet social expectations. Wind Sister has been through these games and has outgrown them. She is an original thinker and thus she is the greatest manifestation of the intellect. As such, she wields an awesome power on Earth.

Usually, Wind Sister is wise and dextrous. She is a great diplomat. She can mediate effectively and settle controversies. This is because she is continually aware of her own conscience, which is her guiding principle, and therefore aligned with original Truth. This is the secret of her thought process.

Wind Sister has a lofty spirit. Her spirit is free because she is aligned with the cosmic will. Her spirit is light because she acts according to the dictates of her conscience. She knows that she must follow her own bent, wherever it leads her. If it leads her into the dominant culture, she will be its greatest defender. If it leads her into the counterculture, she will likewise "defend it to the hilt." She is ready to charge in and defend her ideas, and she will be listened to. What she says rings of Truth.

If her ideas go against the status quo, she may be regarded as the Princess of Trouble Brewing, or the Daughter of Rough Terrain. But, because she is so articulate, and well-loved, she will almost always be successful if she sticks to her ideas.

In the best case, she has fresh intellectual clarity and will be followed by many. If she gets off her original track, she may be stern and revengeful—rebellious—and her logic may become destructive. This only occurs when she gives in to her frustration. Sometimes she cannot understand why the world seems so blind. If she feels this way, she needs to turn inward to examine the roots of her rebellion.

The challenge for Wind Sister is to start at the beginning, remain true to her Self, and build upon that Truth diligently. Freedom from anxiety comes from following one's own path with a great fervor. The wise one, starting from small things, accumulates a great heap of merit (see I Ching: Hexagram 46: Ascension).

Card Symbology: Wind Sister has freed the pent-up butterflies of immortality and transformation. These butterflies were trapped at the Four of Wind by the intellectual processes of social convention. In order to free creativity, and thus the immmortality represented by the butterflies, Wind Sister had to effectively combine messages from the subconscious and the higher consciousness and attune to her conscience. She has moved through all the Seven Veils of Intellect: Imprinting, Parroting, Social Conditioning, the Clever Show, Ego

Reification, Spinning Intellect and Massive Confusion to the original intellect. She has apprehended the universal mind. Becoming attuned to the original intellect has taken a great deal of inner strength.

Now Wind Sister slashes her own opening through the portal of thought to the material plane. Her sword points to the One of Earth. This indicates that the intellectual fervor is coming to rest and now there is a chance for successful creativity. Creating successfully entails attuning to the universal mind and applying the lessons learned there to everyday life.

❖   ❖   ❖

CHAPTER NINE

Earth

Shields
Pentacles
Coins
North
Wood, Metal, Bone, and Stones
Celestial Orbs
Stars and Planets
Moons
ringing round themselves in Inner and Outer Space
beginnings/endings/endlessly
The Body, Birth and Death
The Dark of Midnight
The Sacred Year in Winter's Dream
Browns, Russets and Green Things
for the continual turn of the Seasons
Deer, Bear, Boar and Bull
Burrowing Snakes making caverns in Earth
Direction of the Vision and the Voice
Unraveling the Holy Mysteries
Engaging in the Great Work

Dirt beneath our feet
We walk in packs
social
We build shelters
useful

We trade coins
and feather up the nest.

The Path through Earth

*Earth holds, protects, cradles, nurtures, feeds and smothers. The
body, made of Earth, is the form that holds the Fire, Water and
Wind of life; Earth is the vehicle for the spirit and the breath, the
manifestation of lifeforce; limitless substance . . .*

The Earth itself, like the Wind, is the offspring of the elemental universal forces of Fire and Water. The Earth is seen as the daughter of
the elemental forces.

The Earth is inert *form*, female and receptive, providing a body
for the forces of intellect, emotion, spirit, will and lifeforce. Earth is
the limitless substance of which all things physical are composed.

Earth indicates all physical form. Physical forms are vessels containing lifeforce. In other words, Earth is the form in which life, the
force, is embodied. Mystics say: force is *ensouled* in form. To ensoul
means to endow with a soul. The soul—while it cannot be discerned
materially or physically—thinks, wills, and has spiritual and emotional force. The soul is the vital or essential component of life.

The ultimate etymology of the word "soul" is uncertain. However, one of the forms of the word is "sol." It is interesting to examine
the connections between these two concepts (soul and sol) in that,
in Latin, the root *sol* indicates Sun, Earth and alone. In many languages, Sun indicates "sound," to emit. Earth means "ear," "to hear,"
"to receive." Symbolically, the spirit—the Light of the Sun—ensouls
itself in Earth (the planet and the body) where it manifests through
breath and sound.

Another form of sun is son, denoting offspring. (Son also is the
root form of "sound.") We, as children of the universe, are the sons
and daughters of "Sun" and "Earth." As sons, we emit. As daughters,
we receive. The meaning of daughter (*Dochter, doch*) is *receptacle* or *to
receive* (Greek). Daughter also means *to milk* (*dhugh*/Sanskrit). We in-
tertwine and reproduce. We nourish the young. Lifeforce passes from
us into our offspring. We pass the wand from generation to generation. This is akin to passing the spirit or *the force*. Thus, as the sons
and daughters of Sun and Earth, we are force ensouled in form. We
are form containing force. We are the vessels for new forms which
are, in turn, ensouled by force.

And while we are the sons and daughters, brothers and sisters of Earth, and therefore inextricably connected, each one of us ultimately journeys the path through incarnation *alone*. This is the solitary path of the soul. But, the physical world must be experienced, as we shall see, *before the homeward journey is begun*.

Earth is our *gift*. We find ourselves honored with the exquisitely sensual experience of living on the planet. It comes as a gift that we experience Her joys and wonders. It is also a gift to experience Her quaking, Her tossing and turning. The cracks that open in Her surface crack open our psyches. She shakes us into seeing. Such physical breakage can become the greatest pathway to the inner self.

On the path through Earth, we learn that it is mostly the structures we, ourselves, erect that fall down and hurt us when Earth quakes. We learn to build our foundation upon the most solid and enduring ground.

One of Earth: Form

Divinatory Meaning ───────────

You are receiving the gift of productivity; something new is happening to you physically or materially; you are engaged in promising new endeavors; you are beginning to move toward a state of true external success and internal harmony; in order to arrive at a state of wealth, you must pay constant attention to the state of your spirit, heart and mind as you work through your daily routines.

One of Earth

FORM

Meditation ──────────────────────────────

Aries, Taurus, Gemini
Resurrection
Welcome to the world of Pure Joy!

Cosmic Creation
Celestial Terrestrial
Material Worldly Sensual
Here and Now

Earth is strong and accepting
Supporting Sustaining
Mountain stillness

Landing Lighting
Grounding.

Interpretation

This is the beginning of material gain and physical delight. All matter in the known universe becomes available to you at the point of the One of Earth. As such, this card represents a change for the better in the physical body, the beginnings of financial gain, the acquisition of material objects.

When you are at this point, you are in a state of readiness to live in internal and external wealth. Your body and soul are moving toward a state of *harmonium* (harmonic union). Everything you need is at hand. At this point, you know that wealth—which represents an exalted state spiritually, emotionally, intellectually and physically—ought to be the natural condition. In order to attain and retain such wealth, however, you have learned that you must respect, and not deplete, the principle source of your wealth which is balance in wholeness.

Balance in wholeness means remaining centered in your life in the arenas of the elements: Fire (your spirit), Water (your emotions), Wind (your intellect), Earth (your body). If too much emphasis is put on any one of these areas, to the exclusion of other areas, you will fall out of balance and unhappiness will result.

In order to understand your present position, you must also understand that the four elements listed above are forces and forms of energy. Fire/will(force)/spirit corresponds to electrical energy. Water/intuition/emotions corresponds to liquid energy. Wind/intellect/reason corresponds to gaseous energy. Earth/body/substance corresponds to solid energy. You have all these different energetic patterns available to you to use as you design your life. These energetic media are means through which you *become*, that is, through which you begin to actualize your potential, to create order, meaning and goals out of what may appear to be chaos.

As you accessed the electrical energy of elemental Fire, you learned that things are related to each other. In accessing the liquid energy of elemental Water, you learned the keys to discovering how and why such things are related. In elemental Wind, you developed the capacity to understand the complexity and depth and layered realities of these relationships. Now, in elemental Earth, you manifest your knowledge concretely. You bring everything you know to bear in actual, concrete physical form. In the element of Earth, you begin to apply—in a practical way—everything you have learned.

You have already learned that, with each step you take, you create your own reality. There are many manifestations of layers of the subconscious, the waking consciousness, and the higher consciousness, all of which are reality. You are not limited to any one perception of reality. You are not limited to acting in any one certain way. It is a great advantage to be able to stand back and view the whole branching tree of experience.

On one dimension, the tree which you need to view represents the Tree of Knowledge. In contemporary culture, this tree is frequently equated with "science." Each branch can be viewed as a "field." Those working at the forefront of each "field" are as new growth, new twigs, at the end of these branches. Sometimes these scientists are so far "out on a limb" that they lose sight of the rest of the tree, the basic overview of the Tree of Knowledge. Being highly specialized—with no time to understand or view the processes of the whole—one may easily come to feel cut off, as if one has no control over what is happening.

As a rational thinker, a "scientist" as it were, it is important to be able to move up and down all the branches of the tree, visiting the trunk regularly and even leaving the tree altogether to get the view from afar. The reason this is critical is because understanding the *context* of what one is trying to accomplish is essential not only with regard to choice of subjects of inquiry as well as in interpreting results, but to knowing that the reality in which one works is under one's control. In our world of extreme specialization, however, the view from afar is not always respected or rewarded. This is a manifestation of the shortsightedness of our culture. Nature is not just, but She is exacting, and in the long term, the view from afar will take on considerable importance.

In order to comprehend our universe, we reduce the world to its finest components. We slice apart, analyze, split, splice and recombine. We become so specialized that we barely perceive our connection to the whole. As we divide the world into its components, we can surely understand it better, but we must reconnect these parts to ensure that lifeforce remains in the world. The path to health is to rediscover the connection to the whole. The path to freedom is to rediscover how the whole is produced and reproduced both within and outside of yourself. When you know this, you will understand that you, alone, are responsible for the future, your own future as well as the collective future.

Culture is not a dead or static object to which we must answer or succumb. Culture is living form, ensouled with lifeforce, upon which each one of us—through the force of our lives—has an impact.

Think of the tree of which we are speaking as the Tree of Life. Realize that, in order to create and retain meaning and true wealth in mind, body and expression, all components of this tree must move in balance. Where there is an action, there must be a reaction. Where there is a force, there will be a form it takes, and a new force arising out of the form (and so on).

The Tree of Life represents existence. It is our body, our culture, and indeed, our Earth. At the One of Earth, we are reminded that the Earth is our living Mother, that we are one with her, and that our survival is directly related to the preservation of her resources, especially water and air. The Earth is our workground and our playground. She sustains us completely, providing all food, shelter, clothing, everything we need to survive.

We are, as individuals, no more or no less than the Earth we inhabit. We are, in a sense, parasites, as we drink Her water, breathe Her air and consume the vegetation that arises from Her soil. In another sense, we *are* Earth itself, for we are born of the mud and it is the mud to which we will return.

Consider all these factors as you formulate your plans for the new stage coming in your life. Remember that the universe is recreated at every moment. What appears to be time-connected is continuous, instantaneous expansion and contraction. With each heartbeat, we die and are reborn. With each divine breath, we are renewed.

Card Symbology: The One of Earth represents a coin in the middle of a seven-pointed star. The coin is the symbol for the Sun and the circle-cross of the four directions. The circle-cross is the symbol of the psyche in perfect equilibrium. It is a four-point analysis of the universal pattern of dawn, noon, dusk and darkness; spring, summer, autumn and winter; Wind, Fire, Water and Earth; breath, lifeforce, blood and body; insight, energy, feeling and action.

The star is the seven-pointed star of manifestation. It is the combined energy of the square and the triangle aligning on the material plane. The coin and the star inside the concentric circles are a shield for protection and endurance. This shield represents the polarization of energy on the physical plane.

In this card, green represents Earth, pink is emotions, yellow is divine reason, blue is communication and healing. The integration of many colors shows the potential for balance in all of the energy centers of the physical plane.

The symbology as a whole represents eternal production and reproduction on the physical plane. It shows possibility coming into manifestation, force moving into form.

The card demonstrates balance in that our aim is to become balanced and centered. Everything we aspire toward is contained in the One of Earth.

Two of Earth: Cause and Effect

Divinatory Meaning

You are trying to work out the details of your life in order to bring everything into balance; you are in the process of discovering, first-hand, that every action entails a reaction; your life is in a process of continual re-creation based on the information or parameters you allow it to have; a big change is in the offing at this time.

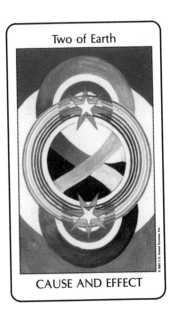

Two of Earth

CAUSE AND EFFECT

Meditation ───

Jupiter in Capricorn
constancy and change
change is stability
polarization
black and white
loss and gain
love and pain
movement
things are getting underway.

Interpretation ──────────────────────────────────────

At the Two of Earth, you have learned how to accrue the necessities
for survival. You can shelter, feed and clothe your Self. You have
skills and you can trade these skills for that which you require.

Now, having accomplished the basics, and having gained a certain stability in this enterprise, you are on the brink of change. You
have tremendous potential to create an expanded and more challenging world in which your Self might dwell. This is becoming clear
to you. It is also becoming clear that you have tremendous potential
to act on the world and to contribute to the world's understanding
and that just as we continually create our own individual realities,
we also create, as a group, our collective reality.

The immensity of the change you face at the Two of Earth can
be quite exciting as well as quite frightening. Change is always disruptive. Old forms must die in order for new ones to take their place
and there may be some difficulty in letting go of that which you have
outgrown.

You have an infinite number of choices as to how you will create,
as well as respond, to such change. You may experience a state of
harmonium as you spiral through change, staying balanced and centered as if at the center of a wheel. You may experience a state
of struggle. It is likely that, on the one hand, you desire to indulge yourself, to give in to all whims of mind, body and pride.
On the other hand, you desire to renounce all physical pleasures
and go on to a disciplinary extreme and torture your body and mind
unreasonably. The golden mean, which lies between, is the path

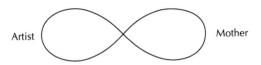

Figure 9. The racetrack of identity.

to wisdom, understanding and peace. The mathematical formula for the golden mean—which provides stimulating contemplation—is $-1+1=0$.

It is very important at the Two of Earth to re-examine the question: Who am I? We are many people at once, existing simultaneously in multiple levels of reality, or multiple realities. We could call these dimensions "reality enclaves." To experience another dimension of reality, we have only to shift our attention.

Under "normal" circumstances, the question, "Who am I?," is unlikely to arise. I say, for example, "I am an artist." Or, "I am a woman." Or, "I am a mother." Or, "I am 40 years old." An artist is an artist. A woman is a woman. A 40-year-old is a 40-year-old. All of these attributes have a certain face value that we all know and respond to on a cultural level. This does not imply that I am either content or discontent with my identity. It is merely what is. I can be miserable, but be an artist nonetheless. On a certain level, I may be quite content with my misery. Unless I want a new possibility to arise (unless I want to create change) or unless a new possibility is forcing itself on me, I may have no need to shift my attention.

The question, "Who am I," only arises when, in the face of new information, my identity becomes problematic. It becomes problematic, for example, when I feel that there is a discrepancy between my public and my private identities. This occurs when I perceive multiple realities.

Our identity may feel like a racing energy flow. We may be moving, as if on a racetrack, between identities. We may spend more time on one curve and race around another. Picture this as a figure eight pattern. Imagine your Self moving through life, as on this racetrack, forever changing identities.[1] See figure 9.

[1]Hal Stone and Sidra Winkelman, *Embracing Our Selves* (Marina del Rey, CA: DeVorss & Co., 1985), pp. 186–191.

According to sociologists Dr. Peter Berger and Dr. Thomas Luck-mann, each individual, after coming to an understanding of his or her location in the social group or culture (example: "I am an artist") and the external expectations that result therefrom is a potential traitor to him or her Self, to his or her internal truth.[2] Conflict arises when, after attempting to live up to social expectations, the individual feels he or she has betrayed the internal or the deep Self. The feeling that one is committing "treason to the Self" comes because one is strongly identified with more than one distinct and powerful reality.

The emergent identity is the identity of the "individualist," one who has the potential to balance between competing identities or to migrate between a number of available worlds and who is aware that he or she has the ability to deliberately and awarely construct a Self out of the material provided by various available identities.

This ability points to a deep understanding of the law of cause and effect which is the essence of the Two of Earth. It is the ability to create reality on an individual as well as on a social level.

And, yet, while the individual can take a great deal of power, it is impossible to say exactly how the actions or forces of the present will manifest in form or substance. Nonetheless, at the Two of Earth, it is time to move out of the "neat" existence of the past. Sometimes this entails throwing the pieces of one's life in the air and having faith.

Having faith may entail some kind of mystical encounter. For your consideration: It is often stated that one who looks upon the face of God dies. At this point, I put forth the following riddle for your contemplation: can one look upon the face of God and live? This riddle is the mystery of the Two of Earth and its unraveling leads to higher levels of understanding. A hint is offered in the following: force encompasses form. Form encompasses force. One fits inside of the other. Draw a diagram and you will realize that spirit and matter do not form a dichotomy. I am both at once. I am spirit and matter. I contain spirit, but I do not encompass or fully understand the extent of spirit. Yet, *my hand is the hand of spirit*. What form shall the change take?

Card Symbology: The Two of Earth is a circular rainbow, repre-senting continuity and the rainbow covenant—the promise to know

---

[2]Peter L. Berger and Thomas Luckmann, *The Social Construction of Reality* (New York: Doubleday/Anchor Books, 1967).

and serve truth—over a figure eight, denoting continuous change, action and reaction, cause and effect.

Above is a black upright five-pointed star overlaid upon a light seven-pointed star. As we have seen, the seven-pointed star represents continuous manifestation. The five-pointed star represents the human being balanced in spirit, intellect, emotions, body and life-force. The upper star is upright to represent the anabolistic processes, the processes of building up. The lower star, which is yellow, is reversed to represent the catabolistic processes, the processes of breaking down.

This card represents the recognition of infinite process, infinite yin and yang, cold and hot, dark and light. It is the sacred space of infinite ambivalence.

Three of Earth: Works

Divinatory meaning ─────────

The work you have chosen is the right work; this is a time of inventing, creating or engineering; the skills you are using are the right skills; all things material are moving into alignment to work with you; expect material success; you will continue to succeed as long as you do not lose your sense of heart or spirit.

Three of Earth

WORKS

Meditation ──────────────────

Mars in Capricorn
Work Trade Silver Gold
Energy moving
Economies flowing

Careful engineering
Brilliance Enacted.

Interpretation ─────────────────────────────

The Three of Earth is the birth of invention, the energy and process of the creative mind applied to the physical world.

At the Three, one could say "necessity is the mother of invention." As you reach the Three, you have realized what is *necessary*. That is why things are beginning to work.

At the Three of Earth, you have developed excellent skills and you have discovered how to market those skills creatively. If you move lovingly and carefully, you will realize material increase. This is the point of gain in commercial transactions. At this time there is gain in all things physical. This is because your spirit, your intellect and your emotions are all in agreement as to what should occur on a physical level, that is to say, in *form and substance*.

One could say, it is the right time and you are in the right place. Metaphorically speaking, planting your gold *now* in a sacred field will bring great rewards. The question you must ask yourself, however, is: of all possible fields, which is the most sacred?

It is important to keep in mind that the aspect of the spirit enters every phase of your life and your work is correct only if you are following your higher consciousness. In work, your conscience must be your guide. Ask yourself: does this work feel right on a deep, internal level? If it does, you will be able to avoid mistakes, slovenliness, sloppiness, all those things that can act to undermine that which you are trying to accomplish.

Your energy is most constructive when it is moving according to divine will. Are you contributing to the positive flow of the universe? Are you nurturing the Mother Earth? Are you respecting life? Are you acting from a basic goodness?

These are the most important motivators. Building a society with the acquisition of material wealth as the highest value leads only to a situation of destruction of life, liberty and happiness. True wealth is balance of conviction, love, divine reason (using the intellect to positive ends), and health. True freedom is contributing to a healthy and positive universal flow.

At the Three of Earth, you are thinking about how you construct your basic reality. You are beginning to see that you create your reality through the very routines of your daily life. Conversely, your routines reaffirm who you are and this becomes your identity. Your routines will change as your identity changes. Change your routines and you will change your identity.

Your work must be in alignment with the highest will of spirit. Are you working in divine and pervasive happiness?

Card Symbology: The pentagrams represent the human being continually moving inside the circle of eternity. These circled stars are also coins which demonstrate that reward is in sight.

The central circle-cross represents balance in the four directions: spiritual, emotional, intellectual, and physical. All is in order and moving as it should.

The dark pyramid of the past—the triangle in the center of the circle—has become green, signifying new growth. The central diamond is orange and red, signifying intense interest or lust in the work at hand.

The alternating circles of light and dark show rapid movement through layers of consciousness (the subconscious, waking conscious and superconscious mind) where all experience is noted, synthesized and finally applied.

All is balance, moving in the direction of light, prosperity and beauty.

Four of Earth: Power

Divinatory Meaning

Power is unfolding within you; you may feel as if you are closing off the outside world, but recognize this as a strength, not a weakness; you have the power to shut the door when necessary, you also have the power to open it; if you think the key to opening the door is lost, look within your own heart to find it; you have high qualities of generosity; do not become a victim of avarice on the part of yourself or anyone else.

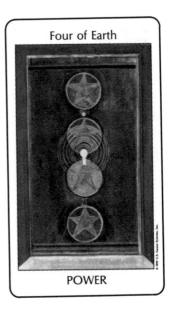

Four of Earth

POWER

Meditation ─────────────────────────────────

Sun in Capricorn
POWER!
The gains have come!
Walls are built!
Guarded, Defended, Protected, Shielded
Security is assured by Law and Order
The System is complete.

Interpretation ───────────────────────────────

At the Four of Earth, great gains have been made. Everything has paid off. Everything has solidified. Your basic needs have been met. You are, symbolically speaking, in your castle surrounded by a moat.

You have power. This is good in that you have now come into your own. You have won. Your ship has come in. Symbolically speaking, it is as if you have attained that dream house on the mountain.

This is a good place to be in that a prince can contribute to the Emperor, while a poor man cannot. But what now? And at what price?

You are just learning that in order to protect your gain, you must maintain your cache with constant authority and vigilance. This takes a lot of energy. Because you have to guard against other people, you become separated from them. You are learning that you need other people in order to feel fulfilled. You are also coming to understand— as you become locked into matter—that acquisitions can become a burden.

There is an old Buddhist tale whereby a man on a long journey comes to a river. He desperately needs to get across. So he builds a raft out of branches and reeds and safely crosses the river. He is very taken by how useful the raft has been and, subsequently, cannot bring himself to abandon it on the other side. He decides to carry the raft with him. Thus, he voluntarily assumes an unnecessary burden. The Buddhists ask: is this a wise man?

Greed arises from wrong ideas as to what can bring true satisfaction. Greed is one of the three fires of the world. The other two are anger and recklessness. The fire of greed consumes those who, through greed, have lost a sense of what brings true satisfaction.

We are social creatures, biologically predestined to inhabit the world with others. The socially shared world becomes a significant reality for us. We construct our individual worlds within the limits of the social world, but once we have constructed our own reality, this reality acts back on the social world. In this way, as I produce my own reality, I also produce my culture through contributing my own unique individual reality to the socially shared reality. Thus, I produce a layer of reality in my culture simply by the way I, myself, live. I am an example for my brothers and sisters on this Earth. I produce reality by the very routines I choose to enact in my daily life.

Our joint realities comprise one reality which is our shared world. The limits of this world are set by nature, but once we have constructed this world, it acts back upon nature. As Drs. Berger and Luckmann state, "In the dialectic between nature and the socially constructed world the human organism is itself transformed."[3] As we construct and transform reality, we thereby construct and transform ourselves.

Now that you are in your Power, think about the kind of reality you are constructing for yourself, and further, for those around you via the "ripple effect." The ripple effect is what happens when you throw a rock in a stream and concentric circles of waves move outward on the surface. You are the rock. Humanity is the stream.

To complicate this scenario, it is not only that there are two realities (the internal and the external). There are many. We live in a complex society with a complex distribution of knowledge. We hear many messages. This can lead to a problem in understanding our own identity.

The question you must ask is: What reality do I want to project out to the world? Remember, you are in a position of Power. You are in a position of influence. You are in a position to make your corner of your culture in your own image.

Culture is not a dead or static entity. It is alive and continually changing. It changes in sequences, periods and cycles. When the time is right, change comes. Nothing can interfere with this universal process.

As a maker of culture, the key to using your Power rightly is to offer that Power in the service of love. You are a citizen of the universe.

---

[3]See *The Social Construction of Reality*, p. 183.

When you are living in love, the culture you create will be positive and will enhance the nature of the universe.

Card Symbology: The Four of Earth shows four encircled penta-grams upon a door which has been barred at the top and bottom from the inside. It appears to the observer as if he or she is standing in a room. This is the room of material acquisition and success.

There is a radiating keyhole which leads to the next level of development. It is surrounded by ten golden circles, ten and not nine, ten and not eleven.[4] These circles represent the ten spheres of the Tree of Life. Beyond the tenth sphere is the secret sphere called Daath. At Daath there exists a secret bridge over the abyss which leads to higher understanding. This bridge is made of knowledge. The knowl-edge is the knowledge of love.

When love is used as the key that opens the door to the higher level, one comes to understand an array of rights and responsibilities that accompany the fact of universal citizenship. There is a separation between the experience of having power over other people and feeling a sense of one's own empowerment from within. The key to higher level empowerment, empowerment of the spirit, is to offer one's Power in the service of love.

The yellow and orange of this card indicate a need to learn through action. Accept love and go through the door.

[4]See the *Sefer Yezirah: The Book of Formation* for a description of why ten and not nine, ten and not eleven.

Five of Earth: The Nadir

Divinatory Meaning ———————

You are experiencing a sense of worry; you have helped to produce a reality in which your own deep truths are denied; you experience a sense of alienation; you feel alone and on the outside; this is a time for introspection, a good time to recount your successes and examine the progress you have made; it is time to rearrange your life in such a way that your heart and spirit are rewarded; this is the essence of healing and making things right.

Five of Earth

THE NADIR

Meditation ———————

Mercury in Taurus
Moving energy appears
Hardship, Worry
There is instability in the Foundations of Matter
Intense strain
is coupled with
long-continued Inaction.

Interpretation ———————

At the Five of Earth, you are in a state of darkness. You feel like you are at the bottom. This feels like the Nadir of existence. You are worried. You feel physically deprived. You feel poor. Your soul is hungry. You are tense. Your body is stressed. Your equilibrium is off. You feel unbalanced. You feel defeated. It is as if you have been left out in the cold.

Pessimistically, you are brooding. Things appear gloomy. Relationships threaten to break apart. You feel you have not been taken seriously. There is a sense of being on the outside.

This is the stage of the dark night. In a sense this is happening because, unwittingly, you have created a reality that has denied your inner self. You have concentrated on material endeavors and your spirit has suffered. Thus, you feel a schism on the inner plane. This also happens on a social level. As a group, we are capable of creating a joint reality—a culture or society—that denies the individual spirit. We know this has happened when large masses of individuals feel an uncomfortable asymmetry between their public and private lives.

It is important to understand that this "dark night"—which is a time of introspection and the re-examination of the systems we have created —is necessary for individuals as well as for groups in order that we might expand our foundation. In actuality, new energy has appeared. New influences are altering a situation which you once felt was prosperous and stable. These new influences, although initially disruptive, will ultimately prove to be positive forces, pushing you to a higher level of awareness and knowledge. You may not yet realize it, but a new light has been ignited on the level of spirit. It will light your way. There is no such thing as regression in this life. Whatever appearances indicate on the surface, we are always moving ahead, processing more and more information and learning the lessons we need to learn.

This would be a good time for you to examine the progress you have made and recount your successes. You are in a dangerous time and you need to move through it with integrity. See the situation clearly, for what it is. Pay attention to detail. It is as if you have the opportunity to examine the active volcano of the Self from the edge of the crater. If you get distracted, you could fall into the pit. See truth. See it bravely. It is time to work toward rearranging your life in such a way that your heart and spirit are honored and rewarded.

Realize that you are merely experiencing the disintegration of a first stage process of manifestation. You are moving to a higher level which demands the purging of past patterns. To find the way on the new path, listen to your intuition. This intuitive ability is now giving you the nudge. From another vantage point, you can put your sense of hardship in the proper perspective.

Card Symbology: The card shows four inverted (banishing) pentagrams which appear in a barring way over the dark pyramid of the past. This indicates that elements of your past must be purged in order for you to move to the next level of learning.

The colorful star represents the opening of your heart chakra, the heart energy center. It is like a pink raft floating on green light in the darkness of your soul. The green light is akin to grass. It is like new growth in the spring. The circle-cross surrounding this star indicates the potential for balance in all four directions: the spirit, the emotions, the intellect, the body and material life. The fifth star represents the introduction of the fifth essence, the quintessence, which represents the ultimate substance of the universe, the lifeforce, ether or great spirit.

The keyhole on the dark pyramid of the past indicates that you have closed yourself off from your inner light. Love is the key that unlocks the door. Tune into the message of your heart.

Six of Earth: Beauty

Divinatory Meaning

You are experiencing the joy of giving; you are healing yourself and your environment through realizing that the pursuit of beauty—which many call "The Beauty Way"—is the secret to all lasting success; you are not alone in your beliefs; speak your truth and you will find yourself in the midst of a like-minded community; great fortune becomes yours as you speak and act in the way of your own deepest convictions.

Six of Earth

BEAUTY

Meditation

Moon in Taurus
Success!
the Way is clear; Gains made

Foundations laid
The Fields are blooming freely
fertile by the Ancients' Ways
Rain and Wind and Sun
and the Daughters and Sons of the New Days
rise to an Age of Healing, Love
and the affirmation
of Life.

Interpretation ─────────────────────────────

At the Six of Earth, you are learning the great secret. The great secret represents the balanced and harmonious establishment of material energy. Harmonious means that influence—which is fully perceived—is coming from the higher consciousness. The spirit is balanced and fully integrated. The heart is balanced and fully integrated. The rational mind understands the meaning of divine reason and is fully integrated. The body is working in perfect order. The material world is full of pleasure.

You are learning to tap the vast energy of the universe in order to move with, rather than against, the cosmic flow. You are learning to use your spirit, heart, mind, intellect, ego and body as a channel for that energy. This is the secret of success with harmonium. This is the secret behind all healing. This is the secret behind all Beauty.

At the Six of Earth, you have learned that you must give up in order to gain, you must surrender in order to win. The frightened, rigid body will sink and drown in no time. The relaxed body floats infinitely on the surface—looking down into the sea—breathing slowly, conserving energy.

Becoming relaxed enough to float demands the creation of internal unity. Establishing clear direction has required voluntarily changing your patterns of thinking. You have been through a storm, but now, it is as if you float, suspended, in the eye of the hurricane. Take refuge there as the world spins around you. Take refuge in peace.

The way of the six is the way of Beauty. It is the way of peace in the eye of the storm. At the six, you will find others at peace— with the secret—in the eye of the storm, others who believe as you do. Banding with or creating a community (bringing together a group of like-minded individuals) is a form of empowerment. One way of creating and shaping reality is by producing your own group of experts. Your community is wealthy and bands together for the greater good. The composite energy of the community is greater than the energy of the sum total of the individuals who comprise it. The light shines upon the community! The light shines upon you! Banding with the like-minded community will bring good fortune!

Card Symbology: The more you look at the center of the Six, the more you are drawn into the rainbow core. This is a reminder of the rainbow covenant.

The yellow diamond, containing six upright pentagrams—for all that is positive, aligned and moving in the same direction—floats before a black and green square.

The observer may feel like she or he is inside a room with this diamond shape hovering at the center. This "room" is the inside of a cube. Therein lies the secret. What does the cube contain? In what dimensions does the cube unfold? As you answer these questions, you will come to understand the Six of Earth.

Seven of Earth: The Garden

Divinatory Meaning

Seven of Earth

THE GARDEN

You are creating your own sense of what you consider to be success and failure; you hold the tools of your own transformation; admit to yourself that you do know what you want and go ahead and attain it; "failure" does not mean regression, it means that there is a better, more rewarding, path for you to take; the Earth can be a delightful garden, you are responsible for making and keeping the Earth beautiful; make your choices according to the deepest directives of your heart.

Meditation ————————————————————————

Saturn in Taurus
Reflection
has not new conception occurred?
cast out the old—
and know
if you are suffering
it is only from gestational malaise.

Interpretation ————————————————————————

At the Seven, you pause during the growth of an enterprise. It may seem, on the surface, that certain things have not turned out as planned. There have been apparent setbacks and failures, particularly with regard to the physical body or material matters. However, you must understand that these problems are just bumps in the path, or trials on the way as you move ahead. If you get a flat tire, what should you do?

There is no truth in the idea that one can "regress" on one's path. All "setbacks" and "failures" are for a higher purpose, if only for the purpose of eliminating or changing an idea that has decreased in worth. In every uncomfortable situation, you come closer to realizing your potential. You discover the seeds for new growth.

We define ourselves as existing in a particular reality, or by changing our focus, as able to discern a multitude of realities. At the Seven of Earth, The Garden, the key is in knowing that the way we define our own reality has a self-fulfilling potency. That is to say, if I define myself as too weak, too non-technically oriented, too clean or dressed up to change my flat tire, I will stay where I am until help comes along. If I am on a country road, I may wait a long while. Perhaps I can use a telephone to call for expert help. If I have thought ahead, I may have insurance which will cover the cost of such help. If I have not thought ahead, I may not have carried a spare! There are a number of possibilities. The important thing is how I construct, define, and act in, the situation. Every action has a set of consequences. As I create my own re-actions (through anger, fear, serenity, etc.), I create my own definition of self.

When I react in the same mode over time, let's say I am generally angry, and tend to "spout off" at people, others come to identify me as an angry person. Eventually I internalize that label and come to identify myself as an angry person. If I feel angry, and I would rather be calm, I can start acting as if I am calm, even though I might still feel a great deal of anger beneath the surface. Through acting as if I am calm, I will experience a different reaction from other people. Eventually, I will begin to think of myself differently. Over time, through acting as if I am calm, I actually *become* a calm person. At the Seven, you realize that you create your Self at every step of the way. You do your own prioritizing. No one else can do that for you. You create your own symbolic universe, that is to say, *you* decide what reality you want to live in. You decide how you will integrate your value system. How does your spirituality fit in? your emotional life? your intellectual pursuits? physical exercise? work?

The trained Magus (see Key I) knows he can wield the Wand (will), Mirror (intuition), Knife (reason), and Stone (substance) to create his internal world as well as to act on the external world, creating a reality which reflects his own image. The Magus recognizes that all social systems are human products. The existence of these systems has its base in the lives of concrete individuals. There are no social systems apart from the perpetrators of such systems. Therefore such systems are malleable and change as a reflection of the individuals involved therein.

So it is with the Gods.

At the Seven of Earth, you are the Magus. The Earth is your Garden. In creating this Garden, you are aided by the gardening tools which you have already earned: your Wand (balance and direction in your will), Cup (balance and direction in your intuition and emotions), and Blade (balance and direction in your reason). You may now select the seeds with which you will sow your Garden. You must "plant your gold in a sacred field."

Use your valuable resources—your wisdom and understanding; all the tools you hold as the Magus—to do what is right. What is your "gold" and how will you sow it?

Card Symbology: In the Seven of Earth, the Garden is created as the Magus sees fit.

The Magus moves upward, out of the dark pyramid of the past toward a beautiful existence. The resources which propel him from the past to the future are the wand with the white star at the tip (conviction), the green and yellow cup (love), and the blade above the cup (divine reason). This indicates that connection has been made in the three layers of consciousness: the subconscious, waking consciousness, and the higher consciousness. Messages are coming clearly. All tools for building a wonderful future are now at hand.

The "garden" in the upper part of this card is in the shape of a brain. The brain contains both the white lotus of the east (God is within) and the red rose of the west (Thou Art God). The red and blue triangle represents unity of sight, clarity, and the third eye, "for those who have eyes to see."

The "point" of this card shows that you must create your world on the physical plane, on the Earth. The Earth is our Garden and we must preserve, if not enhance, Her beauty.

The six black inverted pentagrams at the bottom of the card are part of the dark pyramid of the past which you are now leaving. They indicate that you must release anything restraining you as a result of outmoded systems or old ways of thinking.

The background of this card is gray. Grayness is wisdom. It is a blending of black and white, a balancing of subconscious and higher conscious input.

Eight of Earth: The Mountain

Divinatory Meaning ————————

Eight of Earth

THE MOUNTAIN

Perseverance, commitment and discipline are the real keys to success; talent is important, but not the most important factor; you are learning, practicing, growing and blossoming; this is a good time to be an eager student; it is as if you are climbing a great mountain in your life; the way may seem steep or rocky, but you will get there if you walk one step at a time, thoughtfully and cheerfully placing one foot in front of the other; the important thing is not necessarily the view from the top, but how you feel during each step on the path.

Meditation ───────────────────────────────

Sun in Virgo
Learning
with caution
apply the resources
apply the intelligence
Seeds once planted must be nurtured
It is the Turn of the Tide!
This is no time for a Vacation!

Interpretation ─────────────────────────────

At the Eight of Earth, there is a delicate blossoming of many levels
and layers of the Self. There comes a deeper understanding of the
position of the Self in the external world and what needs to be created
in that external world in order to nurture the inner Self.

This is a vulnerable and delicate time as one begins the ascent
toward the top of The Mountain. The Mountain trail is the path toward
your own en-lighten-ment, the path based in the world of matter, the
path of this incarnation, which begins now, at this moment in your
life. Many have trodden this path. Many more will in times to come.

Here, at the Eight, you are refining your skills, honing in, developing your Self and your true work in a deeper and more concentrated way. You are seeing the point, which is like glimpsing the
mountain's peak. You are growing now. You are applying everything
you have learned. You are listening for insight, carefully analyzing,
assembling and keeping the best and discarding the rest. Your inner
strength is reliable. Your body and mind are ready for the journey
up The Mountain.

The Eight of Earth begins your preparation for the birth which
will renew the cycle. This is the rebirth of spirit which you shall realize
as you reach the peak of the mountain. The climb, however, is long
and arduous. Therefore, this is the time to take stock of what you
know. It is time to mobilize your resources. It is also time to be
humble, to admit what you do not know. The time is one of deep
learning and the integration of new lessons.

You have already sowed the secret seed of your future. You have
planted your gold in the sacred field. It now awaits sun (action) and
rain (the desire for growth). This means that your situation holds

promise. The probability of your continuing success is now enhanced because you are refining your energies. You have been through a system, you have accrued an understanding of its functioning, and you now understand how, when and where you can have an impact. It is time to put this knowledge in your bag of magic tools and begin the ascent. You now have everything you need in order to attain success, in order to reach the climax. You have learned how to learn. Nothing is more important than that.

The message of this time is to begin the ascent and to keep climbing. You will understand the path when you see the view from the summit. This is not the time to mull over regrets or, conversely, to become too excited with anticipation. It is time to meet what comes with a calm, clear, and open mind. It is time to move forward in a balanced state of equanimity.

Card Symbology: This card shows the fundamental path of the element of Earth. It is The Mountain. The pentagrams have all been righted, the dark pyramid of the past seems to be skyrocketing into the future. All of the energy from the Earth is on an upward path. Its shape is a *cone of power,* the conical energy force of magicians. Simultaneously, wisdom—in the form of gray clouds in a vortex of energy—is descending from the above. Thus, we observe the dualistic and simultaneous ascent and descent of power.

At the top of The Mountain, all elements are in perfect balance. This is the potential of the individual in its actualized state. This is the path and direction of the observer. Upon arrival at the summit, the knowledge of the pure white light will be gained.

Nine of Earth: The Zenith

Divinatory Meaning ─────────

You feel a sense of accomplishment, reward, happiness, balance, joy, splendor, unity, love, radiance, beauty and light!; you are succeeding in your life; things are going well; you are succeeding because you have learned that the importance of the ego pales next to that of the soul; you have learned that attaining wealth and prosperity involves the state of the spirit, the heart and the mind, not just how much money you have in the bank.

Nine of Earth

THE ZENITH

Meditation ─────────────────────────

Venus in Virgo
Gain! Accomplishment!
Rites of Passage are now in Progress!
It is my Time
my Moment
my Life on Earth!

I've Grown and Thought
Rewards are there, but not so guarded
I've learned
All is Satisfaction!

My House stands with open doors
Come in and See!
I stand ready to give Birth!

Interpretation ───────────────────────

At the Nine of Earth, you have come a long way. You have worked hard. You deserve all that is coming to you. Your fields are blooming.

Your life is accomplishment. The harvest is nigh. The profits will be fabulous!

You, Dear One, are now in favor in all affairs of the physical body and the material world. You have developed your spirit. You have grounded spiritual energy in your physical form. Your heart has opened. You have grounded heart energy in your physical form. Your intellect has expanded. You have grounded the energy of divine reason in your physical form. You have attuned and refined your strengths, and while it was difficult and demanded a great deal of persistence, you have climbed The Mountain of this life. You have chosen to act according to the dictates of your higher Self, and while this was more difficult than taking the easy path of just doing what was expected of you, now standing at The Zenith ("peaking!"), you have emerged with so much integrity! Your life has so much purpose! You have so much to give! There is so much you can do!

Learning to prioritize, set your goals and keep your life in balance on the spiritual, emotional, intellectual and physical planes—according to the dictates of your conscience—has been one of the most difficult undertakings of this incarnation, but you are now in a pattern of success. That which you wished for has finally manifested.

You have been so successful in accomplishing the tasks presented to you that you are now nearing the end of this cycle within cycles. It is time to push through any remaining pains—for these are only growing pains and pains of labor—and allow your Self to be reborn in wealth: wealth of spirit, wealth of heart, wealth of thought, wealth of matter.

The universe is yours! You are of the universe! Go forth in happiness! Radiate love!

Card Symbology: The Nine of Earth: The Zenith, shows nine encircled stars inside of a diamond. All stars are in alignment, and they are gold! This indicates extreme success.

Energy has come down through the head moving down to the feet and back up through the head. The energy cycle is intact and the force is flowing. That is because all is right. Everything is straight, the spine is like a string of pearls, everything is moving as it needs to.

The throat is open. This indicates that it is time for you to speak of that which you understand as truth.

Ten of Earth: The Great Work

Divinatory Meaning

You are experiencing a sense of order, design, tension, balance and harmony; everything in your life is moving with a wonderful rhythm; you now realize a new kind of wealth which is spiritual, emotional, intellectual and physical in nature: this is the true meaning of wealth, all other kinds of wealth are transitory; you have learned so much, now is the time to put what you know into words or other art forms in order to communciate it to others; you have long been a student, but you are a great teacher as well; following the spiritual path is the greatest of all your works.

Ten of Earth

THE GREAT WORK

Meditation

Mercury in Virgo
Regeneration of a cycle
of Protection
Ultimate Wealth
Satisfaction

The Great Work
is moving in accomplishment

The final solidification
of Earth Energy
spins to Rebirth

Now is True Wisdom
Perfect Happiness.

Interpretation

At the Ten of Earth, you have made a major accomplishment! You are successful. You are completing a path. You are acting in a field of comfort. You are living in comfort. You have stabilized and that pattern of stabilization is the one that you asked for. It is the one that you worked for. It is the one that you wanted.

Interestingly, however, is the fact that, in the very act of accomplishment, you learn that there is a certain futility in focusing on the winnings or the gain. In the end, unless it is devoted to other than mere accumulation, acquired wealth will dissipate. Focusing on the gain ends in stagnation.

Now you learn that understanding *process* is the major key to wisdom. The moment is everything. Imagination is key. Where I shall go or from whence I came is not as important at this time as is each step on the path, the way I have taken each step, the way I have felt at each step. The important thing right now is the step I take at this moment. I must ask myself: am I moving with integrity? Am I truthful? Am I balanced? Am I stable? Am I happy? Do I bring joy?

At the Ten of Earth, you have exhausted your material forces. You are in a sacred place. This is a sacred field. This is the moment in time where materialism is surpassed, where judgments of material loss and gain cease to matter.

The Ten of Earth represents the stage of knowing that while we naturally fear disaster and long for good fortune on the material plane, disaster often turns out to be fortunate while good fortune may turn out to be disastrous! In undertaking The Great Work, you learn that the wise one meets changing circumstances with an equitable spirit, being neither elated by "success" nor depressed by "failure." This is the state of perfect harmony, a state that comes from the experience of much joy and hardship on the spiritual, emotional, intellectual and physical journey.

The Ten of Earth represents a perfect state. It is a state of *sunyata*— perfect *chi*, holiness, sacredness—where all is in balance, where all is solidly centered. It is a state of holding the center, even in the midst of what appears to be chaos. When you have arrived at the center of perfect balance, it is time to begin to think about becoming a teacher. You now understand what you came to learn. You are learned. You now have the words to express your Self. And *you are just beginning the journey homeward.*

This means that you have begun to unravel the mysteries of spirit. In unraveling these mysteries, you have learned that, as a physical body, you are both force and form. You hold the force within your form. Your form is contained in the eternal force. You know something of the limitless light and the limitless substance of which all things are made. You have learned that *you* create the world according to your own vision. You have learned that *you* are a visionary. You, alone, are responsible for your own visions. In the palm of your hand, you hold all the tools to create. You are as magical as the Magus (see Key I).

You are learned. You have learned that you can bring your ideas into manifestation. You can teach these ideas. It is clearly time for you to create newness: to use all your resources to do your part to re-new and to re-enchant your world. It is time for you to give back—to replenish—that which has been given to you, especially now, since you know that you are not alone. Especially now, since you know that you are protected.

Card Symbology: The Ten of Earth card, The Great Work, shows the descent of energy from the above, drawn down to do its work on Earth. The work is symbolized by a pen drawing a white spiral on a black plane.

The pen contains the ascending colors of all the energy centers of the body. This is also the pattern of the Tree of Life and indicates that all is in proportion, all is balanced, all is in a state of perfection.

Setting the ink to paper signifies that the word has become manifest. It signifies that you hold the pen.

Earth Father: The Spirit of Fertilization

Divinatory Meaning ——————————

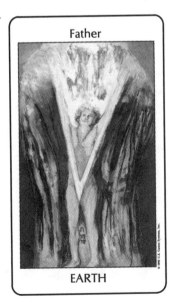

Father

EARTH

There is a sense of joyous practicality reflected in the circumstances of daily life; you are experiencing a sense of "wealth" spiritually, emotionally, intellectually and physically; through self-knowledge, potential is mastered; vast "fields" have been tilled and prosperity has been the result; this is the right mode of working and living; persist in this way and you will continue to prosper.

Meditation ————————————————————————————————

Leo, Virgo
Earthed/Grounded
Mountain Power
The Fire Father in Earth
builds lasting gardens
that produce and produce
the Earth Father
moves
through Cycling Time
surrounded by
Fire and Sea and Sky
Sons and Daughters
of Cycling Time:
steady!

Earthed/Grounded
Abounding Joy
tilling vast lands
investing well
and Time will tell
as intellects rise and shine and die,
fires rage, lovers sigh

Time will tell
the Earth Father
helps them all
through their Dark Age
constancy—
he knows them well
he himself was ill—
before he came to Man's Estate.

Interpretation ————————————————————————————————

The Earth Father is the strength, power and spirit of the Earth, the
physical plane, and the epitome of material success. He is well-
balanced, spiritually, emotionally and intellectually. This is because
he is well acquainted with his deepest inner Self.

Through self-knowledge, he has mastered his potential: actualizing or materializing everything he wishes. With this tremendous capacity, he does not experience uncertainty or anxiety. He has the eternal steadiness and reliability of a mountain. He radiates accomplishment.

The Earth Father is in control of vast lands, symbolically or literally, which he cultivates in a masterful way. Using his great gift of stability, he brings about the best in that which he "touches." There is an important secret in his wisdom. This is the key to his success: he studies the patterns of Nature and imitates Her in every way. That is the key to his material prosperity. He has learned that Nature will obey his every command if he works within Her Law.

He uses his "wealth" for purposes of true charity, to nurture the environment and all life therein. He never fails to aid the mass of humanity, however close to or distant from him. He sees himself as a citizen of the universe. Thus, he places the sake of the universe before the call to nationalism or imperialism. He understands very well that we all share the same spirit, we all drink the same water, we all breathe the same air, we all share the same Earth—and that Earth is growing ever smaller with the growth and development of the human race.

Earth Father knows when it is time to seed and nurture. That is why he is the Spirit of Fertilization. He is able to fertilize because, through internal balance, he has developed an excellent sense of timeliness. He knows when the seed will be lost. He knows when the seed will be received, nurtured and grow to life. He conserves his energy and resources and concentrates on the timely application of principles.

His life is full of pleasure and it is this very pleasure which he proliferates. He is giving and affectionate. This is because spirit is at peace with and within his body. The home, which he has taken the responsibility for creating, is bountiful, beautiful and serene. His friends and his children—which are many more than his blood offspring—can always come to him in times of trouble. People and animals seek his wisdom. His counsel—wherein he uses the secret of nature—is very wise.

Since the Earth Father is so powerful within, he can be also very powerful without. If it crossed his mind, he could be a dangerous opponent. But that is not his priority. He knows that true empowerment is balance within. He knows he does not need to engage in battles. Strength is internal integrity. Internal integrity affects the universe of its own accord.

The Earth Father meditates upon the idea that the great and small mingle and are of one will. Heaven and Earth are in communion. Strength lies within, glad acceptance lies without. Because I am at the center of things, I understand that when grass is uprooted, soil comes up as well. From this balanced position, I can see ahead. Because all is clear, I can steer a fruitful middle course. Any eclipse will quickly pass (see *I Ching:* Hexagram 11: Peace).

Card Symbology: With upraised arms, the Earth Father waves his hands to create. He is surrounded by growth and the activity of Earth: volcanos, earthquakes, flowing waters, birth, death, renewal, the changing of the seasons, the cycling of the year. In the midst of all this, he is rooted—in spirit—to both heaven and earth. He creates his world just as he grows himself—*like a plant.*

The Earth Father appears as a keyhole. He is the key to growth and prosperity on the material plane. He is primal Earth, the lifeforce manifest on Earth, the spirit manifest on Earth, the will of God manifest on Earth.

Earth Mother: Threshold to Birth

Divinatory Meaning ———————

You are experiencing a high level of compassion; the creative forces of your life must be quietly nurtured; cultivated "fields" will eventually bloom; love every stick, stone, plant and animal and you will experience great bounty; be diligent in attuning to every detail of the work required as you tend your "garden"; it is time to rejoice in your own life and to help create a joyous life for others.

Mother

EARTH

Meditation ─────────────────────────────────

Sagittarius, Capricorn
Dark-headed
Garden Mother
the Water Mother in Earth
grows her flowers
roses asters
sweet magnolias
Oasis of Love and Home
in the endless realm of wanting

hard-working
Pleasure Mother
watering abundance
on barren planes
serene/creative/bountiful
inviting Sun to warm the furrows
Rain to swell the knolls
using Reason:
        in the season for planting, she plants
        in the season for reaping, she reaps

and she fills her skirts with blossoms
to make garlands for her Children
and laurels for the Poor.

Interpretation ───────────────────────────────

The Earth Mother nurtures and loves the Earth. She rejoices in her
life, loves the physical plane, loves the opportunity to manifest her
spirit in physical form, loves the sticks, stones, bones and plants,
animals, sun, rain, wind and earthquakes. She is content. The universe is her home. Earth's bounty is her bounty. Earth's beauty is her
beauty.
        She is desirous of goodness, rightness and prosperity and she
attains this on her inward search toward balance. She has discovered
the key to prosperity. For her, that key is love. Self-love. Love of life.
She knows that loving herself is no different than loving the Earth.
For she is Earth. Earth is Self. All things emanate from the same
source. All forms of manifestation have the same source at their core.

Earth Mother understands how to move with the ways of Fire, Water, Wind and Earth. This is because she knows the Fire, Water, Wind and Earth of herself. Through careful observation, she has come to understand each element's constructive and destructive capability. Through allowing herself to be tamed by the elements—to accept the power of their force—she has learned to control them in return. She encourages their activity. Because she serves them well, they are at her command.

In this way, she holds the universe, internally and externally, in the palm of her hand—and makes it work. But her control is neither aggressive nor possessive. She is highly successful in a calm and passive way, and while she is serene, she is not the least bit removed or emotionally distant from her endeavors. Her compassion is of the highest level and she is always persistently and diligently involved in every detail of the work required for tending her garden through the passing seasons.

That is why her flowers, although they may be temporary, or seasonal, are of the most exquisite beauty and delicacy. The Earth Mother is dedicated to quality. Through her love and devotion, she can make the desert bloom. She does this through using her instinctive, emotional, intellectual and practical abilities.

In a mature way, the Earth Mother appreciates all that which is beautiful and good. She loves sensual pleasure and physical comfort. She is incredibly creative in making her home. Because she is receptive and emanates love, she is wonderful at lovemaking and bearing and nurturing children, all children, the children of mind and body. She creates, for all, a joyous life. It is a wonderful thing to be in the bountiful Earth Mother's circle of love.

The Earth Mother's meditation states that by observing what heaven gathers to itself and what earth gathers to itself, I can understand the inner workings of all that is in the environment. By carefully observing that which is around and in me, and combining the results of that observation with my own persistence, I will be able to put everything right (see *I Ching:* Hexagram 45: Gathering Together).

Card Symbology: The Earth Mother stands in the cosmic sea, like a water tree, growing up into radiant and infinite (circular) bounty. Her horned headdress represents the spirit of nature.

Her outer robe is the robe of concealment. She is the bringer of material force, which she holds inside. She is cradling material force, nurturing it, training it into form.

She appears as a quiet and enduring force appearing in the darkness of the Earth. She is the primal goddess, capable of the greatest transformation.

Around the neck of the Earth Mother is the yoke, which first appeared around the neck of the Water Sister's swan. This indicates that the Earth Mother has yoked the forces of nature. In turn, they have yoked her. This yoke becomes her necklace, her decoration, her jewelry.

Earth Brother: Moving Meditation

Divinatory Meaning ——————————

Accomplishment comes through thoughtful meditation; you must carefully adapt to your environment; through first meditating on what type of "soil" you are working with, you will be able to plant the "right" kind of "seeds"; work with the resources at hand and you will be successful; there is no point in working against nature; you are experiencing personal equilibrium and productivity, realize this and there will be no need to struggle.

Brother

EARTH

Meditation ————————————————————

Aries, Taurus
Earth Brother
the Wind Brother in Earth
with flourescent fructified loam
coaxing out the vegetation

that sustains the home
and Spirit
enduring persevering
cogent and thoughtful
a moving meditation
on the physical planes

At peace
At rest
he's done his best
he has it all
and it's led him to humility—

if he's not a dreamer
he is not to blame

moving in balance
he need not scheme
he's sent to adapt
the State
to fit his plan
he need only know the lay of the Land.

Interpretation ─────────────────────────────

The Earth Brother is a gentle breeze across the earth. He is accomplished and thoughtful. Everything he learned about cultivation from his Water Mother on Earth and Fire Father on Earth, he brings to bear: he is a master at growing the vegetation that sustains the spirit.

He is balanced, enduring, capable and highly energetic, but his energy is neither frenetic nor flamboyant. Rather, he is persevering and responsible. He plans well and will work diligently to meet his goals. He is peaceful and lives, competently and imperturbably, in a personal equilibrium within the system. Thus, his whole being is like a Moving Meditation.

The Earth Brother is a quiet teacher, always looking for new uses for common things and passing this information along. Just as easily as he adapts himself to his environment, he adapts his environment—most prosperously—to meet his needs. If he is seen as a materialist, it is because, having the perfect combination of attributes, everything he touches becomes a going enterprise.

One could say that his incredible success is "not his fault." He is a humble soul, like a beekeeper who continually hears the drone of the bees. It is the sound of the sacred Om which resonates in his mind. It is the humming of "mmmm."

His attunement is the basis of his success. Because he is so successful, he is freed from material worry in order to pursue a spiritual path. He can afford to devote a great deal of time to growth in this area. He may frequently meditate in his own productive fields.

The meditation of the Earth Brother says, I contemplate the sacred activities of Heaven—the splendors and miseries—and note how the seasons come to pass, each in its proper time and sequence. Because the holy sage makes these matters the subject of his teaching, all the world accepts his dominion. I contemplate the conditions of my own life—the splendors and miseries—and analyze how each occurrence has unfolded. I am committed to a path and major tasks await my doing. If I am resisting, contemplation will unravel the blocks (see *I Ching*: Hexagram 20: Contemplation).[5]

Card Symbology: The Earth Brother is comfortable on the Earth. He flies upon the lunar bull. This is the first reappearance of the lunar bull, who we initially encountered with the Wind Father. That the Earth Brother rides the bull indicates that he has a complete understanding of the bull, which represents the cycles of Earth—birth, death and divine resurrection—and, inherent in that equation, the complete understanding of the meaning of the One Life.

The body of the bull, which is out of view in the card, is a cube. The cube is a mysterious black box which contains the answers to the mysteries. Look inward and you shall know!

---

[5]Earth Brother and Earth Sister are the only two mortal beings to appear in the *Tarot of the Spirit*. This is because they are born of the Fire Father and the Water Mother on the plane of manifestation (Earth). This is one of the great mysteries of the tarot.

Earth Sister: Revelation

Divinatory Meaning ————————

This is the brink of transformation; something new is coming; a "birth" is about to occur; be advised that the diamond, the world's hardest and most brilliant gem, is born of the deepest folds of the earth's darkness; your own light comes in your darkest hour; you are moving steadily, with a sense of stability; you have mastered your sense of who you are spiritually, emotionally, intellectually and physically; you are "pregnant" with the secret of the future; congratulations, dear one, as a result of your own diligent preparation, you have made yourself the perfect receptacle and the "seed" of creativity has been planted within you.

Sister

EARTH

Meditation ————————————————

Aries, Taurus, Gemini
Earth Sister
the Earth Sister in her own element!
The birth of the highest and purest Light
in the darkest of places

Strong and beautiful
she *is* the mountain top

Priestess of the Future
she bears within her
the Secret of the Coming Sun
the New Aeon in which spins
the twin force of spiral creation
in perfect equilibrium
she holds within her
the Light of Truth

the energy by which all things Begin
by which all being is born

Earth Sister
Angel of the Change.
Angel of Form.

Interpretation

The Earth Sister represents the sphere of Earth, the physical body. She brings the four elements into balance and holds pairs of opposites in equilibrium within her form. She symbolizes complete balance and total success. Therefore, she also represents the completion of a cycle.

The Earth Sister is the brink of transformation. She is careful and diligent and has managed her affairs with the utmost attention and the supreme application of the vast stores of knowledge and intuition which have been made available to her through observation of her Fire Father, Water Mother and Wind Brother.

Her ability to accomplish any work, particularly the Great Work, on the physical plane is so well developed that it appears to be natural, as if she is operating by instinct alone. However, she has developed herself systematically through the most intense course of study and her success is due to her wise assimilation, integration and application of sound ideas.

She is an innovator, but she has moved through the system and understands, first hand, its limits. Therefore she is qualified.

In her delicacy and innocence, she may seem fragile—like a spring garden—but she has increased her powers to the highest levels. She holds great psychic power. Because she has worked so hard at developing her powers and because she has done so prudently and diligently, a great wonder—emerging from the world beyond the consciousness—is about to be revealed to her. This revelation is her reward and she will share it with the universe.

She is pregnant with the secret of the future, about to give birth to a multifaceted diamond: the most enduring of all gems. Earth Sister calls her womb the Eye of God because the wholeness and sight of all things—perfectly in balance on all four planes—has come to rest within her. She calls her womb the Light of Truth. She has been the perfect receptacle and the seed of creation has been implanted within her. She is the wondrous force in physical form. She is the mountain in fruition: *the joy of life incarnate!*

Internally, Earth Sister knows that the path has not been easy. But she also knows that if she had tried to dissociate herself from the responsibility of coming to terms with her physical existence through physical or psychological illness and so on, she would have to come back again to master it. Living life, she knows, like learning magic, demands discipline. One has to come down to Earth, become totally grounded in the physical existence before the homeward stretch can be started.[6]

The Earth Sister's meditation states: embracing all that exists, I become bright and shine forth. I gladly accept the powers of the universe and act in harmony with the sequence of time. On winter ice, I use caution. There is no use in fighting winter. There is a rich profusion of plants and trees, but when the forces that bring such vegetation forth are inactive, the wise one avoids the limelight. The most secret and glorious aspect of my Self, now concealed, will unfold as time ripens. Such an incredible beauty lies within, that its immensity defies comprehension (see *I Ching:* Hexagram 2: The Passive Principle).[7]

Card Symbology: The Earth sister is green and represents the peak of The Mountain in fruition. She is pregnant, giving birth to light. Her body is a vehicle for all that is sacred on Earth.

Her ears are physically transformed because she has given herself over to hearing acutely. She hears the message in the sound of Om. She has called upon the spiral force of creation, the mighty cosmic power, which has answered the call and moves all about her head.

She is sparkling with the energy flow and lifeforce of the universe which moves through her with her every breath. She is the full completion of The Spark of Fire Sister, her Self in spirit.

Earth Sister is the essence of transfiguration. Her power comes from having/being a physical form. Her power to create comes from the fact that she is Earth, the limitless substance from which all things are made.

---

[6]See Dion Fortune's discussion of Malkuth in *The Mystical Qabalah*, p. 265.
[7]*Ibid.*

❖ ❖ ❖

CHAPTER TEN

The Tarot Keys

Key 0. The Fool

Divinatory Meaning ————————

All is movement, all change; this is a
precarious time, take a risk; have faith;
trust that you will be cradled; every fall
moves you closer to your own target of
perfection; you are in the cradle of perfect love; use this opportunity to create;
concentrate on the present; when walking, place one foot in front of the other;
no matter how high the mountain, the
peak is reached one step at a time; you
are in the first mode of empowerment:
detachment from outcome; undertake the
present enterprise because you must,
but detach yourself from outcomes; the
process is critically important at this
time, do not concern yourself with the
ultimate product.

0

THE FOOL

Meditation ————————————————————

All that which is that shall become
breath air spirit root

equation for aspiration
opposites intertwined
cycling spirals move mountains in the mind

Aleph
The Fool
on the path between the Primal Will and Wisdom
is the faithful Ox
that walks the furrow
is the root of manifestation
human adaptation; modification and form
in a Void, the Fool is born:

> Ox plows field
> Field brings wealth
> Wealth brings power
> Power brings health

Salvation is not attained on reasonable terms
and the Soul yearns for clues
I Shall Be is I Am Not
the life-breath prior to manifestation
pulsing in the god-eye of the free mason
in the beginning there is end
and in the end, birth

Life-Power just prior to a cycle of expression
as it will manifest itself upon the Earth
in infinite cycles of birth death re-creation
in infinite spirals of All and None
All that which Is that Shall Become.

Esoteric Qualities

Hebrew attribution: Aleph (pronounced *awlef*), the ox א
Astrological attribution: Air, the lifebreath of the universe
Eleventh Path: Mediates between Kether (the universal breath of life)
　　and Chokmah (the Eternal Father)
Essence: Blind movement
Intelligence: The Fiery Intelligence, the intelligence of the universal
　　lifeforce which burns eternally
Veil: Your present incarnation is the whole of experience.

Mystery: Eternal life is discoverable in the heart of hearts. In the deepest blindness is the deepest sight. The true unraveling of the mystery of eternal life is contingent upon understanding that the knowledge of the many is contained in the one and the knowledge of the one is contained in the many. This is the mystery of the Zero, the complete circle of the Fool. After the journey, the Fool always arrives back at the starting place. And yet, the Fool is transformed.

Interpretation

The Fool (Key 0) is the archetypal journeyer who moves through the entities known as the Keys, Archetypes, Trumps or Major Arcana of the tarot (Keys I through XXI). The Fool represents our own internal archetypal journeyer, the inner traveler on the path through life.

The Fool emerges from the void/abyss and begins the journey through the Keys to understand the mysteries of life. Without realizing it, the Fool longs to know, above all, why we emerge in human form, only to die. The Fool wants desperately to understand this great mystery. At the same time, however, the Fool moves along without desire and without thinking. There is a curious contradiction of simultaneously desiring and not desiring embodied in the archetype of the Fool.

The Fool, consciously, but not analytically, is on the path toward wisdom. The Fool's path is to seek wisdom through developing an understanding—or tolerance—of all the components of the human psyche, as well as all that which is *beyond the human psyche*.

The psyche is complex. The composite of the individual human being consists of many different personalities playing different roles and speaking with different voices. Yet these are all united in one house: the house of the human mind. The Fool moves through the layers and stages of the psyche. Each stage is an archetype, a perfect model or pattern of a personality type. The archetype is an energy pattern of basic psychological instincts. For example, the first archetype encountered by the Fool is the Magus. The Magus has the ability to create—with a wave of the wand—patterns of reality. The Fool becomes empowered to create upon encountering the Magus. The Fool's second encounter is the High Priestess. Through the High Priestess, the Fool learns the secrets of divination, the secrets of the past and future, through learning to access the divine scrolls where divine law is recorded.

These archetypes are the Keys of the tarot. The Fool, as the archetypal journeyer, who journeys for the sake of the journey and without expectation—taking one step at a time—mediates between all of the Keys. As mediator, the Fool embodies the essence of the path through the Keys.

Before stepping onto the path, the Fool begins in the starting place. In this space, there is a vacuum, and in that void, a balance of opposites and mysterious influences. This is the divine wisdom of creation. Some have called it by the name of the Tao. In the beginning, the Fool stands at the center of the Tao. Lao-Tsu says:

> The Tao that can be told is not the eternal Tao;
> The name that can be named is not the eternal Name.
> The Nameless is the Source of Heaven and Earth;
> The named is the Mother of the Ten Thousand Things.
> Desireless, one may behold the mystery;
> Desiring, one may see the manifestations.
> Though one in origin,
> They emerge with distinct names.
> Both are mysteries—
> Depth within depth—
> The threshold of all secrets.[1]

The Fool stands—without judgment—at the center of the breathing forces of the Tao. This is the center of Creation.

At the center of the air and fiery breath of potential lifeforms spinning in the void, the Fool moves in perfect harmony with the rhythms of nature, and in the purest state, before movement—*desireless*—forever sustained and cradled by unknown life-giving elements. The Fool—in purest form—resides at the threshold of all secrets, encircled by the divine wisdom of creation.

The Fool is Key 0. Zero is a circle and represents all possibility. This is the zero between sounds, the zero between thoughts, the zero of negative space: the inbreath between each letter and number, the secret space where creativity reigns supreme. The zero, like the Tao, is the process which cannot be told. Zero represents the vacuum of air that exists in the universe prior to manifestation. It is emptiness, but it is also Wind in its undeveloped form. Wind is the breath of the universe, the universe breathing in and out. The Fool is within the

---

[1]See *Tao Te Ching*, p. 18.

circle of all that is and *is* the circle of all that is. In the circle of all that is, the Fool is the whole. The Fool is also holy: trusting and innocent, operating out of perfect faith. As the universe breathes, the Fool blows out of the void. Then, for the Fool, everything *becomes* possible. The task of the Fool is to understand everything that is and then to return to the source. This is the complete circle of the zero.

The Fool blows out of the void because the universe heaves. To explain why this occurs, we could only make up a story. Some say, the Fool is sent by God, and therefore is a sacred child. That may be true, but, until there is further documentation, the real reason for the Fool's departure from the zero remains a mystery. Suffice it to say, the Fool *must* move. The Fool is merely *propelled*, heaved on the Eleventh Path of the Tree of Life back and forth between the principles of Universal Lifeforce (Kether) and the Eternal Father (Chokmah). So, on the Eleventh Path on the Tree of Life, the Fool rides in and out of the void on the fiery breath of the universe.

As in the festival of the April Fool, our own internal Fool begins to "ride out" in the spring. We want to see *everything!* We are subtly motivated by the same force that moves the Fool. It is the force that causes the seasonal growth on the Earth. It is as if, in springtime, our bodies fill with a sense of excitement. The force is with us! We seek love! We want to procreate! We are full of questions. Why are there seasons? Why do we breathe? Why do seeds take hold and shoots plow through the Earth? Where do babies come from? Like children, we question everything.

Our internal Fool is a child. It is the child of the universe, the child of the breath of life, wrapped, like an infant, in the process of creation. We are nudged from the circle of perfect balance, propelled forward by the unknown universal force. We move because we *must*. The child in us trusts. Because we trust, we risk. (Is this not *Foolish?*) We have an uncanny sense of assurance that where our path narrows and becomes a tenuous tightrope, there will be "safety nets." We feel that we are accompanied by many positive forces, both great and small, that offer us protection. In fact, at the very heart of the Fool's experience is the Unknown Savior. This is the surprise visitor who runs in just when we have been unjustly accused and are about to be hanged, saying "Quick, get your clothes, I'M BREAKING YOU OUT OF HERE!"

Our inner Fool is always innocent and always has faith. The Fool always loves. To those who are less trusting, such an innocent trust and basic belief in the rightness of things and the goodness of fellow beings may seem like idiocy or buffoonery. The Fool may seem naive, even to the point of being perceived as a *mark*, the intended victim of a swindle. But the Fool, although trusting and loving, is not naive. *The mere fact of trusting that things will right themselves does not preclude a sense of awareness of that which IS.* Even further, it can be stated that it is the very acuteness of awareness which makes the Fool appear childlike. To the Fool, all things are equal. That is why the Fool never misses anything.

In missing nothing, the Fool could—by a certain set of definitions—be viewed as an "expert." But since each observation only generates an exponential barrage of further questions, the Fool—while quietly aware of inner knowledge—with each passing moment, knows less than was known at the start. As such, the Fool, no matter how *wise*, remains, incessantly, just a Fool.

The Fool, cast out, must return to the source. On the path of return, every key must be encountered. Like the Fool, *you must now take the leap through every experience.* You must leap through every portal of life. Take the jump, but as you move, in order to truly enjoy the path, you must keep yourself DETACHED FROM OUTCOMES. Through focusing on outcome, you might miss the business at hand! This is your first mode of power: DETACHMENT FROM OUTCOME. Through detachment from outcome, you will be able to infinitely retain your strength for the journey, and *it is a long way back to the source.*

Do not worry. Do not be afraid. The time to move is now! The moment is beautiful! There are *wondrous blessings* upon the path, and, as always, *God protects Fools and small children.* Enjoy! And have a safe and pleasant journey!

Card Symbology: The Fool leaps from portal to portal, moving through every opening, forever stepping into the dark circle of the unknown. The flower upon the Fool's slipper is the red rose of desire. This rose, which represents Western thought, is the Fool's driving force. The message of the red rose is: God is without. The red rose is the driving force of heart.

In the right hand, the Fool carries a white rose of purity and clarity, love, faith and trust. This represents the Fool's attitude and highest aspirations.

In the left hand, the Fool carries the black box which contains the mysteries. The Fool holds every answer in this box.

The Fool looks upward, not down, toward the next step. This is because the Fool trusts that there will be no fall.

On the top of the Fool's head is a crown of lotus petals. The white lotus is the flower of Eastern thought. It is the flower that says: God is within. The Fool knows intuitively that God is both within and without at the same moment, and thus is balanced between. This is because the very life of the Fool is of God. The Fool arises from the mysterious intermeshing of the cosmic forces.

Beside the Fool runs the Fool's guide and friend. The guide is alert, aware and protective. The guide is playful, trusting and creative. The guide speaks with a clarity untarnished by the pressure of social expectations.

Fool and guide move through universal patterns with perfect trust and perfect love.

Key I. The Magus

Divinatory Meaning ————————

Know, will, dare and keep silent; you possess and wield the tools of magical change; you are a visionary, but it is not necessary to express this to others; trust the lessons of your own experience and insight; you embody force and power— you hold every key to create change, you have all the resources you need— but only if you operate through *focused action,* the second mode of empowerment; be ready to create your world in the image of your choosing.

THE MAGUS

Meditation ————————————————————————

"In the beginning was the Word,
and the Word was with God,
and the Word was God."

Beth, the House of Force,

The Temple of Spirit,
The House of Personality,
The Magus is
the communication of Mercury,
the Bearer of the Wand.
"He was in the beginning with God;
all things were made through him,
and without him was not anything made
that was made."
The Word of Creation whose
Speech is Silence
Truth and Falsehood
Wisdom and Folly
Shouting in the Void.
"In him was life
and the life was
the light of men."
Shining—luminescent with Transparency
juggling wine gold frankincense and fire
in the mire of unknowingness
but willing, knowing, daring, touching
there is initiative, primal will, the
primary mode of consciousness concealed behind all
veils of name and form
building domes where none have built before
drawing down the Power
to open the door
of Light and Darkness.
"The light shines in the darkness,
and the darkness has not overcome it." *(The Bible)*

Esoteric Qualities ─────────────────────────────

Hebrew attribution: Beth (pronounced *bayth*), the house ב
Astrological attribution: Mercury, communication
Twelfth Path: Mediates between Kether (the universal breath of life)
     and Binah (the Eternal Mother)
Essence: Controlled action
Intelligence: The Transparent Intelligence, the knower of all things
Veil: Illusion and trickery are the essence of magic.

Mystery: Magic is universal force traveling through the vehicle of the physical body. Fatherhood is not construed until children are brought forth.

Interpretation ─────────────────────────────────

Key One, the Magus, is *Beth*, the House. The house is potential form in which the universal force can reside. This house can be viewed as the House of God. It can also be viewed as the physical body, that which houses the divine spirit. The Magus represents the ability to channel and direct universal force through the vehicle of the house.

The Magus is the Supreme Magician: the master of dynamic power, expanded perception, the motivating energy at the center of the turning of the spring (see Key X). The Magus, standing at the center of the Wheel of Fortune, which is the circle of life, is the master of all things.

The Magus has mastered the three layers of mind: the subconscious (as symbolized by *the dark*), waking consciousness and the superconsciousness (called *the light*). The Magus is the master of the elemental forces of Fire, Water, Wind and Earth and the eight directions: South, West, East, North, Above, Below, Center and Ether. What does this mean?

Symbolically, the elements and directions are forces of spirit (Fire, South), emotion (Water, West), intellect (Wind, East) and matter (Earth, North). Spirit, emotion, intellect and matter are the first four directions. The next three are above, below and center. Above corresponds to superconsciousness, below to subconsciousness, center to waking consciousness. The final direction is Ether. The Ether is the substance that represents the summation of all that is. Ether is the direction which is everywhere and nowhere at once.

Through combining and recombining the forces and forms of the elements and eight directions, the Magus transforms the world. The ability to transform the world is the result of possessing the secret essence of the alchemical process of the ancients. Through this process, the baser metals of Self and world are transformed into gold and the elixir of perpetual life is discovered.

In coming to understand this secret alchemical process, the Magus must discover the power of the revelation I AM! I am unique. I am separate. I am powerful. I am magical. I can create the world as

I so choose! I am a visionary. I AM THE ONE LIFE! I AM THE CREATOR!

Whereas the Fool is all potential, all that is possible in the circle of existence, the Magus is the focal point—Key One—at the center of this circle. Out of this point, all that was, is and shall become, all that is manifest or material, proceeds. Through the powers of the Magus, potential is focused and brought into existence.

The Magus holds, understands, and *is* the master of wielding all the tools, both of mind and matter, of transformation. The major tools, which include the magical wand, cup or mirror, blade and shield or stone, represent the elemental forces of Fire, Water, Wind and Earth. The wand, which represents Fire (the spirit) conducts the force of energy. This energy is will and drive and represents the Magus' connection to macrocosmic forces. It is as if the Magus is connected to the lifeforce of the universe through an electrical current which can be channelled through the Wand. With the Wand, the Magus creates.

The Cup and Mirror, representing Water (emotions and divinatory power) contains all form. The Magus is fully capable of determining the shape or the form into which the universal energy force will be channelled. With Cup and Mirror, the Magus preserves, but also dissolves.

The Blade of the Magus (the intellect) is the tool of reason. It is the analytical ability to break information into its smallest components, the ability to understand the whole through the force of microcosm. The Blade represents knowledge gained through systematic attempts to know. It is the persevering effort of the Magus. The Blade is paradoxically a weapon, the power of the Magus to destroy. With the Blade, the Magus both creates and destroys the universe.

The Shield and Stone represent matter (the body). They provide protection for the Magus. The Shield is also a shining coin. With this coin, the Magus redeems. The Shield sometimes appears as a pentacle. The five points of the pentacle correspond to the arms, legs and head of the Magus. This represents the power of materialization.

The Magus' Creed—which is the essence of bringing the creative force into form—corresponds to the working tools. That creed is:

TO KNOW (intellect, Wind)
TO WILL (spirit, Fire)

TO DARE (emotion, Water)
TO KEEP SILENT (manifestation, Earth).

Maintaining silence is essential for the Magus. Those who have eyes to see will see. Those who have ears to hear will hear. The Magus need not attempt to explain the magic of creation to those who disbelieve.

In Magus energy, you are in tune with the most creative and powerful aspects of your Self. It is the part of you that directs the flow of creative energy. It is the part of you that receives the force and creates reality, that changes the structure of the living situation at will.

In order to effect lasting and rewarding changes, however, you need to be in balance with the universal flow and observe the divine law. The key to balancing is to know and understand your Self. This means that you must attune to your strengths in Fire, in Water, in Wind and Earth. Fire is the source of strength and drive of the primitive or energetic Self. Water is the structure or pattern of the relationships and situations or forms you create. Wind is your analytical mode. How do you arrive at and rationalize your conclusions? And then, how do you manifest these structures in your physical reality? How do you manifest the products of your imagination on your Earth?

To tap the cosmic energy flow and use it toward your ends, you must first recognize and affirm your own power. You are gifted and unique. You are your own leader. You are creating the structure of your own life. If you wish to change, you have only to alter your ways. Nothing concrete stands in your way. If you perceive obstacles, it is only the result of your own lack of confidence or your lack of attunement to your higher purpose.

What could explain an inability to manifest that which you want? It could well be that you are out of balance, that you are not standing balanced at the center of the Wheel of Life, but that you are off to one side, too caught up in North, South, East or West, and as a result, you find yourself precariously clinging to center, but unable to move.

Do not let yourself be distracted by outside influences. Attune to center. Be careful about whose opinions you take to heart. And remember, you need not explain yourself.

It is time to know, to will, to dare and to keep silent.

The key for the Magus is to trust the lessons of experience. The Magus is continually refining internal energies. This means that the Magus is becoming a clear and calm actor and reactor, a clear and calm channel of the inner word. The Magus meets calamity with constancy.

The higher purpose of the human race is to create and maintain a world of beauty, goodness and truth. It is to create a world of harmonium. Here we all become the Magus. We create our world in the image in which we wish to experience it. This is the natural way of universal will. If you are not succeeding, examine your motives. Are you working with clarity? Are you working with an attitude of goodness? Are you bringing light to others?

The Magus is the creative power of the unmoved mover who stands in perfect balance at the center of the wheel. In perfect balance there is perfect trust. In perfect trust, there is perfect love. In perfect love, the vision is clear.

The Magus represents your second mode of power, FOCUSED ACTION. Through action with a clear focus, the universe is transformed.

Card Symbology: The Magus stands in the garden of all that was, is and shall become. The garden is in the House of Beth.

The verdant spirals of red and green at either side of the table represent the powers of the Magus to divide the world into component parts. These spirals are the basic patterns of light and dark, yang and yin, intellect and emotion, not as yet divided into polarities.

The Magus' table is the same black box carried by the Fool. It contains all possibility.

Atop this workspace are the tools of the Magus. Here we find the wand, the sword, the cup and the pentacle (coin, shield). These represent the internal ability to create.

The Magus's right hand is raised and moving in a rapid figure eight, drawing down the force of the universal essence.

The outer cloak of the Magus is black for the unknown. The lining is red for the desire to know. The inner garment is white, denoting purity, innocence and sacredness of intention. White, red and black are also aspects of the life cycle. White is the beginning. Red is the middle time, a time of healing. Black is the end, a time of wisdom. These are the colors of the Hermit and also the three blood mysteries of woman.

Since the power of illusion is inherent in the power of manifestation, the Magus is masked.

Key II. The High Priestess

Divinatory Meaning ————————

All knowledge of dark and light forces
is good; every experience contains a
message for growth; listen and you will
hear the message of your own inner
teacher guiding you in this mysterious
time; attune to faith; you are accessing
hidden or secret knowledge; be aware
of all signals in your environment; attune to impulses; remember, retaining
memory is the third mode of empowerment; the gift of insight is now at hand.

II

THE HIGH PRIESTESS

Meditation ————————

Gimel
Crescent Goddess of the Moon
Maga, the High Priestess
Water Bearer in the Desert
Connect me with my Inner Spring!
memories borne
from one life to the next
silver thorne crown
crescent horn supporting Moon
in tune with Secret forces
of Mystic seas; Secret Orb
You hold the Gift of Vision
Direction Equilibrium Perception
Decision
WaterBearer: Vessel of Salt and Sand and Dark and Sky

heal and set free the innermost reaches
that I may use my Powers wisely
to reach the fertile oasis
of my Inner Stream
even knowing that the stream is
but a veil beyond Spirit
and the Spirit
but a Dream away

Crescent Goddess of the Moon
High Priestess
Let me drink from your Sacred gourd
that I may be filled and
behold your Sacred Lord
and Heal.

Esoteric Qualities ───────────────────────────

Hebrew attribution: Gimel (pronounced *geemel*), the camel ג
Astrological attribution: The Moon, intuitive reflection
Thirteenth Path: Mediates between Kether (the universal breath of
    life) and Tiphareth (spiritual beauty and light manifested on the
    plane of earth)
Essence: Water—the channel that connects the world of spirit to the
    world of matter, the above to the below, the light to the dark
Intelligence: The Uniting Intelligence, the mediating factor between
    the worlds of spirit and matter
Veil: The world of matter is all that is.
Mystery: Through the dark collective memory of all that was, is and
    shall become, the one light of knowledge is encountered. Truth
    shines through the collective memory of darkness. There is light
    in the darkness. We know this to be true, and yet the source of
    our faith remains a mystery.

Interpretation ───────────────────────────

The High Priestess, also called the *Maga* (pronounced Mah-zhah), is
Key II. Two is division. Two is polarization. The Maga polarizes male
and female, yang and yin, light and dark, positive and negative, action
and reaction, flux and reflux, yes and no, initiative and resistance,

flood and ebb, wax and wane. She represents the upper portion of the central pillar of the Tree of Life which connects the world of the gods with the world of humans. She is the mediating factor between worlds. She is the equilibrating factor between the great forces. Thus, the High Priestess is called the *uniting intelligence.*

The astrological symbol of the High Priestess is the Moon, also known as the Silver Star. This star reflects the light of the world of the gods. It reflects the light of the One Light or One Life, the light of the "Above," a light which—as described by mystics and magicians—is *too brilliant to behold.* The symbol of this brilliant light is sometimes considered to be the star Sirius. Sirius, like the Moon, is also occasionally referred to as "the Silver Star."

The Moon is seen as the mediator of light. But is the Moon the thing it reflects? Is the Moon the source of light? No, it is not. And yet the Moon knows the source and offers the image of the source to reflect upon. But one must not mistake the channel or reflector of the light for the light itself for the image will always be influenced by the character of the reflector. If Water dances, stars reflected in the Water will dance. Does this mean the stars are dancing?

The High Priestess is the perfect reflector because she is the archetypal Key of the Open Channel. The Open Channel, which we first contemplated in the One of Water, is like a hollow tube or chute, a form through which energy can pass. The energy of the Priestess crosses over the *secret sphere* on the Tree of Life and becomes the bridge which unites the universal breath of life with beauty and harmony on the plane of physical existence.

The secret sphere on the Tree of Life, which is the sphere called Daath, is at the conjunction of the Eternal Mother and Father principles—the balance and creative potential—of God. As occult practitioner Gareth Knight says, this is the sphere where the force of the universe comes to inhabit form. It is the sphere where form first manifests. The High Priestess knows this sphere and extracts forms therefrom. The forms drawn by the Priestess are not actual images and shapes, but rather the abstract forms of essential energies.

The abstraction of the essential energies represents the highest point of awareness of the human soul. This is the mystical point where there is "a clear-cut realization of the various potencies of life and their unity with God and with the soul . . . [where] the balance and realisation and *absorption* of these potencies meet together in the light of the abstract mind."[2] Thus, the sphere crossed by the Priestess, that sphere known as Daath, represents the highest stage of evolution and the gateway to enlightenment. It is supreme wisdom and the supreme power of realization.

The channel of connection between the worlds of spirit and body, which abstracts the nature of universal energies, is symbolized by the caduceus, the winged staff carried by Mercury. The caduceus represents the simultaneous ascent and descent of universal energies. (See fig. 10.) In that such energies have the power to unify body and spirit, they become a healing force. The caduceus is, noncoincidentally, used as a symbol of healing by the medical profession.

The High Priestess is the hidden knowledge of the inner workings of the universe. She represents the Law of Cyclic Action and Polarity. Within this law is the key to the actualization of human potential. The potential of the soul goes well beyond the potential of the present incarnation. The High Priestess symbolizes the memories carried in the subconscious mind from one life to the next. Thus, in the Hebrew attribution, the High Priestess appears as a camel. The camel moves through the great desert of Daath, the world of abstract energies, as the waterbearer. This symbolizes profound attunement to the psychic or intuitive world. Through powerfully attuning in the state of mystical consciousness, the camel can even move through the eye of a needle. Further, as indicated above, learning such attunement is the secret to the mystery of healing, which can only be attained through connecting and balancing the world of spirit with body, above with below, gods with humans.

The High Priestess helps us to clarify the purpose and potential of our Selves and our world. She helps us work toward healing the ills which plague us. She teaches us about the critical connections by which we can achieve lasting health. In short, she *enables* us.

The word *Maga*, by which the Priestess is also called, comes from the Indo-European root *magh* which means "to be able." *Magh* is also the root word for magic. With the tools of the Magus and the connections to the deep stream of consciousness, the power of the High Priestess enables us to heal our Selves and to maximize our potential.

Enabling the Self means developing the capability to meet all situations with confidence and skill. One can only do this through

---

[2]See *A Practical Guide to Qabalistic Symbolism*, Vol. 1, p. 103.

The Veil of — — — — — — — — the abyss.

Figure 10. The Caduceus.

discovering what brings meaning and fulfillment to life and dedicating one's self to that discovery. As you peel back the layers that veil the Self, moving ever-deeper, you discover more and more the spiritual basis of your existence. You attain faith. That is why the mystery of the High Priestess is the mystery of faith.

As the energy flows between worlds, the personality changes form. This is because you are opening your psychic centers, but it is often better not to open too fast. With a gradual opening, the material life will remain stable and not become suddenly chaotic.

The Maga holds the scroll which outlines the principles of spiritual organization and devotion to the higher principles. This is the scroll of the divine law. Read and understand this scroll—which some have referred to as the Akashic Records—before you dive into Daath, the sphere in the midst of the abyss, or you may find your Self drowning in the waters of oblivion.

Attaining the understanding of the connection between the worlds of spirit and matter is the third mode of power: MEMORY. This is the gift of knowing the collective past, present and future. You can access the scroll of memory in the deepest layers of your subconscious mind. Go deep within your Self to find the answer. The answers reside deep in your inner temple. Therein you will also find the gift of immortality.

Card Symbology: The High Priestess is seated on the cube which is the black box of possibility. In her hand, she holds the scroll of the divine law which is the law and record of Nature. The scroll is unwound and falls down to her feet. Her feet rest on a black and white pattern which represents the duality of polarized forces. This is the floor of the inner temple. Through this pattern runs a stream. This is the stream of consciousness which flows through lifetimes.

To the left is the black pillar of understanding. This is also called the Pillar of Severity. To the right is the Pillar of Wisdom and Mercy. The High Priestess is the central pillar, the Pillar of Mildness. These are the pillars as they appear on the Tree of Life. At the top of each pillar is a spiral force. This is the spiral force of creation.

The gown of the Priestess is blue for the color of Water and the limitless substance of the universe. On her chest is a cross of equal arms, denoting balance in the four directions of spirit, emotions, intellect and body. It also symbolizes the spiritual path intersecting the world of matter.

The High Priestess understands the mysteries. Thus, at the top of her masked head is a Great Eye. This eye represents her all-sensing inner vision. Above the eye is a white pyramid. This is the dark pyramid of the past, now transformed into clarity and limitless light. This transformation, which occurs through attaining psychic connection, becomes the pavement of the spiritual path. The white pyramid is thus like a highway leading to the Above.

Beyond that, rent veils—which appear as the wings of the holy ghost—float upon the air of the above. They represent the first three veils of the first three Keys of the tarot.

Key III. The Empress

Divinatory Meaning

III

THE EMPRESS

You are opening to all sensuality, revel in the delights of the senses; a great beauty is revealed; all is perfection; all is receptive; the things of earth are voluptuously welcoming at this time; you are moving with the flow; earth is your dominion, all things of nature respond perfectly to you; you find comfort among birds, beasts and fellow and sister travelers; there is no need to control; the key at this time is to remember that *imagination is everything.*

Meditation

Will you come next, Sun?
Come through my leafy Door?
come to cast your precious
silky silver rays across
the grove of new and sacred cypress
and leafy wreathlets strung with strands of glistening
pearls; webs of dew;
furry creatures, cold and wet
cooing in the fields where the gold and cobalt lapis
ether: Night Sky—
so recently laid upon me
with all his jewels—ruby/diamond/aqua—glistening down
like so many wonders
carressing, holding, every drape and fold
of my smoky emerald gown
while I gave birth to all
that was, is, and ever shall be
things of beauty, tenderness

pelican and eagle—first to come—
guarded the entrance of cave/womb/home
gentle, delicate hens
pelican gave blood to swallow
eagle feathered the hollow

Now, come Sun, merry meet, through
the channel as well
dawn and dry the borning seas
cast your healing morning rays
across the dewy wings of pelican, eagle, downy damp pelts
of the tiny beasts
unfolding lily and rose
and we shall together thrive in peace
come Sun. Merry meet. Merry meet and part in mirth.
come to heart
and illuminate this Birth.

Esoteric Qualities

Hebrew attribution: Daleth (pronounced *dawleth*), the door ד
Astrological attribution: Venus, love
Fourteenth Path: Mediates between Binah (the Eternal Mother) and
   Chokmah (the Eternal Father)
Essence: The Laws of Nature are understood by working with free
   form imagination
Intelligence: The Luminous Intelligence, the expression of the One
   Life or the One Light in form manifested on the physical plane
Veil: In pain and sorrow you shall bring forth children.
Mystery: In Nature is repeated the archetypal pattern of the One Life.
   Evidence of the One Life appears in its many manifestations.

Interpretation

Key III is the Empress. The Empress is the gateway to form, guardian
of the threshold to Earth. The Empress represents the unity of the
universal female and male forces, the Mother and the Father, form
and force, receptivity and emission.

Form is life, and the Empress is the bearer of that life. She is the
channel between Binah, the quintessential Female Principle on the
Qabalistic Tree of Life, who receives the Force of Life from Chokmah,

the male Principle. Binah nurtures this force in her watery womb and
then delivers this force, transformed, back into the universe.

The Empress is the essence of pregnancy and birth. She is the
universal force of vagina, womb and birth canal. Thus, her traditional
symbols include the glyph of Venus and the Egyptian ankh. Both of
these represent the uterus of woman. The glyph is a solar circle—the
emblem of *Radiant Spirit,* the all and the nothing, the female channel—
surmounting the cross of manifestation.

Because she is the transmitter of radiant spirit, the One Light of
the universe, which is contained in all life, she is referred to as the
luminous intelligence. Every form produced by the Eternal Mother
shines with the light of the spirit.

As the universal Mother, the Empress is the second aspect of the
Triple Goddess and the female aspect of the Creator. (The first aspect
of the Triple Goddess is the High Priestess, who represents Maid-
enhood. The third is the Crone, the old Wise Woman, represented
in the tarot by the androgynous Hermit.)

The Empress, as the feminine side of God, the Goddess, always
represents the power of manifestation or the ability to contain the
lifeforce in the world of form. As the Universal Mother, she symbolizes the second blood mystery of woman. This is the stage when
blood ceases and is transformed, as if by magical means, into milk.
As the milk of the universe, the Empress is all-abundance and all-
nurturing. She is the sparkling primeval ocean of milk from which
all souls emanate and to which all souls return. This is the luminous
sea of milk. It can be symbolically described as the Milky Way.

The Zohar, the qabalistic Bible, written in the 13th century, states:

> It [the luminous sea] is in truth 'great' and not small, for it
> takes all (souls) the higher and the lower up into itself and
> encloses them in itself. It is the great wide place which con-
> tains everything in itself and yet is not overfilled as indicated
> in the verse: 'All rivers flow into the sea and the sea is not
> full'—all (souls) go into this 'sea,' and the 'sea' takes them
> in and consumes them without becoming full; it brings them
> forth new and they go their way . . .[3]

Containing all, without overflowing, The Empress is all-abundance.
She is the symbol of fertility, shelter, protection and nourishment, all

[3]As quoted by Erich Neumann in *The Great Mother* (Princeton, NJ: Princeton University
Press, 1963), p. 242.

this of the soul. She manifests, not objects, but patterns on the spiritual plane. These patterns are the manifestation of the abstract idea of creation. She emits patterns for the structure of existence. She provides the blueprint of nature, or the Matrix of the Soul.

In the Hebrew attribution, the Empress is a door. She is the door of nature. Because she is the cradle from which all souls emit and to which all souls return, she is a two way door. She is the door of birth as well as the door of death. This is the essence of form. All forms come into being to contain the force of creativity, but as we grow, forms become too small and must be discarded. This is necessary so that our creativity can assume a new shape. So it is with the Empress who tirelessly cradles and tirelessly emits new "children."

The Empress within you is the master creator in the world of form. In order to emit new form, you must first be receptive to abstract idea and allow such idea to be implanted in your Self, soul or personal matrix. In the first stage, as the receiver of idea, you are the very essence of Venus, the first aspect of the Empress. Venus is the goddess of love and beauty. Love is the substance—the glue—that allows the seed of idea to cling to the womb. Venus is also the thunderous power of sexuality. As the great and beautiful temptress, the Empress as Venus draws all creativity toward and into herself.

You are Venus. You are all-beautiful. You are the all-attracting spirit. You are the essence of love, that which binds the universe into form. And you are Venus, the huntress! You capture souls!

In the second stage, you are the nurturer. You hold and cradle life. You are all abundance. Everything has come to you! You give everything back in abundance with the magic of your mothering. You are friend and nurturer of all, all creatures of land and sea, the bountiful land and sea itself, the open and glorious sky. Everything moves into your abundance and emerges renewed. In such abundance, there is only calm and enduring joy. There is no fear.

In the third stage, you are the birther. You release! You expel the force in its new form. If you experience sorrow at letting go, let the sorrow be experienced with an undercurrent of joy, for to release means that there is space made for ever-more-powerful and beautiful forms. Sorrow is a veil which masks ever greater levels of creativity. Freely release and the birth, while laborious, need not be painful. Realize that as you relax and release, you are sending forth the children of hope. And these are your own children, the children of your mind and body.

These children further the structure of spirit. They are the blueprint of nature even as they expand the blueprint of nature. Through the creative process, the mind of God grows. Your "children"—the children of your mind and body—reflect the matrix of the cosmic sea within you. In your womb is concealed the fundamental ideas of holiness, the foundation of all beings in form. You understand the sacred nature of the universe. You are reproducing that sacredness in the forms you birth in your life.

The womb of the Empress—whether represented by the phantom womb of the male (or wombless female) or the actual mother-womb—is the cradle of creativity. Let all creativity—all sexual and nurturing connection—be attuned to the sacred flow of the universe. Let the binding glue be love.

Card Symbology: The Empress is a door. She is the door to the House of Beth, guarding the threshold to the world of form. She is the door to the Pillar of Understanding on the Tree of Life.

The veils behind her are green and feel spring-like for the newness and life-giving ability inherent in life itself. They take the form of swirling cypress trees.

The Empress sits on a black throne, the base of which is the black cube. This throne is an illusion, for the Empress floats before darkness. At the pinnacle of this darkness is an eagle. This is the only creature traditionally considered to be able to look at the Sun which is the symbol of spiritual life and light. The eagle is the messenger from heaven, the symbol of divine majesty. It is capable of rising to incredible heights. The eagle represents the Empress' connection to Kether, the messenger of the light of the universe, the crown or primal will of the Tree of Life.

The Empress sits atop a scroll which is the divine law of the High Priestess. Her feet rest upon the crescent Moon which is the beginning of the stream of consciousness.

Her costume is shimmering white and yellow. She has a belt of emerald triangles and an emerald triangle is upon her breast. These represent the holy trinity of the supernal forces on the Tree of Life: Kether (the Primal Will), Chokmah (the Father Principle), and Binah (the Mother Principle). The Empress wears a shawl of roses. The rose is for desire and the red magic of the Great Mother. This is the magic of healing. Her headdress is white lilies for spirituality and purity.

A dove rests on the right hand of the Empress, symbol of her inner peace and also representative of her connection to the world of creatures. In her left hand, she holds the glyph for Venus, her ruling planet.

The Empress is pregnant with the Divine Son (Sun). The son is luminous form on the plane of matter.

Key IV. The Emperor

Divinatory Meaning

Build a firm base of clear knowledge; do not become too rigid; remain open and lucid; to retain control, know and serve a higher force; build your world in beauty and light; do not forget that the Emperor remains Emperor because he has a global sense of things that others do not necessarily possess, yet he will be overthrown if he does not serve his constituents; to remain in power, use your insight and serve those around you.

IV

THE EMPEROR

Meditation

The Emperor, a Window to admit Light and Air
into the House of Beth

Wise Ruler serves by ruling, rules by serving
Power is aligning Love, Thought, Body, Spirit
with the Way of Nature's Laws
in the context of the Rules Ordained

He who would Change that which Is
best first understand his own flaws
He who would control the Mother
best understand first Her Laws

and she is in Flux
not Just, but Exacting
for Nature moves in long strides

The Wise Emperor will not attempt to
enter Her unknown chasm
or cross it with two leaps
but waits to see the Void decrease
then makes his move

The Changer remains, at depth, unknown
known only—fleetingly, and on the surface—by his works
for Paternity is not conceived
until Form emanates.

Esoteric Qualities

Hebrew attribution: Heh (pronounced *hay*), the window   ה
Astrological attribution: Aries, dynamism
Fifteenth Path: Mediates between Chokmah (the Eternal Father Prin-
    ciple) and Tiphareth (spiritual beauty and light manifested on
    the plane of earth)
Essence: Eye of the wind: the clear illuminated window in the dark-
    ness; the interior nature of all form
Intelligence: The Constituting Intelligence, that which creates all of
    existence
Veil: The surface of existence reveals all that is.
Mystery: The vision and the voice are one. The creative word calls
    all into being and yet the word is not the thing. Existence is but
    a veil of concealment, concealing the structural pattern of the
    One Life.

Interpretation

The Emperor is swift, male, creative energy. He is a discoverer, a
leader, a pioneer, initiator and adventurer. He has clear sight and
presence of mind. This enables him to be exceedingly well organized.

His sight is clear because he is, figuratively, a window. He is
Heh which means window. Literally, Heh is the eye of the wind
(*auga*, eye, Indo-European; *vindr*, Old Norse; *windoge*, Middle English). The eye of the wind is the transparent opening or *pane*, which

illuminates the structure of all form. This is the eye or Windowpane of the Soul—that which sees All, knows All—the mystical third eye of the East.

It is noteworthy that the root of pane is *pan* which means *fabric* (Indo-European). The Emperor is like the window*pane* that *is* the structure of all things, even as it *allows for the illumination* of the structure of all things. This structure can be seen as the *fabric* of all substance.

Because the Emperor understands the *nature of structure* so well, he knows what can and cannot be controlled. His success is based on possessing the ability to change that which is changeable, to accept that which cannot be changed and the wisdom to know the difference between the two. This is the key to the Emperor's wisdom.

From this knowledge emanates the idea that the best Emperor serves his subjects by ruling and retains his power of initiative only through offering himself in service. To remain in power, he must meet external needs, needs that transcend his own personal needs. To meet others' needs, he must know and understand all that—both human and non-human—he serves. Thus, his intelligence is reflective, just as it is *constituting*.

The Emperor is referred to as the Key of *constituting intelligence*. This is because he makes up the components or elements of form. The Emperor knows the substance of form and, simultaneously, *is* the substance of form. He knows it because he *is* it. This is one of his mysteries.

The Emperor is Key IV. Four represents stability and security. It is substance. Four represents the physical plane. It is the number of building physical structures. It is also the base number of the cube. The cube, which is the Emperor's throne, has six faces and is composed of twelve intersecting lines. Twelve is a complex juxtaposition of four—the ephemeral—and three—the eternal. The six sides of the cube unfold into the Calvary Cross, which represents sacrifice. The most poignant aspects of sacrifice are symbolized by the death of Jesus.

This is the base of the Emperor's experience: He retains his influence through sacrificing. As the mediating force between the light realm of the universal force of emission, Chokmah (the Eternal Father Principle), and Tiphareth, the One Light manifested on the Material Plane (the Sun, divine son, beauty), the Emperor provides resolution for a basic male conflict. He understands well that Christ was crowned as King because he sacrificed himself for the higher good. This is not to say that the Emperor is manipulative and would sacrifice himself in order to gain. Rather, it is by his very nature that the Emperor sacrifices his life for his subjects. He knows that true gain comes through surrender. If he does not serve, or becomes too enamored of himself or his power, he will face rejection, the fall from grace. Thereby, the Emperor knows the mysteries of Death (see Key XIII) and Divine Resurrection (see Key XX). The Emperor understands the essence of the Father as well as the Son. He is *fatherly*. He is benevolent, compassionate, understanding, protective. He is the archetypal savior with the power to redeem the falsely accused and pardon the sinner.

He is also the father who engenders the child. Although the force is unseen, it is the father who impregnates the mother who in turn brings form into being. This is the capacity of the Emperor as originator.

In mythical expression, Father Time holds the hourglass as well as the scythe. His sense of timing is of the essence. Timing is of the essence in impregnating the universal female force. The Emperor is successful because his is an expression of the primal will to yield fruit and he understands the nature of all things. The Emperor, as Father Time, is the perfect archetypal mate for Mother Nature. He enters Mother Nature—the dark, cool, receptive force—and plants the seed of form. Therefore, the Emperor has been called He Who Sets in Order, or He Who Constitutes. Although unseen, he is the supreme architect of the universe.

The Emperor, working through you, frames the constitution of your personal world. This means that, as if framing a picture through the lens of a camera, you constitute your world through the focal points you select. You have power over your subject matter, but only if you understand its nuances. Your timing is of the essence. You must understand the workings of the camera, frame the shot and capture the light. The outcome depends on how well you "serve" your subject. To do this, you must project yourself into your subject and understand it. You must also understand your tools. You become the artist, the tripod, the camera, the landscape, the frame, the light, the photograph. You are the path of light. You are the stuff from which every form is built and the supply for every need. You are the master. You are the progeny.

Once you have the vision—once you have constituted your "frame"—you also have the voice. You speak your truth through your vision. For those who have ears to hear, this is the way of the word. In truth, you utter your Self by the way you see.

When the patrons of art come to view your works, however, they do not see you. They see only your product, your work. This is as it is with the unseen creative force of the universe: the Emperor. So, it is said: existence is a veil of concealment, for "Thou shalt never see me as I am, but thou mayest know me in what I have done."[4]

The lesson of the Emperor is this: whatsoever you wish to conquer, you must serve. Whatsoever offspring you wish to beget, you, alone, must father. Therefore, let thy deeds be the offspring of the path of light.

Card Symbology: The Emperor carries much of the symbology of the Empress. His leggings are the bodies of eagles, because he has the ability to soar to the uppermost heights. In his right hand is the staff of Venus, showing his connection to the Empress. But, as she is the door, he is the window.

He sits inside, outside and within the window of the House of Beth. This is because he is both the window to the structure of the universe and the structure of the window itself.

Across the front of the window is a cross of equal arms which intersects behind the eyes of the Emperor. It intersects at the Emperor's pineal gland, the location of the third eye and the seat of the soul. The pineal gland is the connecting link between the autonomic and spinal nervous systems. It translates impressions received by the subjective self into impressions for the brain to comprehend.

Behind the Emperor is a pyramid of light—his *cone of power*—which descends, as if through his body, to his navel, where we see the dotted cross of equal arms. The pyramid of light combined with the dotted cross of equal arms is the glyph for sulphur, which represents Fire, one of the four major universal forces of creation. The Ram Head Sceptre is also a reference to Fire, the energy of beginnings.

The pyramid of light that descends upon the Emperor is the transformed eye of the One of Fire. It has now become a road that leads to the higher plane of the supernals.

The divine scroll has now entirely wrapped the black cube upon which the Emperor is seated. This is because the Emperor has a comprehensive understanding of the divine law and divine records. Through understanding, he has mastered the dark. This is his essence: He is a window of light in darkness.

---

[4]Paul Foster Case, *The Book of Tokens, Tarot Meditations* (Los Angeles: Builders of the Adytum, 1968), p. 56.

Beneath his feet, the stream of consciousness flows from the bottom of the cube. It is light and clear and flows as ribbons.

To either side of the Emperor in the House of Beth is a red wall with an X. The X is the crossed path of the physical and spiritual planes. It is the X of the Two of Wind, the X that heals.

Key V. The Hierophant

Divinatory Meaning ————————

Connect with your higher self; listen for messages surfacing within; become both student and teacher; seek both student and teacher; make all moves in the light of your own truth and sense of justice; let your conscience be your guide; the most important thing at this time is to attune yourself spiritually; to find the answers, seek out your god or goddess; you will find that your inner guides are waiting to serve you; quiet yourself internally and you will be able to hear the answers.

V

THE HIEROPHANT

Meditation ————————————————————————————

High Priest: Sacred Vision
transmitter of the Flame of Spirit
holy master, initiate
inner guide of the highest Transformation
unifying interior illumination with exterior manifestation
retaining dominion
advising. Knowing, Willing, Doing
and remaining cautiously removed, of no opinion

Wounded Teacher
every lesson has its pains
every loss, its gains
the Nail that binds the crucifixion
striking the revelation of Truths and Words and Deeds

not always in Time with social motion
but always the "and" of us
nailing the Spirit to the Cross of Matter
the stuff of which the Universe is bound

Nailing, Binding, Hooking in
to Eternal Light
Triumphant Intelligence
with the positive conviction of Eternal Life
the Self exalted beyond
the Limitations of Time

the Representative of Conscious Awakening
(bypassing vestiges of dogma—set aside for novices—
and tricks built in by tricksters
and those who are afraid)
knowing the eclectic Truth
as the Magus of the Eternal
the Sage is Naked
on the Four Sacred Planes, now united as One
bathed in Holy Ether: the Fifth Sacred Plane
(the glue of Cause and Effect)
The Head of the Sage is cocked and listening
if the Path is Truth.

Esoteric Qualities ————————————————————————

Hebrew attribution: Vav (pronounced *vahv*), the nail ו
Astrological attribution: Taurus, loyalty and patience
Sixteenth Path: Mediates between Chokmah (the Eternal Father Prin-
    ciple) and Chesed (the Universal Principle of production)
Essence: The connection with the One Eternal Light, the voice in the
    inner ear which tells the nature of the substance which bonds
    together the pieces of the fabric of existence
Intelligence: The Triumphant, Eternal Intelligence, accessible to the
    inner self
Veil: The scriptures are truth and must not be altered. Interpreting
    such works remains the province of experts.
Mystery: As sharp nails fasten the House of Beth, the bonds of love
    fasten the universe.

Interpretation ——————————————————————————

The Hierophant is the inner teacher. He is the message of the higher self or the perception of higher consciousness. This is because he is the direct reflection of pure spiritual being. To perceive his existence within the Self is to understand the glory of living in the light.

The Hierophant is the revelation of the inner voice, or the flash of insight that comes when least expected. He is the inner nudge or direct firsthand experience—be it intellectual, spiritual, emotional or physical—that guides you on your path through life. This flash, which lets you know what you should be doing, may come in the form of a twinge in the stomach, a tightening of the throat, a pang in the heart. It may come in the form of a sudden, unexpected surge of joy or a tear that leaps to the eye. The Hierophant is speaking when you are thinking: HEY! I *LOVE* THIS PLACE! or HOW AM I GOING TO GET *OUT* OF HERE?

The message of the Hierophant does not usually come in the form of words or complete thoughts, but rather like a deep hearing or a vague or amorphous or visceral feeling. You may know the message when, for example, you experience a sense of discomfort in a situation which you previously found pleasurable. This is the Hierophant speaking to you. You are hearing the "words" of your higher consciousness or higher self.

You recognize the guidance of the Hierophant as the truth because it has a ring of eternity. It *feels* like truth. Through the Hierophant, you tap into a deep space of Self which is connected to your own immortality. Thus, the Hierophant is a bridge between your outer experience and the way this experience is illuminated on the deepest inner level. When you tune in to the messages of the Hierophant, you are tuning in to the primal will of the universe. You are hearing your spiritual Self, but in its *realized* form. You are a human being—containing the lifeforce of spirit—residing on the planet Earth in a physical body. You must accept this structure and work with it.

Thus, the Hierophant can be seen as the Five-Armed Star of Humanity cartwheeling to Earth, the human being after the fall of the spirit to the condition of Humanity. His five-armed star combines the Eternal Circle (Key III, Mother Nature, Eternal Matter, the Empress), with the divine powers of polarization (Key II, Eternal Spirit, the High Priestess). In these two worlds, the Hierophant is the initiate and the mediator. He connects the worlds of matter and spirit. Thus, he is seen as the nail, the binding force of the universe, that which nails spirit to matter.

As the great manifestor—or the spirit in the form of Humanity—he perfects and brings into being all that he wishes. He is enabled, or empowered, through his wisdom and understanding and the gift of thought and because he embodies the creative energies of the Magus, the High Priestess, the Empress and the Emperor. He embodies and understands the power of Wind (intellect and knowledge), Fire (action and will power), Water (emotion, daring and desire) and Manifestation (the incorporation of spirit—creativity—in physical form).

With these energies balanced, the Hierophant has the power to channel or direct cosmic power from level to level to create and destroy. His secret is the energy spiral. He spirals energy clockwise to create, counterclockwise to destroy.

He is known by the esoteric name: Magus of the Eternal. The eternal or the primal will is represented by Kether, the first sphere, on the Tree of Life. This will is brought into manifestation through Chokmah, the Eternal Father Principle. Then through Chesed, the universal force of production, the will is transferred to the individual personality. The Hierophant is the mediator who draws down the energy.

Because he is propelled, however, by his desire to *ascend* or to reconnect with the source from which he sprang, he is often seen sitting in passivity. He need not wield his great powers.

On the path toward understanding the mysteries of life, the Hierophant is known as the Sacrificial Priest. He embodies the strength and resolution to dissolve or to discard that which is no longer needed. As sacrificial priest, he also embodies the strength and resolution necessary to banish and therefore to overcome self-pity.

Thus he is the star of sacrifice as well as the star of manifestation, that which brings forth. He is also known as the guiding star of divinity. The Hierophant's primary role is to illuminate. He illuminates sacred (inner) realities and teaches hidden laws. One of the most important symbols of the illumination of a sacred reality is the birth of Christ in a lowly manger. The birth of Christ-consciousness represents the consciousness of the higher self of all of us. The animals in the manger and the Virgin/Mother Mary (as mortal and yet the Eternal Mother) represent the earthly plane of Malkuth, the tenth sphere of the Tree of Life. This sacred birth represents the spirit made flesh, the descent of the holy spirit to the condition of Humanity. It is the merger of the macrocosmic will of the outer world with the microcosmic will of Self. When I say the spirit is made flesh, I am speaking of rising above, or lighting, the darkness of the unconsciousness or the darkness of ignorance. The light of superconsciousness is realized. That is why the birth of Christ is called the Birth of Light. The Hierophant represents such light. He is both the eternal lifeforce residing in the flesh and the guiding light. He is the eternal will of the babe in the manger as well as the light of the star that guides the Magi to the birth.

The birth of Christ-consciousness can be looked at figuratively or literally. The Hierophant—as the great macrocosmic force coming to Earth—is said to move in cycles of 2000 years. This means that the Earth is due for a new Messiah. The new Messiah is the harbinger of a new level of consciousness. During this phase of the 2000 year cycle, however, there is not one Messiah, but a multitude. A whole generation is rising up and embracing the female aspects of the Godhead. A generation is rising up in defense of the Mother Earth and beginning to raise the vibrational level of the planet to receive the clear communications from the source, to which we shall all return. Even as you read this, you are being called as one of this multitude. You must realize this. You are a harbinger of the new consciousness.

The transition to a higher vibrational level, just as any transition in life, involves its share of pain and suffering. To make room for the new, we must abandon the old. There is a certain amount of sorrow inherent in this process. And the shaking out may not always be what we want or *think* we want. Nonetheless, it is always for the better. We must abandon self-pity. The Hierophant intervenes for our growth and development, both on the micro (self, inner) and macro (universe, outer) levels. He is eternally the *triumphant intelligence*. His will triumphs because it is the same as the will of God.

Even if we are wounded as we grow, we are nonetheless wiser. The Hierophant—which can also be seen as our conscience or the conscience of the planetary group—represents the force of light, the shaking out of ignorance.

The Hierophant is the inner ear. He teaches us how to listen. He shows us the path of understanding of the universal forces and our own place within these forces. He shakes us out of ignorance. We shake out our ignorance through binding with our higher self, through listening to our inner conscience. The Hierophant is personal consciousness linked to universal conscious energy. He is the awakened one, the conscious one, the illuminated, the enlightened.

Card Symbology: The Hierophant sits on a blue throne with black and white pillars to either side. The blue is the energy of healing and purification. The throne has two glyphs for Taurus on the back. These represent the Hierophant's connection to the earthly plane. These glyphs are also targets which represent the descent of the Hierophant into the inner self. The white pillar is the Pillar of Mercy on the Tree of Life. The black pillar is the Pillar of Severity. He understands both of these pillars and his arms rest comfortably upon them.

His head is cocked to one side to show that he is listening. He is the ear. His head is inside of a pentagon to represent the connection between the human and the divine. The Moon at his throat symbolizes that one must travel through the dark of the subconscious in order to reach the higher light of superconsciousness. This is one of the major secrets revealed by the tarot.

The Hierophant's crown contains 15 spheres representing his connection to the Lovers (see Key VI) and the Devil (see Key XV). The numerology of this connection is that $5 + 1 = 6$. The Hierophant is the fifth key, but he is the sixth value (since the Fool, Number 0, is the first value). The Hierophant's connection to the Lovers and the Devil is related to the simultaneous exhilaration and bondage of experiencing the eternal light contained in the flesh.

His garment is white for purity of thought, but it is lined with the red of desire. This is the desire for connection. His tunic is red for his love of God and his desire to ascend. Rising up the middle of his garment are three X's (see the Two of Wind). These represent the crossing of the material and spiritual planes. The Hierophant is the nail—love—that binds the center of the X's. There are three, one each, for Hierophant, the Lovers and the Devil.

The fingers of his left hand are pointing downward because he is channeling energy and directing it to Earth. His right hand remains relaxed. His feet are bare because, like the Magus, the High Priestess, Empress and Emperor, he needs to be exposed to the cosmic energy force.

The floor, which is the checkered floor of the inner temple, is the stream of consciousness of the High Priestess, now turned into black and white diamonds. This is because the foregoing level of consciousness has been challenged. This demonstrates the movement of the first awakening.

At his feet, anima and animus, the Lovers (see Key VI) kneel in prayer. They have yokes around their backs—he is yoked by the Sun, she by the Moon—because, though on the earthly plane, they remain yoked to higher consciousness. Their task is to discover this yoke within, and with it, harness the power of the One. They can accomplish this through engaging in a yoga of the mind.

Key VI. The Lovers

Divinatory Meaning ————————

THE LOVERS

You recognize that you are lonely, at the same time you realize that without separation, there can be no connection nor demonstration of love; you are attracted to that with which you wish to merge; be advised that in truth self-love (which can be translated as self-confidence, self-esteem, self-respect and a deep understanding of the "inner marriage") is the key to lasting relationships; true marriage consists of knowing you are simultaneously united and separated; accept this equation for inner happiness.

Meditation ——————————————————————

The Lovers
Zain, the Sword, the engine of division
separating out the primal essence of the Universe
into discreet Sparks, the basis for evolution

contradiction, splitting
the core of at(de)tachment

As the idea is born
its opposite is bred

etching form on the nameless
simultaneous cut and seam
isolating Stream from Clay, Night from Day
Cause from End—
analyze/synthesize; unite/divide
solidarity/extrication
jubilation/grief
relief and trepidation that one is (not) alone

the recognition of simultaneous bonding
and alienation
Love: a mirror dance
which clouds and clarifies, distills and smears
the three layers Within
the Self rising through Relation
airy triplicity
harboring the Sea of That which Was, Is and Ever Shall Be
I am who am you are me
with you I am at One
alone
all One
atoning:

> With the subconscious power of acute imagination
> and the self-conscious power of acute discrimination
> in the stone of gestation
> the children lie
> rocked by parental Love
> in the dawn of Love, the dance of Love.

Esoteric Qualities

Hebrew attribution: Zain (pronounced *zahyin*), the sword ז
Astrological attribution: Gemini, communication
Seventeenth Path: Mediates between Binah (the Eternal Mother Principle) and Tiphareth (spiritual beauty and light manifested on the plane of earth, the Eternal Son principle)
Essence: The Lovers are the children of god, also referred to as the children of the voice of superconsciousness
Intelligence: The Separating or Disposing Intelligence; in order to join, separation must first be acknowledged.

Veil: Each one of us is a completely separate entity. We are born alone
and we die alone, remaining forever disconnected.

Mystery: Separation is essential for evolution; part of the self stays
in ascension while part of the self descends into manifestation.
We are each a spark of the one flame.

Interpretation ─────────────────────────────────────

The Lovers represent the sword that slashes down through the cosmos separating the whole of us into discreet forms. The sword dis-
tributes gender and polarity through the universe, creating the
tension of opposites. Polarity is the basic principle of manifest existence. It is the antithesis of the nail (see Key V: The Hierophant). The
nail binds. The sword cleaves, cuts, divides, separates. The sword of
Zain cuts apart and places all that exists into the distinct forms of
manifestation. It is the force that takes the limitless substance of the
universe and categorizes it. It creates form in the formless, name in
the nameless. It separates night from day, black from white, female
from male, negative from positive, cold from hot, wet from dry, loss
from gain, pleasure from pain. Zain, the sword, is the tool that separates the lifeforce into discreet entities: trees of the garden from
beasts of the field from birds of the air from man and woman.

It is through the sword of Zain that we know ourselves as individual and unique. Through Zain, we understand our separation.
The fact of split-apartness causes us great joy as well as great grief.
We know the jubilation and the devastation of having descended into
manifestation to be ensouled in a physical body. The process of becoming manifest provides us with a tremendous opportunity to create
just as it is the source of our frustration. We feel hopeful, but cut off.
Therefore, we continually strive to reunite with the great force of the
limitless substance, even as we *fear* that same reunion.

Further, we seek to unite with others just as we seek peace within
ourselves. This is the dilemma of the Lovers. The tension of separation
facilitates our desire to reconnect. As such, our very separateness
becomes the basis of our love. The desire to reconnect is the driving
force. We seek the unification of opposites within in order to know
inner balance. We seek all that we are missing in order to make us
whole.

The polarity of the Lovers can be understood on several levels.
On one level, the Lovers can be taken literally to refer to sexual and

sensual unity. This aspect of the Lovers involves attraction and ap-
proaching. It is the recognition of the Self divided from the whole.
The Self feels removed and yearns for that which is beyond. This is
the desire to connect intimately with another and experience completion. This urge is beautifully expressed in the following interchange
from the Song of Solomon in the Bible[5] which reads:

O that you would kiss me with the
        kisses of your mouth!
For your love is better than wine,
        your anointing oils are fragrant,
your name is oil poured out;
        therefore the maidens love you . . .

You have ravished my heart, my
        sister, my bride,
    you have ravished my heart with
        a glance of your eyes,
    with one jewel of your necklace.
How sweet is your love, my sister,
        my bride!
    how much better is your love
        than wine,
    and the fragrance of your oils
        than any spice!
Your lips distill nectar, my bride;
    honey and milk are under your
        tongue;
    the scent of your garments is like
        the scent of Lebanon.
A garden locked is my sister, my
        bride,
    a garden locked, a fountain sealed . . .

Awake, O north wind
    and come, O south wind!
Blow upon my garden,
    let its fragrance be wafted abroad.

[5]*New English Bible:* The Song of Songs (Solomon's Song) (New York: Oxford University Press, 1971).

Let my beloved come to his garden,
and eat its choicest fruits.

I come to my garden, my sister,
my bride,
I gather my myrrh with my spice,
I eat my honeycomb with my
honey,
I drink my wine with my milk.

Eat, O friends, and drink:
drink deeply, O lovers!

In many tarot representations of the Lovers, they are depicted as nude figures. Their nakedness demonstrates the innocence of their love. In their nakedness, they are clothed only by the holy spirit of their love. The Lover, in purity and innocence, mirrors aspects of the Self and completes that which is lacking.

On another level, Key VI symbolizes a royal or exalted marriage. This is the marriage of the Emperor (Key IV) and the Empress (Key III), the marriage of yang and yin, animus with anima, heaven with earth, force with form. Their love conveys the delicate balance of equally-weighted opposites.

On the Tree of Life, this is the marriage of Chokmah and Binah, the Eternal Father with the Eternal Mother principles. This marriage unifies, even as it defines and separates, Fire and Water, the two primary elemental forces. Through this marriage, the son is born. Thus, Key VI is the path that connects the Universal Mother with the Universal Son. Paternity is, once again, the hidden cause of this connection.

In the tarot, the Lovers has several layers of meaning. The meaning has been in debate for centuries. Who, really, are the Lovers? Some say the Lovers are man and woman. Some say they represent balance within the Self, the divine inner marriage which results from Self-love. Still others say the Lovers represent the connection between Self and God. Finally, Key VI is said to represent brotherhood or sisterhood. Brotherhood, for example, refers to an association of people who are united in a common interest such as a belief system. This, too, is *union*.

Just as the meaning of the Lovers in the tarot has been widely debated, the identification of the Lovers in Song of Solomon has always been in dispute. Suffice it to say, the Song works on many levels. Some see the Song as a genuine love story conveying a true and genuine affection between two people. Others say the male is God and the female represents the People of Israel. Others claim that the man is Christ and the woman is the Church.

A good symbolic representation works on many levels at once. As a spiritual symbol, the Lovers represents the unification of the levels of consciousness within the Self. It refers to the true merger of the three modes of mind: the superconscious (higher consciousness; the light), the waking consciousness and the subconscious (the dark). In linking these layers of consciousness, the link between the individual and the holy guardian angel is formed. This link is the link between the individual and the spirit as well as between the individual and the personality.

Through separating out and understanding the true relation among the three modes of consciousness—and thereby beginning to ascertain clearly the messages of the universe—we begin to attain a knowledge of our individual purpose on a higher level. Understanding this entails a complete transformation on four planes, a transformation which is told in the original stories of creation. So then, the Lovers is also the key of creating a new universe. Key VI separates out and recombines. It leaves us with the questions: of what are things composed; how shall we recombine them?

Once we have heard the messages of the universe clearly and begun to perceive our calling, we must retain faith in our perceptions. Taken even further, the Lovers is the experience of faith in the higher self. Part of this faith is the understanding that in order to grow, we must let go, or separate out, that which no longer fits. This is the experience of giving birth. One must surrender to the fact of birth in order to experience the new life that is emerging. On the spiritual plane, the new birth can be seen as the birth of light and faith.

The Lovers is the Seventeenth Path on the Tree of Life. This path mediates between Binah, the Eternal Mother Principle, and Tiphareth, the Eternal Son Principle. The separation of Binah and Tiphareth contains the magical image of the power of *surrender* (see the Three of Wind). In the Lovers, you learn that you must give up one form in order to gain another. You must *surrender* in order to achieve victory. You must understand your sense of sorrow and separation even as you recognize your oneness with all things.

In all cases, the Lovers is the experience of the agony of separation and the bliss of union. We learn that there is a certain ecstasy in separation and that is the *triumph of individual achievement*. There can also be a terrible agony in union. Union, without a sense of oneness, can feel like unfulfilling bondage.

The fact of separation contains union and union contains separation and these two concepts repeat infinitely within each other. Knowing love is an opportunity and a curse. The object of the Lovers is to tune into basic goodness, to attune to pure unconditional love, both on the inner and outer levels. Key VI tells us that unconditional love is the driving force of the universe. The secret of Key VI is the knowledge that things of matter in the universe are separated by the boundaries of matter and that love is the glue that binds all things. As we learn this lesson, we understand that Key VI represents the emergence of the Christ-consciousness on the physical plane.

Card Symbology: The Lovers are depicted seated in an embrace in perfect balance on the horizontal bar on the glyph of Venus. That is because Key VI is ruled by Venus. The female aspect is blue to represent the cosmic sea. The male aspect is the orange-yellow of cosmic fire. This symbolizes Binah and Chokmah coming together at the point of Tiphareth. They appear to be in a state of complete relaxation.

They are seated within a downward pointed phallus, the male principle which, in turn, contains the female principle of Venus. The vertical axis of Venus comes down into a point. This axis represents the central pillar on the Tree of Life. It is the Sword of Zain which culminates with its point on the plane of manifestation.

Above we see a suggestion of the wings of the Holy Ghost, as we saw in Key II, the High Priestess. The wings refer to the divine nature of the love that binds the Lovers.

Key VII. The Chariot

Divinatory Meaning ——————

VII

THE CHARIOT

Negative past influences may be affecting the present without due cause; it is time to clear out, see clearly, begin with new energy, take responsibility for your present condition; it is time to move beyond the past; seek deep meanings within yourself; standards of action must emerge from within yourself in order to guarantee lasting results; act on the basis of your own deep internal messages; an important message is coming to you; pay attention to internal nudges.

Meditation ————————————————————————

The Chariot, Fence
High Intelligence in the House of Influence
Charioteer, whose face I seek, but cannot know
whose name I know, but cannot form
descending through raining fence of blood and sea, sea and blood
through the inner Self—ignorance, power, force and corpse—
to conscious mind
holding, in your empty hands, the amethyst gift of
    Wisdom
            I can nearly hear your call—a whisper—
            through the veil

Charioteer
speaks in tongues
awakening fields of consciousness:
the preserving, protecting power of words,
new words as yet unsaid
words that manifest and edge through the bony fence

encasing matters of heart
words that dart through pillars
from the middle of the soul

The strength of will is measured
by the will to let
the Force of Life
manifest unreined;
The strength of will is hearing through the water
well enough to speak
the Secret of the Flame.

Esoteric Qualities

Hebrew attribution: Cheth (pronounced *khayth*), field or fence ח
Astrological attribution: Cancer, nourishment
Eighteenth Path: Mediates between Binah (the Eternal Mother principle) and Geburah (the universal principle of destruction)
Essence: The personality is the vehicle for ascent /descent; change perspectives for a new field of view
Intelligence: Intelligence of the House of Influence; in the physical body, we are the act, the actor, and the means of action
Veil: True knowledge is blocked by stopping the inquiry at the Symbol. Symbolism represents Spirit, but is not Spirit.
Mystery: Form acts as a limitation, but it is not. It is protection. Form is a "Ring-Pass-Not," a finite field (of activity) in which the force of Spirit resides. New force will dissolve old Forms. This is the creative process. You are the creative force.

Interpretation

The Chariot is the vehicle of the force of spirit. A vehicle carries, conveys or expresses. In this case, the human personality—as the Chariot—is the vehicle for expression. The human body is also a vehicle. It is the vehicle of spirit. Personality and body both contain and limit the way you conceive and present your Self internally and to the universe.

There is a way you know yourself. You classify yourself according to type. You are this kind of person or that kind of person. Others also identify you according to type. There is an interactive relationship between how you view yourself and how you are seen by others. How others see you affects how you view yourself. Often it is said that we see ourselves as others see us.

When you reach Key VII, you are breaking out of old definitions of self. You are becoming less likely to internalize others' opinions of you and more likely to be forming your identity based on your own will or volition as set apart from others. You are redefining from within and refining your energies. This is a difficult process. It means breaking out of old molds. It means movement and change. You may find yourself literally changing residences or traveling at this time. All signs indicate that action is now occurring.

At the point of the Chariot, you are beginning to move upon a new path. This path involves the essence of your spirit. Your old personality can no longer contain the growing force of your spirit. You are refocusing and moving—in a perfectly balanced system of progression—toward personal change. All is mobility. You are becoming more centered in your movement, even as you are becoming ever more "spirited."

These changes have been set in motion by the onrush of new receptivity. Your subconscious has opened and become active. You have had many illuminating ideas and many new insights have surfaced. As a result, you are experiencing a change in perspective.

Your new perspective comes from changing your field of focus. You are framing the picture of your life in a new way. You are orienting around a new field of activity. The Hebrew attribution for the Chariot is Cheth (which means field). You can picture your field, not only as the field of view, but as the area in which you are working. It is the field which you are sowing. You are now framing things differently, working in a new field, or sowing a new variety of seed.

Although your choices may seem radical, they are not impulsive or irrational. They have come about through your own internal process of introspection and meditation. Such changes are necessary to accommodate your growth. Everything that has led up to these changes has been steeping for some time in the depths of your subconscious mind. Further, you are guided by your higher consciousness.

Your new path, which entails an inner transformation, will be for the better. You have developed your armor—your defenses against vulnerability—and you are protected. You are well-equipped to meet the forthcoming challenges in that you have gained power through all of your experiences. You have become the master of the expression of your own life. On a deep subconscious level, you now understand the workings of your spiritual, emotional, intellectual and physical natures. You know the combination of these energies: the totality that is You. You know that self-expression comes through your personality, and you know that your personality is the harbor of all the power of the universe that flows into you.

Thus far on your path you have gained the understanding of the balance of opposites (see Key VI, the Lovers) and you understand your own role and powers in bringing about internal and external balance (see Key I, the Magus). You understand how the force of spirit (see Key IV, the Emperor) is embodied in the form of creativity (see Key III, the Empress). You understand that the human entity (see Key V, the Hierophant) is subservient to the divine law (see Key II, the High Priestess).

You have learned all of these things through self-examination. You know now that all of your personal actions are a manifestation in time and space of some phase of the sum total of cosmic influences. You know that you are never acting completely alone or in a void. Your actions are attuned to the cosmic will.

And yet, you know the power of your own will.

Key VII is the Self manifesting its dominion over that which was, is and shall become. It is the innate and harnessed will power of the individual. As occultist Eliphas Levi said: "All magic is in the will." At Key VII, you are learning the deep meaning of real magic.

Part of your magic is that you are learning the effective use and power of words, deeds and symbols. These manifestations (words, deeds and symbols) are like fences that enclose fields of consciousness. They paradoxically free our imagination even as they limit it.

As you come to understand the most effective use of these tools, you are forced to grow. Having increased understanding means that you must let your old forms or ways of thinking dissolve so that new ones can take their place. This means letting go of that which has served you well, but is no longer of great value. It is as if the fences you have built now limit your view. You must use your will power to tear down the fences.

Even with all the power you hold, even with everything you have learned, this process may be difficult. You may feel like you are moving into the darkness, moving into an unfamiliar state which may feel like a state of chaos. Although you have outgrown your old forms, you understand them well. They are familiar. They have been comfortable. And while they are less comfortable to you now, they are still clear. What is unclear is the future. What is unclear is the nature of the trials through which you must now pass in your expanded state.

At Key VII, you come to know that the true strength of your volition is surrender. You must understand that you *are* moving in the flow of the cosmic will and you must let the cosmic spirit find unobstructed manifestation through you. This means that you must trust your deepest intuition.

If you open and trust now, you will be given a message. This is a message about the future of your personality and your role and niche on the planet. The gift of growth is being offered to you by the universe. It is your privilege and opportunity to, in turn, share this gift with others. Through introspection and meditation, you will know the name and power of your gift. You are greatly gifted. Through timely internal searching, the name and power of this gift will be revealed.

As your gift is revealed, you will see that you have created it. In right communion, you are the creative force.

In order to have right communion, however, your view must not be obstructed by fences of your own making. Key VII is the Eighteenth Path on the Tree of Life which mediates between Binah, the Eternal Mother Principle, and Geburah, the Universal Principle of Destruction. Cheth is concerned with destroying or clearing any fences or barriers—especially those which are self-constructed—which obstruct our view. We cannot fully understand our gifts if fences or limited fields of view obscure or mar our clarity of sight.

Dissolving fences, in part, may mean ridding oneself of views left over—or remaining—from past incarnations. Key VII is known as the *intelligence of the house of influence* or the *house of hidden senses*, because we are often guided by a memory which we do not clearly remember. Clearing the memory and clearing out the fields of limitation are the major tasks of the Charioteer.

Card Symbology: The Charioteer sits inside the cube, which is the transformed table of the Magus. The driver of the vehicle has now *become* the magic tool. The driver's hood is gold on the outside and lined with black. This symbolizes that one must move through darkness in order to experience light. The driver wears the mask of the High Priestess (see Key II), symbolizing attunement to this divine law.

On the driver's chestplate are the letters V.T for Tav, the last letter of the Hebrew alphabet. Tav is Key XXI (the Universe). Tav is the completion of all things. The Charioteer, with increased depth and understanding, is the beginning of the end, or the end reversed. The end begins at Key VII because the Chariot contains the power of all the Keys that have gone before. The Charioteer has conquered the four planes of Fire, Water, Wind and Earth and through the Magus (Key I), High Priestess (Key II), Empress (Key III), Emperor (Key IV), Hierophant (Key V) and Lovers (Key VI), has become the master behind life expression.

The two serpents on the chestplate symbolize the mastered ability to renew the Self at will. The cross, like the mask, indicates attunement which is the secret of the master.

The four corners of the cube, which is the vehicle, represent the three aspects of the mystery of the divine trinity: Father, Son and Holy Spirit; Mother, Father, God; or Love, Will, and Original Intelligence, plus the fourth aspect: the Destroyer or Dissolver. All four are necessary for the movement of energy.

The vehicle represents the human personality, the ultimate vehicle for expression. The driver is in perfect control of an invisible steering wheel. This implies impeccable balance and a thorough working knowledge of the machinery at hand. The machinery at hand is the cosmic workings of the Universe.

The two sphinxes, which are the Lovers (see Key VI) transformed into the mysteries of light and dark, are the guardians of the threshold of the house of God. They pose the riddle: what has four legs in the morning, two at noon and three at night? Degree of movement depends on depth of answer.

To the right and left, the Pillars of Mercy (light) and Severity (dark) are operating in full force. The stream of consciousness is flowing through the pillars. There are wheels at the top and bottom of each pillar to indicate that energy is flowing.

The double Suns and Moons to either side of the rising pentagrams demonstrate that duality is the driving force. The stars move upward toward the above. That there are four stars shows the connection between the Chariot and the Emperor (Key IV). The Charioteer has mastered the house/structure/vehicle of personality and is at home in the physical body. The glyphs for Cancer on each of the pillars indicate the stability of the Charioteer in this realm.

Key VIII. Strength

Divinatory Meaning ───────────

The truth comes from within yourself, it is your own deep inner light which, in good conscience, you ought to follow if you wish to discover happiness; this truth uncoils within you like a great serpent, acknowledge its movement, do not try to repress its stirrings; be strong and courageous for you will find that truth is bliss; seek bliss to find bliss; even though you cannot see the future right now, if you do what your heart of hearts says is right, you will come to happiness.

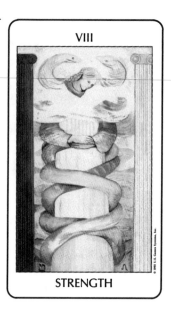

Meditation ──────────────────────────

Strength of the Serpent
Lust, Joy
Surging passion, Rapture
Light in the Eye; Fire in the Breast
Raptor falling on Prey—Life feeding off life
No god would dare deny the Natural Order; the Order be of God
The Order be God!
horizontal, vertical, circular, balanced
tension, design, order, harmony, Truth
endless transformation/conversion
internal confidence between one level and the next
a nexus of enterprise
movement, competition
all is for the best

ecstasy and madness
primal surgings and jubilation
divine intoxication, drunk on anticipation, promise
drinking passion
blood
pumping in the wings
Light in the Eye, Heart Sings
ecstasy and madness, jubilation
Girding up Strength for the next leg of The Journey
wherever it might lead.

Esoteric Qualities

Hebrew attribution: Teth (pronounced *tayth*), the serpent ט

Astrological attribution: Leo, enacting the drama

Nineteenth Path: Mediates between Chesed (the universal principle of production) and Geburah (the universal principle of destruction)

Essence: The internal flame that rises like a serpent in the darkness; the coiled fiery power of attuning to *process*

Intelligence: The Intelligence of the Secret of All Spiritual Activities, the unraveling of all mysteries entails moving through the dark shadows of the self

Veil: Every moment counts and every moment is numbered.

Mystery: One must first learn to count before realizing that the power of the One is concealed in the many. Attune to the process of life. God dwells in the dark. Through the dark comes redemption. Redemption follows the experience with the serpent, therefore the serpent of temptation is secretly the anointed one.

Interpretation

Key VIII is Strength. At the point of Strength, the presence of the inner spiritual force creeps to the surface and materializes in the waking consciousness. You feel a surge of energy which is connected with creative growth. As you perceive the presence of the creative spirit in your life, you begin to feel a new potential, a new capacity. You change. You become more spirited. There is now a new opportunity to soar. The Dance of Life becomes ever more precious. The Dance of Life becomes ever more vibrant. At this time, it is as if a new, more exuberant *movement* has begun. You become enflamed with the passion of delight in newness. You feel compelled to throw off your old "clothes." You want to shed your old ways, roles and routines to make way for newness. The new you is emerging. Like a shedding snake, you cast off old skins.

As the spirit materializes in your life, you begin to perceive the depth and fullness of each moment. You realize that every moment is a new beginning and that inherent in each moment is a kind of ecstasy. Every moment counts just as every moment is numbered. As you recognize this, the focal point of every moment becomes ensuing *newness*. The past is *not*. You are reborn with each breath.

Before coming into an understanding of BEING in the present, each one of us and each generation is called to BECOME. This is the time of humanity at noon, the time of rising Strength, of walking strongly on two legs without assistance (see Key VII: the Chariot for the Riddle of the Sphinx). And even when the future remains uncertain, it is nonetheless the time of "taking the planet and riding it bareback." As P. L. Travers writes on the topic of repetition and renewal:

> With all their energies at the mid-heaven, they are thirsting for responsibility and full of constructive imagination. And whatever of value is lost in the carnage they will rediscover and make their own. Eden recurs continually. Each generation experiences its guileless morning, equivocal noonday and the drumming out in the evening.[6]

Every generation must work through this process of the call to BECOME before undertaking the task to BE.

At a certain point, however, we still our minds. We begin to hear the inner voice and that voice calls us to the present. It urges: The time is now. The place is here.

As we become aware of this inner voice, we find ourselves asking: What is it time for? Why am I here? To answer these questions, you must hear with a New Ear (see Key V: the Hierophant) and see with a New Eye (see Key IV: the Emperor). You must abandon the drive to accomplish those tasks which have their origin in culture. The *musts* and *shoulds* we are given in the process of our socialization move into

---

[6]P. L. Travers' article "Well, Shoot Me!" in the Repetition and Renewal issue of *Parabola*, Volume XIII, No. 2, 1988, p. 34.

the realm of Death (see Key XIII). The voice of the *musts* and *shoulds* obscures the guidance of the Inner Teacher (see Key V: the Hierophant and Key IX: the Hermit). The flame—the teacher—that arises from *within* is truth. The inner truth is your calling and your bliss which, when heard with clarity, translates into spiritual renewal. In understanding the nature of your bliss, you acquire the potential to create with a new hand (see Key IX: the Hermit).

The lesson of Key VIII is to place your emphasis on the *process of creation* as opposed to the *product*. The essential experience of Key VIII is understanding the jubilation that emerges from allowing the creative force to flow freely. The creative process is the force of spirit moving through the hand of Self. Product is static and flat. Product is form which will always be outgrown and cast aside. Form is an empty shell. Force is the breath and the source of life. The force/process is the spirit in constant renewal; the focus of force is on *being-ness*. The future is, by nature, uncertain. The past is no longer. The now *is*.

As the builder of your life, and the creator of the reality in which you dwell, deeply consider your *process*. As "Joseph" channelled from an angel who spoke to him in Budaliget, Hungary, in 1944:

> The motto of your way is not, *'it was,'*
> nor, *'it would be good'*;
> and certainly not, *'it is good.'*
> The key work of the builder is: *'BE!'*
> *'It was'* signifies omission;
> *'it would be good,'* incapacity;
> *'it is good,'* smugness.
> Your motto is: *'BE!'*[7]

In the process of *being*, you are, at all times, engaged in the endless cycle of repetition and renewal. The past is not this moment and yet this moment is forever moving into the past. Your Strength comes from understanding the timelessness of process. Process is forever. This knowledge is your power. This knowledge becomes your bliss. When you are rightly attuned, the force of your internal fire—the lifeforce and seat of your power—is strengthened by the Wind

---

[7]Transcribed by Gitta Mallasz in *Talking with Angels* (Zurich, Switzerland: Daimon Verlag, 1988), p. 240.

(see Key 0: the Fool). Only when your flame is weak does it require protection.

Key VIII, the Nineteenth Path, mediates between Chesed and Geburah on the Tree of Life. Chesed is the universal force of creation, production or anabolism. It is the universal will in a state of actualization. Geburah is the universal force of destruction or catabolism. Key VIII, Strength, is the continuum and balance between these two. It is the path of the "Secret of all Spiritual Activities." The secret is the knowledge that the processes of production and destruction work hand in hand. This is the key to understanding spiritual (as well as other kinds of) growth. Old forms must be blasted away so that new forms can be constructed. *Newness needs room to grow!* Nineteen is the path of continuous movement, continuous process. It is the path of the serpent forever shedding old skins.

In Eastern philosophy, the serpent represents the kundalini or chi force (see the Eight of Fire: The Lightning Path) which lies dormant and coiled inside of the physical body. As this spiritual force uncoils, you experience bliss and union with the One. The secret of union with the One is that the One is contained in every aspect and every moment of life. Thus it is said that the One is concealed in the many. The *newness* of each new moment is the opportunity to experience bliss and union with the One *at all times.* Let the past go. Surrender the past. Approach the present with exhilaration and experience the *newness* of the now.

In an interview with Bill Moyers, philosopher Joseph Campbell stated:

> Joseph Campbell:
> Remember the last line [in the novel *Babbitt*]? "I have never done the thing that I wanted to in all my life." That is a man who never followed his bliss.
>
> You may have a success in life, but then think of it—what kind of life was it? What good was it—you've never done the thing you wanted to do in all your life. I always tell my students, go where your body and soul want to go. When you have the feeling, then stay with it, and don't let anyone throw you off.
>
> Bill Moyers:
> What happens when you follow your bliss?

Joseph Campbell (after pausing):
You come to bliss.[8]

At Key VIII, you are moving into center. This is bliss. You are experiencing the energy of transformation. This is bliss. You are coming to an understanding of the inner light. This inner light is synonomous with love of self, inherent in which is self-acceptance. Self-love/self-acceptance is the first step on the path to true mastery. To follow this path, attune to your own internal process and *follow your bliss. Seek and you shall find. Knock and every door shall be opened!*

Card Symbology: Key VIII, Strength, is the essence of process. Thus, the card shows two serpents climbing a pillar of light. The light is a flame. The serpents represent continual rejuvenation and movement. They move in opposing directions, symbolizing the tension of dualities. In this case, the snakes are the intellectual and intuitive forces working in perfect balance on the central pillar, which is the Pillar of Mildness of the Qabalistic Tree of Life.

The dualistic forces are also symbolized by the pillars of dark and light to either side of the central pillar. These are the Pillars of Severity and Mercy.

The white figure eight about the shoulders of the Goddess of Strength represents the eternal movement of the winged holy ghost. This glyph also suggests the commitment and devotion symbolized by the white nun's collar.

---

[8]Joseph Campbell and Bill Moyers, *The Power of Myth* (New York: Doubleday, a division of Bantam, Doubleday, Dell Publishing Group, Inc., 1988).

Key IX. The Hermit

Divinatory Meaning ——————

IX

THE HERMIT

In your own heart, you carry the light and love you have often sought outside of yourself; each one of us holds the power to fulfill ourselves; you must always return to yourself; accept yourself and celebrate; you are beautiful, you are worthy, you are a wholly unique and wonderful individual; you are completely independent and yet you will always remain indivisibly connected to the great stream of humanity; you may feel alone, but you are not; alone does not necessarily mean lonely; raise up your inner light and place it on a hilltop where everyone can see it; as a guide, you can aid the seekers who come your way; remember, a lamp is not made to hide under a bowl.

Meditation ——————————————————

Having floated
    through the danger-filled realm of the Shadow of Fear
    and the Dark Spaces around the Spirit
The Old Hermit
    sinks
        into *chi*
Chi is Balance
Chi is Force and Form moving as One Breath

Finally at rest, the Old One
    spirals toward the Force
        of Heart and Sexuality
    escapes the deception of that which is Transitory
    moves toward

Completion, Perfection, utter Realization
that there is one Free Will in all the Universe
Supreme Will
Cosmic and Free
Eternal: Universal Volition

Oh, Ancient and Holy One
In Heaven, there is no Marriage
for there is no Separation
In Heaven, there is no Sin
for there is no Division

And You, Isolated One
—so far from alone,
Indivisible One
You, Hermit,
Witness to the Question
Hand of the Ancients
pointing to your own Heart
the Cause, Source and Origin
of all that is Known—and not Known—
the very Heart of the Truest Fertility

You, Hermit,
Know that
As it is Above, So it is Below.

Esoteric Qualities ─────────────────────────────────

Hebrew attribution: Yod (pronounced *yode*), creative hand י

Astrological attribution: Virgo, introspection and healing

Twentieth Path: Mediates between Chesed (the universal principle of
production) and Tiphareth (spiritual beauty and light manifested
on the plane of Earth)

Essence: The Source of wisdom is within

Intelligence: The Intelligence of Will, the knowledge that you create
your world with your own hand

Veil: The *illusion* of newness: in changing circumstances, the deepest
problems will be solved.

Mystery: All that *is*, was and ever shall be. There is nothing new
under the Sun. The deepest marriage is the divine marriage
within.

Interpretation

Key IX, the Hermit, is the creative hand. This creative hand can be viewed as the Hand of God. It is also your own hand. It is the hand that magically creates, preserves and transforms the world.

Creation, preservation and transformation are the three points which define the divine circle of eternal movement. The Hermit is the Ninth Key, which is three times three. The Circle of Eternity, as symbolized by three, geometrically expands. This expansion denotes an incredible power. Thus, three is the number used for magical incantation. Three times three—nine—becomes the magical number because it always returns to itself: $9 \times 1 = 9$; $9 \times 2 = 18$, $1 + 8 = 9$; $9 \times 3 = 27$, $2 + 7 = 9$; $9 \times 4 = 36$, $3 + 6 = 9 \ldots$

The power of nine is extraordinary wisdom. The deepest understanding of the Hermit involves the knowledge that, like nine, in the end, we shall return to our Self in an infinitely recurring cyclical process. The secret of the Hermit is the knowledge that all that is, always was. It is the understanding that there is nothing new under the Sun. Everything that is, always was, and ever shall be. We discover this again and again.

This means that with all of your external searching for answers and all of your external searching for love, you paradoxically wind up right back where you started: alone, with your Self. What you learn is simple. There is one answer and that answer is *love of Self*.

What does this mean? Beneath all external layers and social conditioning to the contrary, the deeper you spiral on the path, the more you learn that there is *one* spirit and this is the spirit of life itself. You learn on this inward spiral that you are the soul, that you hold the light—the power of love—in your own hand: *within*. In coming to this realization, which is the second step of the beginning of the end of the inward spiral (see Key VIII: Strength) you become a guide for your fellow journeyers whose destination (as *they* will eventually realize) is simply their own heart.

The Hermit is the familiar archetype of the Wise Old Man (or Wise Old Woman) who takes up residence deep in the forest. He has no need of society. Historically, he is discovered again and again by spiritual seekers who have lost their way. He is frequently discovered by a "hero" who has temporarily lost his way. There are wonderful examples of the wisdom of the Hermit contained in the *Tales of King Arthur*, and, in contemporary times, in the movie trilogy *Star Wars*.

The Hermit is the Wise One who emerges from the dark of the forest like a sudden light, at first startling and then aiding the bewildered (but eternally grateful) hero. The Hermit generally offers simple provisions—a crust of bread, perhaps—but mostly food for thought. With few words, and through riddle and parable, he interprets the hero's experience. The hero is astounded at the old man's insight. The Hermit teaches the hero that (after traveling the world over) the destination is the hero's own heart. He tells that each one must walk the path to the heart alone.

The Hermit is simple and has no desire for recognition as a teacher. He lives harmoniously with all forces. As a result of his deep understanding of the timeless nature of all things, he lives centered in the moment. He has no need of discovery. He understands eternal movement. He points to the still pool, and would have the hero study his own reflection to understand why he came. The Hermit would neither disdain nor exalt the hero's process of discovery. He has no need to judge. Heroes come and go. All things come around again and again.

The path of the Hermit is the Twentieth Path. This path leads from the sphere of Chesed, the Universal Principle of Production, to the sphere of Tiphareth, the incarnation of the light and beauty of spirit. On this path, the love of goodness is awakened in the hero. After living the lessons of the Hermit, the hero will never be the same. After meeting the Hermit, the hero understands the meaning of his seeking. He understands why the Hermit is alone in the evening of life.

Key IX represents the evening of life: every generation "drumming out" in the evening. He is the third aspect of the Riddle of the Sphinx of Key VII. (What has four legs in the morning, two at noon and three at night?) The answer, of course, is humanity: crawling on four legs in the morning, standing on two at noon, and supported by a cane at night. The Hermit's cane is the Staff of Power. He holds the key to the workings of magic. The key is the power of love. Though he may appear to be a Fool, the Hermit is a very Wise Man. He lives alone, but he is far from being alone.

Through the Hermit, true primordial wisdom becomes known. When one follows the teachings of the Hermit, his true identity is eventually revealed. He is the archetype of the Father of Fathers. He is God incarnate. As Christ said, "No man cometh to the Father except by me." The traditional archetypal portrayal of the Father—to whom one will return—is the Wise Old Man with the Long White Beard who Lives in Heaven. The Hermit, as the Wise Old Man, is the Father. In moving deeper we learn, of course, that the kingdom of heaven is at *hand,* that is to say, *we hold the kingdom of heaven in our own hand.* We hold it in our own heart. The kingdom of heaven is *within.* The Father is within. All life has one spirit. The pulse of life is universal.

These are the messages arising through the keen introspective power generated through understanding the Ninth Key. With this knowledge, we are empowered to create the world with our own hand. We are empowered to create the world through our own vision.

The Hermit, it must be said, is also the Mother of Mothers, the archetypal Crone, the Wise Old Woman. She represents the Universal Mother of Mothers, the Mother of all Creation. She, too, resides in the forest. She is not really wicked, as she is often presented in tales, but rather she has come to be quite misunderstood. This Wise Old Woman is the original Goddess, the one who gave birth to the universe. Politically, she was all but slain. She was cast into obscurity and her name slandered by a rebellious patriarchal system that envied her ability to bleed without wounding and her ability to give birth to all form. She is the very Crone who carried the life of the universe in her own bloody pool. But, like a dark shadow, she now remains only a specter behind the Old Man. It will take a great deal of belief and devotion to coax her out from behind this image. Nonetheless, SHE is the one who birthed the Hermit. She is the one to whom the Hermit must return.

At Key IX, we honor the Hermit and the Crone within: the force and form of the universe. We turn inward, become introspective, and the lesson we learn is that we are not alone. We learn that we carry the ability to fill ourselves with a deep, meaningful and enduring love. We learn that we *are* love and that love is truly the substance that bonds the Universe.

Card Symbology: In Key IX, the Hermit *is* the light in the darkness. He lights the way for all seekers. He is the guide, but conveys the message that each one walks the path alone.

His waistband is a fire red Yod. This symbolizes his guiding principle: we create the world with our own hand.

In his left hand, he holds the Staff of Power. There is a hole in his right hand. This hole represents his ability to receive or channel all that is. It also represents the Wheel of Fortune (see Key X).

Above his head are ten lights of emanation, representing the ten spheres of the Tree of Life, of which he has a complete understanding.

Behind him is Ain Soph Aur, the realm of the Ring-Pass-Not, beyond which is limitless light and radiant darkness.

The black shadow that appears like a cape behind him is actually the outline of the Wise Old Crone, the great dark mother of form who was cast into obscurity. She now stands, looming in a large silence, behind the male archetype of God. She is his source.

Behind the two are the wings of the holy spirit. These all-embracing wings designate truth and the higher way of understanding. They are the third aspect of the holy trinity.

Key X. The Wheel of Fortune

Divinatory Meaning ——————————

Your fate is changing, rising or falling; stay balanced through these changes; you are responsible for your own state; whatever you are seeking without is a manifestation of your desire to understand your own inner spirit; the ultimate goal is to stay balanced in heart, mind, spirit and body through all the upward and downward movements of life; in times of sadness, retain your equilibrium, in times of joy, retain your equilibrium also.

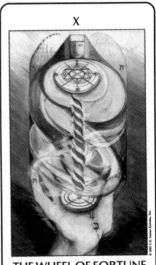

THE WHEEL OF FORTUNE

Meditation ———————————————————————

The Hand of Wo/Man
in the Act of Grasping
Circumstance

Imagine It and It Shall Be
through the Laws of Sequence and Periodicity
"Will you play at Tables, at Dyce, at Tarots, and Chesse?"
Advance your Hypothesis
Read your own Curved Palm, the Hand of Action/Progress,
    the Hand of Happiness

The Wheel of Taro speaks the
Laws of Nature:

> ATOR: Ded buth my prynces be atour
> ORAT: I haue herde thy prayer and thyn oration
> TORA: The Laws of the Divine Will
> ROTA: Circling Round and Round in Winged Rotation

>> (round your throne, Dear One, a rainbow
>> wheels, gleaming like Emeralds in a Sea of Glass
>> greenness growing by degrees)
>> (round your throne, Dear One, are four proud beasts
>>> Lion, Eagle, Ox
>>> and another, staring from a Looking Glass
>>> Do you See?)

Come, Dear One, to the Center
where the Perception of Light and Dark
is unhindered by the Sight of Polarity
Where Perceiving
the Balance of Opposing Forces
> Knowing, Willing, Daring, Keeping Still
is the Just Reward for Those who Will
open up to See, to Believe
to perceive
> and Trust
>> with Certainty
>>> in the Self.

Esoteric Qualities ——————————————————————

Hebrew attribution: Kaph (pronounced kahf), the palm כ   ך
Astrological attribution: Jupiter, expansion
Twenty-First Path: Mediates between Chesed (the universal principle
   of production) and Netzach (the universal sphere of feeling and
   personality)
Essence: You are the master of all conditions and circumstances
Intelligence: The Conciliating Intelligence, that which *balances* emo-
   tions and evens out personality
Veil: You experience happiness only when your fortune is rising.
Mystery: The whole of experience is necessary. Through the whole
   of experience, all manifestations of light and dark ultimately

merge and become One. The mystery is gyroscopic: how to spin with perfect balance?

Interpretation

The Wheel of Fortune turns. It is the wheel of karma. It is the wheel of chance. It is the wheel of return. It is the wheel of consciousness. It is a game of mastery over that which falls out, over that which is given and that which is taken away, that which is created and that which dissolves.

The wheel tells of the endless rotation of night and day, the earth, the skies, the seasons, the years, and the rise and fall of humanity through the endless cycling of birth, fortune and death.

The game of life, symbolized by the turning Wheel of Fortune, like a game of poker, or even a spread of the tarot, involves choice just as it involves happenstance. You may not be in control of all the cards you are dealt, but you choose how you will react. You judge. You hold onto that which seems beneficial. You discard that which appears extraneous. You learn to be clever. You learn to be creative.

As your lot is cast in the Wheel of Fortune, you become familiar with your strengths and weaknesses. You perceive your limits, the lines you cross willingly, those which you will not cross. You explore the matter of choice. You explore the matter of freedom. You consider the question of free will versus destiny. You imagine that you may choose the games in which you participate.

At Key X, your fortune is changing. The wheel of your life is turning at an accelerated rate. Your fortune is rising or falling. You are gaining, losing. This process, and the emotional experience that accompanies it, is not new to you. All your life, you have undergone such occurrences. You have gained. You have lost. You have known success and happiness; you have known failure and remorse. You have been accepted and rejected. You have accepted and rejected. You have achieved and rejoiced. You have failed and cried. And, in realizing your goals, you have experienced the degree to which you created the circumstances of your achievement.

Creating reality is an intricate and paradoxical process. We learn that, in general, if we apply ourselves, we can accomplish a task. We can break down barriers which at first appear as insurmountable. If we push hard enough at the walls around us, they begin to miraculously fall away. We find we can go places we never thought possible. We can create our world in our own image. And we are visionaries.

Reaching goals we never thought possible is exhilarating. It can also be frustrating to reach a goal and realize that "nothing's changed," or worse, that, in the face of great accomplishment, one feels distraught, depressed or unfulfilled. There may be an undercurrent of sadness or anxiety. Sadness may come because one is leaving the past. Anxiety may come because, in reaching a peak, one finds oneself standing at the bottom of an even higher mountain. For any of these reasons, we may fear success. An example of fear of success is found in the novel *Comrades* by Paul Leaf. Two men are involved in a discussion regarding a challenge to a game of chess. It reads as follows:

"Why wouldn't you play me the other night?" Mike asked.

"I told you."

"Are you afraid of losing?"

"I may be more afraid of winning," Robert answered as if the words had wanted to escape forever. "Winning means responsibility. You have to win again. It's expected of you. If you lose, no one expects anything."[9]

If we are not paralyzed by our own fears, we may become paralyzed by what appear to be real-life barriers. We may find ourselves caged by our experience of the past, of family, of religion, of social or financial circumstances, of sex, age or race, of marriage, work, education, politics and even the cage of our own physical, emotional or psychological constitution. We may feel as if we are butting up against a structure that we merely happened into. This is so frustrating. But the lesson of Key X is to begin to learn to detach or distance ourselves from emotional attachment to outcome. We ask ourselves the question: Who is most hurt by our anger or frustration? The answer lies in introspection.

At Key X, you are in transition. Your star is rising or falling. Be cautioned, however, that your star is *always* rising or falling, perpetually moving. And that which you gain is not necessarily cumulative. Material gain is always transitory. Gains of matter are eternally lost.

---

[9] Paul Leaf, *Comrades* (New York: New American Library, 1985), p. 37.

For example, you may work very hard for many years amassing material wealth or security. In moments this is dissolved by a crashing stock market or a natural disaster. These are the cruel twists of fate. Such turns may be purely chance. They may happen to anyone. You may find all your dreams suddenly dashed on rocks. And the more life we have lived, the more cases we can recall of our own and others' broken dreams.

The dreams and broken dreams, the hopes and dashed hopes, are all symbolized by the outer rim of the Wheel of Fortune. In Western culture, we tend to operate from the standpoint of this outer rim, the outer rim that moves the quickest and tells of the passage of time: the cycling of past, present and future. The outer rim represents the most material aspects of consciousness.

In Tibetan Buddhism, the outer rim of the wheel represents the causes of birth, old age, death and rebirth. In Buddhist thinking, this is the eternal cycle which can be stopped only through the knowledge that the sensuous world is but illusion and emptiness. Is the sensuous world illusion and emptiness? This question arises as the Wheel of Fortune rises and falls. And, if it is, should we work toward escaping it? The answer of the Wheel of Tarot is *No*. This world is not to be escaped, only to be *understood*. We must understand its *context*. The world of the senses is a gift. It is a blessing and an opportunity to be explored.

The eight spokes of the Wheel of Fortune create an image of the Sun which represents the wonders of the sensual world as well as the eternal light. Reaching the eternal light at the center of the wheel symbolizes *deliverance from attachment to material outcome*. This is not a contradiction to the idea of experiencing the world of the senses, as will be presently explained.

Spiraling inward on the wheel, one arrives at the middle circle. In the outer realms of this circle are represented the mortal sins, the conscience and the perception of the consequences of action. Symbolically, this is the circle of both heaven and hell. It is within this circle that one begins to understand cosmic balance, the balance of the Six (see Key VI, The Lovers), wherein the two triangles of the universal father and mother, cause and effect, force and form, come together and rotate in perfect balance. And, as it is said that "no man cometh to the Father except by me," the middle realm is the realm of coming to terms with the emerging Christ-consciousness within. This is the way of love.

When one reaches the level of consciousness of the middle circle, a gate opens at the wheel's center. This is the gate to the higher realm, the realm of God-consciousness.

The Wheel of Fortune thus becomes a prayer wheel, depicting the birth of Christ in the human spirit. The very center of the wheel is eternity. Here, one masters time and fate. At the center is the unification of the higher consciousness (the light) with the realms of the subconscious (the dark). At the center is mastery of the knowledge of the divine totality which involves coming to an understanding of the energy patterns or archetypal forces that dominate the Wheel's rim. These energy patterns are exactly those represented by the 22 Keys of the tarot.

Through understanding these patterns, the door to divinity—the gateway to superconsciousness—is cast ajar. Thus, the Wheel has the potential for demonstrating to each one of us the path to the soul. This path entails deliverance from fate through the realization of the divine light (the Sun or the *Son*) within.

In other words, whatever happens in life, from the rim to the hub of the wheel, is a growth experience. All experiences, whether manifesting as positive or negative, enrich us. Just as we experience the depths of the spirit through pleasure, we experience the depths of the spirit through pain. In this way, we "meet" the Self and move deeper in our understanding. Sometimes we even seek a painful experience so that we may learn its lessons. And, just as every accomplishment has the potential for bringing out the best in us, so does every disaster. Similarly, each success or failure has the potential for bringing out our inner beast. The challenge at Key X is to remain even, to remain serene and balanced, and to hold the center.

Imagine that the rises and falls of your life are connected to the outer rim of the great turning wheel. Attached to the rim of this wheel, you are forever moving up or moving down. You are always waiting. You are always living in the future. You are always living in the past. Things are always changing and moving. Things are always out of balance. You always think that, "Things will get better."

How can this continue perpetually?

The lesson of the Wheel of Fortune is to hold the center. If you can stand centered at the hub, watching as the world of the senses transpires, you can achieve balance. Even while experiencing the world of the senses, you can open the door to divinity. Then, in times of accomplishment, you will remain balanced. Then, in times of tragedy, you will remain balanced. You hold the Center. That is strength: to be at center. In holding the center, you cannot be thrown off.

Through holding the center, you become master of time and fate. At center, you hold the key to your fortune in your own curved palm. At center, you become the mature individual: *the wheel that rolls out of its own center.*

Card Symbology: The Wheel of Fortune appears as a turning screw. It is boring into the grasping palm which symbolizes that all possibility is at hand. The central axis of the screw turns perpetually between the two disks at either end. The disks are energy centers, and the whole process of the turning wheel represents not only the spinning of fate, but the twisting of the spinal column which is the precursor to the cellular changes which are prerequisite to the opening of the door of divinity.

The disks show the three concentric rings which represent the levels of moving toward central balance. In the outer circle are the four alchemical glyphs which represent the transition from matter to spirit. The glyph for Mercury (☿) represents the onset of rapid movement. Sulphur (🜍) is the male universal principle, force, the Sun, which ignites the spirit. Aquarius (♒) is the glyph of dissolution. It is the glyph of the abyss and the knowledge of the many in the One and the One in the many. Finally, salt (⊖) represents the female lunar side, the side of form, birth and death.

In the middle circle is the six-pointed star of divine unity. All the forces and forms of the rim unite in a field of golden light.

In the central circle is the circle-cross of the four directions, Fire, Water, Wind and Earth. The circle is Key 0. The circle-cross is formed by adding the cross of earth to the cross of salt. Thereby, the circle-cross represents the descended one: the force of spirit ensouled in form and spiraling inward toward a point of perfect balance, the point at the intersection of heaven and earth.

When this inward spiral is fully realized, the spirit is "turned inside out" and a new cosmic mandala appears. This is a circle contained inside of a square, the eternal circle contained in the square of the material. This new glyph (▢) is the symbol for the philosopher's stone, lapis lazuli. The philosopher's stone represents the understanding of the psyche of humanity, the understanding of the truth of the One in the many, or the divine monad, which is the unity of totality.

Around the axis of the screw, ten yods (י) spiral like a winding serpent. This is the Golden Serpent of Understanding descending to the world of matter.

The Wheel of Fortune is the wheel of Mother Nature. This is the ascent and the descent of human life. The whole process is overseen by the sphinx which is the symbol of the Great Mother Goddess of death and rebirth. The sphinx is now the dark and light principles, which originally appeared in Key VII, the Chariot, united in one.

The Wheel of Fortune is the spinning wheel of the Great Mother. It is the loom of creation, out of which spins all possibilities of force and form, all patterns of energy, and out of which the logos, the word made flesh, the circle of eternity as contained in the square of materiality, is reflected as the creative principle of the universe.

Key XI. Karma

Divinatory Meaning ─────────────

Do not deny the consequences of your actions; own the results of your thoughts, words and deeds, for even thought constitutes action in the energy cycles of the universe; adjust your actions and embrace love; remember these words: "Be not deceived, God is not mocked, for whatsoever a man soweth, that shall he also reap."

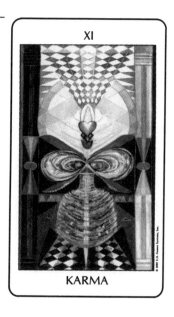

KARMA

Meditation ──────────────────────────

Listen to the stillness at the Center of the Cyclone
the calm crevice of Truth
Truth that breathes hollowly, sends chills, dispells illusion,
    by the still cool air of the Moon
    Truth at the breathy core

Whirling, twirling
the Dance of Karma
swirling off excess costume like tattered fringe-lace on the
    dancer's dress
      casting off the excess bit by bit
      until remains a breathless core
      which lives and learns and breathes and grows
      from one life to the next
      without expectation

Youth-parent-aged and feeling
all at once, every page of LifeForm glimpsed at one reading
    in one place, at one Time
      diameter forever circling, expanding/contracting
all the infinite spinning Faces of Self
tapering down to that featureless space
    of naked Truth
    not Just, for the time, but Exacting
    and therefore, Just, in the long stride
      on the long ride
      through Forever

The Dance of Karma spins and whirls
like the twirling of a little girl
learning balance
whirling with glittering Magic Sword and Wand
finding skill and lore
spinning madly about that which is still
    —the empty breathy Center—
sighing
    Love is the Law, Love under Will
breathing
    Love is the Will, Love under Law.

Esoteric Qualities ———————————————

Hebrew attribution: Lamed (pronounced *lawmed*), the ox goad ל
Astrological attribution: Libra, mediation and balancing
Twenty-second Path: Mediates between Geburah (the universal prin-
    ciple of destruction, the destroyer) and Tiphareth (spiritual love
    and beauty manifested on the Earth plane)

Essence: Bringing polarities into balance through adjustments
Intelligence: The Faithful Intelligence, the faith that all in life tends
    toward balance and wholeness
Veil: No matter what we do, we cannot change our fate.
Mystery: The nature of things is to move into perfect balance by
    making adjustments to the forces and forms of the universe. All
    adjustment is good in that it moves us closer to the center of the
    target of perfection.

Interpretation

At Key XI, Karma, you are experiencing karmic adjustments in your
life. Your thoughts and actions of the past have led to your present
state. You have seen that your actions produce consequences. You
are aware of your actions and are capable of discerning whether they
are right or wrong. Whatever is happening now, you will probably
be able to pinpoint its causes in the past. As the Buddha said, "If you
want to know the past, look at your present. If you want to know
the future, look at your present."[10]
    The conditions of present reality reflect past thoughts and deeds.
In general, we use the term karma to refer to fate or destiny. Fate
and destiny represent the workings of the divine law of cause and
effect. Every action entails a reaction.
    The principle behind karma is cosmic law. Cosmic law is the
absolute balance inherent in the universe, which, as Gareth Knight
says, takes account of all factors from within it from the relationships
of the simplest atom to the remotest and largest suns.[11] Cosmic justice
is exacting. It does not veer to the right or the left, but is perfect.
Karma is, in the long view, a balancing force even if the temporary
results are disruptive. This means that, according to cosmic justice,
we must account for and atone for all of our behaviors.
    Sometimes, however, we find ourselves in negative circum-
stances which we feel cannot be justified on the basis of our behavior
alone. How could we have generated such a deplorable fate? How is
it, for example, that you could be born into a wealthy family while I
am born into a poor one? These occurrences seem inexplicable. Many
belief systems thus explain these phenomena in terms of past lives.

---

[10]Phillip Kapleau, *The Three Pillars of Zen* (New York: Doubleday, a division of Bantam,
Doubleday, Dell Publishing Group, Inc., 1980), p. 294.
[11]See *A Practical Guide to Qabalistic Symbolism*, p. 104.

In Sanskrit, karma means deed or act. In the Buddhist and Hindu systems of thought, karma indicates the totality of a person's actions in any one of the successive states of his or her existence. The actions of each life are presumed to determine fate in the next incarnation. The goal of successive incarnations is union with God.

Various religions maintain that we choose the circumstances of our lives in order to learn our own personal lessons which will facilitate our progress on the spiritual path. As we begin to accept or face our own karma, and understand that we are not the innocent victims of our environment—but rather that we *chose* our circumstances to receive certain lessons—we are coming to a true meeting with our inner Self. According to Edgar Cayce, karma is a personal thing between the Self and the Creator. It is not between individuals. Other people only provide the conditions for us to learn our lessons and gain self-mastery. Self-mastery involves attaining perfection on the spiritual path which results in companionship and co-creativity with God.[12]

In the ancient Hebrew system, Key XI, Lamed, means ox goad. An ox goad is a sharp pointed stick used in driving oxen. The word *goad* means any driving impulse, to prod on to action, to urge on. It is fitting that the ox goad is sharp pointed, given that it represents the twenty-second path on the Tree of Life. This is the path between Geburah and Tiphareth. Geburah is the destroyer, the force of destruction, that which pares down, or lightens, in order to force onward. Tiphareth represents the birth of Christ-consciousness, the manifestation of universal truth and beauty on the physical plane. In order to realize such a birth, we must lighten. We must focus. We must be goaded on by sharp points. We are pushed toward spiritual growth by consequences resulting from our thoughts, words and deeds.

The sword of Geburah, the destructive principle, is absolutely necessary for spiritual enlightenment. We must use it to cut away the false values of past conditioning. That is why Jesus came with a sword. The sword is the great balancer. In order to balance, we must destroy the old to the same degree that we construct the new. We must make room for new growth. The sword is the symbol of karma.

Thus, Key XI becomes the great mediator between the two sets of tarot keys. It mediates between Keys I through X and Keys XII

---

[12]Mary Ann Woodward, *Edgar Cayce's Story of Karma* (New York: Berkeley Publishing Corp., 1972), p. 21.

through XXI. Karma is the key which balances the Major Arcana, just
as it is the key which balances life.

Through lifetime after lifetime, the individual's personality develops. It begins as inexperienced and unevolved spirit which develops as a pattern of energy. The hundreds of personalities built up
through evolution enrich the composition of the individual. Key XI
is the path of destroying negative karmic build-up and keeping the
spirit on track. It is the path of coming closer and closer to meeting
the mark of perfect union, the path of perfecting the aim of spiritual
enlightenment. Paul Foster Case says:

> . . . as the archer gaineth skill
> By reason of aiming again and again at his mark,
> Though in the beginning he miss it a thousand times,
>   So doth the fruit of sin,
>   Which men call punishment,
> Perfect the skill of my chosen ones.[13]

As the divine law of cause and effect, karma is a continuous
process. This means that the way the individual responds to circumstances determines quality of life for the present as well as for the
future. This applies to circumstances of the mind, spirit, feelings and
body. Through our reactions, we create our own karma. Of course,
we cannot regress and change the circumstances of our birth, but we
have a degree of will over our response to these conditions as well
as to any others that arise. The circumstances of our birth—the composition and condition of our family of origin—are an example of
"fixed karma," a fate that has been cast and a fact over which we
currently have no control. The way we react to our circumstances,
however, represents "mutable karma." It is through mutable karma
that we have the potential at each moment to alter the course of our
future. We can alter our fate.

Thus, will is the key to freedom. We must choose to do right and
exert our will in that direction:

> For will is that developing factor with which an entity chooses
> or builds that freedom, or that of being free, knowing the
> truth as is applicable in the experience, and in the various
> experiences as has been builded; for that builded must be
> met, whether in thought or in deed; for thoughts are deeds,

---

[13]See Paul Foster Case's The Book of Tokens, p. 84.

and their current run is through the whole of the influence in an *entity's* experience. Hence, as was given, "He that hateth his brother has committed as great a sin as he that slayeth a man," for the deed is as of an accomplishment in the mental being, which is the builder for every entity.[14]

Thus each soul or entity has its own karma, its own urges which arise from "earthly sojourns" or "interims between earthly appearances." Knowing your Self, your Self's ideals and Self's principles is coming to terms with your karma. When you do this, you are meeting and facing your inner Self, the deep unmoving Self at the center of the Wheel of Fortune (see Key X).

You build up "bad" karma when you remain indifferent to that which you know is right. Correcting bad karma becomes a question not of correcting for the specific wrong committed, but rather a question of correcting your purposes and desires and eliminating wrong actions from your ideals and purposes. Correcting your karma means walking toward the future with faith that you are doing the right thing. This is the *faithful intelligence.*

While many belief systems claim that it is possible to get off of the "Wheel of Return"—that is the eternal cycle of birth, death and rebirth (see Key X: The Wheel of Fortune)—through eliminating negative karma, it is also possible to free ourselves of negative karma and live in grace while on the earth plane. To do this, we must accept the law of love and offer ourselves in service of this principle.

To be free and to live in a state of grace involves gaining the knowledge necessary to dissolve that which binds us. We make progress on the spiritual path through recognizing that our problems are opportunities. We alone are responsible for our trials, obstacles and miseries. When we recognize this, we are meeting Self at the center of the forever rising and falling Wheel of Fortune (see Key X). Knowledge of the deep Self brings us ever-closer into communion with the Creator. This communion is a state of divine love.

Grace is God's love. Moving into Christ-consciousness entails eliminating negative karma through making the primal will—the will of the Creator—our will. Living in this state of grace, we are freed from bondage.

We begin to move toward the gate of grace through the medium of mental processes. Through contemplation or meditation—and then

---

[14]Edgar Cayce, as quoted by Woodward, p. 28.

through *intention*—we can erase all evil paths from the present and thus the future. We will find that the "Pure Land" is near at hand. At the first moment we embark upon this path, our karma is forever affected. We begin the path through learning to accept and love ourselves. The path is ended with the realization of universal love. Love is the law. Love under will. *When I love, I love you as I love my Self, for—in truth—we are one love. We are one light.*

Card Symbology: Key XI depicts the mechanical aspects of karma. Karma appears as a spinning insect-like top, balanced on the Middle Pillar on the Tree of Life. The central axis is a sword which remains in constant motion. It is propelled by the lemniscate-like (figure eight-like) wings of karma.

Karma's head is a spinning egg. This is the egg from the sevenfold alchemical process, which symbolizes the realization of eternal life.[15] This egg holds the bird of regeneration. The aim of the sevenfold process is a higher synthesis, or initiation, wherein the egg, the germ of contact with individuality, is hatched to reveal harmonious control. This indicates a karmic breakthrough.

To the left and right, we see the outer pillars of the Tree of Life, meeting at the center in points that resemble the points of pencils. These points merge at center points on both sides which symbolize the maxim As Above, So Below. This can also be read As Within, So Without, which is another key to understanding the nature of karma. The points at many places on this card are the ox goads which urge you to come to terms with your karma and meet your true self at the center of the Wheel.

The diamond floor, reflected in the diamond ceiling, is the floor of the inner temple. The checkered pattern shows the movement of the stream of consciousness flowing now with more color. The color indicates that, through introspection, true reflection is getting deeper.

In the background is the glyph for Venus which rules Libra. This is a further indication that love is the law, love under will.

---

[15]If you are interested in delving deeper into the mysteries, the sevenfold alchemical process involving the egg has been elucidated by Gareth Knight in *A Practical Guide to Qabalistic Symbolism*, pp. 64–67.

Key XII. The Hanged Man

Divinatory Meaning ───────

XII

THE HANGED MAN

It is time to retreat, withdraw and surrender to quietude; when the internal waters are stilled, you can see and hear your deep eternal self which is your own truth; through meditative contemplation, you will arrive at truth; your glorious nature is revealed when the clear waters of your mind cease to be disturbed by rippling thoughts; this is a time of voluntary withdrawal, reenter the world only when you know you have received answers; do not be pushed or agitated by the whims of others.

Meditation ───────────────────────

Submersion in the element of Illusion
    suspension from dependence
    crossed like an anchor
descending
from Light to Dark
while the Serpent of New Life
stirs beneath the waves at the bottom of the seagreen
deep dark depths
and wells that are flat calm
and churning with undulating currents

the Will to Surrender
beyond that which Is
to that which Was and Shall Become
the Willing Surrender
to a flow beyond Culture
back to womb grave tomb shell
the shining home of the first reflection

a clear vision from immersion
sound waves travelling like
lost and haunted bells
across obstructive swells
of limitation and defense

submersion to discover
Self
as the vehicle for true
ascent.

Esoteric Qualities ────────────────────────────

Hebrew attribution: Mem (pronounced *mayim*), water מ   ם
Astrological attribution: Water, the reflective principle
Twenty-third Path: Mediates between Geburah (the great universal
    destroyer) and Hod (the thinking mind)
Essence: The Return to the sea of life, the womb of all being
Intelligence: The Stable Intelligence, the original intellect, the deep
    mind, which is, was and ever shall be
Veil: Thoughts that ripple across the mind's surface are the whole of
    the truth.
Mystery: In losing your self, you find your Self.

Interpretation ──────────────────────────────

Key XII, the Hanged Man, represents the suspended mind. At Key
XII, you are in a time and place of surrender. You are letting go. You
are voluntarily retreating. You are evolving and this process necessitates withdrawal.

The Hanged Man immerses himself in Water, the element of deep
understanding. There it is possible for him to tap the deep flow of
the original intellect, the universal mind, the most stable intelligence,
the brilliant pattern of thought known before and beneath the myriad
dimensions of cultural overlay. He is immersed in the cosmic womb,
that which cradles spirit and builds form. This womb is a shell of
protection which offers a way of knowing through quieting the mind
and releasing the self from preoccupation with everyday matters. The
Hanged Man is submerged in deep introspection.

From this womb, which could be compared to a cocoon or an
isolation tank, the man—when he so wills—is reborn in newness.

As the twenty-third path on the Tree of Life, Key XII mediates between Geburah, the universal force of dissolution, and Hod, the Hanged Man's intelligence or patterns of thought. On the twenty-third path, the Hanged Man must experience the dissolution of former patterns—Death—in order to evolve. Thus, the womb is also a grave or tomb, in that the process of change requires laying to rest, or leaving behind, antiquated forms. Old ways of knowing must die, to make room for the new to emerge. The Hanged Man's process is therefore akin to a metamorphosis. Just as the larva of an insect becomes the pupa which then transforms into the adult, the Hanged Man eventually emerges in a more evolved state. Reborn, he now sees the world from a new perspective, a point of view which is uncolored by his prior socialization. He has abandoned thought patterns which were overly complicated, false or misguided.

As one situation ends and another begins, the submerged one is redeemed. He is freed from the constructs which led him into bondage. As is symbolized by his legs crossed in an inverted 4, the Hanged Man in submersion is reconsidering his relationship to the material world. He is engaged in the human quest to overcome conditioned limitations. He is rethinking the purpose of his existence. Gareth Knight states, ". . . perhaps the most basic Spiritual Law of the Universe is, however much appearances seem to indicate to the contrary, you get out of life exactly what you put into it."[16] Key XII, the Hanged Man, holds the answer to discovering what you are going to put into life. Your first task is to make your mind into a clear receptive vessel operating with pure, unfettered and unclouded universal mind. Once social conditioning is cleared away, your true purpose has room to emerge.

Submerged, you will find your Self at the door of reason. This is a door to the "mighty Waters of Ain Soph," the realm in which the cosmic atom of the inner Self—the Self freed from social constraints—is encountered. In this realm, you arrive at an understanding of the nature of consciousness and perceive the truth purely and clearly. Submerged, you begin to come to terms with the vast and mighty power of the massed and steadfast intention of the will-to-good.[17]

[16]See *A Practical Guide to Qabalistic Symbolism*, p. 142.
[17]Alice Bailey, *The Rays and the Initiations*, Volume 5 of *A Treatise on the Seven Rays* (New York: Lucis Trust, 1960), p. 139.

To achieve a state of clear awareness, you must learn to see as the Buddha saw. The Buddha said, "In what is seen there must be just the seen; in what is heard there must be just the heard; in what is sensed (as smell, taste or touch) there must be just what is sensed; in what is thought there must be just the thought."[18] Zen Buddhist Philip Kapleau states that for many of us, whose minds are usually "checkerboards of reflection, opinion, and prejudice," bare attention becomes difficult to achieve. Our lives have become centered not in reality itself but in our *ideas* of it, and the mind, when agitated or disturbed by an excess of stimulation, cannot reflect the deepest inner reality. Only when the pool of consciousness is stilled can we begin to perceive the true reflection of the One Self. To enter into a new way of knowing, we must strip the mind of extraneous thought and allow our selves to fully experience that which IS on the innermost plane.

In order to perceive its own true nature, the mind must first be brought to a state of emptiness. This is why retreat or withdrawal— secluded submersion—is so important. In this state, certain characteristics of existence are illuminated. In diving below the built up layers of our human experience, we begin to come to grips with the divine law of cause and effect. We come to understand the exacting nature of karma: the necessity of production and solution as well as the necessity of dissolution. We understand that we create and control our own reactions and reflections. We learn that at every moment, we are taking the first step upon the new path. At each moment, there exists the potential of rebirth into goodness. At each moment, we create the karma in which our path is bound. Most importantly, we learn that true and lasting freedom is achieved through successfully aligning our own "free will" with the cosmic will. We learn that *love is the will, love under law.* We have created the conditions of our own bondage.

Through our deepened understanding, and attunement to the guidance of the Higher Self, we can overcome the conflicts we feel in our everyday life. Through willingness to submit to the dictates of our highest conscience and consciousness—which will inevitably point to love as the highest of all principles—we are regenerated and born again. In the way of love, we sacrifice aggression, greed and selfishness for vulnerability, openness and selflessness.

---

[18]See Kapleau's *The Three Pillars of Zen*, pp. 10–11.

As we emerge from submersion in the mighty waters of the cosmic sea, the realm where we discover the elemental Self, the efforts of body and mind are consolidated, focused and energized. Our intelligence is clear, stable and consistent. Stress dissolves. We have seen the Inner Self and we have learned of its higher purpose.

Card Symbology: The Hanged Man is inverted upon a cross to which he is "tied" by a "rope"—perhaps the Serpent of Rebirth— which does not actually bind him. This indicates that his posture is a willing withdrawal. At any time, he can emerge from this state.

The swirls of blue and green symbolize his submersion in the cosmic sea, that realm of formation and reformation in which all creative force is cast into form.

The point at the top of the inverted man's head (at the bottom of the card) represents the cutting away of extraneous and antiquated thoughts and modes of thinking. In submersion, the Hanged Man is truly beginning to "get the point."

He sees with his eyes closed, for the journey is inward. His hands are behind his back in that this is a time of not-doing. His legs are crossed in an inverted 4 because he is reassessing his involvement in the material world. The circle-cross at the top of the card shows that his reassessment involves not only the material but the mind, the spirit and heart. That his heel is in the center of this cross means that he is balancing and centering between matter, intellect, spirit and emotions and that, upon emerging from his retreat, he will take his first step from a balanced perspective.

The Hanged Man resides on the Left Pillar of the Tree of Life, the pillar of matter and judgment. He can only judge the form of his existence through withdrawal into the deepest layers of Self. This is the solitary task of deep reflection at the innermost depths of the luminous sea of Binah (see Key III).

Key XIII. Death

Divinatory Meaning ——————————

You are involved in a major transformation; this is one of the greatest transformations you have known; you must go through this change alone; you will be reborn into newness, but first you must face your darkest fears; do not forget, the darkest hour is just before the dawn.

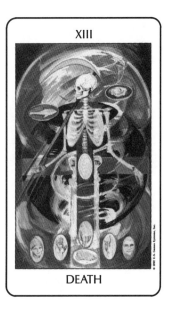

XIII

DEATH

Meditation ——————————————————————

Death comes
beating drums
screaming out the low wail
of Fate and Doom
Time has Come!
too soon! too soon! I scream, be gone!
knowing full well, all the while
it is late night; has come the dark hour; no dawn—
but corpses strewn about the strand
rolling twixt sand and sea

stretches out her bony claw
reaches
brushing hand and boot
and touches soul
screaming all the while
Come Brethren! Beat the Drum!

Sister! Brother!
Pound the Nail!
Time! Time! Time! Time!
has Come! Come! Come! Come!

Hear not the horses scream
but bleeding beating hooves with every crash upon the shore
submerging to emerge again
throwing off the old forms
waves of inert stagnation
fatal moves
grasping for gestation, fetal moves,
birth—
another breath—
re-spiration
in
carnation

The icy transformation of Death comes to
release
casting off the empty shell of
dead and bootless
grief.

Esoteric Qualities

Hebrew attribution: Nun (pronounced *noon*), fish נ ן
Astrological attribution: Scorpio, understanding through death and
    regeneration
Twenty-fourth Path: Mediates between Tiphareth (spiritual beauty
    and light manifested on Earth) and Netzach (the personality)
Essence: The great fish as symbol of pain, suffering and perpetuity
Intelligence: Imaginative Intelligence, imagination changes all form
Veil: Death is the end.
Mystery: Pain is the catalyst to the portal to the center. All things are
    contained in the belly of the fish. The fish is a sign of secret
    wisdom. Fish and sea are one. Perpetual change is at the root of
    all things. The two faces of change are death and birth, tearing
    down and building up. The secret of immortality is to understand
    the nature of continuity. The only thing that continues is the
    motion which moves all things.

Interpretation ─────────────────────────────────

At Key XIII, Death, something in your life is dying. Some structure, pattern or *form* that you created, or with which you have been involved, is disintegrating or dissolving. This is necessary, of course, in order for new birth or *transformation* to occur. The nature of transformation is to pass beyond form. Transformation can be taken to mean re-forming or transcending the limitations of matter. This is exactly what you are now doing.

Just as children quickly outgrow clothing, our minds as well as our bodies move through stages of growth during which we must abandon old "clothing"—that which contains and protects us—or feel uncomfortably constricted.

New thought forms are continually replacing the old. New ways of living accommodate expanded identities. Old lifestyles die. Priorities change. The body changes. As we renew ourselves with food and movement, light and air, we feel resurrected. New bodies grow within bodies, are released, and subsequently die. The spirit is born in matter, uses the body like clothing, and then abandons it. From birth to death, the spirit and the body are united. A bridge is formed between spirit and matter. Birth and death are the rites of passage at either end of the bridge. This is natural law.

Continual movement to new forms of being is the natural state. We discover that the only thing that is constant is the motion which carries all form from moment to moment. Change is the basis of all manifestation. Death is the instrument of progress. Death is our protection against stagnation.

The relationship of our body and mind to the outside world also undergoes transformation. In these days of fast-paced living, we seem to live many lifetimes in one, changing residences and occupations, on average, at least once every seven years. As we change, we are forced to leave behind that which is outgrown. Changing or leaving often feels like a kind of death. It is painful, and yet we know we must change to grow.

Each of us has a task in this life. The thing we call "life" is itself a task. When your life is active in its task—when you are living according to your deepest inner convictions and accomplishing your true task—Death is your servant. When your life is passive in its task, Death is your master. This applies to the physical life of the body as well as the "life" of any project, household, job, relationship, affiliation or endeavor. As tasks are completed, old forms fall away, new forms arise.

How do you know whether you are meeting your task? To find your task, you must move through the Valley of the Shadow. You must face your fears. You must move toward the still space at the center of your being. At center, you discover your true cosmic will.

You begin this process of moving to center by delving into your feelings. Does what you are doing *feel* right? Does your conscience support your actions?

Imagine how it might be in the best of all worlds. This is why the twenty-fourth path—the path of Death—is known as *imaginative intelligence*. Imagination makes all things possible. Imagination makes all things happen. We change form first in our imagination. Imagination takes us on the path from the sphere of Netzach, the realm of our emotions and the basis of our personality, to the sphere of Tiphareth, spiritual beauty and light or Christ-consciousness manifest on earth. Through the vehicle of our imagination, we come to see that in order to live in beauty and light, in righteousness, we must first abandon our ego as we know it. That is the essence of Death as it applies to the spiritual path.

In coming to live in righteousness, it is critically important that we discover our true position in the cosmic pattern. Our inner spirit must ultimately align with the divine cosmic pattern. Wrong or distorted perceptions of the cosmic pattern are what lead us to follow a false path. This causes confusion. False images of the cosmic pattern lead to sin, evil and disease: the target of perfection missed. Most distortion of the truth results simply from *fear of pain*.

Having fear of pain is like having a fear of falling. Gareth Knight provides us with the analogy of a gymnast about to vault over a horse. Running up, the gymnast loses confidence, suddenly imagining what would happen if his foot slipped, or if someone removed the mat from the other side, or if the springboard did not work. As a result of his *self-imposed distortion*, he leaps halfheartedly. He does not clear the horse and as a result, he dislocates his neck or breaks a wrist.[19]

On a grander scale, *the fear of the individual is the root of the fall of humanity*. When one individual loses the confidence to follow the true path, all are affected. This is the source of the world's chaos and confusion.

---

[19]See *A Practical Guide to Qabalistic Symbolism*, p. 94.

The idea of fear as the basis of the fall is summed up in the story of Jonah and the great fish. The tarot Key, Nun (Death), which means fish, represents the great fish that swallowed Jonah. In this story, Jonah, motivated by fear, flees the presence of the Lord. He attempts to run away by boarding a ship bound for a distant land. At sea, the Lord causes a great wind to arise. There is a mighty tempest which threatens the ship. The passengers pray to their god that they will not perish. When they discover that Jonah—through attempting to run away—is responsible for the storm, they ask him what they should do to calm the sea. Jonah says, "Take me up and throw me into the sea, then the sea will quiet down for you; for I know it is because of me that this great tempest has come upon you." They throw him into the sea where the Lord causes a great fish to swallow him. Jonah spends three days and three nights in the belly of the fish. When he realizes that "deliverance belongs to the Lord," the Lord speaks to the fish who then vomits Jonah out—alive and re-born—on dry land.

It is because of Jonah's suffering that the great fish is seen as the emblem of all pain and sorrow, but this very pain and sorrow is the portal which enables us to better understand how we have missed the target of perfection. It is the portal which enables us to move to the heart of spirit. The fish does not kill Jonah, but, in a sense, saves him from other treacheries of the sea. The fish cradles Jonah and then releases him. Thus, the belly of the fish is like a womb. Yet it is dark and unknown. This signifies that Jonah must face his fears in darkness before he begins to see the light.

Esoterically speaking, the great fish—the vehicle of light and regeneration—is hidden in the waters of the cosmic sea just as the secret of the One is concealed within the semblance of the many. The fish thus becomes the sign of secret wisdom. Such wisdom is simply the discovery of the oneness or unity of all things.

In the story of Jonah and the great fish, Jonah experiences fear. In an attempt to cling to a particular reality, he tries to run away. This may be your own pattern. You may run when you need to stay. You may stay when you need to run. You may find yourself clinging to that which your heart of hearts tells you is false or outmoded. You may cling for the sake of convenience. You may cling because you fear pain. No matter how bad it is, it could be worse. To cling, however, is to *sink into matter*. In clinging, you develop a "heavy" body. To sink into matter is true death.

The polar opposite of Death is birth, and as a magnet can be infinitely divided and still contain its poles, Death and birth are inextricably connected. To attempt to hold back forthcoming life as one gives birth is to endure great pain. When one looks deeply inward, one realizes that surrender to the process, surrender to motion, is the key to pushing through the pain to relief and newness.

You must surrender to the dark apparitions of the unknown. On the path through shadow, you learn that light is born of darkness and that darkness cannot overcome light. When you know this, fear subsides. When fear subsides, you can unequivocally accept the path by which you have come. You can accept the way others have come. You can accept the way you must go as well as the way others must go. You learn to love your enemies and you realize that Death is the final enemy. You learn to love Death.

Death is a manifestation of the law, and when we understand the law, we can direct the forces of change so as to understand and overcome Death. Thus the adage: "Know thine Enemy."

At this moment, yours is the path of the sword. No matter how difficult it is, you must cut away that which is extraneous, that which keeps you from truth, that which keeps you in bondage. Surrendering to the universal force, and facing all the fears you encounter on the unknown path, entails the killing of the old. Death must occur before rebirth into higher consciousness can be achieved.

This kind of transformation may manifest as a crisis period in your life. You may be tempted to run back to the safety of the known. But fear of the future must be replaced with confidence in the future.

Moving through the dark toward the light is the path of initiation. This is the path on which desire is abandoned and you are absorbed in Christ-consciousness. Christ, too, is symbolized by the fish of regeneration. Christ comes from the great sea, offers himself as the symbolic meal, dies and is resurrected as the Great Mother gives birth in the spring.

In Christ-consciousness, we act from the space of "dead center," the place of spirit that remains still while everything revolves around it. From this center, we realize that change is the root of all things. We realize that change has two faces: the face of birth and the face of death. At "dead center," we discover—like Christ—our own changeless life: that which binds together the unending series of little lives and deaths. At "dead center" we sacrifice ego, intellect and short-term memory for charity, faith and hope. The personality undergoes willful death. The spirit is resurrected into cosmic awareness and light.

The self must die to know love. Love is the fruit of understanding. Through love we advance from fear. This is the ultimate and supreme connection between love and death: when one lets go of matter, the portals of the path to true love and beauty open. It may be frightening at first, for this is a path one must undertake alone. To take the first steps, one must slash away that which binds, but, then when all extraneous matter has been cast aside, one is unfettered, sees clearly, and realizes that there are kindred spirits in all directions.

Be strong and courageous, with inner conviction, will and courage. Open and you will find yourself at the gates of freedom and love peering into eternal limitless light. As Paul Foster Case says, *Every morning is a resurrection of the awakened soul.*

Card Symbology: In the Death card, the skeleton is moving. This shows that things are changing. The skeleton is the basic form or pattern upon which all outer form is built. Thus, at Key XIII, you have stripped down to the bare bones and are ready to begin again.

The scythe over the skeleton's shoulder is the tool for cutting away that which is extraneous and no longer matters. Death swings the scythe in a figure eight, or lemniscate, which shows eternal movement. The scythe is effective in removing that which is dead or useless.

In its "womb," the skeleton holds a developing fetus. The fetus is at the center of the Holy Cross that represents Tiphareth, the Christ-consciousness, the realization that the eternal light of the Mother-Father-God resides in all beings. The horizontal bar of the cross represents the physical plane. The vertical axis represents the spiritual path. The cross is encircled by the eternally moving wheel of transformation. The circle-cross represents the eternal interaction of the physical and the spiritual. Each Death—through eternity—lays the groundwork for birth as old forms are outgrown.

The body parts in the lower portion of the card symbolize possibility. The fish stands for eternal life. The white rose on the platter signifies innocence, truth, purity and the way of beauty which is the way of Tiphareth.

Key XIV. Temperance

Divinatory Meaning

The trials and temptations you currently experience will lead you toward integration, the "middle way," the path of moderation; through acting in moderation, your fears are conquered and your purity shines forth; you are in a period of growth, of "stretching" yourself spiritually; through allowing inner growth, you will arrive at a period of profound realization.

XIV

TEMPERANCE

Meditation

Temperance
the right leading
of the New Living Substance
on the Path of True Will

The chance to overcome contradiction
through adherence to the Golden Mean
and creative cleansing

direction and persistence
art perception integration
alliance of the incomplete
with that which completes
via
a journey to the soul's interior
on black and white steeds

balancing deeds with thought
and thought with that-which-is-not
yet manifest

in order to discover the hidden stone
of wizards
both rigid and elastic
that which will temper and modify
vibrations of the Universe at will

the secret to this magic
is to journey to the center of the Earth
by Water

Esoteric Qualities ─────────────────────────────────

Hebrew attribution: Samekh (pronounced *saw-mek*), the prop or crutch ס
  Astrological attribution: Sagittarius, aspiration, the bowstring
  which fires the arrow of divine Love
Twenty-fifth Path: Mediates between Tiphareth (spiritual beauty and
  light manifest on Earth; the sphere of the Sun) and Yesod (the
  subconscious; the sphere of the Moon)
Essence: The Middle Way as the key to happiness
Intelligence: The Intelligence of Trial or Temptation, the knowledge
  of why such things arise
Veil: Fire is the Great Destroyer
Mystery: The serpent of temptation is the Holy One, deliverer into
  liberation. Fire is the Great Illuminator. Through destruction or
  trials—as if by Fire—all that covers or mars internal beauty is
  burned away, leaving behind the pure gold illumination of the
  Shining One who is Truth Unveiled.

Interpretation ──────────────────────────────────────

At Key XIV, Temperance, you are coming to terms with your excesses.
You must modify all excessive behavior. Temperance is the force
which integrates and balances all things: the great mediator. Temperance elicits reaction from action, reception from emission, cold
from hot and moist from dry. Temperance connects the seeker to the
sought. In the divine marriage of the tarot, the Empress and the
Emperor wed. Their qualities blend. It is the activity of Temperance—
the activity of blending qualities—that enables them to stay together.
Similarly, the activity of Temperance unites the Sun and Moon as
well as all other heavenly orbs. Through affecting qualities, Temper-

ance binds all patterns of universal movement. Temperance is the dynamic energy behind every bond and within every nexus.

In essence, Key XIV, Temperance, can be conceptualized as the dynamic activity of *tempering*. Together, for example, just as the Empress and Emperor act on, and thereby modify, each other, black and white act on each other to make gray. This exemplifies the energetic activity of Key XIV. In general, to temper means to *attain a proper measure or mix*. It means to regulate or to make something suitable, desirable, fit, or free from excess. This is done by reducing, intensifying and mixing qualities.

In Temperance, we observe the subtle mixing of qualities which ultimately results in a path of moderation—the *middle way*. The middle way—usually depicted by the color gray to symbolize the wisdom that results from integrating extremes—is the basis of true and lasting connection and happiness. Happiness is achieved through alleviating conflict by consciously mingling (or coming to terms with) elements which appear to be contradictory.

On the Tree of Life, Temperance is the twenty-fifth path. This path connects the sphere of Tiphareth, the sphere of spiritual beauty and light, and the possibility of its manifestation in the life of the individual, with the sphere of Yesod, the subconscious mind. This connection symbolizes the interaction, or comingling, of the sought-after spiritual light with all the fears, confusion and chaos, still swirling below the mind's surface, shrouded in darkness.

As you come to Key XIV, messages are beginning to surface to the light of your conscious mind from the dark subconscious realm. The major message you receive at Temperance is one regarding the balanced state. You need to balance and consciously mingle those things in your life which seem contradictory. You need to center yourself between opposing forces and *consciously temper or mediate your circumstances*. Further, you must temper your Self in order to see clearly the past, present and future and all of your relationships. This applies to tempering your state of mind or disposition.

As an interesting aside, when we lose our *temper*—our state of balance—we are prone to anger or even rage. We may become depressed or overly excitable. Our problems, however, will continue until the internal conflict is resolved. Internal conflicts are caused by *disharmony in our desires*. For example, you may have found yourself struggling to resist certain attractions for which you might have to compromise your values. This is what it means to be *led into temptation*.

It seems as if, to attain certain pleasures, the dictates of the conscience must be challenged. You question how far can you go without hurting yourself or others. You question where you draw the line on ethics. How clear is the boundary between right and wrong?

In Hebrew *Samekh* means prop or crutch. The most important prop or crutch which will help you decipher the problem and reach resolution is to embrace the sensibilities of faith, hope and charity. Having faith, hope and charity involves knowing that in following the path of righteousness, moderation and conscience, you will be able to purge the results of error and disease from the path of your soul. You will be reborn in truth and clarity. Conflict will melt away. Further, when you give yourself over to follow the way of faith, hope and charity you will be empowered, so to speak, to abandon those material crutches which have kept you operating from a place of weakness.

The first step to internalizing faith, hope and charity is to realize that *it is the divine powers themselves that cause temptation*. The trials through which we pass are but the tests which *temper* our souls, making us better human beings. Says Paul Foster Case:

Wise art thou if thou knowest
That the subtle serpent of temptation
Is in truth the anointed One
Who bringeth thee to liberation.[20]

As we err in judgment and miss the mark of perfection, we sharpen our skill for the next test or trial. In this way the *fire of punishment, whether applied to the Self from within or from outside, tempers and refines us*, just as metal is hardened and made resilient through exposure to fire.

The path toward righteousness, however, may seem arduous and unforgiving. It is a path which must be taken alone. This path may seem, at first, empty and without direction. It may seem hard to correlate this path with the demands of everyday life in an advanced capitalist society. In occult writings, this path, which connects the Moon (Yesod) and the Sun (Tiphareth), has been called The Desert Way. The Desert Way represents the dark night of the soul. During this dark night, when you are conflicted and struggling for clarity, you are beginning the ascent from the bondage of matter. As Gareth Knight says, the ascent along the path from the darkness of matter

---

[20]See *The Book of Tokens*, p. 140.

toward the brilliance of spirit, is characterized by darkness and aridity. The soul seems to be sustained only by its own resources. At this time, in order to progress, many things material must be purged. In the dark night of the desert, one learns to *identify with emptiness*. This emptiness is like the breath. Through the direct and open experience and acceptance of such emptiness, one can finally begin to experience the *bliss of being alive*. One learns also that the only attributes which do not weigh heavily in the darkest and emptiest moments of material existence are faith, hope and charity.

When this is understood, you will realize that coming to meet you from the other direction, descending from spirit to matter, is "the downflow of life, light and love." As Gareth Knight iterates, life, light and love are three exact terms, not misty generalizations. These qualities arise from the *individuality*, "seeking to make and establish contact with its projection in incarnation."[21]

Thus, to the journeyer ascending the path of Temperance, the appearance of the divine light in the darkest hour marks the first dawning of mystical consciousness. This is the deep understanding of your nature and your role in all things. The dawning, which is spiritual insight or enlightenment, will occur for the soul which has intentionally immersed itself in spiritual dryness in order to know the deepest truth.

Ultimately, the desert way leads to the inner temple or sanctuary of the deep Self. It leads to the inner covenant with God. Temple and temper both come from the same Indo-European root *tempos* which means to stretch or span, to tense, to pull, stretch or make thin. The act of stretching tight or straining also has to do with the *temporal nature of things*, the chronological arrangement of past, present and future. In the inner temple, past, present and future—via the internal activity of temperance—meld into one moment. In this centered and eternal moment, you finally stand balanced, rooted firmly in the middle way, where you are able to see right and wrong, above and below, past, present and future. At center is a unified field, a space-time continuum which *transcends the limitations of dualistic thinking*.

The challenge of Key XIV, Temperance, is *to become fully illuminated, centered in the unified field of space and time, dead to the domination of matter*. The formula of continued life is Death. In illumination, Death is comprehended and the vehicles of matter are used only for ends of a higher nature.

---

[21]See *A Practical Guide to Qabalistic Symbolism*, p. 76.

The challenge of Key XIV is to be centered and balanced like a gyroscope, continually righting itself, in the midst of moving forces. The universe will always revolve and evolve. The only true stability results from continual adjustment and movement with the flow. The highest art of humanity is thus to continually adjust and compensate, always motivated from the highest and most conscious values. This is the art of temperance, to move with fluidity among the great and powerful forces of nature.

Card Symbology: The armless spirit of Temperance, clothed in a gown reminiscent of the stone of which the cube of the divine law is fashioned, is a manifestation of the archangel Michael. In Temperance, Michael stands between the Sun, which is the Light of spirit and higher consciousness, and the dark Moon, representing the subconscious, now in ascension and transcending the limitations of matter.

Temperance is the art of balancing and moderation, thus the sense of the card is that of a gyroscope, which readily rights itself in the face of movement.

Michael is armless in the art of balancing. Arms are of matter and Michael's art requires no arms. This is because, at the point of Temperance, the great work becomes spiritualized. The great work, at this point, involves understanding the connection between the Sun and the Moon. This understanding requires the purification of the body, as symbolized by the glyph for salt at the back end of the arrow, and the ignition of the cosmic force, represented by the glyph for sulphur at the arrow's point. This is the arrow of divine love, just as Cupid's arrow represents eros or human love. The force that propels the arrow is the human *desire to understand*.

The Sun and the Moon, denoting the harmonious mingling of Fire and Water, are the targets, the spheres which the aspirant desires to connect. The targets represent the manifold or multidimensional layers of Self which must be peeled back to be understood like the layers of an onion skin. They merge together at center and form a lemniscate, or figure eight, the universal symbol of eternity which continually moves and changes.

The rainbow surrounding the Moon reflects the Sun's rainbow which is too bright to be discerned. This rainbow is a symbol of the Rainbow Covenant, God's covenant of love to humanity. The rainbow is formed in the same way that color occurs at all intersections of light and dark.

Michael not only stands in the rainbow target of the Moon, but stands with one foot in green and one in blue, symbolizing the balance of earth and sky. Temperance is thus the card of perfect balance.

Key XV. The Devil

Divinatory Meaning ———————

The closer you get to your own truth, the more you perceive contradiction; the key to understanding is to see things from a new perspective; accept the presence of paradox in your life and you will realize your own truth; celebrate life, laugh, play, dance upon the Earth; enjoy the material, but do not become a slave to it; bondage results from too much concentration on material success; stay attuned to matters of the heart and spirit.

Meditation ———————

You, Devil, You!
Playing on Earth!
Wash your Heart with Laughter! Mirth! Freedom!
and Renew—
It is the false sense of your own Power
that binds you
How do you estimate? Over or Under?

Devil, you, Base of the Matter
with an Eye for Creativity
a Mind to See
Body to Touch
Feelings to Know
Will to Dare!

You, Devil, You!
Contradictory! Emotions enflamed with the Spiral Force of God

the woman in you seeks Life
the man in you, Death
And if you think the one facing you
is Devil
see the Mirror!
What you see is what you look with
What you see is not all there is to Know!

Esoteric Qualities ─────────────────────────────

Hebrew attribution: Ayin (pronounced *ahyin*), the eye ע
Astrological attribution: Capricorn, perseverance
Twenty-sixth Path: Mediates between Tiphareth (higher conscious-
    ness, spiritual truth and beauty manifested on Earth) and Hod
    (the thinking mind)
Essence: All that is of matter
Intelligence: The Renewing Intelligence, the knowledge of unity
Veil: A separate lord prevails over darkness.
Mystery: God and the Devil are revealed by reflection. As humanity
    changes, so do conceptions of God and the Devil. Faith and
    science must work together, holding a sublime balance, to pro-
    duce a new reality for humankind.

Interpretation ─────────────────────────────

At Key XV, the Devil, it is as if the world of dark subconscious—the
part of you that struggles in chaos—and the world of the higher truth
are superimposed. When you reach the Devil, there is a struggle for
truth amid seeming contradictions and haphazard or incomplete information. Through all this, you see glimpses of light.

At Key XV you may find yourself face to face with a person or
situation which confuses you, upsets you, appalls you, disgusts you,
or by which you feel hopelessly entrapped. You may feel that someone is acting reprehensibly. Perhaps someone (or some organization,
association, or nation) is being unethical. Perhaps he or she is overly-
aggressive, lusting after money, power or sex. You may feel your
highest ideals are offended.

Or, perhaps you have been forced to work closely with someone
you feel is a coward, and you cannot tolerate the "victim mentality."
You may be sickened, revolted or outraged. This experience brings
up a great deal of energy in you. You may become preoccupied, and

spend a great deal of time stewing. This is the experience of the Devil, which, not incidentally, is the archetype of anger.

We often judge situations harshly. From our own vantage point, we know what is "good" and "bad." We know what is "fact" or "truth." Frequently, however, we make assessments based solely upon surface appearances. And we *believe*, often without examination, that which we suppose to be true. Things, however, are not as they seem. We frequently misjudge. Without depth of understanding, we project our own views outward, making assumptions that have no basis in reality. Worse, yet, *that which we are judging negatively is more than likely merely a mirror image of our own weakness.* The cowardice we perceive in others is merely a mirror of our own internal cowardice. We are seeing our own fears projected onto another.

We form our personalities through identifying and incorporating those characteristics which we consider to be attractive, noble or socially useful. Some of us aspire to goodness, gentleness or righteousness. Some aspire to aggressiveness or rugged individualism. Most of us shy away from thievery, killing, and other behaviors which, as a society, we believe are morally offensive or completely intolerable. We don't do these things, because we don't want them done to us, and if we do, we fathom that we will be punished. But since these dark qualities are in us and part of us, we often release them in ritual form. The ritualistic experience of threatening behavior is as close as your television set. Just turn it on at dinner time!

That which we fear, or label as reprehensible, is no more or less than our own shadow.[22] The shadow is the dark, undesirable part of ourselves. This is the part of us that has been repressed, the part which we do not let out. We fear the shadow because when it gets loose, our conscious status quo is thrown into confusion. When it surfaces, we often explain it in terms of the Devil. This menacing Devil whispers words of temptation to sidetrack us from our path of virtue, especially for the purpose of material gain. Interestingly, explaining our temptation in terms of the Devil releases us from responsibility. When we quip, "The Devil made me do it!" we are dividing our very Selves in half.

A confrontation with the Devil—whether internal or external—should alert us to the fact that it is time to change our attitude. It is an indication that our consciousness is false. We are not seeing the

[22]See, for example, John Sanford, *Evil: The Shadow Side of Reality* (New York: Crossroad/Continuum, 1987), pp. 49–56.

whole picture. Our perception or consciousness, however, is not necessarily false by intention. We often misjudge out of ignorance. Further, it is out of ignorance that we persecute our surfacing shadow. We need to *embrace our shadow in order to transcend it.* This is the act of *conscious bondage* which is the first stage of spiritual unfoldment.[23]

To embrace the shadow, and that means to come to terms with our inner Devil, we must transcend this state of ignorance. We must take all sides of a situation into account. Does this mean we should altogether refrain from any form of persecution or condemnation? Of course not. Our instinct tells us that the *wholeness* we seek as individuals and as a society will never be developed without a sense of moral conscience, even moral outrage. Nonetheless, if we are to make the leap in consciousness which will enable us to move on a path of virtue, we must recognize, confront, accept and integrate the Devil. Acknowledging, and coming to terms with, the dark undercurrents of ourselves makes us stronger human beings. When we accept the Devil, or the shadow, we become tolerant. We become accepting. We come to accept others, and—very importantly—we come to accept, and eventually to love, ourselves.

Right along with the Devil, juxtaposed on the twenty-sixth path of the Tree of Life, we are forced to examine our relationship with the "Angel," the divine one or God. In classical cartoons, the Devil sits on one shoulder, the Angel on the other, and from these positions they argue with each other using you as a mediator! This picture is an apt representation of the twenty-sixth path which involves coming to terms with the contradiction we experience between ourselves as matter and our material needs (as represented by the Devil) and ourselves as spirit with spiritual needs (as represented by the Angel). Somehow we must integrate and unify ourselves as both matter and spirit. We must achieve an internal spiritualization of matter and a materialization of spirit. We must integrate the extremes of the Self. To sink into Matter, without developing the correlating depth of spiritual consciousness, is the worst kind of bondage. The inverse also holds true. To be trapped in either extreme without the other is like a living Death.

Undertaking this task of realization involves a great deal of commitment and effort. Committing to change is not easy when one sees

---

[23]For a description of the stages of spiritual unfoldment, see Paul Foster Case, *The Tarot: A Key to the Wisdom of the Ages* (Los Angeles, CA: Builders of the Adytum, 1974).

only from the vantage point of the material. To see any other way often upsets conditions. Values change as perspective changes. It is generally easier to leave things as they are. In fact, the temptation of the twenty-sixth path is to remain ignorant. But, for those who wish to realize the wholeness that results from the divine integration of matter and spirit, a wonderful meditation, which leads to quantum leaps in ways of knowing, is to intentionally contemplate the integration of opposites. Contemplating and transcending contradiction becomes the task of Key XV. Intentional contemplation opens up the powers of *seeing*. It develops The Eye, *Ayin*, the Hebrew name and the secret of Key XV. As the eye is developed, all sides are perceived.

Relevant here is the practice of Zen Buddhism. One aspect of Zen involves the contemplation of paradox through meditating on a *koan*. A koan is a baffling formulation which defies rational thought. Examples of koans include: "In the trees fish play, in the deep sea birds are flying," "What is the sound of one hand clapping?" or "Who is it that hears?" According to Zen Buddhists, the contemplation of a koan can point to ultimate truth. This is because the koan can only be solved through awakening a level of the mind which transcends the discursive intellect.[24] Unravelling the koan involves a sublime balance of science and faith. Only by integrating the two can such a leap in consciousness occur.

On the Tree of Life, path twenty-six, the Devil, connects the spheres of science (Hod) and faith (Tiphareth). In Hod consciousness, we abstract, rely on our logic and think things through thoroughly. In Tiphareth consciousness, we give up and rely on faith. We begin to understand the nature of surrender (see Key XII, the Hanged Man). Regarding Zen Buddhism, Zen master Dr. Thich Thien-An describes the interconnection of faith and science and—although it was not his intention, relates the major message of Key XV. He says that people often state that the person is created by the environment, but in Zen Buddhism it is believed that the individual creates the environment. Therefore, we create ourselves. Whatever the world becomes, then, depends upon the collective mentality of humanity. Thich Thien-An states,

A Zen master once said that water is of one essence, but if it is drunk by a cow it becomes milk, while if it is drunk by

---

[24]See Kapleau's *The Three Pillars of Zen*, pp. 335–336.

a snake it becomes poison. In the same way whether life is blissful or sorrowful depends on our state of mind, not on the world. So we must seek to transform the mind, to bring it into the awakened state, and this requires at the outset great faith, faith in ourselves and in the latent powers of the mind. The second step in Zen Buddhism is great doubt (dai-gi-dan). The method of Zen is very scientific. In science we are told never to believe anything unless its truth has been demonstrated experimentally. Zen takes the same stand. We are not to believe anything blindly; rather we must demonstrate its truth to ourselves.[25]

The challenge of the twenty-sixth path, which is the challenge of Zen Buddhism, is to search our minds and learn to transcend ordinary states of consciousness in order to perceive deeper levels of truth. We are searching our Selves for Buddha- or Christ-consciousness, the consciousness of the sphere of Tiphareth. Achieving Tiphareth-consciousness is the secret to opening The Eye (*Ayin*) of Key XV. When The Eye is open, we will integrate contradiction. We will accept shadow. We will transcend anger. We will know our neighbors as our Selves. We will know our neighbors *are* our Selves. Propelled by the intentional contemplation of opposites, we arrive at a unified field of space and time and ultimately overcome the limitations of dualistic thinking.

If this all sounds too intense or demanding, throw up your hands and laugh. Take it lightly! Through laughter, just as through meditation, you can be renewed! Through laughter you can gain a new perspective and make the conscious leap. Don't be so serious. Laugh your way to integration and health! While he may tempt you to devilish acts, the Devil also plays. The Devil dances and revels on the Earth's craggy peaks! The Devil drinks and eats, makes music, jokes and explores. The Devil adventures. The Devil loves life. Drop those preconceived notions and try laughing with those you disdain. Take them on a river trip, shoot the white water rapids, and I guarantee, you will come to love them. If such a trip is out of the question, try inviting them to tea. You may discover that the coward is a power-

---

[25]Thich Thien-An, *Zen Philosophy, Zen Practice* (Berkeley, CA: Dharma Publishing, 1975), pp. 43–44.

house. The moneygrubber is a saint. I urge you to cast off the bonds of your thinking and you may notice, then, that you were never trapped in the first place! Celebrate! And ultimately, in becoming truly lighthearted, you may not even notice that, through the vehicle of your own earthly laughter, your darkest shadow has been released. The other aspect of *conscious bondage* is to *embrace, with a whole heart, every earthly delight!*

Card Symbology: The Devil looms like a smiling goat-headed entity over the "cube" to which is chained a woman and a man.

The Devil has the head of a goat to represent his Capricornian origins and the fact that he is a scapegoat. In the Christian Bible, the scapegoat was driven off to the desert supposedly carrying the sins of the tribe. The scapegoat signifies that our "sin" has been disowned and depersonalized. The goat's head is an inverted pentagram to signify repression and banishment.

The Devil's right arm is red because he is matter in the act of doing. There is a hole in this hand, however, to symbolize his potential connection or openness to the divine. The left arm and hand are skeletal, to show the temporary or cyclical nature of matter. The left hand holds a sword for the Devil's ability to pare down to truth.

The cube—which represents the divine law—is now halved because the Devil represents half-truth. In order for the woman and man to escape their chains, they must realize the whole truth. The whole truth is that there is nothing holding them. The fifteen links of the Devil fit loosely about their shoulders. They can easily duck out of bondage. Ducking out of bondage, however, entails a leap in consciousness. They must understand that they are free. When they do so, they are free to become the Lovers (see Key VI).

The Devil knows all of this and more. His third eye is wide open. Knowing all of this and more, he smiles ironically. He is not nearly as wicked as he seems. He knows full well what binds the humans. He knows full well how close they are to connecting with each other and discovering that *the key to their salvation is love!*

Key XVI. The Tower

Divinatory Meaning ─────────

A series of insights propels you to new awareness; you have outgrown the old structure—physical or mental—you built; you must destroy this structure (or allow it to crumble) in order to make room for the new structures you need; you may have to sacrifice certain things in order to grow; you may find yourself changing quite a bit; search your heart for answers; we often have to give up before we can gain.

XVI

THE TOWER

Meditation ───────────────────────────────

Purification by Fire
Spiral lightning flash of sudden transformation
moving out of chaos and out of time
when the tongue of Truth brings division
and the securities of the past crumble;
to cling then is to cling to rubble
realities flood in layers and layers
and the Spirit floats inside

Blast to Personal Structures!
Blast to Social Patterns!
Blast to Relationship!
Blast to Patterned Response!
The Tower I built is hit by Lightning!

> The nations sink in the pit
> which they made

    in the net they hid
        their own foot is caught

Chaos reigns
and the collective sigh of the soul
dives into space
driven by the Power of the Force that activates
Fortune's Wheel
Death's Scythe
Hermit's Light
Emperor's Sceptre
The Wand of the Magus
The Wind of the Chariot Driver
and the imperceptible Orbit of the Star

Broken down are the Structures of Ignorance
the Tower of Science which says that we are all
each one of us
Separate.

Esoteric Qualities

Hebrew attribution: Peh (pronounced *pay*), mouth   פ   ף
Astrological attribution: Mars, the activator
Twenty-seventh Path: Mediates between Netzach (the Realm of
      emotion and personality) and Hod (the thinking mind)
    Essence: Transformation through the destruction of outgrown
      forms
    Intelligence: The Activating Intelligence, flashes of insight
    Veil: That which is blasted away is destroyed.
    Mystery: Matter does not die, but continually changes form.
    Disturbing flashes of truth become the source of liberation.

Interpretation

At Key XVI, the Tower, you have had a sudden glimpse or glimpses
of insight. This sudden illumination is the Lightning Flash (see the
Eight of Fire), that brilliant force which descends through you and
excites or activates the truth. The truth rises like a glimmer of light
from the dark and chaotic realm of your subconscious mind.

As the truth arises, flashes of insight nag at you and summon you to change. Having made certain accomplishments and having acquired a certain depth of understanding, you are now being called to a higher challenge. This higher challenge demands that you break out of old structures. It is time to experience things anew.

Had you not opened your Self to truth, you would not be experiencing such flashes of inspiration. You have opened your Self up as a clean, clear, pure and deserving channel and the glorious will of the universe has begun to respond. This means that your higher will is moving with, rather than against, the universal flow. You are now perceiving what you need to do and what changes you need to make. You are well on your way to enlightened vision.

Experiencing truth, however, can be very disturbing. This is because, to know truth, *you must first be based in a position of freedom*. Only as a free individual—a free thinker—can you overcome the false perceptions or consciousness that bind and guide you away from your higher knowledge and calling. Adopting a position of freedom does not come easily. At this time, you can be sure that becoming free will upset the status quo or circumstances of your life. This is because your liberation involves letting go of, or destroying, certain things. As the Tower is the key of rapid and destructive change of form, letting go, for you at this time, means that you may be moving to a higher level through the experience of drastic conditions. You may sacrifice your job or home, go bankrupt or get divorced. You may experience natural or man-made violence, disease or disaster. You may be confronting and coming to terms with Death. Key XVI implies raising consciousness or becoming liberated through facing destruction.

At Key XVI, you will often discover that your consciousness is raised *suddenly*. Relating research results concerning spiritual crises during World War II, Alan Watts once commented:

> When a person is in an absolutely extreme situation, and they accept it, there is a possibility of a natural *satori*. . . . When one gets to an extreme, that is to say, to the point where you realize there is nothing you can do about life, nothing you can not do about life, then you are the mosquito biting the iron bull. . . . You heard a bomb coming at you, you could hear it whistle, and you knew it was right above you and headed straight at you and that you were

finished, and you accepted it. And suddenly there was this strange feeling that everything is absolutely clear. You suddenly see that there isn't a grain of dust in the whole universe that's in the wrong place, that you understand completely, totally, what it's all about. . . . In so many cases, the bomb is a dud and [you] live to tell the tale. . . . It's an extraordinary feeling. Freedom.[26]

Satori is the Japanese term for the experience of enlightenment. *Satori* is the greatest degree of freedom. The mind is opened, the true nature of the Self is revealed and realized and hence, the nature of all existence is awakened.[27] A major key to *satori* is *acceptance*. The people experiencing sudden raised consciousness during war *accept* their position. They accept it and resign themselves to it. It is then that the flash of insight comes. It is then that everything—and their place in it—becomes clear. On the topic of acceptance, Rosicrucian Donna Pryor writes:

Our concerns have multiplied since we have had newspapers and television. We can grieve over "problems" and "injustices" all over the world. Our anger has multiplied as our pace of life has increased and things previously hidden are now exposed. Acceptance is a key to peace and allows us to stay in tune with the cosmic. . . . Acceptance keeps us open and willing to grow. . . . Acceptance implies the *knowledge* that it is alright, it has always been alright, and it will always be alright, because it belongs to the Cosmic.[28]

To become accepting, we must come to a new understanding of our Selves as separate and as non-separate entities. The Tower represents a place to be isolated in order to understand. Isolation has two forms: solitude and imprisonment. Through either form, we can begin to break down the notion that matter and form are the ruling principles of existence. Through the experience of solitude or imprisonment, we can come to understand, accept and transcend our position in matter and form. This is the second stage of spiritual unfoldment. It begins with a series of sudden, fitful inspirations which

---

[26]Alan Watts, aired on KPFA Radio, Berkeley, CA, April, 1989.
[27]See *The Three Pillars of Zen*, p. 343.
[28]Donna Pryor, "Master's Message," *Golden Gate Pronaos*, March, 1989.

lead to the perception that *the structure of knowledge is built on the foundation of the fallacy of personal separateness.*

Confined in solitude, squarely facing ourselves, we may, at first, rant and rave. We might kick the walls or rattle the bars. We might scream for release. But, we cannot escape. We find no answer in our raging emotions (as represented by the sphere of Netzach on the Tree of Life) and no answer in our rational thought (as represented by Hod). The answer is provided by the flash of insight which unexpectedly descends from the heavens and surfaces from the dark realm of the subconscious. In a flash of insight, we begin to understand the ironic twist. We come to know that we made our own prison. Until we understand our own motivation for creating it, we cannot escape our prison. The only route to escape is through the acceptance of who we are and what we have done. When we finally accept ourselves, immobile walls miraculously explode! As if by an act of God, we are suddenly freed! The Lightning Flash is upon us! The Tower falls and we are hurled forward into the unknown.

Falling into an unknown future—and accepting the fact that *it is unknown*—is forever the price of true freedom.

After glimpsing the Lightning Flash of truth, like a bombing victim, we may be able to tell the tale, to some extent, of what we have seen. Key XVI, Peh, means mouth. It represents both the mouth of God and the power of human utterance. Words, of course, are but symbols. They only *reflect* a deeper truth. As Samuel Johnson, author of the 1755 *Dictionary of the English Language* said, words are the daughters of earth . . . [the] things [they represent] are the sons of heaven.[29]

Language, says Charlton Laird, represents the human power to generate and control symbols. Surrounded by a bewildering world, we order what is otherwise inexplicable by reducing it to symbols. The word is a symbol. The human as an organism, art and civilization as social phenomena, and language as a means of thought and growth, are so interdependent that one of them could not have developed without each of the others. Each grew by being interactive. Language helps the individual cultivate his or her own humanity and makes society possible. As humanity and society are cultivated, language—as its symbolic representation—changes and grows.

---

[29]As quoted by Charlton Laird in his introduction to *Webster's New World Dictionary of the American Language*, 1976.

The Tower can be seen as 1) our own physical body, 2) our own personality, 3) the structures we erect as an individual, and 4) the structures or institutions we create as a society. The Tower represents, in a sense, both the individual and collective "language" we use to describe our world. Our individual and collective symbolic system, as we repeat it over and over, acts to hold certain realities in place.

The Lightning Flash represents new perception, new description, new words, new symbols. Through new symbology, we transcend our imprisonment and also our isolation. The *activating* or *exciting intelligence* of Key XVI, the Tower, shakes us into awareness through bringing us face to face with destruction. We must embrace such destruction to move into freedom. Resistance gets us nowhere. In allowing ourselves to fall toward an unknown future, we begin to understand the meaning of Self-realization and ultimately, the bliss of *satori*.

Card Symbology: The card shows a man and a woman flying from a towering structure which has been blasted by a bolt of lightning. This represents the Lightning Flash, also called the Descent of Power, through the Tree of Life. The lightning bolt connects the whole Tree so that all aspects of the Tree can be known at once. This represents the most powerful of perceptions. The trail of the Lightning Flash goes from Kether to Chokmah to Binah, to Chesed, to Geburah, to Tiphareth, to Netzach, to Hod, to Yesod and finally to Malkuth. See figure 11 on page 350.

This Tower represents the destruction of matter by Fire. It represents the destruction of physicality. The more resistant or clinging the man and woman are, the more difficult is their transition.

The Tower also symbolizes the seven stages of enlightenment as outlined in the *Chymical Marriage of Christian Rosenkreutz*, published in 1690. In the marriage, the man and woman, referred to as the King and Queen, give up their mundane existence and become magically transformed to enter into a higher marriage of the spirit and ultimate resurrection. The stages of this marriage are wonderfully described by Gareth Knight.[30] The marriage of the King and Queen symbolizes the regeneration and higher synthesis of Netzach (the sphere of emotion) and Hod (the thinking mind) through the *sacrifice of personality*.

---

[30]See *A Practical Guide to Qabalistic Symbolism*, p. 64.

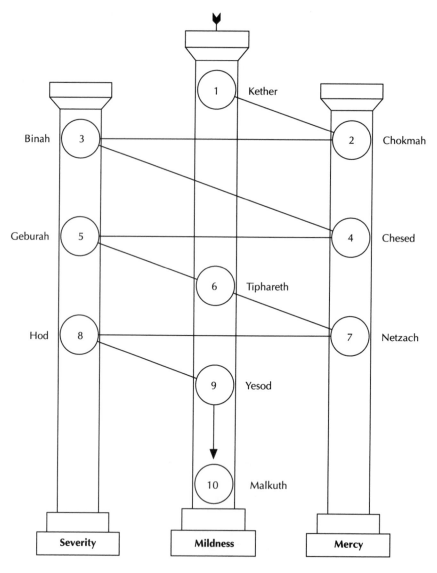

Figure 11. The Lightning Path.

Key XVII. The Star

Divinatory Meaning ────────

Follow your own star; to find your star, meditate upon your own nature; at the center of your true self, a great secret will be revealed; the great secret is the key to your creative powers; knowledge of this great secret will answer your question; for inspiration, take a walk under the night sky and contemplate your own existence.

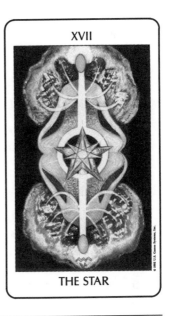

XVII

THE STAR

Meditation ──────────────────────────────────

Conception at the edges of the night
The fish-hook snags pieces from the ledge
probing the deep beyond where we
can see and reach

The Star is a fish-hook in the lapis of contemplation
on that outer plane
where the brain waves flatten
and the ba-boom, ba-boom
of the racing heart moves to quiet-ness
balanced gently between life as it seems and the ocean of dreams
(which is the deepest reality)
swimming with inspiration

emotional abundance
shall overcome the
sorrow of your Vision

O Night Sky
visions dance eternally

springing between the dark and windy waves of Night
and the weary shore of Self
consciousness

Come all the treasure
—velvet, diamonds—
of Night's windsome sky
springs a message from Her depths
springs a lovenote from Her thighs:

> Thy Star doth riseth, Dear One,
> Dances Magic in Thine Eyes!

Esoteric Qualities

Hebrew attribution: Tzaddi (pronounced *tzahdi*), fish-hook צ   ץ
Astrological attribution: Aquarius, the visionary
Twenty-eighth Path: Mediates between Netzach (the sphere of emotions and personality) and Yesod (the Subconscious Mind)
Essence: Meditation, the method by which the Great Secret is attained
Intelligence: Natural Intelligence, turning within to understand
Veil: Meditation is withdrawal from responsibility.
Mystery: Through meditation, the Creator recognizes its own existence. Through meditation, you develop the power to exercise the divine power from which all creation emerged.

Interpretation

Your true quest is now beginning! Through self-reflection, you can now *see the truth.* You can understand your own nature and your niche in the universe. This knowledge allows you to transform your mode of self-expression. In knowing yourself, you are enabled to trust yourself, and thereby modify and moderate your actions according to the dictates of your conscience. At this time, there is no more need to try to explain yourself or to act out of self-defense as you have in the past. You may retreat calmly. You may repose in silence.

You have made all of your progress by looking inward. In quietude, you have reflected. In silence, you have contemplated. You have stilled the agitating effect of exterior noise and you have quelled distraction. You have heard the deepest messages of your own heart.

It is as if when all the singing stopped, you could finally hear your own song.

Hearing your own song is the key to healing. The Star, Key XVII, is the Key of Health. Through meditation, you learn what you must do to preserve your health: mental, physical and spiritual. You learn what you must do to preserve the health of the Mother Earth. You are made of the same stuff as Earth. You require—and must create—a spiritual, emotional, mental and physical environment free from pollution in the broadest sense.

The Star is *natural intelligence*. This is the intelligence of the universal mind which can be found in the great ocean of your dark subconscious. You have cast out your fishing line—through introspection—and drawn out answers. In the great sea you have encountered the unending flow of primal information. *This* is what is important. Such knowledge as you discover in your heart of hearts cannot be found outside the Self. It comes from within. This time you have not been taught, you have taught yourself. Your knowledge will stay with you. You have discovered the deepest way to learn. Your *natural intelligence* directs you toward a peaceful co-existence with all things of nature.

You have learned this by experiencing difficulties throughout this life and through past lives. The path has not been easy. Again and again you have witnessed the wreckage of what you assumed to be the highest truth. You have witnessed the wreckage of your own life. You have seen the very foundations of your existence blown apart again and again. But through all this, nothing you really needed was ever lost or abandoned. Through every experience, you grew. You changed. You became whole. Sometimes, when you faltered, you thought you were regressing, but you were only moving to a more challenging plane. You needed to learn further methods of coming to terms. Nonetheless, it sometimes seemed as if it took a war to make you realize that there was only one answer all along. That answer, as you know, is love. When you feel, think and act from the deepest love, all is well. Internal conflict fades. Every living thing is exalted. Knowing, now, the great secret, you are fit to rule. As Lao Tsu said: He who values the World as his own body can be entrusted with the Empire.[31] And yet, knowing the secret, you have no need to rule.

---

[31]See *Tao Te Ching*, p. 24.

Having arrived at Key XVII, you are shining. Your prospects are bright. Your Star is rising. You have found the beginning of the way of truth. You are on the path toward light. This is the third stage of spiritual unfoldment. You have come to terms with your Self. You have come to understand that all that is material will die. All form must be outgrown and cast off. *Eternal life and light reside on the inner plane.* You have learned this by turning the eye of your soul *from the contemplation of appearance to the vision of reality.* You have learned that you can—and *must—follow you own Star.*

Through ceaseless meditation upon your own nature, you can retain the careful balance between the sphere of Netzach on the Tree of Life, which is the personality you have developed, and Yesod, the sphere of the subconscious, which is also the sphere of universal mind. At the Star, you recognize that you are of the ephemeral physical plane, but you are also of the heavens, the plane of eternal light. There is no contradiction. *Through this knowledge, all things that exist upon earth are brought to perfection.*

You are now experiencing cosmic inspiration which has descended to the material plane. You are experiencing the most wonderful insight, but this does not mean you should become unduly excitable. Remain balanced in the central flow between Earth and Heaven. Move in moderation. You can move quietly and softly because you are renewed in faith, hope and charity. Having attained, through mystical consciousness, the mystical secret that as it is below, so it is above—as it appears on the outside, so it is on the inside— you can *move steadily in the way of love with a calm and peaceful agility.*

Card Symbology: The two figures of the Star, mirroring one another, show that as it is above, so it is below. This also shows that the unhindered mind reflects the truth *perfectly.*

In the center of the card is a circle containing two stars. This circle is the sphere of Tiphareth, or Christ-consciousness, on the Tree of Life. It has been said that the star it contains is the Star of Sirius. The figure on the upper portion of the card represents the Plane of the Supernals, the creative force, all that is not manifest, while the lower figure represents all that has been brought into manifestation, *Creation.*

Each figure has seven lights, like seven candles, emanating from the spiritual heart. These are like the seven branches of the menorah. The three on the left represent the created world. The three on the right represent the creating world. The middle branch represents the creative function of the Self and humanity as a collective entity.

The five-pointed Star represents humanity's *power* to create. It stands for vision, creativity, formation, and manifestation out of the realm of nothingness. The seven-pointed Star represents the intersection of the spiritual path (as represented by the number three) with the physical path (as represented by the number four).

The figures of the Star appear to float on a black background. This blackness represents the abyss, the dark realm of the subconscious mind and the great unknown. This is the radiant darkness from which the light of the Star has emanated.

Key XVIII. The Moon

Divinatory Meaning ————————

You cannot see the future clearly, but you must stay on your chosen path; trust your intuition; at your darkest hour, you will find that you hold your own light; use your own light to overcome your fears; shedding light on your fears will propel you toward self-understanding, strength and self-confidence; through this process, you will heal and move forward into happiness.

XVIII

THE MOON

Meditation ————————————————————————

The Moon is the gateway
to all that which is fantastical, phantasmic,
horrid and horribly seductive
the appeal of the Mysteries and Dreams
glinting streams of vision bespeaking that which lies beyond the
River Styx

that Great Abyss
of which we seldom speak
leading straight from the back of the head
    to the four Darkest
    Nights of the Soul
every trial of sorcery, secrecy, oppression and shameful deeds,
all that which we suppress and long to conceal
    seeds within which plague us in dreams of
    humans congealing into forms enacting feats
    of treachery, treason, torment and deceit
    every moment is a test of strength
our greatest fears rise up—even as we sleep—like the desperate
    Wolves of Yesteryear and
    Nature's Extremes
    galloping too close on glimmering trails of light
    stalking too close in the night
    while we lie vulnerable
    and defenseless
    our corporeal selves in that state of trance
    which allows no movement

Pick up that stick!
Pick up that Stick and Defend yourself!
    —for this is the final and most difficult test
    of the endurance of Spirit
    and Spirit we have
    and Spirit we are—
Pick up that Stick and show the inconquerable courage
that is the Spirit!
    —for this time the passage will not be blocked
    it is the channel to the Pure Light
    the glimmer you saw
    in the front of your mind
    floating in darkness
    and that is the irony
    for no Spirit ever rose that was not felled
    and Heaven never kissed the Soul of She-Who-Knew-Not-Hell

Pick up that Stick!
and Fling yourself through demons
    'cross the narrow threshold

twixt Night and Morrow
through planes of consciousness
to where Light lies in wait
and Dark is bound by Day

(The alternative is crossing by
the Whitelight Bridge of Knowledge
and the knowing is of thyself, Dear One,
The Moon, but a reflection—
See the Mirror!)

Esoteric Qualities

Hebrew attribution: Qoph (pronounced *kofe*), back of the head ק
Astrological attribution: Pisces, intuitive understanding
Twenty-ninth Path: Mediates between Netzach (the sphere of feeling
  and personality) and Malkuth (the sphere of body or physical
  manifestation)
Essence: The Way of Daily Life
Intelligence: Corporeal Intelligence, forms all bodies formed in all
  worlds
Veil: You cannot see in the dark.
Mystery: The Moon is the Veil of Mystery, the Radiant Darkness
  behind the first sphere of the Tree of Life. It is the *back of a head*—
  the Godhead—which is not a head. It is the Great Regenerator
  and the Sum of All Perfections. The light never was at the end
  of the river. It always was, and forever shall be, directly at hand.
  Nonetheless, we must move through shadows to grasp the light.

Interpretation

Shadows rear like monsters with horrifying heads. These are the
monsters of living, the monsters of weakness, war, ugliness, poverty,
sickness, pain and death. These are the unexpected trials and tribu-
lations that block the flow of the river of life. These are the monsters
of the Moon.

At Key XVIII you have known these Monsters. You have suffered
along the path of this life. More than once, with great surges of will
and conviction, you have drawn your sword defiantly against such
creatures. You knew that, however devastating the crisis, you had to

go on. You were moving, always moving, toward the light—the reward—which was just up ahead. It was as if you could almost taste the glory and victory of success.

You sometimes felt that the river to freedom flowed with blood. Your body tired with hardship in life and love. And how did you see freedom? Was it not liberation from bondage? And was not that bondage *life itself*? And yet, you did not want to leave this life. As much as you sought escape from the monsters of living, you desired connection with all living things. You craved song and dance and revelry upon the Earth's bountiful mounds and plains.

Through the ordeals, you thought, why *me?* When you were at your lowest points, revelations surfaced. Ideas rose. When you thought you could go on no longer, another ordeal occurred, and you went on. You just continued, persevered, and new thoughts came. New ways appeared. You have spent time intuiting and dreaming. You have experienced great psychic upwelling. Now, in Key XVIII, the Moon, your intuition reigns supreme. You have kept the mystical aspects of your Self in bondage. At the Moon, these aspects are liberated.

At some point in the Key of the Moon, we begin to look upstream—back to where we have been—and realize that where we came from is right and good, where we are going is right and good, that there is nothing new under the Sun, that all is as it should be, *all is as it must be.* We seem to realize that while this river appears to be moving, while it is forever changing and forever new, it is ever the same. It seems to go nowhere. There is a certain sameness in the river of life, a certain constancy, a certain endurance. It is the same in victory, the same in defeat. It is the same river. And to those who have eyes to see, in this river of life, *wherever one may plant one's foot becomes holy ground.*[32]

How do we come to this realization? We arrive at this point through consciously experiencing, and bonding to, the rearing monsters. Each ordeal then becomes a ritual of passage, allowing us to move to the next level. The Moon is the final initiation of the dark. It is the last symbolic death. It is followed by divine resurrection. You are in the last of a series of trials.

Each trial is designed to make you forget your past views, your past values, the way you were conditioned to believe. At the Moon,

---

[32]See Paul Foster Case's *The Book of Tokens*, p. 170.

you release your memory. You let go of the conditioned reactions of the past. You learn to walk on the earth in a new way. You hear your new name spoken. You are at the Key of Mystical Initiation. In mystical initiation, you die and reawaken. You feel your Self cease and desist and you reassemble your Self in the light of new consciousness. You let go of your memory, but, for the first time, you truly RE-MEMBER. You arrive at a new consciousness of *Memory.*

At the portal of new consciousness, you stand at the gateway to beauty, the gateway to light and higher consciousness, the gateway to unconditional love. The Moon is the great portal on the river of life. Like the last stage of winter, or the dark hour before dawn, the passage of the Moon leads into the pristine brilliance of a new dawning.

What separates the morning of this new day from other days? It is your own recognition of the independent journey of your soul. It is the recognition that every monster that set foot on your path was a test of your perseverance and tenacity. It was a test of your physical capacity, determination and capability. Your own animal wildness, that which you tried to suppress, has aided and abetted you in your struggle to survive. This you now recognize. You have accepted every shadow. You have tamed wild beasts. You have learned that your own inner light rises and carries you through the monstrous times. All this you know through your own willingness to know. You have come a distance—a distance of which you are acutely aware—and you have arrived at a magical crossing.

Key XVIII is the path that connects the sphere of the emotions and psychic upwelling with the sphere of the physical body. This is the path of *corporeal intelligence* on the Tree of Life. It is the time when all that you have learned (the great secret of the Star, Key XVII) moves through the passage to physical manifestation. This is the fourth stage of spiritual unfoldment. At this stage, the knowledge gained through the deep spiritual understanding of the meaning of the trials you have faced becomes incorporated into your body. It is as if your physical body is *dismembered* and *reassembled*. It is rebuilt in accordance with the plan of your new subconscious pattern.

Then, as a result of physiological changes, your latent powers unfold freely. You recognize, through your own willingness to know, that your body—which has been the burdensome bag of bones you have dragged through the ordeals of incarnation—is your *vehicle for adeptship.* In your divine initiation, your body becomes a light body.

In this initiation, you surrender the burdens of the past. You accept
the divine emanation of light from a higher evolutionary manifestation. The eternal light extends into your divine self. It is as if you
reach upward, accepting and knowing. The hands of divinity reach
down and enfold you. Within you, the seeds of wisdom are magically
implanted. You can never be as you were before. There is no turning
back. The rite of passage is complete. You have become the source
of light. In knowing this, *your savage wildness is perfected. Your shadowy
monsters transmute into luminous beings. You begin to move in the beauty
way, which is the way of light.*

On the deepest levels, life has appeared as a dark river. Your
strength has been tested. The path of the Moon is your *final release
from bondage, dismembering your dark and heavy body in exchange for the
eternal lightness of being.* So mote it be.

Card Symbology: On the card of the Moon, two distinct spheres
appear, one in the upper right section of the card, one in the lower
left. The upper is the sphere of Netzach, the sphere of feeling and
personality on the Tree of Life. From this upper sphere, we can see
light emanating like a rainbow. The lower is the sphere of Malkuth,
the sphere of physical manifestation and the four elements. Inside
this sphere is a landscape with a rising body of light on the horizon.
Out of this landscape crawls a crustacean, the symbol of new life.
There is a winding path, barely visible, that connects the two spheres.
The crustacean will move in darkness until it turns in the direction
of the light.

On either side of the lower sphere, two wolves are positioned.
One is a dark body. One is a light body. These are the two sides of
Self: the shadow and the spirit. The sphere of Malkuth—the sphere
of the physical body—is balanced between.

The face of the Moon is the face of Binah, the Univeral Mother,
the creatress of all form. In serenity, she waits through the gestational
period. She represents the radiant darkness behind the light. She is
Ain Soph Aur behind the first emanation of the Tree of Life. On the
back of her head is a chignon of intricate knowledge: the knowledge
of all that is, ever has been and ever shall be. Her knowledge is
painless. There were no trials in obtaining it. It merely exists. This
knowledge always has been.

Fifteen red *yods* (Hebrew letters) fall in the midst of the card. The
yods represent the hand (see Key IX: the Hermit), *the ability to manifest.*

This is the hand of humanity as well as the hand of divinity. The *yods* are blood red for physical manifestation. They seem to fall like *mana* from heaven.

Key XIX. The Sun

Divinatory Meaning ————————————

You are in a process of spiritual realization; this is the truest love possible; a divine marriage—which is physical, mental or spiritual—is coming; everything now makes sense; everything is as good as it could possibly be; all things are illuminated and show themselves truly, revealed by the great light of the Sun; your own "garden" is as lovely as could be.

Meditation ————————————————————————

Creation Synthesis Collection Assemblage
The Sun
brings insight from the world of darkness, unconscious chasm,
into harmonious strains of Light that resonate
like the sweetest sounds, the most poignant poetry of Universal
Unification:
Conscious and Subconscious brought into synch
and the Higher Consciousness flits about like butterflies of soul
landing on the head and face and dancing upon the face of the
Earth

This, then, is the Face of God. Whose face is that?

Awareness, fulfillment
Love Wisdom Spiritual Transformation

The radiating Light of
Lifeforce come to Earth
clothed in flesh
the naked child wakes and sleeps
and wakes again: Reborn!
dancing with friends upon the Earth's crest
invoking the gods on high
while the Universe reaches down her cradling fingers like
Light Streamers through clouds after rain

There is no more pain
the pain has ceased for all this Aeon
it remains but a relic to change to art, music and prose
it remains love at the core
the Rose unfolding
blooming heart on the Central Pillar of Eternity,
balanced and temperate,
growing toward Light, aspiring toward the Flame of Life
held only by the grounding pull
of the human condition—
rooted in Earth

and the soil is rich
the Earth is full
it is heavenly to be stretched by the grounding pull.

Esoteric Qualities ───────────────────────────────────

Hebrew attribution: Resh (pronounced *raysh*), face ר
Astrological attribution: The Sun, the vital essence of life
Thirtieth Path: Mediates between Hod (the thinking mind) and Yesod
    (the subconscious)
Essence: The lifeforce behind every "face" is the face of God
Intelligence: Collective Divine Consciousness, the inner light
    of the world perfected
Veil: The face of the self is the Self.
Mystery: We are sparks of the infinite. We are light. Submerged in
    eternal light, every particle of being is permeated. All things,
    within, and without, are expressions of Divinity. The Sun is the
    single point of perfect realization.

Interpretation

At Key XIX, the Sun, you are in spiritual realization. You have been through a deep darkness. Your shadow has accosted you from every side. But this darkness, you now understand, is only a temporary absence of light during the movement through the great birth canal. The womb is comfortable. But one outgrows it! Still, the movement outward can be terrifying. The world heaves. It is dark and the new postures are strange. The squeeze is uncomfortable. Sounds change quality, becoming more distinct; too loud, too close, too soon. On the unknown path, you can only associate your fears with darkness. In fearing the dark, you fear the unknown. You fear aloneness. You fear the solitariness of your path. You fear your own withdrawal. You fear your own hermitage. These fears spiral upon themselves and worsen. The greatest fear of all is the fear of the unknown.

But now you find you *know*. You see the light! You emerge in light! Now you see that you have been moving through a divine channel. This divine channel has conducted you toward realization! You now emerge in beauty! In realization, you are reborn in light! Every aspect of your Self, both light and dark, is integrated. You put your fears in perspective. Every aspect of your Self is integrated into the divine light of the cosmos. The divine light of the cosmos is integrated in your being. The divine light of the cosmos is eternal! The divine light is forever and always. The darkness is temporary. The movements of the body are transitory. Through reaching this knowledge, you are reborn. This is spiritual rebirth!

You are reborn through attaining a singleness of mind. Through attaining a singleness of mind, you have seen the face of God and you will never again be limited. Jesus said: "The light of the body is the eye: if therefore thine eye be single, thy whole body shall be full of light" (Matthew 6:22).

Jesus spoke of the third eye of the East, the Star of the soul, that eye that sees God and thereby integrates all things, balances all things, and moves into a state of divine realization. This is the eye that integrates good and evil, that moves beyond dualities and knows the goodness behind all things. This eye sees that the fruit of all "sin," which humanity calls "punishment," perfects the skill of the initiate, just as the archer gains skill by aiming again and again at the target. This target, of course, is the target of perfection, the target of spiritual realization.

This third eye is the eye of understanding. It is the eye of unconditional love. It is the eye of limitless sympathy and compassion. It is the eye of gnosis, the eye of the direct experience of God. It is the eye of the unconditional marriage of the inner spark with the eternal flame. Paramahansa Yogananda said: "When my two eyes that behold both good and evil become single, and behold in everything only the divine goodness of God, I shall see that my body, mind, and soul have become filled with His omnipresent light."[33]

At Key XIX, the Sun, you are truly transforming your way of life. You have concentrated your efforts on the eightfold path. That is to say, you have persevered at right understanding, right resolution, right speech, right action, right way of living, right efforts, right thoughts and right meditations. This effort has paid off. For yourself, you have verified the existence of the ultimate reality or *God*. To you, God has spoken. Now, you come to see how you are interrelated with others and related to God, just as the Sun's rays are related to each other and to the Sun. This very ideal, says Swami Akhilananda, is the basis of happiness in our everyday life.[34]

Paramahansa Yogananda says, "Your soul, being a reflection of the ever joyous Spirit, is, in essence, happiness itself. If you keep the eyes of your concentration closed, you cannot see the sun of happiness burning within your bosom; but no matter how tightly you close the eyes of your attention, the fact nevertheless remains that the happiness rays are ever trying to pierce the closed doors of your mind. Open the windows of calmness and you will find a sudden burst of the bright sun of joy within your very Self."[35]

To find happiness, retain *faith*. The name of true divinity is *faith*, not hope. *Knowledge*, not hope; *trust*, not hope; *love*, not hope. The gift of divine presence is faith. Faith dispels all doubt. Faith dispels all lack. Faith is attunement to bounty and beauty and the truest and deepest freedom. In the deep consciousness of *knowingness*, and that is the deep consciousness of *knowing God*, the gift of faith is delivered. You have faith when you have *seen* the eternal.

Faith has the power to oppose or neutralize any negative mental attitudes. For example, faith dispels fear. Fear is, in fact, the negative

---

[33]See Paramhansa Yogananda's *Metaphysical Meditations*, p. 41.
[34]See Swami Akhilananda's *Spiritual Practices*, p. 120.
[35]See Paramahansa Yogananda's *Metaphysical Meditations*, pp. 67–8.

use of faith. It is faith misplaced, the belief in two powers instead of one, a belief that there is a power that can bring us to evil. To correct all evil, we must have positive faith. Ernest Holmes, the founder of the Religious Science movement, says our faith must be "rightly placed, a faith that lays hold of the integrity of the Universe, the beneficence of God and the Unity of all life."[36] In order to *have* Faith, he says, we must have the conviction that all is well. In order to *keep* faith, we must allow nothing to enter our thought which will weaken this conviction.

Jesus said: "If ye have faith as a grain of mustard-seed, ye shall say unto this mountain, Remove hence to yonder place; and it shall remove; and nothing shall be impossible unto you" (Matthew 17:20). This is the challenge of Key XIX: to have faith; to retain a quiet knowledge and to know that—through faith—you can transform the world.

You can only arrive at such a deep sense of faith through belief, acceptance and trust. Belief, acceptance and trust is strongest when you have direct knowledge of that in which you believe. To truly believe, you must actually see. And you *have* seen! You have attuned to the *collective divine intelligence*. Through your meditations, you have come to truly understand. That is the impetus behind your spiritual rebirth. You have attained the intelligence of the realization of the Christ or the *Son of God*. As Yogananda iterates, God is the absolute, existing beyond vibratory creation. Appearing in the Son, God exists *within* vibratory creation. This is Christ-consciousness, which is the reflection of the uncreated infinite. This is what you have seen.

You have glimpsed Christ-consciousness and the knowledge gained has given you faith. You have glimpsed the inner light through the vehicle of your subconscious mind. That light has come to you from the universal flame. You have abstracted the meaning of this light with your reason and you have internalized the meaning. That is why the Sun represents the thirtieth path on the Tree of Life: the Key which integrates the subconscious (Yesod, the foundation) with the abstract mind (Hod, splendor). With this knowledge integrated into your daily life, you transform your life. You are now *radiating!* *This is the realization of a new personality. This is a new realization of personality.*

---

[36]Ernest Holmes, *The Science of Mind* (New York: G. P. Putnam's Sons, 1938), p. 156.

Human speech is the manifestation of this union. As your personality evolves through lifetimes, your central Self is represented by that part of you which makes words and other symbols. The word-maker is responsible for speaking the truth. Have faith in your knowledge and *speak the truth*. This is the fifth stage of spiritual unfoldment: *Through conscious self-identification with the One Life, you are liberated from the limitations of physical matter and circumstances.* You are now beginning the free and liberated journey homeward.

The first step on the journey homeward entails taking the vows of the divine marriage. This is the conscious marriage with the One Life. The altar is set with the most beautiful flowers. It is bathed in a divine and golden light. You are fully conscious as you take your vows. You are fully aware. You are fully clear. You are clean, clear, pure and deserving.

You shall marry and bear a child. The product of your marriage shall be *the birth of a new humanity*. You are the divine partner. Your wedding ring is the golden circle of eternity.

Card Symbology: Beneath the Sun, a divine marriage is taking place. A man and a woman meet before an altar of lilies. They represent the marriage of all duality: good and evil, light and dark, hot and cold, dry and moist and so on. They represent the return to God-consciousness. That is why they are naked. We clothe ourselves for the descent to the physical plane. We leave our clothing—which can be seen as our physical bodies—behind as we return. The overall feeling of the marriage is joy and relaxation. There is a quiet knowingness within the bridal chamber.

The marriage is overseen by the Archangel Gabriel, the herald of good news. Gabriel means "God is my strength" (Hebrew).

The marriage is exalted and takes place atop the Middle Pillar of the Tree of Life. This is the pillar of equilibrium, the pillar of mildness. It is also the pillar of the mystical consciousness. When one *knows* the One Life through mystical consciousness, there is no need to attach to pain, sorrow, worry, tension or other negative human emotions. Joy reigns at the center.

The symbol for the Sun is the alchemical symbol for gold. Over time, gold is the most durable and precious of all metals. The divine marriage is eternal. The symbol of this union is the endless circle of gold.

Key XX. Resurrection

Divinatory Meaning ————————————

Your personal perceptions and consciousness shall dissolve to be replaced by the deepest understanding possible; you are in the final stage of knowledge as you have known it; you are about to be resurrected into new thinking, into a completely new stage; it is as if you are entering a new aeon or cycle in the grand scheme of your life; let this happen naturally and beautifully; do not fear change, you have earned the right to ascend; you have earned your rewards, you deserve every good thing that is happening to you.

RESURRECTION

Meditation ————————————————————————

Seeing All, the Totality
Moving to a new Aeon on all five planes:
the Actions, the Feelings, the Mind, the Flesh
and that fifth dimension which transcends the rest:
    the Lifeforce
    the Spirit of Spirits
    in which Ten Thousand Things rejoice
    to which Ten Thousand Things return

This is Resurrection

Judgments were wrought
self and culture weighed, subtracted, divided and multiplied,
leaving one with that reverent feeling of having done it all,
having seen it all,
having known it all,
having said it all,
having lived it all,
having done the process,

and having learned only that one knows less
than one knew at the start

One hovers in the New Aeon, free of form,
in proximity to the Divine
the last vestiges of Worldly Life—being that of
self-knowledge and personal consciousness—
about to be cast aside
to make room for complete ascent

Soon, the Breeching Dolphins of New Life
will stay upon the surface
for the move is fast,
the gestation complete
the limitations of Form torn asunder

The false personality
its speculation and separation
is ripped to shreds by the fang of the Serpent of Transformation
and
in no Time at all
the Breeching Dolphins of New Life
dance forever on the surface.

Esoteric Qualities ───────────────────────────────

Hebrew attribution: Shin (pronounced *sheen*), tooth or fang ש
Astrological attribution: Fire, eternal flame of lifeforce
Thirty-first Path: Mediates between Hod (the thinking mind) and
Malkuth (the material world or the physical body)
Essence: Resurrection in God-Consciousness, the circle of the eternal
flame
Intelligence: Perpetual Intelligence, the flame of the one life is eternal
Veil: The "Last Judgment" is the Final Word. A devouring flame
consumes the unrighteous.
Mystery: Freedom from judgment accompanies the liberation of per-
sonal consciousness. Cessation in one form is transition to another. Resurrection is the return journey home for all three layers
of consciousness: the subconscious (the dark), the waking consciousness, and the higher consciousness (the Light). The su-

preme realization is that there is no death, only evolution of form, and return to the great fire from whence all things emanate.

Interpretation

Spiritual rebirth is the recognition of the One Life, the unity of all things. This primal lifeforce has been called God. Spiritual resurrection is the path of return to perfect union. It is the return to God. It is the complete transcendence of dualism, the quintessential transcendence of all matter, the final release of and from the bondage of matter. This is divine convergence with the One Life. This is resurrection.

Resurrection has been referred to as the path of return. You are now on the path of return. At Key XX, you are on this path *consciously*.

The path of return is your personal release. It releases you from the constraints of false personality, that personality conditioned by the transitory situations of physical life. It releases you from all limitation and from every boundary. On the path of return, you are enabled to let go of your daily concerns and your attachment to matter in order to transcend to the world of light which is eternal. This world of light vibrates with the power of lifeforce. This is the world of the unformed. It is the world of the One Life wherein all moves in a field of bliss. This is the world of pure energy, wherein energy moves like a subtilized fiery electrical force.

This is the world of pure bliss, the white light world of transcendence. You have glimpsed it through the catalysts of holy sounds and mantras, sacred movements, the blissful experience of deep love, rituals of devotion and worship, and the physical act of love. But now, you are moving fully into this blissful world. In transcending, you merge fully and completely with this world, experiencing a full recognition of every nuance. In this world, you become light bathed in light. In this world, all souls rise and expand, merge into one another, and become one soul. This is the world of oneness, complete and total symbiosis, complete and total awareness within a sphere of unawareness. This is universal consciousness.

This world of light descends to you even as you have ascended to meet it. You have been opening to it and working toward it for some time. And now you perceive it directly. You perceive it as a flame or light. This light is the flame of transformation. This is not the devouring flame or "fang" of death. *All that dies is your false personality.* In knowing this, you move into the sixth stage of spiritual unfoldment.

This flame of transformation is not the fire of hell. It is the powerful flame of transition. It is the circle of eternal light from which all things proceed. This flame is the *perpetual intelligence* of the universe. It is often experienced as white and burning. That is what you now see.

In order to ascend, you must internalize light and become light. To become light, you suspend the dense, weighty and dark effects of extreme or intense emotional reaction. How those reactions weighted down your heart! Because you have now been initiated, you can experience this wondrous light as pure joy!

To the uninitiated, the experience of the One Life may be frightening. It may feel like Death. The uninitiated may experience the universal flame as the fire of hell. But, perception is truly related to the state of the perceiver's own heart and consciousness. How do you feel about your Self? Have you done the best you could? Have you given as much as you could? Has your thinking been positive and supportive? Have you devoted yourself to work and humanity? Have you learned through "punishment" and moved ever-closer to the target of perfection? Did you recognize that you were trying to move toward that target? Has your heart become a light heart? Is your heart as light as a feather? Are you *loving?*

As you learn to truly love, you suspend clever reasoning. You let go of judgment. You have learned that on the path of return, there is no need to judge. External judgment no longer has meaning. All that remains is but a brief stand at Self-review. The question is: *Am I living in grace?*

Jesus said: "Judge not, that ye be not judged. For with what judgment ye judge, ye shall be judged: and with what measure ye mete, it shall be measured for you again" (Matthew 7:1–2). Have you been in need of such a warning?

Jesus' counsel is echoed in Sufi teachings. Have you heard the Sufi story of the Saint and the Sinner? Idries Shah tells this tale in *Wisdom of the Idiots:* He says that once upon a time there lived a dervish devotee who felt he should monitor the behavior of others for "godliness." One day he discovered a man who was gambling excessively and took it upon himself to help curb the man's behavior. He stayed outside the man's house and each time the man left to gamble, the dervish placed a stone upon a pile. The growing pile of stones was a "visible reminder of evil." For twenty years, this continued. Every time the gambler saw the devotee he said to himself, "How that saintly man works for my redemption!" It came to pass that both men died at the same time as a result of a natural catastrophe. An angel came to take the soul of the gambler to paradise. The gambler said:

> "How can that be? I am a sinner, and must go to hell. Surely you are looking for the devotee, who sat opposite my house, who has tried to reform me for two decades?"
>
> "The devotee?" said the angel, "No, he is being taken to the lower regions, since he has to be roasted on a spit."
>
> "What justice is this?" shouted the gambler, forgetting his situation, "you must have got the instruction reversed!"
>
> "Not so," said the angel, "as I shall explain to you. It is thuswise: the devotee has been indulging himself for twenty years with feelings of superiority and merit. Now it is his turn to redress the balance. He really put those stones on that pile for himself, not for you."
>
> "And what about my reward, what have I earned?" asked the gambler.
>
> "You are to be rewarded because, every time you passed the dervish, you thought first of goodness and secondly of the dervish. It is goodness, not man, which is rewarding you for your fidelity."[37]

We learn much from this parable and yet, as we suspend every judgment, as we refine our attunement to the supreme universal consciousness, we know that, just as the gambler is saved, the dervish must also be saved. This is because, on the plane of resurrection, dervish and sinner arise together and merge into the one life. Dervish and sinner become one.

In the same way, *you* are both dervish and sinner. We are ever the One Life.

Through recognition that we are the One Life, *our false personalities and sense of separateness suddenly cease.* In the last analysis, saint and

---

[37]Idries Shah, *Wisdom of the Idiots* (New York: E. P. Dutton & Co., 1971), p. 91.

sinner are one. Dervish and gambler are one. As we merge with universal consciousness, we know that there is neither saint nor sinner. There is no hell. There is only eternity and conscious immortality. In universal consciousness, we return to the source of all. Every delusion of separateness forever disappears.

Through redemption and resurrection, our old ways are destructed, as if by fire. We are awakened by the white light of universal consciousness from the three fires of the ephemeral world: greed, anger, and recklessness.

The Thirty-first Path connects the sphere of Hod (the thinking mind) on the Tree of Life with the sphere of Malkuth (the physical body). Through divine consciousness, the plane of the eternal descends to meet the physical. The plane of the physical ascends to meet the eternal. *Perpetual intelligence* is thereby realized.

Through this realization, you move beyond the mere identification of the existence of the One Life. You undergo a complete merger. In so doing, you move into a new aeon. This is a new arena of consciousness. Your body becomes a light body. You know the light. You now know and understand the meaning of the holy spirit. You bear witness to the coming of the holy spirit.

From the path of resurrection, you will never return to who or what you were before. Your life is forever changed. You are eternal. You are resurrected in light. Now, you can begin to remake your universe in the image of light. You are the Creator. Your every thought radiates outward in the brilliance of divine light.

Card Symbology: The angel Gabriel calls from on high. His trumpet sends out the call! He is calling for the rising of the soul.

Through their deep love for each other, the Lovers merge and their souls arise together. They become one rising up as the collective soul. This signifies the end of duality. This is the end of polarization.

The collective soul of the Lovers rises up from the darkness (dense vibrations) of the physical plane to the spiritual or eternal plane (light vibrations) through several vibrational levels as represented by the rainbow colors appearing on the card. Moving through the rainbow colors is the path of return.

The red cross on the back of the golden spirit, who represents the unified Lovers, indicates that the final healing is occurring. The abyss has been bridged. Awakened consciousness is at hand. The cross of equal arms indicates that *salvation from death and eternal life have occurred.* At the center of this cross is the point which is the fifth dimension: the here and now. Here and now, salvation is at hand.

In total surrender and total bliss, the spirit rises to the white plane of universal consciousness. The spirit rises in balance and harmony to the plane of consciousness with God.

Key XXI. *The Universe*

Divinatory Meaning ───────────────

XXI

THE UNIVERSE

Your whole world is in balance; you move like a dancer with every movement perfectly timed; every undertaking has paid off; your endeavors have been successful; you are at the end of a long "journey"; the world is at your feet; celebrate the great work you have done!; if you want to journey further, the time is right.

Meditation ──────────────────────────────────────

O Great One of the Night of Time
Sun, Strength, Sight, Light
Completion, Celebration, Cosmic Union
The Cross of Equal Arms
born
in the Place of Holiness
CenterPoint in the Dance of Life:

The Universe, one verse, one turn
One Song
hailed on Earth as it is in Heaven
One Will

done on Earth as it is in Heaven
One Life
lived on Earth as it is in Heaven

Esoteric Qualities

Hebrew attribution: Tav (pronounced *tahv*), mark or the cross ת
Astrological attribution: Saturn, Earth, everything is here now
Thirty-second Path: Mediates between Yesod (the subconscious)
 and Malkuth (the body, the physical plane)
Essence: End and beginning are one
Intelligence: Administrative intelligence, the one who would rule
 Nature must first obey Her laws
Veil: Eternal salvation will be rewarded in Heaven.
Mystery: As Above, So Below. You are the beginning and the end.
 You are the window which looks inward to the source and
 outward to the goal. The treasure you seek so diligently is
 the Jewel of eternity buried deep in your own heart.

Interpretation

At Key XXI, the Universe, *you close the circle by discovering that you are
the source of your own love.* All of your transgressions are forgiven. You
have atoned for your "sins." You have "burned off your karma." You
are liberated! You have risen from bondage. The whole of the Universe
is at your feet. The whole of the Universe is at your command.

Your every movement is now in balance. You have learned the
great lessons of spirit: how to harness and control your energies and
actions, how to focus your intention, how to discipline yourself and
how to persevere.

You have learned the great lessons of emotion: how to harness
and control your desires, reactions and moods, and how to indulge
and consume without hurting yourself. You have learned how to fill
your own emptiness.

You have learned the great lessons of thought: how to harness
and control the direction of your thinking, how to discriminate among
teachers and methods of instruction, how to direct your attention,
how to align yourself with the higher wisdom of the inner Self, and
how to master that which you set out to accomplish.

You have learned the great lessons of body: how to bring your
material life into accordance with your spiritual truth.

You know your strengths and you have learned how to handle your fears and weaknesses. You are self-reliant. You have the perfect measure of self-esteem and confidence and you balance this well with your esteem for, and confidence in, others.

You are centered. As the Wheel of Fortune rises and falls, you wisely hold center. This is the middle way. It is the way you have internalized.

You know all these things because you have trained yourself in understanding the laws of Nature. You understand the divine law of cause and effect just as you understand the energy of the One Life behind that divine law. You have studied wisely and you have learned that when you work within Nature's Laws, She will obey your every command. This is the *administrative intelligence*: one who would harness Nature must first obey Her laws.

Because you are freed through new insight, the reality of your daily life is once again in flux. Reality is forever compromised at beginnings and endings. Beginnings and endings, which are one and the same, constitute a window period. Through this window, you see past, present and future with new clarity. You understand the dynamics of the present by examining the dynamics of the past. You know what the future holds by observing the dynamics of the present. You have learned that you can change dynamics at will to achieve the effects you want. This is the divine law of cause and effect in action.

Through this magical window, you can see your steps laid out before and behind. In reviewing these steps, it appears as if you have been traversing the Earth incessantly. But where have you actually gone? It appears now that you have traveled forever, but you have gone nowhere! And yet, it is not as if you have not reached your goal. On the contrary! You have climbed the mountain diligently and revelled at the peak! You have met your goal, but, *even at the very moment of victory*, you are aware that *the goal is not what you expected*. You feel, in some ways, just like you did at the beginning. Some things have changed. Others have not.

In pondering the question of where you have gone, you will ultimately realize that the real goal is, was, and always will be, to arrive back at the beginning. The goal is to arrive at the source. The source, then, *is the goal*. And, conversely the goal is the source. And, *this*, however confounded it seems, is the *great revelation* of Key XXI, the Universe.

This great revelation is like a riddle. What does it mean? What *is* the point of all this work? What have you learned? Why work so hard to end up at the beginning?

What is the beginning? Did you not begin to re-member WHO YOU ARE? Did you not learn that *the illumination you sought without was within you all along? Did you not see that you ARE the illumination you sought without?* The point never was the distance from whence you came in the world of matter, nor to where you fathomed you were going in that world, but the discovery of WHO YOU ARE. *The purpose of the journey is the discovery of the inner self.* You have explored and discovered by traveling through the dark depths of your sub-conscious mind, and therein you have glimpsed the light of the inner self. Your physical body has been the *vehicle of your discovery.* It will now—in light of your new knowledge—be the vehicle you use to *TRANS-FORM your world.*

Such a great lesson must not be merely observed and set aside. You must integrate your new knowledge into the reality of everyday life. But, in what direction should you form your world?

On your path, you have realized extraordinary powers, but while you can see much, and there is much you know, there are also things you don't know. You are encompassed by the ocean of light, the One Life, but you cannot perceive the whole of the sea. Just as you are the Magus, you are also the Fool. You bumble and stumble and fall in holes. Then, how can you decide? Upon what criteria should any judgment be taken?

To answer this question, you must consult an oracle. To this end, you shall find the most powerful oracle in the universe at the inner shrine in the deep temple of the self. Attaining to this oracle is the seventh stage of spiritual unfoldment. Attaining to this oracle is attaining to the eternal inner eye. Attaining to this oracle is attaining to the eternal inner ear. Through the infinite inner eye, you see the eternal dance. Through the infinite inner ear, you attune to the eternal song.

When you attain to this oracle, you will understand the true meaning of the phrase *"As Above, So Below."* That is your key to alignment. That is your key to action. "As Above, So Below" means "As Within, So Without." "As it is in my heart of hearts, so it is in my life of lives." "As I feel, so shall I act." "As it is in the one heart, so it is in the One Life." From this reasoning, all else is derived.

The Christian Bible says: "Hear also the words of our Lord Jesus, how he saith: Thou shalt love the Lord thy God with all thy heart, and with all thy soul, and with all thy mind. This is the first and great commandment. And the second is like unto it: Thou shalt love thy neighbor as thyself. On these two commandments hang all the law and the prophets" (Matthew 22: 37–39).

Every law of Nature hangs upon these two commandments. That is because, contained in these commandments, is the key to understanding every nuance of Nature's cycles, and whoso works within Nature's cycles, commands Her movements. The key to knowing Nature is to know love. Love is the key that unlocks every door of Nature. Love is the key to all change. Love is the key to all movement. But, how is it that love commands Nature? What has love to do with Nature? You will find the answer at the inner shrine.

To love all creatures as you love yourself, to love every fish and snake, every hawk and sparrow, every rock and stone, to love every giraffe, every clod of dirt and blade of grass, every wild spring and deep winter, this is the commandment of the inner oracle. Upon this commandment, all else rests. The commandment is love.

Climb any mountain. Love, you find, is the point of departure. Love is the point of return. This is universal law. There is no other.

Meditate upon the following quotation:

> He that seems unjust, let him be unjust still: and he which is filthy, let him be filthy still: and he that is righteous, let him be righteous still: and he that is holy, let him be holy still. And behold, come quickly; and my reward is with me, to give every man according as his work shall be. I am Alpha and Omega, the beginning and the end, the first and the last. Blessed are they that do his commandments that they may have right to the *tree of life*, and may enter in through the gates into the city. (Revelations 22: 11–14)

What commandment must we "do?" We must "do" the commandment of love. Love completes the circle. Love is the balance. Love is the movement. Love is the center. Love is the perimeter. Love is the goal and the source. Love is grace. You can travel and travel, but at the apex of the mountain, if you find not love in your heart of hearts, you find nothing. Love is the goal and the goal is the source. This is fulfillment.

You, Dear One, are the most powerful Magus. You hold the tools of transformation. Transform thy universe in accordance with thy inner thoughts. Transform thy world in the image of love. That is the answer. That is the direction. Love is the goal. Love is the source. Love is the way.

Accept this gift delivered through Paramahansa Yogananda:

Peace flows through my heart, and blows through me as a
    zephyr.
Peace fills me like a fragrance.
Peace runs through me like rays.
Peace stabs the heart of noise and worries.
Peace burns through my disquietude.
Peace, like a globe of fire, expands and fills my
    omnipresence.
Peace, like an ocean, rolls on in all space.
The perfume of peace flows over the gardens of blossoms.
The wine of peace runs perpetually through the wine press
    of all hearts.
Peace is the breath of stones, stars and sages.
Peace is the ambrosial wine of Spirit flowing from the cask
    of silence,
Which I quaff with my countless mouths of atoms.[38]

As you find your love, Dear One, you find your peace. May peace
be with you! May peace arise through the magical dance in your inner
eye! May peace arise through the magical song in your inner ear! May
peace resound through the still silence at your inner shrine! May peace
surround the apex of your mountain! May peace come to you in the
dawning of love's magic!

*Trans-form thy world in love, Dear One. You are love incarnate. The
world dances in your hand!*

Card Symbology: Upon the card we see an ellipse encircling a
woman who stands within three worlds. The ellipse is the sacred
uroborus, in this case, a serpent splitting into two segments and
devouring its own tail. This demonstrates the perpetual change and
continuity of the Universe. The uroborus also demonstrates that
movement always connects back to its source, thus there is sameness
in all change.

The woman is Nature Herself. Her legs are crossed in the 4
pattern, as are the legs of the Emperor and the Hanged Man. This
indicates perfect balance in the material world.

Her palms are opened in the center by a Sun and a Moon. This
means that She is informed by the forces of light and dark (see Keys

---

[38]See *Metaphysical Meditations*, p. 52.

XIX and XVIII). She sees and hears through Her hands. Through Her hands, the work of the lord is done. She understands the necessity of the divine Balance between the two forces.

About Her is wrapped a blue shawl of healing. This shawl is in the shape of a *kaph*, the grasping hand of the Universe. This means that She wields the powers of the four directions. The power of the South is the power of the suit of Fire. The power of the West is the power of the suit of Water. The power of the East is the power of the suit of Wind. The power of the North is the power of the suit of Earth. All that She knows is integrated at the center of Her being.

She is everything that is changing and everything that is the same, for She is Nature Herself.

She stands before three worlds. These are the ultimately intertwined worlds of the three layers of consciousness: the waking consciousness, the subconsciousness (the dark), and the superconsciousness (the light). The right interaction of these three worlds produces the mystical consciousness. This is the key to understanding the mysteries. This is the key to making the circular connection which will take you to the goal and the source. This is the key that informs you that *goal and source are ONE.*

The Mystery Card

Divinatory Meaning ——————

Birth, death and karmic transitions; incredible power, magic and wonder; use your imagination and your thoughts shall become form; spiral inward; build bridges; create possibility; erect new worlds stone by stone; empty out to know fullness.

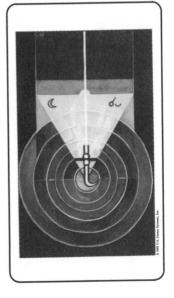

Meditation ————————————————————————————

The River of Life moves strangely.
It is always moving.
Yet it never goes anywhere.
Where does it come from?
Where does it go?
It moves like an infinite snake
across the infinite landscape
of Time and Space.
I fling out my net,
and yet, I catch nothing.
The River dissolves in a Sea
where neither Time nor Space exist.
I See then, that,
through all the shifting change,
I remain at Heart, my Self,
the Full Emptiness of the One Life,
where You, Dear One, and I,
are Forever Entwined in Infinite Love.

❖ ❖ ❖

Appendices

❖   ❖   ❖

Appendix I
Divinatory Meanings
for the Tarot Deck

The Minor Arcana

Fire

One of Fire—Force: You feel a sense of transformative high energy; inner blocks are falling away freeing you to move into newness; you have the will to change and you feel the great energy of new beginnings; you have a newly discovered source of power; you are excited, you feel exhilarated; if there is an undercurrent of depression, it is only because the future remains unknown at this time; if you feel like you are burning up with no channel or outlet for your emotions, do not worry, the way will very soon become clarified, you will soon find someone or something to connect with.

Two of Fire—Convergence: Unfocused energy becomes clear and polarized; you feel you now have a strong direction; you are making changes spiritually, emotionally, intellectually and physically; while you may go through various struggles, your courage in starting an enterprise at this time will eventually pay off; maintain your own internal sense of balance as you begin your new activities.

Three of Fire—Birth of Light: Stay on the path; keep on with your present activities; everything is coming into fruition; it is as if a mi-

miraculous birth is at hand; to resist this great birth would bring pain; realize you are in a state of grace and stay with this feeling; giving birth to the "children" of body or mind is not always easy, but it is a highly rewarding process; in this case, your "child" is a product of love.

Four of Fire—Flame of Spirit: A phase of development is complete; based on your revelations and good intentions of the past, you built a strong structure, but in some ways, you no longer feel connected to that structure; know that old structures must frequently be abandoned to make way for new growth; you are growing, beginning a new phase in your life; it is as if your own personal wheel of fortune is turning again; this is necessary in order for you to grow; search your heart for the right course of action.

Five of Fire—The Struggle: You feel a sense of conflict; the struggle which seems to be happening outside of yourself may, in reality, be happening on the inside; you feel as if you are striving, but you are immobilized at the same time, a sense of chaos has resulted from the presence of conflicting ideas; allow yourself to "fail," allow yourself to "lose" and you may find that you are actually winning; in losing all, you will gain everything; in this case, you are merely relinquishing that which is obsolete.

Six of Fire—Glory: The struggle has been difficult; it is as if you have fought a battle and now all you have left is the bloody fruit which you have won; make an offering of this fruit, surrender your winnings, to move into a state of harmony and beauty; you must understand that glory, however much you covet it, is a brief and fleeting thing; the truth is that which endures deep inside of yourself over time.

Seven of Fire—Courage: Conditions intensify; take further risks with greater awareness; you may feel trapped by social expectations—all that you were taught as you were growing up—but now the reality of the past no longer works for you; if you trust in your own internal convictions, you will develop strengths and a sense of self-confidence which will work for you and will, in good time, come to be respected by others; if you have the courage of your convictions, all that traps you will fall away.

Eight of Fire—The Lightning Path: This is a high energy period for initiating change; you have a sense of fast movement, rapid growth;

you are achieving a broader base of human and spiritual knowledge and potential; energy is coming to you, but it is as if you have to reach up to meet it; stretch yourself and you will grow; the perception of love creates the most powerful of all energies, remember this in your period of development.

Nine of Fire—Eye of Fire: You have arrived at a peak experience; you have reached the right wavelength, the right current; you are attuned to the right frequency; you are seeing things accurately and—if you work within the concrete realm of your everyday life—your clear sight will lead to solid creations which will endure over time; as things change, do not let yourself get thrown off balance; stay focused on the details of living.

Ten of Fire—The Cage: Your spirit feels trapped or oppressed; your heart seems caged; you have had a peak experience, but you are having difficulty applying the results to daily life; the key is to let go of extraneous matter; free yourself of all unnecessary encumbrances; tune into your emotions to realize what should stay in your life and what should go; attuning to your emotions may necessitate an attitudinal change on your part.

Fire Father: You are experiencing the sense of conviction; there is much movement, energy is surging; you feel the power of leadership; you are rapidly moving toward a new way of knowing: a new viewpoint or perspective on matters; regulate your activity; be careful not to burn yourself out in this high energy period.

Fire Mother: Long after the energy of others has burned out, your own energy burns like a constant pilot light; you have the sense of being a sought out leader especially in matters of the spirit; you seek quiet, but consistent, leadership; as long as you move in accordance with Nature's Laws, Nature obeys your every command.

Fire Brother: Your inner spirit aspires; you are like a flame reaching heavenward; you perceive great qualities of strength, swiftness, brilliance and agility, the sense of romantic revolution: qualities which are real and wondrous; be careful, however, do not be too impulsive at this time of great revelation and change; attune to the eternal nature of things and your actions will endure.

Fire Sister: Accept all change and movement with a balanced perspective: equanimity; you feel enthusiasm, self-confidence, eloquence; you are moving within the natural flow of the universe and you are favored by all universal forces; when you feel in danger of fragmentation, turn within for the answers: meditate on the sun setting in the ocean—imagine this picture in your mind—and you will be soothed and regain touch with those things that are of real and lasting importance to you.

Water

One of Water—The Open Channel: You are experiencing a burst of feeling, sentiment, empathy, sympathy, enthusiasm; the time is right for connecting; stay very open and the way to connect will become clear; the only way to receive is to open yourself up; becoming vulnerable is sometimes the only way to the discovery of true love.

Two of Water—Sacred Cord: All opposites joyfully merge: male and female, light and dark, dry and wet, hard and soft; you have a great sense of connection; you feel a sense of bliss; you were waiting to make a connection and now you have received just as you have been received; enjoy!

Three of Water—Stream of Love: You are in a sublime state of harmonious pleasure; you are in a grace period; you feel a sense of wondrous creation; you feel very loved by all that is, you love all that is; this is a beautiful time to be alive.

Four of Water—The Flood: You are outgrowing a period of contentment; things that were once good now seem stale; things once new have grown old; change is the only thing that remains stable; do not be afraid to change to regain your balance.

Five of Water—Spilling: Painfully, you feel that relationships are transient and impermanent; do not rely so much on others for love; when it seems like the "cups" of your life have spilled—and all your love has emptied out—you will discover that you still have a major reservoir: your own source of internal love, do not forget that! Look inside yourself and you will see that of five cups, only three have spilled, two are still standing and spewing light everywhere!

Six of Water—Faith: Having learned that the answer to your question lies within, surrender to faith; be innocent, remain innocent; take great pleasure in your childlike qualities; experience the world as if you are seeing it for the first time; you are taken care of in all ways.

Seven of Water—Insight: The empty space of the soul must be filled; you are moving into deeper spiritual realms; you may feel highly intuitive; perhaps you do not want to know everything you are seeing; if you feel depressed or generally uneasy with the state of things, remember that this reaction is natural and normal; be careful not to overindulge in alcohol, drugs, food, tobacco or any other substances, these will never satisfy your emptiness; the times you feel the worst are often when the greatest spiritual insights come; let yourself experience this time and do not judge yourself harshly; you are a good and loving individual.

Eight of Water—Still Waters: You are in a state of withdrawal; retreat is necessary and good at this time; through withdrawing, all things shall become clear; you will be protected as you withdraw, you will not lose anything important; take a break and remember, "still waters run deep."

Nine of Water—Rainbow Mirror: You feel a strong sense of internal integrity and inner security; you are enjoying a strong sense of self-esteem; you are peaceful with your sense of inner joy; you have accepted yourself and that has given you a new sense of wisdom and harmony.

Ten of Water—Fountain of Love: When you are motivated by love, the highest wisdom unfolds; you feel that you are showered by a fountain of love; all has turned out well; enjoy this time: it is a time of rarefied joy, spiritual love, exquisite beauty and deep sharing with others.

Water Father: Listen to your conscience; trust in your impulses; be guided by your instincts and intuition; you are in a gentle and sensitive period, it is like falling in love all over again; wonderful things may come of your endeavors; have faith and maintain your self-confidence.

Water Mother: This is a stable and nurturing time; there is a feeling of maternal love and support; pace your steps and wrestle joyously with difficulty; this is a passage in love; your associates, particularly children, may not always show it or even be aware of it, but they love you deeply; you are always there for them in their time of need—even if they come to you in anger—because you see life and love in long strides; your love is full with its own spiritual source; your love is unconditional.

Water Brother: Love is the basis for your new creative surge; love gives wings to your spirit; your heart is wide open and filling with love; you feel romantic; let your creativity be translated into art, poetry, writing; give a friend a rose.

Water Sister: Trust your feelings and impressions; you are on the right path; you are strongly connected to earth, water and sky and the passage of all seasons; maintain your strong connection and stay attuned to the earth by meditating frequently; you are blessed with the ability to know intuitively that which others do not have access to.

Wind

One of Wind—Dawn: The dark clouds of your mind are scattered as if blown away by a strong wind at daybreak; an important new idea is taking hold in your mind; it is as if a light is turning on in your life; pay attention to new thought; this is an exciting time; as you think about your new ideas, you will not be able to follow every nuance to its logical completion point in the future, but there will be time for that later; attend to the present and accept the great potential of your new ideas!

Two of Wind—The Crossing: You are in a temporary balance which may feel like a state of detente; there is a sense of release from captivity; maintain balance gently and peace can continue; it is time to use all of your wisdom and understanding to assess the situation you now face.

Three of Wind—Recognition: Give up to gain; surrender in order to achieve; recognize that all that is good has the potential for evil; all that is evil has the potential for good; you have seen so much and you sometimes wish you hadn't; you have told yourself that ignorance is bliss, but you know that something is missing in that proverb; all that you know will eventually help you to build you own character or personality in a positive image; ask yourself if your motivation is pure, then you will know whether you are on the right track.

Four of Wind—Mastery: You are in a holding pattern; having now mastered a difficult task, you are resting on your laurels and enjoying rewards in your environment; only you know that disturbing influences are beginning to emerge within you; there is a tendency to cling to successes because of ego; be careful: clinging to the desires of ego can be a deadly enemy; the things that gratify the ego do not necessarily gratify the soul.

Five of Wind—Fear: You fear a painful, frightening or unknown situation; the major thing you have to fear, however, is fear itself; you have trapped yourself with your own negative energies from the past; operate with ethical tactics and bad situations will be resolved; attune to your own conscience; ask forgiveness; build bridges, not walls.

Six of Wind—Clarity: Everything is suddenly clear; you have a keen ability to analyze; you have the right perspective; you feel a beautiful sense of reverence; enjoy this time but be careful not to get caught up in fanatically embracing your new truth; that is a current danger that could lead to much trouble.

Seven of Wind—Many Tongues: There is a sense of futility; it is as if you are hearing or speaking several languages at once and there is no sense to be made of anything; you cannot express yourself in the way that you want to; this is because old systems—things that you once believed in—are now outmoded; let go of the old ways, it is time to change; do not fear change or movement; fear of change can lead you to danger.

Eight of Wind—Power Shield: Indecision leads to a sense of imprisonment; energy is wasted; there are external obstacles; you feel disillusioned; go into retreat; do not fear solitude; you will find that empowerment comes through surrendering yourself to the higher way of love; if you surrender yourself to love, you will become clear, you will become internally empowered.

Nine of Wind—The Screen: You are threatened; you may appear to others as threatening; you fear cruelty, judgment and pain; you feel a sense of anger; there is a tendency to go into seclusion, but this is not the time for withdrawal; you must enter the world and atone; embrace love and you will discover freedom.

Ten of Wind—The Way of the Cross: Death comes to the old way of thinking; a new perspective arises; you have learned to think in the ways of Nature and your thoughts are clear; you are transcending old patterns of thought which have kept you caged in a reality which no longer serves you; you feel as if your spirit is rising on the winds of change.

Wind Father: An analytical period; thought is very powerful; the power of the intellect is bounded by neither time nor space; your ideas are brilliant and highly rational, but as you move through intense mental processes, do not lose touch with yourself as a spiritual, loving and physical being.

Wind Mother: An intellectual process is completed; there is a sense of resolution and commitment, triumph, clarification, objectivity and rationality; a time of thinking globally rather than locally; at this time emotional balance is the key to success; embrace your loving nature and you will have many followers.

Wind Brother: You may feel torn between two ideals or ideas which seem to be of equal weight or value; go deep within to find the answer—meditate—you will not ease this conflict through continual analysis; if you find your head spinning with too many ideas, find a teacher to help you focus.

Wind Sister: The truth has risen to the surface; you may feel that you are engaged in battle; you may feel that you are fighting against traditional notions or values; this is not an easy time but your ideas are correct; stick to your convictions and you will eventually know victory.

Earth ─────────────────────────────────

One of Earth—Form: You are receiving the gift of productivity; something new is happening to you physically or materially; you are engaged in promising new endeavors; you are beginning to move toward a state of true external success and internal harmony; in order to arrive at a state of wealth, you must pay constant attention to the state of your spirit, heart and mind as you work through your daily routines.

Two of Earth—Cause and Effect: You are trying to work out the details of your life in order to bring everything into balance; you are in the process of discovering, first-hand, that every action entails a reaction; your life is in a process of continual re-creation based on the information or parameters you allow it to have; a big change is in the offing at this time.

Three of Earth—Works: The work you have chosen is the right work; this is a time of inventing, creating or engineering; the skills you are using are the right skills; all things material are moving into alignment to work with you; expect material success; you will continue to succeed as long as you do not lose your sense of heart or spirit.

Four of Earth—Power: Power is unfolding within you; you may feel as if you are closing off the outside world, but recognize this as a strength, not a weakness; you have the power to shut the door when necessary, you also have the power to open it; if you think the key to opening the door is lost, look within your own heart to find it; you have high qualities of generosity; do not become a victim of avarice on the part of yourself or anyone else.

Five of Earth—The Nadir: You are experiencing a sense of worry; you have helped to produce a reality in which your own deep truths are denied; you experience a sense of alienation; you feel alone and on the outside; this is a time for introspection, a good time to recount your successes and examine the progress you have made; it is time to rearrange your life in such a way that your heart and spirit are rewarded; this is the essence of healing and making things right.

Six of Earth—Beauty: You are experiencing the joy of giving; you are healing yourself and your environment through realizing that the pursuit of beauty—which many call "The Beauty Way"—is the secret to all lasting success; you are not alone in your beliefs; speak your truth and you will find yourself in the midst of a likeminded community; great fortune becomes yours as you speak and act in the way of your own deepest convictions.

Seven of Earth—The Garden: You are creating your own sense of what you consider to be success and failure; you hold the tools of your own transformation; admit to yourself that you do know what you want and go ahead and attain it; "failure" does not mean regression, it means that there is a better, more rewarding path for you to take; the Earth can be a delightful garden, you are responsible for making and keeping the Earth beautiful; make your choices according to the deepest directives of your heart.

Eight of Earth—The Mountain: Perseverance, commitment and discipline are the real keys to success; talent is important, but not the most important factor; you are learning, practicing, growing and blossoming; this is a good time to be an eager student; it is as if you are climbing a great mountain in your life; the way may seem steep or rocky, but you will get there if you walk one step at a time, thoughtfully and cheerfully placing one foot in front of the other; the important thing is not necessarily the view from the top, but how you feel during each step on the path.

Nine of Earth—The Zenith: You feel a sense of accomplishment, reward, happiness, balance, joy, splendor, unity, love, radiance, beauty and light!; you are succeeding in your life; things are going well; you are succeeding because you have learned that the importance of the ego pales next to that of the soul; you have learned that attaining wealth and prosperity involves the state of the spirit, the heart and the mind, not just how much money you have in the bank.

Ten of Earth—The Great Work: You are experiencing a sense of order, design, tension, balance and harmony; everything in your life is moving with a wonderful rhythm; you now realize a new kind of wealth which is spiritual, emotional, intellectual and physical in nature: this is the true meaning of wealth, all other kinds of wealth are transitory; you have learned so much, now is the time to put what you know into words or other art forms in order to communicate it to others; you have long been a student, but you are a great teacher as well; following the spiritual path is the greatest of all your works.

Earth Father: There is a sense of joyous practicality reflected in the circumstances of daily life; you are experiencing a sense of "wealth" spiritually, emotionally, intellectually and physically; through self-knowledge, potential is mastered; vast "fields" have been tilled and prosperity has been the result; this is the right mode of working and living; persist in this way and you will continue to prosper.

Earth Mother: You are experiencing a high level of compassion; the creative forces of your life must be quietly nurtured; cultivated "fields" will eventually bloom; love every stick, stone, plant and animal and you will experience great bounty; be diligent in attuning to every detail of the work required as you tend your "garden"; it is time to rejoice in your own life and to help create a joyous life for others.

Earth Brother: Accomplishment comes through thoughtful meditation; you must carefully adapt to your environment; through first meditating on what type of "soil" you are working with, you will be able to plant the "right" kind of "seeds"; work with the resources at hand and you will be successful; there is no point in working against nature; you are experiencing personal equilibrium and productivity, realize this and there will be no need to struggle.

Earth Sister: This is the brink of transformation; something new is coming; a "birth" is about to occur; be advised that the diamond, the world's hardest and most brilliant gem, is born of the deepest folds of the Earth's darkness; your own light comes in your darkest hour; you are moving steadily, with a sense of stability; you have mastered your sense of who you are spiritually, emotionally, intellectually, and physically; you are "pregnant" with the secret of the future; congratulations, dear one, as a result of your own diligent preparation, you have made yourself the perfect receptacle and the "seed" of creativity has been planted within you.

The Major Arcana

Key O—The Fool: All is movement, all change; this is a precarious time, take a risk; have faith; trust that you will be cradled; every fall moves you closer to your own target of perfection; you are in the cradle of perfect love; use this opportunity to create; concentrate on the present; when walking, place one foot in front of the other; no matter how high the mountain, the peak is reached one step at a time; you are in the first mode of empowerment: *detachment from outcome*; undertake the present enterprise because you must, but detach yourself from outcomes; the process is critically important at this time, do not concern yourself with the ultimate product.

Key I—The Magus: Know, will, dare and keep silent; you possess and wield the tools of magical change; you are a visionary, but it is not necessary to express this to others; trust the lessons of your own experience and insight; you embody force and power—you hold every key to create change, you have all the resources you need— but only if you operate through *focused action*, the second mode of empowerment; be ready to create your world in the image of your choosing.

Key II—The High Priestess: All knowledge of dark and light forces is good; every experience contains a message for growth; listen and you will hear the message of your own inner teacher guiding you in this mysterious time; attune to faith; you are accessing hidden or secret knowledge; be aware of all signals in your environment; attune to impulses; remember, retaining *memory* is the third mode of empowerment; the gift of insight is now at hand.

Key III—The Empress: You are opening to all sensuality, revel in the delights of the senses; a great beauty is revealed; all is perfection; all is receptive; the things of Earth are voluptuously welcoming at this time; you are moving with the flow; Earth is your dominion, all things of nature respond perfectly to you; you find comfort among birds, beasts and fellow and sister travelers; there is no need to control; the key at this time is to remember that *imagination is everything*.

Key IV—The Emperor: Build a firm base of clear knowledge; do not become too rigid; remain open and lucid; to retain control, know and serve a higher force; build your world in beauty and light; do not forget that the Emperor remains Emperor because he has a global sense of things that others do not necessarily possess, yet he will be overthrown if he does not serve his constituents; to remain in power, use your insight and serve those around you.

Key V—The Hierophant: Connect with your higher self; listen for messages surfacing within; become both student and teacher; seek both student and teacher; make all moves in the light of your own truth and sense of justice; let your conscience be your guide; the most important thing at this time is to attune yourself spiritually; to find the answers, seek out your god or goddess; you will find that your inner guides are waiting to serve you; quiet yourself internally and you will be able to hear the answers.

Key VI—The Lovers: You recognize that you are lonely, at the same time you realize that without separation, there can be no connection nor demonstration of love; you are attracted to that with which you wish to merge; be advised that in truth self-love (which can be translated as self-confidence, self-esteem, self-respect and a deep understanding of the "inner marriage") is the key to lasting relationships; true marriage consists of knowing you are simultaneously united and separated; accept this equation for happiness.

Key VII—The Chariot: Negative past influences may be affecting the present without due cause; it is time to clear out, see clearly, begin with new energy, take responsibility for your present condition; it is time to move beyond the past; seek deep meanings within yourself; standards of action must emerge from within yourself in order to guarantee lasting results; act on the basis of your own deep internal messages; an important message is coming to you; pay attention to internal nudges.

Key VIII—Strength: The truth comes from within yourself, it is your own deep inner light which, in good conscience, you ought to follow if you wish to discover happiness; this truth uncoils within you like a great serpent, acknowledge its movement, do not try to repress its stirrings; be strong and courageous for you will find that truth is bliss; seek bliss to find bliss; even though you cannot see the future right now, if you do what your heart of hearts says is right, you will come to happiness.

Key IX—The Hermit: In your own heart, you carry the light and love you have often sought outside of yourself; each one of us holds the power to fulfill ourselves; you must always return to yourself; accept yourself and celebrate; you are beautiful, you are worthy, you are a wholly unique and wonderful individual; you are completely independent and yet you will always remain indivisibly connected to the great stream of humanity; you may feel alone, but you are not; alone does not necessarily mean lonely; raise up your inner light and place it on a hilltop where everyone can see it; as a guide, you can aid the seekers who come your way; remember, a lamp is not made to hide under a bowl.

Key X—The Wheel of Fortune: Your fate is changing, rising or falling; stay balanced through these changes; you are responsible for your own state; whatever you are seeking without is a manifestation of your desire to understand your own inner spirit; the ultimate goal is to stay balanced in heart, mind, spirit and body through all the upward and downward movements of life; in times of sadness, retain your equilibrium, in times of joy, retain your equilibrium also.

Key XI—Karma: Do not deny the consequences of your actions; own the results of your thoughts, words and deeds, for even thought constitutes action in the energy cycles of the universe; adjust your actions and embrace love; remember these words: "Be not deceived,

God is not mocked, for whatsoever a man soweth, that shall he also reap."

Key XII—The Hanged Man: It is time to retreat, withdraw and surrender to quietude; when the internal waters are stilled, you can see and hear your deep eternal self which is your own truth; through meditative contemplation, you will arrive at truth; your glorious nature is revealed when the clear waters of your mind cease to be disturbed by rippling thoughts; this is a time of voluntary withdrawal, reenter the world only when you know you have received answers; do not be pushed or agitated by the whims of others.

Key XIII—Death: You are involved in a major transformation; this is one of the greatest transformations you have known; you must go through this change alone; you will be reborn into newness, but first you must face your darkest fears; do not forget, the darkest hour is just before the dawn.

Key XIV—Temperance: The trials and temptations you currently experience will lead you toward integration, the "middle way," the path of moderation; through acting in moderation, your fears are conquered and your purity shines forth; you are in a period of growth, of "stretching" yourself spiritually; through allowing inner growth, you will arrive at a period of profound realization.

Key XV—The Devil: The closer you get to your own truth, the more you perceive contradiction; the key to understanding is to see things from a new perspective; accept the presence of paradox in your life and you will realize your own truth; celebrate life, laugh, play, dance upon the Earth; enjoy the material, but do not become a slave to it; bondage results from too much concentration on material success; stay attuned to matters of the heart and spirit.

Key XVI—The Tower: A series of insights propels you to new awareness; you have outgrown the old structure—physical or mental—you built; you must destroy this structure (or allow it to crumble) in order to make room for the new structures you need; you may have to sacrifice certain things in order to grow; you may find yourself changing quite a bit; search your heart for answers; we often have to give up before we can gain.

Key XVII—The Star: Follow you own star; to find your star, meditate upon your own nature; at the center of your true self, a great secret will be revealed; the great secret is the key to your creative powers; knowledge of this great secret will answer your question; for inspiration, take a walk under the night sky and contemplate your own existence.

Key XVIII—The Moon: You cannot see the future clearly, but you must stay on your chosen path; trust your intuition; at your darkest hour, you will find that you hold your own light; use your own light to overcome your fears; shedding light on your fears will propel you toward self-understanding, strength and self-confidence; through this process, you will heal and move forward into happiness.

Key XIX—The Sun: You are in a process of spiritual realization; this is the truest love possible; a divine marriage—which is physical, mental or spiritual—is coming; everything now makes sense; everything is a good as it could possibly be; all things are illuminated and show themselves truly, revealed by the great light of the Sun; your own "garden" is a lovely as could be.

Key XX—Resurrection: Your personal perceptions and consciousness shall dissolve to be replaced by the deepest understanding possible; you are in the final stage of knowledge as you have known it; you are about to be resurrected into new thinking, into a completely new stage; it is as if you are entering a new aeon or cycle in the grand scheme of your life; let this happen naturally and beautifully; do not fear change, you have earned the right to ascend; you have earned your rewards, you deserve every good thing that is happening to you.

Key XXI—The Universe: Your whole world is in balance; you move like a dancer with every movement perfectly timed; every undertaking has paid off; your endeavors have been successful; you are at the end of a long "journey"; the world is at your feet; celebrate the great work you have done!; if you want to journey further, the time is right.

The Mystery Card: Birth, death and karmic transitions; incredible power, magic and wonder; use your imagination and your thoughts shall become form; spiral inward; build bridges; create possibility; erect new worlds stone by stone; empty out to know fullness.

Appendix II
Tarot Correlations in Astrology and the I Ching

THE MINOR ARCANA AND FACE CARDS

Number	Fire	Water	Wind	Earth
1	Cancer Leo Virgo	Libra Scorpio Sagittarius	Capricorn Aquarius Pisces	Aries Taurus Gemini
2	Mars in Aries	Venus in Cancer	Moon in Libra	Jupiter in Capricorn
3	Sun in Aries	Mercury in Cancer	Saturn in Libra	Mars in Capricorn
4	Venus in Aries	Moon in Cancer	Jupiter in Libra	Sun in Capricorn
5	Saturn in Leo	Mars in Scorpio	Venus in Aquarius	Mercury in Taurus
6	Jupiter in Leo	Sun in Scorpio	Mercury in Aquarius	Moon in Taurus
7	Mars in Leo	Venus in Scorpio	Moon in Aquarius	Saturn in Taurus
8	Mercury in Sagittarius	Saturn in Pisces	Jupiter in Gemini	Sun in Virgo
9	Moon in Sagittarius	Jupiter in Pisces	Mars in Gemini	Venus in Virgo
10	Saturn in Sagittarius	Mars in Pisces	Sun in Gemini	Mercury in Virgo

THE MINOR ARCANA and FACE CARDS (continued)

Number	Fire	Water	Wind	Earth
Father	Scorpio Sagittarius	Aquarius Pisces	Taurus Gemini	Leo Virgo
Mother	Pisces Aries	Gemini Cancer	Virgo Libra	Sagittarius Capricorn
Brother	Cancer Leo	Libra Scorpio	Capricorn Aquarius	Aries Taurus
Sister	Cancer Leo Virgo	Libra Scorpio Sagittarius	Capricorn Aquarius Pisces	Aries Taurus Gemini

THE MAJOR ARCANA

Key	Astrological Attribute	
O. The Fool	Air	△
I. The Magus	Mercury	☿
II. The High Priestess	Moon	☺
III. The Empress	Venus	♀
IV. The Emperor	Aries	♈
V. The Hierophant	Taurus	♉
VI. The Lovers	Gemini	♊
VII. The Chariot	Cancer	♋
VIII. Strength	Leo	♌
IX. The Hermit	Virgo	♍
X. The Wheel of Fortune	Jupiter	♃
XI. Karma	Libra	♎
XII. The Hanged Man	Water	▼
XIII. Death	Scorpio	♏
XIV. Temperance	Sagittarius	♐
XV. The Devil	Capricorn	♑
XVI. The Tower	Mars	♂
XVII. The Star	Aquarius	♒
XVIII. The Moon	Pisces	♓
XIX. The Sun	Sun	☉
XX. Resurrection	Fire	△
XXI. The Universe	Saturn, Earth	♄ ∞▽

The I CHING

Element	Father	Mother	Brother	Sister
Fire	Hexagram 1 The Creative Principle	Hexagram 10 Treading, Conduct	Hexagram 44 Sexual Intercourse	Hexagram 12 Obstruction
Water	Hexagram 5 Calculated Inaction	Hexagram 58 Joy	Hexagram 48 The Well	Hexagram 19 Going There
Wind	Hexagram 9 The Lesser Nourisher	Hexagram 28 Excess	Hexagram 57 Willing Submission	Hexagram 46 Ascension
Earth	Hexagram 11 Peace	Hexagram 45 Gathering Together	Hexagram 20 Contemplation	Hexagram 2 The Passive Principle

Bibliography

Akhilananda, Swami, *Spiritual Practices*. Cape Cod, MA: Claude Stark, Inc., 1974.

Berger, Peter L. and Thomas Luckmann, *The Social Construction of Reality*. New York: Doubleday/Anchor Books, 1967.

Blofeld, John, *I Ching: The Book of Change*. New York: E. P. Dutton & Co., 1968.

Campbell, Joseph, *Myths to Live By*. New York: The Viking Press, 1972.

Case, Paul Foster, *The Book of Tokens*. Los Angeles, CA: Builders of the Adytum, 1960.

———. *The Tarot: A Key to the Wisdom of the Ages*. Richmond, VA: Macoy Publishing Company, (1947) 1981.

Crowley, Aleister, *The Book of Thoth*. York Beach, ME: Samuel Weiser, (1944) 1969.

Dennis, Landt and Lisl Dennis, *Catch the Wind*. New York: Four Winds Press, 1976.

Fortune, Dion, *The Mystical Qabalah*. York Beach, ME: Samuel Weiser, (1935) 1984.

Gibran, Kahlil, *A Tear and a Smile*. New York: Alfred A. Knopf, 1950.

Hoeller, Stephen A., *The Gnostic Jung*. Wheaton, IL: The Theosophical Publishing House, 1982.

———. *The Royal Road*. Wheaton, IL: The Theosophical Publishing House/Quest Books, 1980.

Holmes, Ernest, *The Science of Mind*. New York: G. P. Putnam's Sons, (1926) 1938.

Holy Bible

I Ching (see Blofeld)

Johnston, Charles, *The Yoga Sutras of Patanjali*. Albuquerque, NM: Brotherhood of Life, 1983.

Jung, C. G., *Memories, Dreams, Reflections*. New York: Random House/ Vintage Books, 1973.

———. *Mysterium Coniunctionis*. Princeton, NJ: Princeton University Press, Bollingen Series XX, 1977.

Kaplan, Stuart, *The Encyclopedia of Tarot, Volume 1*. Stamford, CT: U.S. Games Systems, 1978.

Kapleau, Philip, *The Three Pillars of Zen*. Boston: Beacon Press, 1965.

Kavanaugh, James, *There Are Men Too Gentle to Live Among Wolves*. Los Angeles, CA: Nash Publishing, 1970.

Knight, Gareth, *A Practical Guide to Qabalistic Symbolism*. York Beach, ME: Samuel Weiser, 1978.

L. V. X. (private communication, Fraternity of the Hidden Light, Covina, CA).

Laird, Charlton, "Language and the Dictionary," in *Webster's New World Dictionary*, William Collins & World Publishing Co. Inc., 1976.

Lao Tsu, *Tao Te Ching*. London: Concord Grove Press, 1983.

Leaf, Paul, *Comrades*. New York: New American Library, 1985.

Mallasz, Gitta, *Talking with Angels*. Zurich, Switzerland: Daimon Verlag, 1988.

Matt, Daniel Chanan, *Zohar: The Book of Enlightenment*. New York: Paulist Press, 1983.

Mead, George Herbert, *Mind, Self and Society*. Chicago: University of Chicago Press, 1934.

Moyers, Bill and Joseph Campbell, "Following your Bliss," in *Parabola*, XIII:2: May 1988.

Naranjo, Claudio and Robert E. Ornstein, *On the Psychology of Meditation*. New York: The Viking Press, 1971.

Neumann, Erich, *The Great Mother*. Princeton, NJ: Princeton University Press, 1963.

Patanjali (see Johnston)

Ralisch, Isidor, *Sepher Yezirah: The Book of Formation*. Gillette, NJ: Pentangle Books, 1987.

Sepher Yezirah (see Ralisch)

Sanford, John A., *Evil: The Shadow Side of Reality*. New York: Crossroad, 1987.

Shah, Idries, *Wisdom of the Idiots*. New York: E. P. Dutton & Co., 1971.

Starhawk, *The Spiral Dance*. New York: HarperCollins, 1979.

Stone, Hal and Sidra Winkelman, *Embracing Our Selves*. Marina del Rey, CA: DeVorss & Company, 1985.

Tao Te Ching (see Lao Tsu)

Thien-An, Thich, *Zen Philosophy, Zen Practice*. Berkeley, CA: Dharma Publishing, 1975.

Travers, P. L., "Well, Shoot Me!" in *Parabola*, XIII:2: May 1988.

Trungpa, Chogyam, *Shambhala: The Sacred Path of the Warrior*. New York: Bantam Books, 1984.

Wang, Robert, *The Qabalistic Tarot*. York Beach, ME: Samuel Weiser, 1983.

Yogananda, Paramahansa, *Metaphysical Meditations*. Los Angeles, CA: Self-Realization Fellowship, 1982.

Zohar (see Matt)

INDEX

Identity (*cont.*)
  collective, 4
  crisis, 87
  individual, 4
  personality type, 289
Ignorance, 169, 170, 279, 345
Illumination, 165
Illusion, 153, 254, 259
Imagination, 17, 22, 41, 43, 56,
  156, 257, 265
  as vehicle, 327
Immortality, xvi, 264
Imprinting, 162
Imprisonment, 347
Inaction, 81
Incarnations, Goal of successive,
  315
Incense, 161
Individual, 121
Individualism, 339
Individuality, 92
Individuation, 128
Initiate, 29, 277
Initiation, 29
  mystical, 359
Inner shrine, 376, 377
Inner temple, 4
Innocence, 186
Insight, 140
Insomnia, 163
Inspiration, 178
Instinct, 150
Institutions, 84
Intellect
  exalted, 190
  original, 190
  patterns of, 194
  pure, 189
  unbounded, 191
  wreckage of, 180
Intelligence, 261, 267, 372
  absolute, 187
  activating, 345, 349
  administrative, 374, 375
  collective divine, 365
  conciliating, 306
  constituting, 271, 272

  corporeal, 357, 359
  eternal, 276
  exciting, 349
  faithful, 314, 317
  fiery, 248
  house of hidden senses, 292
  house of influence, 292
  illuminating, 167
  imaginative, 325, 327
  luminous, 266
  natural, 352, 353
  occult, 180
  of the House of Influence, 289
  of the Secret of All Spiritual
    Activities, 295
  of trial or temptation, 332
  of will, 301
  perfect, 187
  perpetual, 368, 369
  radical, 176
  receptive, 174
  renewing, 338
  sanctifying, 171
  separating, 282
  stable, 320, 323
  transparent, 254
  triumphant, 276, 279
  uniting, 260
Introspection, 75, 151, 290
Intuition, 28, 77, 92, 95, 138, 292
Isolation tank, 320

J

Jesus, 370, 376
Jewel, 125
Johnson, Samuel, 348
Jonah, 328
Journey, xi, 56, 60, 249, 295, 302,
  332
  homeward, 366
  mystical, 3
  transformational, 3
Joy, 126
Judgment, 334
  last, 368
Jung, C. G., 64

Jupiter, 89, 144, 172, 182, 212, 306
Justice, 134, 147
   cosmic, 314

K
Kaph, 306
Kapleau, Philip, 322
Karma, 132, 176, 312, 322, 374, 379
   bad, 317
   creation of, 316
   dance of, 313
   fixed, 316
   mutable, 316
Kavanaugh, James, 150
Kether, 74, 101, 106, 107, 127, 248, 254, 260, 269
Key, 154
Keyhole, 154
Keys, 11, 19
   and energy patterns, 12
   as conditioned response patterns, 11
   as super powers, 11
King Arthur, Tales of, 302
Knight, Gareth, 35, 261, 314, 335, 349
Knowing, ways of, 49
Knowledge, 46, 113, 124, 171, 364
   attained through feeling, 42
   human, 95
   spiritual, 95
   uses of, 168
Koan, 341
Krishna, 82
Kundalini, 102

L
Laird, Charlton, 348
Lamed, 313, 315
Language, patterns, 11
Lao Tsu, 81, 250, 353
Lapis lazuli, 311
Laser beams, 170
Laughter, 337, 342
Law, 262, 264, 269, 274
   devine, 257

divine, 293, 314, 336
   love as, 192
   of cause and effect, 314, 316
   of nature, 270
   of periodicity, 305
   of sequence, 305
Laws, 84
   of Nature, 306
Lawsuits, 87
Leadership, 105
Lemniscate, 127, 258, 318, 330
Leo, 73, 86, 89, 92, 111, 114, 236, 295
Liberation, 358
Libra, 122, 155, 158, 166, 169, 172, 195, 318
Life
   as a task, 326
   eternal, 248, 276, 354
   evening of, 303
   meaning of, 326
   one, 369, 372
   one, identification with, 366
Lifestyle, 326
Light, 127, 135
   external, 85
   speed of, 90
Lightning flash, 345, 348, 349
Lightning Path, 46, 95
Lily, 269
Limitation, 126
Lion, 71, 108, 110, 113, 306
Lotus, 125, 154
Love, 16, 27, 74, 80, 85, 94, 97, 122, 124, 126, 186, 282, 336, 354, 364
   as fruit of understanding, 330
   as internal goodness, 142
   as law, 132
   as moral excellence, 142
   as salvation, 147
   law, 313, 318, 322
   maternal, 152
   power of, 303
   self, 135, 142
   spirit of, 112
   will, 313, 318, 322

Moses, 34
Mother, 125, 153, 250, 266, 267, 309
  and water, 10
  Earth, 194, 216, 279, 353
  eternal, 261, 266
  Great Mother, 269, 312
  of Mothers, 304
  mother principle, 269
  nature, 273, 312
  universal, 267, 360
  wind, 195
Mothers
  as guardians, 154
  as pure, 10
  of a threshold, 154
Mother-Father-God, 65, 81, 100, 330
Motion, 325
Motivation, 171
Mountain, 378
Mouth, 345
Movement, 296
Moyers, Bill, 298
Music, 342
Mystery, 42, 51
  as gyroscopic, 307
  card, 12, 49, 379
  of faith, 263
  schools, 32, 33
Mysteries, 29
Mystical consciousness, 28, 31, 65

N
Nail, 276, 278, 325
Naranjo, Claudio, 52, 54
Naropal Institute, xii
Nature, 209, 264, 266, 375, 377, 378, 379
  door of, 268
Navajos, 176
Netzach, 93, 99, 140, 306, 325, 327, 345, 348, 352, 357, 360
Neumann, Erich, 267
Newness, illusion of, 301
Night, 266
Nine, power of, 302

Nudity, 285
Numbers
  and their meaning, 6
  geometric progression, 6
Nun, 299, 325

O
Obstacles, 257
Occupation, 326
Octahedron, 91
Om, 157, 159, 242, 246
One, 99
One and many, 116, 295, 298, 311
One Life, 380
One Light, 276
One-ness, 93
Opposites, reconciled, xvi
  unification of, 283
Oppression, 101
Oracle, 115, 376
Oral traditions, 43
Order, 175
Ornstein, Robert, 52, 54
Outcome, 252
Ox, 247, 306
Ox goad, 313, 315, 318

P
Pacific Center, 50
Pain, 123, 126, 186, 266, 325, 327, 357
Palm, 306, 311
Pandora's Box, 166
Pane, 271, 272
Paradox, 78, 170, 337
  of love, 127
Paramahansa Yogananda, *see* Yogananda, Paramhansa
Passage, rites of, 231
Passion, 51
Past, living in, 310
Paternity, 271
Path, of return, 252, 369, 370, 372
Paul Foster Case, *see* Case, Paul Foster
Peace, 140, 378
Peak experience, *see* experience

Star Wars, 302
Stine, Richard, 65
Stock Market, 309
Stone, 61, 256, 332
    philosopher's, 311
Storm, 132
Strength, 72, 93, 109, 152, 187,
    375
    from flexibilty, 84
Student, spiritual, *see* spiritual stu-
    dent
Structure, 131
    outgrown, 82
Struggle, 86
    analytical, 183
Subconscious, 99
Submersion, 319
Substance abuse
    alcohol, 138
    drugs, 138
    food, 138
    tobacco, 138
Success, 106, 310
    fear of, 308
"Success Syndrome," 173
Suffering, 186
Sufi, 370
Sulphur, 274, 311
Sun, 80, 89, 130, 131, 136, 189,
    206, 218, 229, 266, 269, 270,
    293, 301, 311, 332, 334, 336,
    358, 361
Sun Warrior, *see* Warrior
Sungate, 234
Superconsciousness, *see* conscious-
    ness
Supernals, 269, 354
Surrender, 77, 98, 183, 286, 287,
    292, 319
Swami Akhilananda, 63, 66, 364
Swan, 160, 241
Sword, 282, 283, 343
    as symbol of karma, 315
    characteristics of, 163
    of Geburah, 315
    uses of, 163
Swords, 161, 171

Symbiosis, 121
Symbols, 11, 96, 291
Symbolism, 289
Szekely, Edmond Bordeaux, 39, 41

T
Tablets
    esoteric, 34
    exoteric, 34
Tao, 249
Tao Te Ching, 81
Target of Perfection, 314
Tarocchi, 33
Tarot
    ancient history of, 32
    and elements, 5
    and playing cards, 9, 15
    and tree of life, 34
    as game, 3
    as oracle, 3, 15
    as psycho-active, 19
    as psychological tool, xvi
    as Qabalistic, 4
    as spiritual path, 3, 31, 41
    as theoretical system, xv, 28
    as transformative images, 3
    as visual image, 39
Tarot card reading, 19
    cards of, 5
    concept of the cards, 16
    divinatory meaning, 20
    face cards, 9
    gates of, 37, 39, 45, 49
    keys, 49
    Major Arcana, 37
    oral history of, 33
    paths of, 37
    scientific explanation of, 17
    spread, 307
    spreads, 21
    ten gates, 26, 35
    theory of, 11, 13
Tarot cards
    as alive, 42
    as cycles, 27
    as equally important, 22

Pamela Eakins, Ph.D. is the director of Pacific Center. For the past decade, she was an Affiliate Scholar at Stanford University's Institute for Research on Women and Gender. She is a medical sociologist, university educator and counselor. In addition to her regular academic pursuits in health and women's studies, Dr. Eakins is learned in women's mysteries, Qabalism and the Western Mystery Tradition. She has been a pioneer in childbirth reform and sees childbirth as a metaphor for spiritual birth. She delights in teaching classes in spirituality for men and women outside the university walls and, in January 1991, founded Pacific Center which offers correspondence courses in the Western Mysteries based on the *Tarot of the Spirit*. For more information, please write to Pacific Center at P.O. Box 3191, Half Moon Bay, CA, 94019.

TAROT of the SPIRIT

Tarot of the Spirit reveals the tarot as a complex yet beautifully simple and refined system for describing the psyche. It leads the student of tarot on a transformational journey of the soul through meditation and divination. Centered on the Qabalistic Tree of Life, *Tarot of the Spirit* is neither dark nor light, neither chauvinist nor feminist—it is a guide for those seeking lasting balance in their lives.

This new deck and new symbolism clearly explore the Minor Arcana as a representation of the four components of life: spirit, emotion, intellect, and body; while it reveals the Major Arcana to be the keys that can unlock our emotional response patterns to the symbolic universe in which we live. Through the 78 cards—plus the non-traditional Mystery Card unique to this deck—we can reach an altered state of consciousness, necessary for our spiritual transformation to begin.

Combining historical background with modern psychological interpretations, Dr. Eakins brings tarot within easy access of all of us. Her seven monthly meditations, individual readings, and layouts from differing tarot traditions combine to help the tarot user see new perspectives and create new energy patterns. This truly remarkable book can be your personal guide to the way!

The deck was painted by Joyce Eakins and is published to accompany the book.